TRIBES OF THE HINDOO KOOSH

TRIBES OF THE HINDOO KOOSH.

BY

MAJOR J. BIDDULPH, B. S. C.

GYAN

Published by

Gyan Publishing House
5, Ansari Road
Daryaganj, New Delhi-110002
Phone: 011-47034999, 9811692060
E-mail: books@gyanbooks.com

Distribution Network
gyanbooks.com
India, USA, Canada, UK, Australia, France

ISBN: 978-81-212-8023-5 (PB)
First Published, 1880

2nd Impression 2023

Printed at: Gyan Press, Delhi.

TRIBES OF THE HINDOO KOOSH
Author: J. BIDDULPH

TRIBES OF THE HINDOO KOOSH.

BY

MAJOR J. BIDDULPH, B.S.C.,

POLITICAL OFFICER AT GILGIT.

CALCUTTA:

OFFICE OF THE SUPERINTENDENT OF GOVERNMENT PRINTING.

1880.

Zincographed at the Surveyor General's Office, Calcutta.

TIRICHMIR FROM CHITRAL.

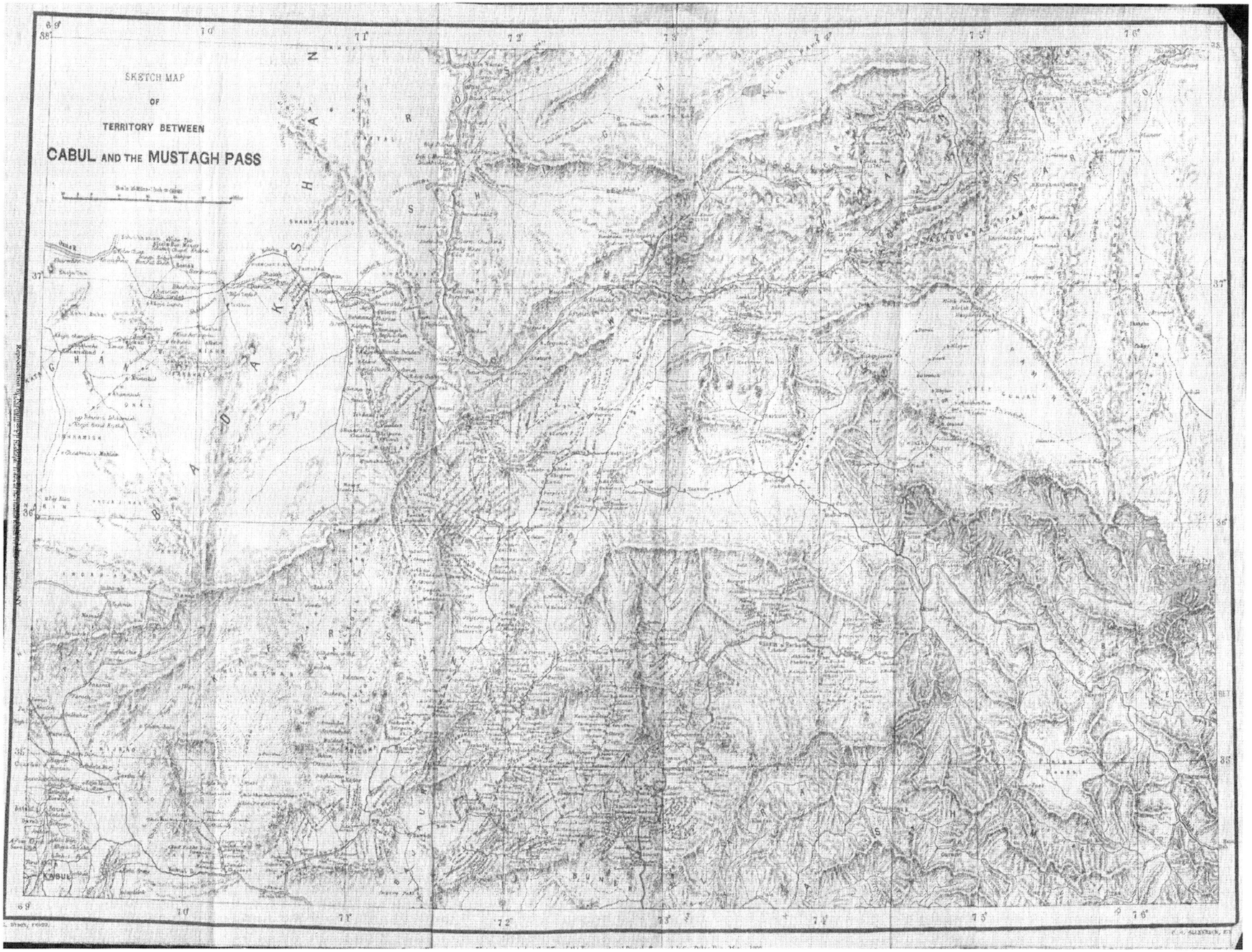
SKETCH MAP
OF
TERRITORY BETWEEN
CABUL AND THE MUSTAGH PASS
KABUL

PREFACE.

DURING the last six years it has been my good fortune to visit a number of countries on both sides of the eastern portion of the Hindoo Koosh range of mountains, all of which are very little known, and some of which have never before been visited by any European. In 1873 I formed one of Sir D. Forsyth's mission to Kashghar, and in the spring of the following year crossed the Pamir and visited Sirikol and Wakhan. In 1876 I visited Gilgit, Hunza, and part of Yassin, and in 1877 was appointed by the Indian Government to reside at Gilgit in a political capacity. In 1878 I visited Yassin and Chitral, and was only prevented by the outbreak of hostilities with Cabul from prolonging my journey.

In the following notes I have endeavoured, to the best of my ability, to record all that I have deemed worthy of general interest regarding the countries and their inhabitants, without going over ground already trodden by more competent observers. In some places I have found it necessary for the preservation of the unity of the subject to repeat what has already been written by Mr. Shaw, Mr. Drew, Dr. Leitner, and others; but where possible, I have purposely avoided doing so. The sketches given of countries I have not personally visited, as in the case of the countries described in the first chapter, are compiled from the accounts of natives of the countries in question, or, as in the account of the Siah Posh tribes, from the accounts of persons who have visited their country; the last two years having brought me in contact with great numbers of both classes. But I should explain that what I have written regarding caste observances, habits, customs, and religious ceremonies, should, as a rule,—except, of course, where I make special reference to particular places,—be understood to be chiefly the habits and observances of Gilgit and its immediate neighbourhood, as this is naturally the part of the country with which I am best acquainted.

On the other hand, though I have visited Sirikol and Wakhan, whose peoples would properly come within the scope of a treatise on the Tribes of the Hindoo Koosh, I have avoided making special mention of them, because I can add little or nothing to what has already been published about them.

Apart from political considerations, the countries about which I write, possess much of great ethnological interest, and recent events make it probable that opportunities for further and better organised enquiry will soon be afforded. I shall therefore be satisfied if the information I have gathered is found, by persons more competent than myself to make scientific use of it, to throw light on what has already been made public.

I would deprecate the application of a severe scientific criticism to my endeavours to give an insight into some of the languages and their grammatical constructions. The difficulty of attaining to an accurate knowledge of a language, when one can only learn it from illiterate peasants through very poorly-educated interpreters, can be easily understood.

The plates have been elaborated by my friend Captain H. H. Cole, R.E., from rough sketches of my own.

The spelling of some of the names in the text will be found to differ from that used in the survey map.

CONTENTS.

CHAPTER I.

Page

THE INDUS VALLEY, FROM BRITISH TERRITORY TO BOONJI.

Inaccessible nature of country — Difficulty of communication — Climate — Cultivation —Palosa — Poorun Valley — Chakesar — Nandiar — Alai — Kanra — Ghorbund— Pathans and Neemchas — The Indus Kohistan — The Dards — Doobeyr — Koli — Batera — The Gawaré — The Chiliss — Palus — Puttun — Seo — Kandia — The Maiyons — Sazin — Herbund — Tangir — Darel — Kandbari — Hodar — Talpin — Gies — Gor — Thalich — Chilas — System of government — The Jushteros — Curious custom — Slavery . . . 1

CHAPTER II.

GILGIT—HUNZA—NAGER—PONYAL.

Boonji — Gilgit — Ancient name — Ruins — Shina — The Ras — Mountainous country — Description — Gold — Bagrot — The Hunza River — Chaprot — Rakiposh — Hunza and Nager — Rivalry — Shimshal — Raskum, Pakpooh, and Shakshooh — Sirikol — Kunjoot — The Ayeshé — The Moghloté — Their origin — Relations of Hunza with China — Plundering caravans — Relations with Gilgit — Hunza — Faith — The Boorish — Forts — Ponyal — The Boorooshé — Cher — Gahkuch — The Karoomber Valley — The Ishkoman Pass 19

CHAPTER III.

CASTES—ADMINISTRATION.

General distribution of castes — The Ronos — Their origin — Personal appearance — The Shins — Physical types — Position relative to other castes — Brokpas — Shin feeling as to cows and domestic fowls — The Yeshkuns — Syuds — Krammins — Doms — Shoto — Cashmeri immigrants — Goojurs — Shin administration — Taxes — Officials — Measures . . . 34

CHAPTER IV.

BALTISTAN—THE BROKPAS.

Dards of Haramosh — Origin of Brokpas in Baltistan — Position of Brokpas towards Baltis — Name of Rom — Brokpa castes — Physical differences among Baltis — How caused — Mixture of Aryan and Mongolian blood — Intermarriage — Balti castes — Buddhist Dards of Dah-Hanu — Mr. Shaw's account — Relics of earlier immigration . . . 46

CHAPTER V. Page

YASSIN—CHITRAL.

Frontier of Ponyal and Yassin — Narrow defiles — Yassin territory — Woorshigoom valley — Village of Yassin — Durkot — Scene of Mr. Hayward's murder — Pass — People of Woorshigoom — Origin of name — Ruling family — Title of ruler — Reminiscences of ancient rulers — Present ruler — Peihlowan Bahadoor — Roads to the Chitral Valley — Toowi Pass only available in summer — Route by Ghizr and Laspoor — Chashi — The Kho Valley, inhabited by Shins — Ancient stone-tables or circles, probably burial mounds — Pandar Lake — Ghizr — Road to the Swat Valley — The Kho race from Kashkar — Shandur plateau — Two lakes — Laspoor Valley — Mastooch — Yarkhoon — Kashkar Bala — Tirich Mir (mountain) — Tirich, Moolkho, and Toorikho Valleys — Toorikho, residence of Chitral heir-apparent — Kashkar River — Ludkho stream — Change in scenery and climate — Chitral — Birkot — Bushgali Siah Posh — Bailam — Asmar — Boundary wall — Chitral town and fort — Ruling family — Aman-ul-Mulk — Products — Manufactures — Population — Kho — Khowar language — "Fakir Mushkin" — Privileged class — Their clans — Yidghâh — Kalashgoom and Bidir Valleys — Gubbers or Narisati — Origin of tribes — Manufacturing castes — Revenue system — Justice — Administration — Officials — Slave-trade — Weights and measures 55

CHAPTER VI.

TORWAL AND BUSHKAR.

The Torwalik — Their kinship to the Chiliss — Former home in Boneyr — Relations with the Afghans — The Bushkarik — Their degraded state — Quarrelsome character — Payment of tribute to other States — Language — Peculiar construction of villages — Forests 69

CHAPTER VII.

HABITS AND CUSTOMS.

Old customs — Some modified or abolished by Mahommedanism, but many still remaining — Difficulty of tracing their origin — Physical features of the men — Disposition — The women — Dress — Ornaments — Hair — Mode of salutation — Polygamy — Marriage of widows to husband's brother — Terms expressing relationship — Traces of communal marriage — Infidelity — Morals in Hunza and Nager — Infanticide — Marriage ceremonies — Burial of the dead — Rules of inheritance — Foster kindred — Hidden treasures — Storing clarified butter — Wine cellars — Wine drinking — Polo playing — "Buz-kushi" — Shooting — Dancing — Music — Singing — Specimens of songs in Shina and Khowar — Oral traditions and genealogies — Weapons — Warfare — Forts — Computation of time — The Nager calendar — Days of the week — Chitral calendar — Bushkar and Torwal calendar — Constellations — Theory of earthquakes — Points of the compass — Fairies and demons — Guardian fairy — Yoodeni drum — Magic — Charms — Divination — Dainyals — Crimes — Punishments — Nomenclature — Shin and Yeshkun names 72

CHAPTER VIII.

FESTIVALS.

Semi-religious festivals survive in spite of Mahommedanism — Mostly connected with agriculture — 'Shiné baradesi' — Nôs — Taleni — Dushti-Daiko — Bazono —

Aiboi, now obsolete — Similarity to the Holi — Ganoni — Domenika — Chili — Thumer Bopow in Hunza and Nager — Binesik in Yassin and Chitral — Curious custom in Yassin — Similarity of this festival to the Dussehra — Cedar worship in Gilgit . . *Page* 100

CHAPTER IX.

PAST AND PRESENT RELIGIONS.

Fire worship — The Taleni — Buddhism — Buddhist remains — Rock-cut figure of Buddha — Fah-Hian's route — Fable — Feeling with regard to the cow — Burning the dead — Funeral urns — Suttee — Idolatrous customs — Mixture of Spirit-worship — Ancient Sanscrit inscription — Names suggestive of Hindooism — Tree-worship — The sacred Cedar — Forms of Mahommedanism — Introduction into Gilgit, Iskardo, Nager, Chitral, and Yassin — Soonnees and Shiahs — Maulais — Their veneration for Agha Khan — Sketch of origin of the sect — The Kalam-i-Pir — Tenets — The Noor Bukhshis — Their origin — Mixture of Soonnee and Shiah tenets 108

CHAPTER X.

THE SIAH POSH.

Kaffiristan — Their origin — Tribal divisions — The Rumgalis — The Waigalis — The Bushgalis — The Kalashis — The Kittigalis — The termination "gali" — No general name — Physical characteristics — Dress — Habits — Curious head-dress — Intercourse with their neighbours — Products — Houses — Stockades — Arms — Jushts — Religion — Deities — Form of sacrifice — Traditions — Relations with Chitral — Bragamatal —The Kalashis — Slavery among the Bushgalis — Dancing — Polygamy — Morality — Tribute of children 126

CHAPTER XI.

THE GILGIT PRINCES.

Genealogies of the Trakhané, the Moghloté, and the Ayeshé — The historical legend of Gilgit — Shiri Buddutt — Azor — The introduction of Islam — Mirza Khan — Trakhan — Soomalik — Mirza and Jowari — Gowrithum Khan — Mahommed Khan — Gilgit conquered by Suleiman Shah, Khushwaktia — Azad Khan — Tahir Shah — Sekunder Khan — Gohr Aman, Khushwaktia, establishes himself in Gilgit — His cruelty — Karim Khan established under Sikh protection — Alidad Khan — Slavery — The story of Bira Khan 134

CHAPTER XII.

THE BALTISTAN PRINCES.

Genealogy of the Makpons — Ibrahim Shah — Meaning of Makpon — Non-Mahommedan names — The founders of the Rondu, Khurmang, and Astor Makpons — Ali Shah, the conqueror of Chitral—Superiority of the Makpons over other families — The Shigar Princes — Their appearance — Table of the Amachahs — Iskanderia, and the claims of various families to descent from Alexander the Great — Bolor 144

CHAPTER XIII.

THE YASSIN AND CHITRAL PRINCES.

Genealogies of the Katooré, the Khushwakté, and the Boorooshé — Chitral formerly known as Katoor — References to the name — The Yuechi in Chitral — Ancient figure and inscription — Tradition of king Bahman — Chinese invasion — Baba Eyoub — Shah Sangalli — Khush Amad and Khush Wakt — Feramorz — Chinese invasion and siege of Mastooch — Corroborated by Chinese records — Chitral identified with Bolor — Suleiman Shah . . *Page* 148

CHAPTER XIV.

DARDISTAN.

Languages — Yidghâh — Khowar — Shina — Boorishki — The term "Dard" — Mention of the Dards by ancient writers — Probable origin of the name — Division of Ghalchahs and Dards into groups — How the differences arose — The Boorish — The Shin invasion — The Tartar invasion — The Gawaré, Torwalik, and Chiliss — The Kho — The Siah-Posh — A decadent race 155

Map in pocket.

APPENDICES.

APPENDIX A.

Boorishki. (Nager dialect.) The language spoken in Hunza, Nager, and Yassin . iii

APPENDIX B.

Shina. (Gilgit dialect) xl

APPENDIX C.

Chiliss. Spoken in the Indus Valley lxv

APPENDIX D.

Torwâlâk. Spoken in Torwâl, in the Swat Valley lxxvii

APPENDIX E.

Bushkarik. Spoken in the upper part of the Swat and Punjkorah Valleys . . xcii

APPENDIX F.

Gowro. Spoken by the Gawáré in the Indus Valley civ

APPENDIX G.

Narisati. Spoken by the Gubbers in the Chitral Valley cxvi

APPENDIX H.

Khowar. Spoken by the Kho in the Chitral Valley cxxi

APPENDIX I.

Bushgali. Spoken by the Bushgali tribe of Siah Posh cxlv

APPENDIX J.

Yidghah. Spoken in the upper part of the Ludkho Valley and in Munjan . . cliv

TRIBES OF THE HINDOO KOOSH.

CHAPTER I.

THE INDUS VALLEY, FROM BRITISH TERRITORY TO BOONJI.

WITHIN the last half century, war and private adventure have contributed so largely to making known the least accessible regions of the continent of Asia, that few parts remain of which a fair general knowledge does not exist. Certain localities are, however, still sealed to European travellers, and chief among them is the country lying between the 35th and 38th parallels of latitude, and the 70th and 76th degrees of longitude. Though situated within easy reach of the Punjab, and containing a population fairly numerous for its capabilities,—one indeed far denser than that of the better-known province of Ladakh,—it has hitherto attracted little attention.

The apparent neglect has been caused by the almost inaccessible nature of the country. In no other part of the world, probably, is there to be found such a large number of lofty mountains within so confined a space. This immense mass of mountain is intersected by numerous deep valleys, and these, owing to some peculiar geological formation which I have not remarked in other parts of the Himalayas, are generally narrower at their mouths than higher up. It is not unusual to see among them valleys of from 10 to 30 miles in length, supporting a population varying from 500 to 5,000 souls, with an embouchure so narrow that it is difficult to find a pathway beside the torrent which issues between overhanging rocks. In addition to this, the enormous rush of water during the summer months from numerous and extensive glaciers and snow-fields impedes communication.

Thus aided by nature in preserving their independence, and partially isolated from one another, the people of the country have formed themselves into a number of separate communities which have existed for generations within the same narrow limits. Living the same life, and following the same customs as their forefathers did hundreds of years ago, they have remained unaffected by the changes that have taken place around them, and but slightly moved even by their own internal wars. Several valleys exist, into and out of which cattle and horses can only pass during two months of the year, and in which the continual falling of huge masses of rock from the steep mountain sides under the action of frost, snow, and sun, frequently sweeps away the narrow and frail pathways.

The roads are of the rudest kind, and necessity has made the inhabitants intrepid cragsmen; they pass with ease over places so dangerous that even experienced mountaineers would frequently hesitate to follow them.

Communication is maintained over the rivers at certain points by hanging bridges of plaited birch twigs—a means of crossing which tries the steadiest nerves.

The bridge is formed of nine plaits of twigs, suspended across the river at a suitable place where the stream flows between precipitous rocks. The plaits are bound together at intervals by threes. One triple plait forms the foothold about 5 inches wide; the others form a hand-rail on either side about 2 feet above the middle plait, and held apart at intervals by forked sticks which have to be straddled over in crossing. There is not a nail or piece of rope in the whole structure; the ends are secured round logs of wood held in their places by heaped-up rocks. The whole bridge sways about with every gust, making it very unpleasant to cross in a high wind; and when the river, as often happens, requires a span of over 300 feet, the steadiest nerves feel the trial. As no great strain can be put on the twig plaits, there is always a dip in the middle; and when, as not unfrequently happens, one bank is considerably higher than the other, the difficulty of crossing is greatly enhanced by the steep incline. Where there is much traffic, these bridges are renewed yearly; but where little used, they are left for two or three years without repair, and become very dangerous. Notwithstanding their fragile appearance, they are safe enough when renewed yearly, and accidents are few.

A good twig bridge will bear ten or twelve persons at once with ease. Men accustomed to them carry large and cumbrous loads across, and pass and repass each other on them without fear; and accidents by falling from them are unknown. I have even known cases of men being carried across a twig bridge on the backs of others. Sheep and calves are also carried across on men's shoulders.

The danger of the bridges is nothing compared to that of some of the hill paths, where precipitous rocks overhang the boiling torrent, and the sole means of progression is by a rough log thrown across a chasm, or a rude ladder placed against the face of the rock, where a false step or slip entails fatal consequences. Over such places, which many a good mountaineer would turn from with a shudder, the inhabitants pass with a *sangfroid* only equalled by the wild goats of their own craggy mountains. The old Chinese travellers seem to have been much impressed by the rugged character of the country. Fah Hian relates: "Steep crags and precipices constantly intercept the way. These mountains are like walls of rock, standing up 10,000 feet in height. On looking over the edge, the sight becomes confused, and then on advancing, the foot loses its hold, and you are lost." Sung Yun writes: "For a thousand li there are overhanging crags, 10,000 fathoms high, towering up to the very heavens. Compared with this road, the ruggedness of the great pass known as the Mang Mun is as nothing, and the eminences of the celebrated Hian mountains (in Honan) are like level country."

Besides these difficulties in internal communication, the only roads which link the country to the outer world can be traversed freely for little more than half the year.

The River Indus, which would seem to offer an easy channel of communication, is in the upper part of its course subject to the same conditions as the smaller streams, and in the lower its banks are inhabited by fanatical and warlike tribes, whose lawlessness and feuds effectually bar the way to traders and travellers.

The division of the country into a number of small isolated communities has placed great restrictions on free intermarriage, which have, in some places, been further increased by caste observances. Continued intermarriage for many generations within a circumscribed area has had a most pernicious and deteriorative effect on the population.

Eight or nine miles above Derbund, where the River Indus enters the Punjab, the traveller leaves British protection and enters the independent territory of Yaghestan—literally, the rebellious country—a name given to all republican communities.[1] No natural feature marks the boundary, but the difference in the appearance of the country is at once evident,—fewer villages, less cultivation, more cultivable ground lying idle. The road, though still allowing the passage of horses, grows worse as it proceeds; and the people, though retaining the Afghan speech, differ both in appearance and clothing from those in British territory. The difference in feature, though not very striking at first, becomes more and more apparent at each stage, till the Afghan language and features imperceptibly disappear and are replaced by a different type. From Derbund to within a few miles of Boonji the course of the river, for about 150 miles, lies between two continuous and lofty mountain ranges,—the breadth of the tract, from watershed to watershed, averaging about 50 miles throughout its length. Though the general character of this tract is rocky and barren, it is intersected by deep valleys of great fertility. In spite of the rocky nature of the soil, water seems the only thing required to produce crops of great richness. Mulberries, peaches, apricots, apples, figs, melons, and grapes grow in the most wonderful profusion; while the ground yields year after year without exhaustion two crops, one of which is invariably wheat or barley, the alternate one being rice, cotton, or millet. This undiminished fertility is probably due to the large amount of alluvial deposit brought down from the mountains with the melting snows, and spread over the land by irrigation. The climate is dry and wholesome, though the heat in summer, owing to the radiation from the enormous expanse of bare rock, is oppressive; but the nights are cool and fresh, and above 3,000 feet there is a short but sharp season of dry cold, increasing in length and intensity with the elevation. There is no rainfall to speak of, it being almost entirely intercepted by the neighbouring lofty mountains. These characteristics extend beyond Boonji up the Indus Valley to beyond Iskardo, and up the lateral valleys to nearly the same altitude. At 5,000 feet the season of intense cold lasts for more than a month, during the whole of which time the thermometer remains below freezing point; it then gradually breaks, and the spring which follows is exceedingly brief. Hardly have the first cornshoots shown themselves well above ground when summer makes itself unmistakeably felt. Ear is added to stalk, and fruit succeeds

[1] The name is sometimes erroneously applied to the small neighbouring Meerships.

blossom, with marvellous rapidity, and by the beginning of June harvest has commenced. At this elevation, at the end of March the spring crops are not more advanced than they are in the south of England at the same season; by the middle of June harvest is over, and the ground is immediately planted with rice. The production of two such crops yearly, without intermission, from the same ground, testifies to the favourable qualities of both soil and climate.

In the lateral valleys, however, above 6,500 feet the year yields only one harvest, as the second crop cannot be sown in time to ripen before the winter frosts set in.

In the Indus Valley, owing to the great heat generated by the large expanse of bare rock, a double crop is grown up to 7,500 feet, if the first be barley. Wheat, which takes longer to ripen, will not admit of a second crop being sown on the same ground.

Soon after leaving British territory the mouth of the well-known valley of Boneyr is passed, and a few miles beyond it the Wahabi colony of Palosa is reached, on the right bank. Here is the refuge of Hindustani Mussulman irreconcilables, whose avowed object is unceasing war against the Christian power of the British Empire. They are regarded with suspicion and dislike by all their neighbours.

In preference to the native name of Palosa, they call their place Kila Mujahideen, "the fort of warriors of the faith." They number about 500 men, of whom only eight or ten are married. Their whole time is employed in drill, of which the words of command are given in Arabic. Their two forts of Garai and Nawa Kali are armed with cannon made of leather, which become useless after a few discharges. They subsist entirely on contributions from their sympathisers in Hindustan, and make no attempt to cultivate the soil. Their neighbours credit them with the possession of great treasure. They yield obedience in all things to a Moulvie from Swat.

Continuing up the right bank of the river, the village and fort of Kamach, with 120 houses, is passed, and 8 miles further up the large village and fort of Kabalgram, with 500 houses. Above Kabalgram a considerable stream, whose banks are cultivated by the Chagherzai, Ferozai, Mokhozai, and Balole Khel, joins the Indus. The upper portion of the valley of this stream is called Poorun. The principal forts are Titiwalan, 500 houses, in the Chagherzai country; and Chogah, 1,000 houses, in that of the Mokhozai. The smaller villages of Senelah, Sumdooi, Bingalai, and Alooch in Poorun, and Topai and Baikhaneh in the Ferozai country, are fortified. It is said that the entire valley can furnish over 20,000 fighting men; but the number is probably much exaggerated.

Seven miles above Kabalgram on the same side, the Chakesar stream joins the Indus, and 7 miles from its mouth are the fort and group of villages of Chakesar, numbering about 400 houses. Two miles further up the Indus, on the left bank, are the fort and village of Daur, about 100 houses, above which the valley makes a bend at right angles to its general course, the river flowing from east to west for more than 5 miles, instead of from north to south. In the bend several small villages are situated.

At Sarkul the course of the valley is again nearly north and south for more than 10 miles, in which space two streams, from the extensive valleys of Nundiar and Alai, join the Indus on the left bank. These two fertile valleys, which stretch eastward for many miles, support a dense and flourishing population. Nundiar can furnish about 8,000 fighting men. Their recognised leaders are Gufar Khan of Trand and Zuffer Khan of Batgram. The principal villages are Takot (fort), 400 houses; Batgram (fort), 500 houses; Batkool (fort), 400 houses; Giborai, 400 houses; Shingolai, 400 houses; Hilleh (fort), 220 houses; Piriarai (fort), 200 houses. Besides these, the smaller villages Karg, Kotkala, Nilishang, Banda, Gania, and Lergram are also fortified.

The Alai Valley can furnish about 7,000 fighting men, who acknowledge Bahadoor Khan of Sakergah and Ursulla Khan of Pookal as their chiefs. The principal villages are Sachbehar, 300 houses; Karg, 800 houses; Banna (fort), 400 houses; Bateleh, 300 houses; Pashtai (fort), 300 houses; Nogram, 300 houses; Beorai, 400 houses; and Rashung, 300 houses. The smaller villages of Roopganai, Sakergah, Tandawal, Robat, Bandai, Pookal, and Kanteyr are also protected by forts. One branch of the Alai Valley stretches up towards the head of the Palus Valley, from which it is separated by a low pass. Increase of population and the scarcity of land cause the men of Alai to cast longing eyes on the Palus land, and disputes are already beginning to arise concerning settlers from Alai, who have found their way across the pass. The tract on the right bank of the Indus opposite the mouths of the Nundiar and Alai valleys is called Sandakai, and contains several small villages, of which Daood and Jaba are fortified.

A few miles above the fort of Shung, where the river makes a sudden bend, a large stream, which forks about 6 miles from the main valley, enters the Indus. At the bifurcation is the village of Karorah, which marks the junction of the two important valleys of Kanra and Ghorbund. Both valleys are extremely fertile and productive, and sustain a large population. The northernmost valley, Kanra, is divided into two districts. Pirkhana, the upper part of the valley, is inhabited entirely by Syuds. Their peaceful habits and the reverence due to their descent secure them from attack, and there is not a single fort in the district. The principal village is Bilkanai, 400 houses. In the lower part of the valley, or Kanra proper, the chief villages are Damorai, 400 houses; Bar-Kanra, 300 houses; Dalai, 500 houses; and Kooz-Kanra, 400 houses; all of which have forts. No road leads out of the head of the Kanra Valley. In the Ghorbund Valley the chief villages are Kotgai, 300 houses; Kotgai Bazargai, 800 houses; Aughan, 250 houses; Derai, 300 houses; Shahtool, 200 houses; and Ranihal, 200 houses; all fortified. Between the junction of the two valleys and the Indus is Kormung, 320 houses. The two valleys of Ghorbund and Kanra can together furnish between 6,000 and 7,000 fighting men under their chief, Fuzl Ahmed Khan of Dalai, his partner in authority and frequent rival being Lallookeh of Kotgai.

A good road, much frequented by traders, leads from Ghorbund into the Swat Valley, by which Sedoo is reached in four days from the Indus. The Gandao Pass has snow on it in winter, but never sufficient to close the road.

The whole of the people on both banks of the Indus, so far, with the exception of the fanatics of Palosa, call themselves Pathans, and claim to belong originally to Swat; but there is a considerable difference between them. Those on the right bank and in the lateral valleys to the westward are pure Pathans, who still maintain close connection with Swat. Those on the left bank and in the lateral valleys to the eastward, including the people of the Pukli and Agror Valleys in British territory, though speaking Pushtoo, are styled Neemchas, or half-breeds, by the pure-blooded Afghans of Yusufzai, who refuse either to intermarry or make common cause with them in their local quarrels. They are apparently descended from mixed marriages between Afghan settlers from Swat and the original inhabitants, whose race individuality has here become merged in the more vigorous Afghan type, but is still found untouched a little further north. The Neemchas refuse, on their part, to associate with the tribes to the northward, and are said to be easily distinguishable from pure Afghans by their accent.

Above the junction of the Kanra-Ghorbund Valley with the Indus, the traveller enters the Kohistan, a name also used by the Afghans in the valleys to the westward as far as Cabul, to denote the districts inhabited by an older race whom they have displaced.

The Kohistan of the Indus Valley, which is also called Shinkari, "the country of the Shins," by the people themselves, is inhabited by what are apparently the remains of a number of tribes of cognate race, whose progenitors once inhabited the valleys skirting the Punjab, and possibly extended into the plain country below. They and the tribes to the north and north-west have been hitherto confounded under the name of Dards—a name which, practically, has no real signification.

Notice was first drawn to the Dards in modern times by Moorcroft. Later, Vigne, who travelled through Cashmere and Baltistan in 1835, made an attempt to reach Gilgit, which unfortunately was unsuccessful. It is much to be regretted that so observant a traveller did not succeed in entering this country while a phase of native rule was existing which has since passed away. Following in his footsteps, Cunningham contributed further to our knowledge of these races from information gathered in Baltistan in 1846. The part of the Indus Valley between Torbela and Boonji still remains a sealed book to European travellers. The first to cross the Indus at Boonji and penetrate to beyond Gilgit were Young and Vans Agnew, two officers of the Bengal Army who were employed by Government in 1847 to report on the north-western frontier of Cashmere territory. Their report, unfortunately, was never made public.[1] Nearly twenty years later Dr. Leitner reached Gilgit under circumstances of considerable difficulty, and, after a brief stay of a few days only, brought back a mass of interesting information, which has been supplemented by Mr. Drew in his valuable work on Cashmere. Dr. Leitner was the first to bring into prominent notice the existence of an Aryan race of great ethnological interest in these remote valleys. His scanty opportunities, however, have caused him to fall into the error of believing that the tribes which he has classed under the name of Dard are all of the same race, and he has applied the term of Dardistan, a name founded on a misconception, to a tract of country inhabited by several races, speaking distinct

[1] It is doubtful whether this report was ever presented to Government, and it is believed to have been lost at Mooltan when Vans Agnew was murdered, directly after his return.

languages, who differ considerably amongst themselves. As, however, there is no one name which will properly apply to the peoples and countries in question, it will be perhaps convenient to retain the names of Dard and Dardistan when speaking collectively of the tribes in question and the countries they inhabit.

The first 50 miles of the Kohistan of the Indus Valley is inhabited by tribes of cognate race, who still speak a variety of dialects and languages. Their distribution seems to show that they represent tribes who formerly lived apart, but have been forced by circumstances into contiguity. In addition to their own languages, Pushtoo is universally spoken, and they present the appearance of a decadent race in process of absorption by one of greater vigour. The country is somewhat poorer and less fertile than that already described. Long intervals of barren sand intervene between the patches of cultivation, the villages are smaller, much cultivable land lies idle, and all agriculture is of a slovenly description. The men are small and clean-limbed, with dark complexions, quick eyes, and sharp features. Women are not secluded from the public gaze. Men shave their heads in a manner more suggestive of Hindoos, and many strange customs still linger amongst them, showing that Mahommedan fanaticism is not incompatible with ignorance of the Koran. In some of the more inaccessible villages idolatry can hardly yet be said to be extinct. Instead of the loose ample garments of the Pathan, the men wear tight-fitting clothes, like the natives of Hindustan.

Some 15 miles above the mouth of the Kanra-Ghorbund Valley, on the right bank of the Indus, is the extensive but thinly-populated valley of Doobeyr, which extends nearly due north for a distance of about 40 miles. Five miles from the Indus the village of Ranooliyah, 200 houses, is reached; above this the habitations are scattered broadcast over the whole valley, instead of being collected into villages. The only village of any size is Jarg, 100 houses, 6 miles above Ranooliyah. From the head of the valley a road leads into the Swat Valley near Payeteh, and another into Kandia. The valley can furnish about 1,500 fighting men, and the ground, where cultivable, is said to yield excellent crops.

On the opposite bank of the Indus and above the mouth of the Doobeyr Valley are the neighbouring and rival communities of Koli and Palus, which are often spoken of as forming a single tribe. They were formerly close allies, but a feud, arising out of a dispute concerning some land to which both lay claim, has existed between them for several years past. It is seldom that two or three months pass without a raid from one side or the other.

Koli proper consists of three villages—Honinkot or Barkali, 400 houses, Batangai, 200 houses, and Kirkot or Koozkali, 100 houses.[1] In local feuds the inhabitants of the Kohistan villages on the left bank of the Indus, below Koli, side with the people of Koli against Palus. Land is scarce in Koli, and a considerable number of the people are forced to support themselves by trade. A large settlement of Koli people exists in Gilgit, being favoured by certain privileges conferred on them by the Cashmere Government, in recognition of services performed in the wars which led to the establishment of the Dogras in that district. They carry on a large trade as pedlers between the Punjab and Gilgit, whence they occasionally find their way into Yassin, Chitral, and the Punjkorah Valley, where the ground is chiefly occupied by Kaka Khel traders from Peshawur. The Neemchas of the Alai, Nundiar, Pukli, and Agror Valleys make common cause with the people of Koli. On occasions of great emergency, Koli can furnish about 3,000 fighting men.

Within the Koli limits four dialects founded on Sanscrit are spoken, in addition to Pushtoo. In the small village of Batera, consisting of 120 houses, a language peculiar to this village only is spoken.[2] In Pâto, Bhimkot, Mahrin, and Jamrah, about 300 houses in all, the people speak a dialect known as Gowro,[3] and call themselves Gawaré, or Gabaré: they are sometimes also called Mahrons, from their principal village. According to their traditions, they came originally from Râshung in Swat.

Scattered through the different villages are about 200 families, who are called Chiliss by their neighbours, but Galos by themselves. They have a tradition that their home was originally in Boneyr, whence they emigrated to Swat to escape being forced to become Mussulmans. Being further persecuted, they resolved to stake their all on a battle, after which, if defeated, they would consent to embrace the religion of Islam. They were defeated, but a certain number of them, clinging to their old faith, migrated to the Indus Valley. This did not, however, save them from being forced later to become Mahommedans, but they no longer form a

[1] Many of the villages in this part have a Pushtoo as well as a Dard name.
[2] This I have not yet succeeded in obtaining.
[3] See Appendix F.

separate community. Like the Gawaré, their language is founded on Sanscrit.[1] They are treated with much respect by their neighbours, and occupy, as a rule, the best land in the country. A few of them are found also in Jalkot and in Palus on the same bank of the river. In addition to the above, a dialect of Shina is spoken by the greater number of the people of Koli, who belong to the Shin race.

The people of Palus, who are also Shins, inhabit a valley of considerable extent, stretching in a south-easterly direction, and having easy communication from its head with the Alai valley. Land in Palus is plentiful, and much remains uncultivated. As has been already observed, this abundance has for some time caused the envy of the more crowded populations of Alai and Koli. The population of Palus is much scattered, and embraces the inhabitants of all the valleys on the left bank of the Indus up to the Shorai nullah, where the boundary is marked by a solitary olive tree, which is the subject of a local legend. The principal village is Jalkot, 400 houses, which was formerly jointly tributary to Koli and Palus, and has now become a bone of contention between the two communities. Palus with its allies can muster about 5,000 fighting men.

Nearly opposite to Palus, on the right bank of the Indus, is the settlement of Puttun, which, with the group of villages in adjoining valleys dependent on it, can muster from 4,000 to 5,000 fighting men. Puttun is the largest and most flourishing place in the Kohistan. The land is noted for fertility, and the crops raised from it are of great richness. Here, again, a too redundant population has caused difficulties about land, and has forced a portion to seek a living by trade. The valleys of Chilas, Darel, and Tangir are frequented by pedlers from Puttun, to whom this portion of the local trade has been abandoned by the Koli people.

A few miles above Puttun, on the right bank, is the little settlement of Seo. This, with its outlying villages, the principal of which is Mandraza, can muster 400 fighting men.

Above Seo, on the same side, is the extensive valley of Kandia, running due west and then bending suddenly to the north. From the upper part of the valley, roads lead into Doobeyr, Bushkar, and Tangir. The population being widely scattered, this valley can only furnish some 1,500 fighting men, and the villages in it are small. The people are extremely poor, and the valley very inaccessible, the road from the

[1] See Appendix C.

Indus being impracticable for horses. There are no forts in Kandia.

Up to this point in the Kohistan, the people along the right bank of the river—that is to say, those of Bunker, Doobeyr, Puttun, Seo, and Kandia—speak a separate language[1] and call themselves Maiyon. The Afghans apply the name of Mair to them. Very little is known of these people, who are the poorest of all the Kohistan communities. They combine against all others, and refuse to intermarry with any but their own people and those of Puttun and Jijál, who have, of late years only, begun to intermarry with the inhabitants of Koli and Palus. They apply the name of Dard to the people living on the left bank of the river. This is the only use of this term found among all the tribes to which it has been applied. Above Kandia, on both banks of the river, and in the lateral valleys up to and beyond Boonji, Shina[2] is the only language spoken.

Following up the course of the river, on the left bank, the small communities of Sazin and Herbund are reached. They can respectively furnish about 400 and 500 fighting men. Between the two is the small valley of Shatial, which belongs to Sazin. The people of Sazin keep themselves apart from all others and refuse to intermarry. They have the reputation of being warlike and brave.

Immediately opposite Sazin, on the right bank, is the fertile valley of Tangir. The people, like those of Sazin and Herbund, are Shins intermixed with Yeshkuns and Krammins. They are looked upon as the rightful owners of the soil, but the fertility and abundance of the land has attracted Afghans from Swat of the Mundi Khel, Akhoond Khel, and Khuddoo Khel, and Syuds, who have begun to settle in the valley. Of late years, too, the overflow from the redundant populations of Koli and Palus has found its way into Tangir, so that now the immigrants outnumber the rightful owners of the soil. A bad feeling also exists between Tangir and Sazin on the same account. The valley can muster about 1,200 fighting men, of whom only one-third are furnished by the three villages of Kami, Shekho, and Diemar, the only villages in which none of the recent immigrants are found. The principal village in the valley is Kami (fort), 250 houses; after this, the fortified villages of Juglot, Loork, and Diemar. From the head of the valley, which is thickly covered with pine forest, two roads lead into the Yassin territory, besides the

[1] This I have not yet succeeded in obtaining.

[2] See Appendix B.

road already mentioned leading into Kandia. Another road leads into the Swat valley and is a favourite route for traders.

Tangir and the neighbouring valley, Darel, are celebrated for the number and fine quality of their flocks and herds. Large numbers of sheep are here annually reared for sale to the inhabitants of the neighbouring valleys. Being somewhat straitened for summer pasture, the people of Tangir have long been in the habit of driving their flocks across the watershed to the Yassin country. In return for permission to graze, they pay to the ruler of Yassin a fixed tribute of salt and tobacco from each village. Besides this tribute, they give sheep and goats in varying numbers as a free gift. These payments have led to the Yassin rulers claiming the nominal allegiance of Tangir; but they make no attempt to exercise authority in the valley, which is to all intents and purposes a republican community like others in the Kohistan. Any attempt by the Yassin rulers to enter Tangir is resisted by force of arms, but the connection between the two communities has led to Tangir being regarded as the place of refuge for Yassin princes in misfortune. The people of Tangir pride themselves on giving asylum to all such who claim it, and it is seldom that the valley is long without some exiled member of the Khushwakté family. On such occasions the inhabitants contribute to his support as if he were their legitimate ruler, and if any attempt is made to seize him by force, they take up arms for a sufficient time to secure his safe retreat. Many a deposed ruler of Yassin has found a welcome in Tangir, where in the days of his power he would have been opposed by force of arms. Though Mahommedanism is of comparatively recent introduction, the people of Tangir are more fanatical than any of their neighbours, except those of Chilas, owing probably to their more intimate relations with Swat. They say of themselves that they have been Mussulmans for six generations. They marry with Yassin women, but refuse to give daughters in return, on account of the slave-selling practised by Yassin rulers.

Six miles above the mouth of the Tangir stream, the Darel Valley joins the Indus. Though small, this valley is extremely fertile and well populated. From its head, roads lead into Tangir, Yassin, Ponyal, and Gilgit. The principal villages are Birokot (fort), 800 houses; Doodookot (fort) 700 houses, in the Samangal district; Manikal (fort), 140 houses; Rashmal (fort), 120 houses, in the Joomeh district; and Gaiyal (fort), 500 houses. The whole community, including the dependent valleys of Doodooshal and Kandbari, can muster about 3,000 fighting men, but the people are neither fanatical nor turbulent. Since 1860 Darel has paid a yearly tribute to Cashmere of four tolas of gold dust; but no Cashmere officials ever enter the country, and the state of the community differs in no respect from that of other Kohistan republics. In the autumn of 1866 the Cashmere troops invaded Darel in two columns, to chastise the people for joining the rulers of Chitral and Yassin in an attack upon Gilgit. The only resistance met with was at the foot of one of the passes, where a breastwork had been erected across the defile. After a day's resistance the Darelis fled, fearing probably to be taken in rear by the flanking column, and in the pursuit suffered considerably. The whole population fled to the mountains, and no further resistance was offered. A few of the Darel leaders were hung, and after a brief stay the troops returned, not without considerable difficulty owing to an unusually early fall of snow, which caused the loss of over a hundred men. Since then Darel has given no trouble to Cashmere. The Kandbari Valley is popularly credited with great mineral wealth, from which probably it derives its name. No mines, however, are now worked there.

Above Darel is the small community of Hodar, which has paid a yearly tribute of two tolas of gold-dust to Cashmere since 1860. From the head of the Hodar Valley a road leads into the Gilgit Valley. In Hodar there is a small settlement of Cashmeri refugees, who fled from the severity of the Pathan rule about a hundred years ago.

Above Hodar are the small valleys of Talpin and Gies, which support a scanty population. The former is a dependency of Chilas, but Gies is claimed both by Chilas and Gor, between which communities disputes have of late become frequent in consequence. From the heads of both of these, good roads lead into the Gilgit Valley. Continuing up the right bank of the Indus, Gor, the last Yaghestan community on that bank, is reached, standing on a high plateau two miles from the river. Notwithstanding its exposed position and its proximity to Chilas, idolatrous customs have lingered in Gor longer than in any other place in Shinkari, and are even now scarcely extinct. Gor can furnish 500 fighting men, and in ancient times was always closely connected with Gilgit. Since the establishment of the Sikh rule across the Indus, Gor has paid to Cashmere a yearly tribute of twelve goats, and is bound to furnish one man from each house for military service in time of war. It also gives three hostages for good conduct, who are changed periodically. The people of Gor claim to have been Mussulmans for only three generations, and are all Soonnees.

There are three forts in Gor, named Loosonotkot, Doolotkot, and Tunelkot. The people of Gor have always been friendly with Chilas. At present Gor is noted in the Kohistan for the good quality of the wool it produces. The tradition is still preserved of the god Taiban, who was the tutelary deity of Gor, and whose worship was continued to a very recent date. A rude sculpture of a horse still exists, which is named "Taiban's horse." Even now Taiban is invoked occasionally as a witness of a solemn covenant. Along the river, at intervals the whole way from Gor to Seo, are said to be a number of ancient rock inscriptions.

A few miles above Gor the small detached village of Thalich forms the extreme limit of Yaghestan, consisting only of 11 houses: it forms, as Mr. Drew observes, the smallest of independent communities. The people of Thalich make common cause with those of Chilas, of whom they are an offshoot, and are protected by them against more powerful enemies.

Above Herbund, on the left bank, is the large community of Chilas, which embraces six valleys. The principal villages are Tor, 200 houses; Chilas, 140 houses; Geen, 5 houses; Takk, 80 houses; and Booner, 60 houses. Chilas can furnish about 1,500 fighting men, without counting a number of immigrants from other communities who have lately settled in the country. Roads lead from Khaghan in the Hazara country by the Babusar Pass to the Indus in seven days, and from Shardi in the Kishengunga Valley by the Shotô Pass in five days. There is also a road from Astor by the Mazenoo Pass, only practicable at any time for men on foot, and closed in winter, by which Booner is reached in four days. The road up the Indus from Chilas is difficult and almost impassable even for men on foot. This difficulty of access has given the Chilasis a spirit of independence, and a distinctive character among all the Kohistan communities. Though but comparatively recent converts to Islam, they are bigoted and fanatical beyond all other Dards, owing, it is said, to Chilas having been at all times a favourite resort of Moollahs from Swat. Being Soonnees, every Shiah who falls into their hands is put to death without being reserved for the usual alternative of slavery. The whole community can muster 3,000 men capable of bearing arms, and have at all times borne a high reputation for bravery. In former days, Chilas, with the neighbouring valleys of Darel and Gor, owed allegiance to Gilgit, but the Chilasis were notorious for the way in which they tyrannised over the whole surrounding country, making frequent raids, plundering and carrying off men, women, and children into slavery. The Cashmere, Kishengunga, Astor, and Gilgit Valleys were frequently laid under contribution, and they boast of having once plundered Iskardo. During the Sikh occupation of Cashmere, an expedition was sent against Chilas, but sustained a disastrous defeat. Permission was granted by the British Government, in 1851, to the Maharajah Golab Sing to exact reprisals for a successful raid, and two columns entered Chilas,—one from Cashmere by the Lolab Valley, and one from Astor by the Mazenoo Pass. The Chilas fort was taken, and the Chilasis made submission, agreeing to pay a yearly tribute of a hundred goats and five tolas of gold, and engaging that the fort of Chilas should not be re-built. Takk is now the only fortified place in Chilas. Since then Chilas has given no trouble to the Cashmere Government. Three hostages reside in Cashmere, and are changed yearly. Cashmere officials do not, however, visit the country, and any attempt to exercise authority would probably be resisted.

The love of music, dancing, and polo, which are so marked among all the neighbouring communities, are unknown in Chilas; and ponies, which are common enough elsewhere, are scarce.

The country is bare and treeless. The village of Chilas is situated about half a mile from the Indus, on a plain three miles in length, and from a mile to a mile and a half in breadth, sloping gently down to the river. Booner, though a dependency of Chilas, has paid a separate tribute to Cashmere of twelve goats and three tolas of gold since 1842. The Chilasis relate that in former times a Hindoo Rajah, named Chachai, ruled in Chilas over the whole of Shinkari, but that, dying childless, his country became divided into republican communities, as at present. In later days a disastrous civil war broke out in the community between two brothers, Bôt and Matchuk, which ended in the defeat and expulsion of all the partizans of the latter. The Bôte are now the most prosperous family in Chilas.[1] Tradition still preserves the name of Naron, a

[1] This is perhaps the origin of the name "Bôte," applied indiscriminately to all Dards by Cashmere officials.

tutelary deity of Chilas whose worship was practised in former times.

The system of government is the same in all these small republics, and differs somewhat from what obtains among the Afghans. Each village, according to its size, has a certain number of Jushteros, or elders, who are appointed according to the general estimation in which they are held for bravery, liberality, and eloquence. They receive no benefit from their office, and are more the servants than the leaders of those they represent. Each village manages its own affairs irrespective of its neighbours, and it is in the superintendence of these details that the Jushteros are mostly occupied. All matters affecting the village are discussed in public. A meeting for this purpose is called *Sigas*. At the Sigas all who please join in the discussion, the Jushteros apparently encouraging individuals to give their advice, and when the general opinion has thus been elicited, the Jushteros announce the decision they have formed. At a Sigas of several villages, a single Jushtero is appointed by each village at a meeting previously held. At the close of the general discussion, which is open as before, a loud whistle is given, after which none but the representative Jushteros are allowed to speak. If war with a neighbouring valley is determined on, the Jushteros settle the way in which those they represent shall take part in it; but beyond their personal influence they have little voice in determining the general policy to be pursued. It is for them to decide who shall stay at home and who shall take the field, and in the innumerable disputes about land their decision is respected; but should the dispute involve men of another village, they are expected to do their best for their own townsmen. In more serious disputes the whole valley makes common cause against its neighbours; but this does not prevent all the communities combining, when threatened by an external foe. Criminal offences are not dealt with by the Jushteros, but by the Moollahs, who profess to administer the law according to the Sharyat; this is, however, set aside in many instances in favour of ancient custom, which is very strong in some communities, and the prompt redress of grievances depends greatly on the personal influence of the aggrieved. Murder is regarded as a personal matter to be avenged by the nearest relative; but should the case be of a very wanton nature, and the family of the murdered individual have sufficient influence with the community, reparation is enforced by general consent. Blood feuds are not permitted to last for an indefinite period, as amongst the Afghans, and after a time the parties are brought together and made to swear peace on the Koran. The crime of murder is rare, and the readiness to spill blood on slight occasions so noticeable among the Afghans is unknown. No public measure can be carried out except by general agreement, the details being left for the Jushteros to arrange.

The communities in the lower part of Shinkari, being more exposed to Afghan influence, and having been longer converted to Mahommedanism, have lost many of their characteristic customs; but the remoter valleys of Chilas, Gor, Darel, and in a lesser degree Tangir, are probably little changed from what they were two hundred years ago. A very singular custom exists in these valleys, by which the sexes are kept strictly apart during the summer, from May till September. The custom is apparently very ancient, and any attempt to evade it is punished by fine; the old women of the family being specially charged with the responsibility of seeing that the rule is observed. Great difficulty is said to be experienced in rearing children in Chilas. The great mortality among them is ascribed to the climate, but it is more probably due to too close intermarriage.

Agriculture is left entirely to the women, with the exception of ploughing, which demands more strength than they can afford. In summer the men spin wool and attend to their flocks on the mountain pastures; but in winter the duty of caring for the herds is relegated to the women.

Slavery is a recognised institution in all the Shinkari republics—a matter in which they contrast unfavourably with the Afghans and Neemchas of the Indus Valley, among whom it is unknown. Prisoners taken in war, and the children born of slave parents, form the servile class.

CHAPTER II.

GILGIT—HUNZA—NAGER—PONYAL.

CLOSE above Gor the traveller leaves Yaghestan and reaches Cashmere territory. On the left bank is the extensive Astor Valley, of which so good a description has already been given by Mr. Drew. Twelve miles below the point at which the Indus, after a north-westerly course of nearly 500 miles, turns between precipitous rocks abruptly to the south, is Boonji, the name of which has been converted by the Sikhs and Dogras into Bawanji. This was at one time a flourishing settlement, and is said to have contained eight forts, which would represent a population of between 2,000 and 3,000 souls. Its prosperity began to decline under the influence of the wars undertaken at the beginning of the present century by the rulers of Yassin and Chitral, which finally led to the Sikh occupation of Gilgit. In 1841 Boonji only contained 200 houses, and it was then finally ruined by the disastrous flood, of which Mr. Drew gives so interesting and able an explanation. The water-courses, on which the prosperity of such alluvial spots entirely depends, were swept away, and the amount of labour and expense necessary for their repair are beyond the power of a small village community. The Cashmere Government has lately taken them in hand, with a view to encouraging the resettling of the place, which at present only contains a colony of convict horse-stealers and a small garrison.

Immediately opposite Boonji is the narrow but fertile Sai Valley. Six miles further up, the Gilgit river falls into the Indus. The lower part of the valley of this river, nearly 40 miles in length, forms the Gilgit district. Gilgit itself, situated 24 miles from the Indus, at an elevation of 4,890 feet, combines the advantages of a good climate, a considerable extent of fertile land, and a central position, and appears from ancient times to have been the seat of a succession of rulers who, to a greater or less degree, exercised authority over the surrounding valleys and states.

The ancient name of the place was Sargin. Later, the name of Gilit was given to it, and this has been changed to Gilgit by the Sikh and Dogra conquerors; but among the inhabitants it is still known as Gilit or Sargin-Gilit. Its identity with the Gahalata of ancient Sanscrit literature has been suggested.[1] A few remains still exist of ancient stone buildings, apparently of the same description as the Martund and Pandrethan temples in Cashmere. Their presence indicates that a considerable amount of wealth and scientific skill must once have existed in this remote valley, of which not even the tradition has survived.

The settled population of the Gilgit district, which is very mixed, amounts to about 4,500 persons. The language spoken is Shina, though the Shins are numerically inferior to the rest of the population. The Gilgit pronunciation of Shina is supposed to be more refined than the dialects spoken in neighbouring valleys, but of late it has received a large infusion of Cashmeri, Dogri, Hindustani, and Punjabi expressions. The former rulers had the title of Ra, and there is reason to suppose that they were at one time Hindoos, but for the last five centuries and a half they have been Mahommedans. The names of the Hindoo Ras have been lost, with the exception of the last of their number, Shiri Buddutt. Tradition relates that he was killed by a Mahommedan adventurer, who married his daughter and founded a new dynasty, since called Trakhané, from a celebrated Ra named Trakhan, who reigned about the commencement of the fourteenth century. The previous rulers, of whom Shiri Buddutt was the last, were called Shahreis. The present Ra of Gilgit, Alidad Khan, belongs properly to the ruling family of Nager, but was installed as representative of the Trakhané on account of his descent from that family through his mother, on the failure for the second time of direct male heirs.

The population must have been at one time at least six or seven times as numerous as it is at present. High on the mountain sides up to an elevation of 10,000 feet, wherever the presence of water and the contour of the hill side permit, the ground is terraced and levelled, showing that it was once cultivated; but many generations have passed since its cultivation was abandoned. The period of greatest prosperity was probably under the Shin Ras, whose rule seems to have been peaceable and settled. The whole population, from the

[1] McCrindle's *Ancient India.*

Ra to his poorest subject, lived entirely by agriculture. According to tradition, Shiri Buddutt's rule extended over Chitral, Yassin, Tangir, Darel, Chilas, Gor, Astor, Hunza, Nager, and Haramosh, all of which were probably held by tributary princes of the same family. The first decline of prosperity was due apparently to the introduction of Mahommedanism, by which the Shin kingdom was broken up into a number of small independent states, which, from that date, commenced to make periodical wars with one another; but the final blow to the prosperity of the country was administered by the establishment of a warlike ruling race in Yassin, three centuries later.

A glance at the map will show that Gilgit is situated in the centre of the most mountainous region of the Himalayas. Nowhere else in the world, probably, is there to be found so great a number of deep valleys and lofty mountains in so small a compass. Within a radius of 65 miles from Gilgit the survey maps show, amidst innumerable smaller peaks, eleven varying from 18,000 to 20,000 feet, seven from 20,000 to 22,000 feet, six from 22,000 to 24,000 feet, and eight from 24,000 to 26,600 feet; while half of the tract thus included still remains to be surveyed. A rival to Everest and Kinchinjunga may yet be found among the mountains of Kaffiristan.

From Gilgit, mountain roads radiate into all the surrounding valleys, and it is easy to see how favourable is its position for the establishment of the head-quarters of a confederacy of small states. The lofty mountains around it, though barren and rocky at their bases, are covered with verdure higher up; and everywhere above 7,000 feet are thick fine forests, grassy glades, deep glens, and running streams, of which a view of the mountains from below gives little promise. Here the wild goat (*C. Falconeri*) roams in great numbers almost undisturbed, his chief foes being the snow ounce (*F. Uncia*), and the wild dog (*C. Rutilans*), of which packs are sometimes seen. In winter, when forced down to lower ground by the snow, a few fall victims to village matchlocks; but the number thus slain is few, as the Dards are not keen hunters. Above the forest, where innumerable peaks tower up in their panoply of eternal snow and glacier, ibex (*C. Sibirica*) are found in great numbers. The solitudes which they share with the red bear (*U. Isabellinus*) and the snow cock (*T. Himalayanus*) are rarely disturbed by the hunter's voice. On the lower and more barren hills, below the forest, are to be found numerous flocks of the wild sheep (*O. Vignei*). At an elevation of 11,000 feet, wild onions grow in great profusion, and to this fact the range is indebted for its Chinese name Tsungling. (The Onion Mountains.)

The principal difficulty in communication is caused by the rivers, which in winter are shrunk to small dimensions, but in summer, fed by snow-fields and glaciers of enormous extent, become impassable torrents, bringing down tons of soil in their turbid waters. Many of the streams are rich in gold; especially those flowing from the great Rakiposh Mountain, and it is probable that a scientific search for minerals would be well repaid. The natives believe that the gold is generated by the glaciers, because the greatest quantity is found in the glacier mud, and there are traditions of small but rich veins of earth having been occasionally laid bare by earthquakes. Gold-washing is only practised in winter, and then by none but the poorest and meanest of the population, though the quantity found even with the rude apparatus employed is sometimes very remunerative. The gold itself is of fair quality, the best being of twenty carats.

Nearly half way between Gilgit and the Indus is the Bagrot Valley, which contains several flourishing villages, and is capable of supporting a population of 2,000 or 3,000 souls. The Bagrot gold-washings are celebrated for the quantity and fine quality of the gold they yield, and the valley contains many signs of mineral wealth. It was a favourite summer resort of the old Gilgit rulers, and was their last place of refuge when hard pressed by external enemies. The Bagrot people belong almost entirely to the Shin caste.

A mile below Gilgit itself the Hunza River joins that of Gilgit. Though fordable in winter, this is in summer a deep and rapid torrent more than a hundred yards in breadth, bringing down with it an enormous quantity of soil from the lofty mountains it drains. Cashmere jurisdiction extends some 25 miles up the valley to a point at which the river makes a sudden bend from a westerly course to south-south-east. As generally happens where these abrupt changes of course in a stream are found, the river here flows between perpendicular rocks, across the face of which none but the most expert cragsmen can find a path. On the occasion of my visit to Hunza in 1876, I suddenly found myself confronted with a more difficult and dangerous piece of ground than I had ever traversed in a tolerably large experience of Himalayan sport. For nearly half a mile it was necessary to scramble over rocky ledges, sometimes letting oneself down nearly to the water's edge, then ascending 300 or 400 feet above the stream, holding on by corners of rock, working along rocky shelves 3 or 4 inches wide, and round projecting knobs and corners where no four-footed animal less agile than a wild goat could find a path.

Immediately above the bend of the river is the district of Chaprot, consisting of the fort and village of that name and three other villages. This has always been a fruitful source of contention among the rulers of the three states of Hunza, Nager, and Gilgit, between which it is situated, principally on account of the fort, which, according to local ideas, is impregnable. It is situated in the angle formed by the junction of two streams, with high precipitous banks, and can therefore only be approached from one side. It has belonged in turns to all three states, but at present is garrisoned by Cashmere troops. Continuing up the valley to the eastward, at about 52 miles from Gilgit, the residences of the rulers of the two states of Hunza and Nager are reached, the river forming the boundary between the wild two.

The view of the great Rakiposh Mountain from the north side is truly striking. From the water's edge it rises without a break for 19,000 feet to its topmost peak, which is over 25,000 feet above the sea-level. Its lofty sides, girdled with dark pine forest and seamed with glaciers and *mers-de-glace*, some of which reach nearly down to the water's edge, overlook numerous fertile settlements which are nourished by streams flowing from the great mountain. Above the forests extensive fields of snow sparkle and glitter in the summer sun, while, overtopping all, great points of granite, on whose steep sides the snow can scarce find a resting-place, give emphasis and unity to a scene not easily forgotten.

Above Hunza the course of the river, which rises in the Hindoo Koosh, lies entirely in Hunza territory. The people of these two states, of whom so little is known, have been counted as mere robber tribes, who have brought themselves into notice by their depredations on the caravans between Yarkund and Leh. This is, however, scarcely a just estimation of them. They are of the same stock as the people of Yassin, Ponyal, and the majority of the people of Gilgit and the neighbouring valleys. So far from being mere robber tribes, they are settled agricultural communities, living under rulers who boast of their long unbroken descent from princes of native blood. Hemmed in by lofty mountains, they are proud of the independence they have always maintained, and they probably present the spectacle of a race living under almost the same conditions now as their forefathers did fourteen centuries ago. The rulers are called *Thum*, and their families are descended from twin brothers, Moghlot and Girkis, who lived about the end of the fifteenth century. General Cunningham makes the somewhat natural mistake of confounding Girkis with Kirghiz, and suggests that the former inhabitants of Hunza must have been Dards (?), who have since been displaced by the nomads of the Pamir. From this he goes on to argue that the rulers of Shigar must also be of Kirghiz blood; and following the same line of argument he states that the Astor district must once have belonged to the Tibetan race, because the ruling family are Makpons. He also mentions the Gilgitis as a race of Dardo-Tibetans, for which assumption there is no adequate foundation.[1]

I have been told by a Nepaulese gentleman that *Thum* is a Chinese title, meaning Governor, and that it is used in a reduplicated form *Thum Thum*, to signify a Governor General.[2] Its existence in these countries, where its origin has been completely lost sight of, is curious and must be extremely ancient.

The rulers of Nager, who are descended from the first-named of the two brothers, are called Moghloté, the present Thum being Jaffer Zahid Khan. Though the smaller of the two states, Nager has the larger population, owing to the greater amount of cultivable ground which it contains. The population is about 10,000 souls. The land where cultivable is extremely fertile and bears exceptionably heavy crops, and the Nager streams are rich in gold. The country is especially famous for its apricots, which are dried and exported to the Punjab in considerable quantities. Nearly opposite Hunza, the Myetsil River, a considerable stream, joins the main river from the south-west. The fort of Nager and the Thum's house are on the southern side of this stream, about 3 miles from the junction, at an elevation of 8,000 feet above the sea. Both sides of this valley belong to Nager, and it forms the eastern boundary of the state. At the head of it is the difficult and dangerous road over the Hispar Pass into the Shigar Valley, which is never used except in cases of necessity. When Cashmere authority was temporarily

[1] Cunningham's *Ladakh*, pages 27, 38, 58, 295.

[2] It is perhaps a corruption of the word Tung, which appears in many titles. The Chinese Governor of Kashgharia is called Tsung Tung, and the officer who commands the troops is styled Tung-lung.

expelled from Gilgit, between 1852 and 1860, communication with Nager was maintained by this road. In the prosperous times of the Shin rule, the Thums of Nager acknowledged the Ras of Gilgit as their feudal superiors, and tradition relates that the villages of Nilt, Gulmit, Toll, and Pussunt, which now belong to Nager, were given as dowries to different Thums who married daughters of the Trakhané. At the time of the Sikh occupation of Gilgit a very close connection existed between the rulers of the two states of Gilgit and Nager. Between Hunza and Nager a great rivalry, which has frequently resulted in open hostility, has always existed, but they are generally ready to combine against an external foe. Though possessing a common origin, the people of Nager are distinguished for timidity and incapacity for war, and no instance is recorded of their being victorious over their rivals of Hunza, at whose hands they have suffered many disastrous defeats. The people of Nager are Shiahs, and slavery does not exist among them. Since 1868 Nager has been tributary to Cashmere, to which it makes an annual payment of twenty-one tolas of gold and two baskets of apricots.

Between the two states the river flows between perpendicular banks, 300 feet high and 600 feet apart at the top. The banks can only be ascended in a few places, which are carefully guarded.

Hunza, which comprises a considerable extent of territory, has an agricultural population of about 6,000 souls. North of the great range of peaks which bisects the principality from south-east to north-west the country opens out into rolling grass steppes, supporting a scattered pastoral population. Here the great wild sheep (*O. Poli*) roams in large herds. This tract is known as Little Goohjal, to distinguish it from Wakhan, which, south of the Hindoo Koosh, is known as Goohjal proper.

From the north-east the Shimshal stream, draining the valley of that name, brings down a great volume of water in summer, and effectually closes all access from the south, except to men on foot. The only direct route in summer to the Shimshal Valley from the south, is by the high and difficult Moorkôn Pass, which is only open for two months in the year. From the head of the Shimshal Valley a road, only passable for men on foot, leads to Koolanooldi in the Yarkund Valley. It was by this road that attacks on the caravans were organised. Another route leads by a somewhat difficult pass on to the Shimshal Pamir, from whence a road goes to Ujadbai in the Sirikol Valley. On this Pamir dwell a number of Kirghiz, who pay tribute to the Thum of Hunza, and here the wild yák (*P. grunniens*) and the kyang (*E. Hemionus*) find their most western limit. The Pamir appears to lie north-west and south-east. From its north side the Kara Kuchkar Pass leads to Raskum, once a flourishing settlement, situated on one of the many branches which form the south-western source of the Yarkund River. Considerably further to the north-east are the two small communities of Pakpooh and Shakshooh, situated on different tributary streams. Pakpooh is said to contain about 4,000 and Shakshooh about 5,000 souls, and they are situated respectively at an elevation of about 10,000 and 9,000 feet. Both pay tribute to the ruler of Hunza. These curious people, of whom very little is known, are of Aryan race, and are described as being of very fair and ruddy complexion. Their language is Chagatai Turki, but, like the Ghalchah tribes of Sirikol and the countries north of the Hindoo Koosh to the westward, many of them speak Persian also. Dr. Bellew,[1] who met some men of the tribe, speaks of them as being a tall, very fair, and handsome race, of a purely Aryan physiognomy, and describes them as poorly clad, carrying matchlocks, of timid and subdued demeanour, and very cautious of giving any information regarding themselves. He mentions that they spoke Turki to other people, but conversed among themselves in a totally different language. He says that they are Mussulmans of the Shiah sect, like the Wakhis and Badakhshis,—that is, Maulais.

Nearly due north of Hunza is the small mountain state of Sirikol. The rulers of the two states have ever maintained a close friendship in spite of the mountains which separate them. From Girtchah in Goohjal, Tashkurgan is reached in eight days. Horses can only travel by the Kilik route, which is longer than that by the Kirish Pass ; but the road is excellent and open all the year to both horses and camels. For about two months in summer the road by Misgar is impracticable for horses on account of the depth of the stream that has to be forded. The route by Rishipjerab and Derdee is then used, but men on foot can travel by Misgar at all times. Good roads also lead to Lungar and Kabr-i-Bosai in Wakhan territory.

In Wakhan, Sirikol, and Yarkund, the name of Kunjoot

[1] Bellew's *Kashmir and Kashghar*.

is given to Hunza, though this name is not in use among the inhabitants themselves, nor among any of the people dwelling south of the Hindoo Koosh. The name, according to the pronunciation of the inhabitants themselves, is more properly Hunzoo. In ancient times it was called Challaj Bultum, a name which has now fallen into disuse.

The ruling family of Hunza is called Ayeshé (heavenly), from the following circumstance. The two states of Hunza and Nager were formerly one, ruled by a branch of the Shahreis, the ruling family of Gilgit, whose seat of government was Nager. Tradition relates that Mayroo Khan, apparently the first Mahommedan Thum of Nager some 200 years after the introduction of the religion of Islamin to Gilgit, married a daughter of Trakhan of Gilgit, who bore him twin sons named Moghlot and Girkis. From the former the present ruling family of Nager is descended. The twins are said to have shown hostility to one another from their birth. Their father, seeing this and unable to settle the question of succession, divided his state between them, giving to Girkis the north, and to Moghlot the south, bank of the river.

Age did not diminish their enmity, and Girkis, while out hunting, was one day killed by an adherent of Moghlot, a native of Haramosh, named Mogul Beg, who under pretence of a quarrel with Moghlot took service with Girkis, and persuading him to look up at some game on the cliff above him, drove an arrow into his throat. Girkis left only a daughter, who, according to the custom of the country, became Queen or Ganish of Hunza. Her first care was to avenge her father's death. The tradition relates that having sworn to tear the murderer's liver with her teeth, she carried out her vow to the letter. Left without a chaperon, she was not long without getting into a scrape, as young ladies in similar circumstances are apt to do. The young prince Kamal Khan of Nager, a younger son of Moghlot, crossed the river by night, serenaded her, and won her heart. Night after night the lovers met, unknown to the rest of the world, till serious consequences ensued; and one fine day it was announced in Hunza that, though Providence had not yet provided the princess with a husband, it had seen fit to bless her with a son. Morals in Hunza are not of the strictest even now, so that few questions were asked, and the good people generally contented themselves with beating their drums, dancing, and the usual festivities proper on the occasion of the birth of the prince Chiliss Khan. Kamal Khan seems to have "behaved badly" all through, as the above story is concealed in Hunza under the fiction that a prince of Shighnan became the husband of the princess, but that his name being forgotten he is known only as Ayesho (Heaven-sent), from which the present ruling family of Hunza takes the name. The present Thum of Hunza is Ghazan Khan.

The rivalry of the two brothers has been perpetuated till the present time, and has become almost an article of faith between the people, as well as the rulers, of the two states. The people of Hunza have a greater reputation for bravery than those of Nager, but they are not warlike in the sense that the Afghans may be said to be so. Secure in the inaccessibility of their country, they have preyed upon all their neighbours without fear of retribution. At the time of the insurrection of the seven Khojas in Yarkund in 1847, Shah Ghazanfur Khan of Hunza rendered assistance to the Chinese in overcoming the rebellion. In recognition of this service a jagheer was granted to him close to Yarkund, and a brass tablet inscribed with a record of the friendship of Hunza towards Pekin, and its reward was placed on the gates of the city. A fixed subsidy was paid by the Chinese to the Thum of Hunza, who in return gave a nominal allegiance. Under these circumstances, the caravans between Yarkund and Leh were regularly plundered in the valley of the Yarkund River near Koolanooldi by the Hunza people, whilst the Chinese authorities winked at a proceeding which they were unable to prevent or punish. The raids were organised by the Thum, and looked upon as a right conferred by the proximity of the caravan route. His agents in Yarkund sent notice when a rich caravan was about to start, and a party was at once despatched by mountain paths known only to themselves, to lie in wait for it. Besides the plunder carried off, young men were generally seized and sold into slavery, which caused Hunza to become the chief place of resort for slave-merchants from Badakhshan. The last exploit of the kind, and the most successful recorded, took place in 1865, when no less than 50 camels and 500 ponies laden with merchandise were driven from Koolanooldi to Hunza by way of Ujadbai without opposition. Kunjooti eyes still glisten when they talk of that day, but the establishment of the firm rule of the Atalik in Kashghar put a stop to future proceedings of the kind. On the re-establishment of Chinese power in Kashghar in 1878, Ghazan Khan preferred a formal request to me that he might revive his ancient right of "striking the road." The Nager people were never concerned in these raids.

With the former rulers of Gilgit the people of Hunza seem to have lived on tolerably good terms, rendering them a nominal allegiance in the days of their prosperity, but asserting their independence as the later Trakhané Ras grew weak. The Sikh and Dogra governors found their most troublesome enemies in Hunza, against which country they never gained a single success. Hunza raids against Gilgit villages were incessant, till in revenge an expedition was organised in 1848 by Nuthoo Shah, the first Sikh governor of Gilgit. Falling into an ambuscade, Nuthoo Shah and Karim Khan, the Ra of Gilgit, were both slain, and their army defeated with serious loss. In the beginning of 1865 a second attempt was made in alliance with the ruler of Nager, whose lukewarmness or treachery caused the expedition to fail. In the succeeding year a third attempt was made, but the Nager ruler's treachery was now evident, and while the Hunza force looked on from across the river, a skirmish took place between the *quondam* allies, in which the Dogra governor was badly wounded. The unexpected defection of their allies and the loss of their leader so disheartened the Dogras that the whole force took to flight, and reached Gilgit with the loss of only two men. Their artillery, which had been at first abandoned, was recovered by the presence of mind of one of the Dogra officers, who, with a few men, preserved the semblance of order in their retreat. The expedition having been undertaken without permission from Jummoo, the governor was recalled and his proceedings ignored.

In 1869 the raids from Hunza were at last put an end to by the present Thum consenting to yield allegiance and pay a yearly tribute of two horses, two hounds, and twenty ounces of gold-dust, which has since been paid regularly.

The elevation of Hunza is 8,400 feet. It may be described as an elongated crescent with the points towards the south, formed by the hills receding from the river. At each end is a strong torrent flowing from the glaciers on the peaks, which are just visible to the north. The cultivation extends about 7 miles in length by 1½ in depth. This is terraced down to the river, but in parts is broken and undulating. It is divided into eight districts,—Naraydass, Assanabad, Doorkun, Hyderabad, Aliabad, Ganish, Baltit, and Altit. Each district has its own fort. Baltit is the Thum's residence. The ground is thickly wooded, and the whole eastern end is covered with orchards of fruit trees. The cultivation is extremely good, and fruit of all kinds grows in abundance.

Mahommedanism sits but loosely on the Hunza people, who make no secret of their preference for easy-going tenets. Though professing to be Maulais, they are disowned by their own Pirs, who refuse to visit the country, and no contributions are sent by them to their spiritual chief. They are great wine-drinkers, and are reproached by their neighbours for their readiness to eat unorthodox food,[1] and for the immorality of their women. Firearms are scarce, and bows and arrows are still not quite obsolete.

The people of Hunza and Nager belong to the caste called Yeshkun by the Shins, but amongst themselves known as Boorish. They differ slightly in appearance, the Nager people apparently showing an infusion of Tartar blood, derived, no doubt, from their Iskardo neighbours. The Hunza people, who are a somewhat taller race, have finer features and are distinguished for being more deliberate and less vivacious in their actions. The language, called Boorishki or Boorishaski, is identical in both states; the Hunza pronunciation being rather more broad and drawling than that of Nager. This language was first published by Dr. Leitner. All their songs, however, are in Shina,—a language which is supposed to lend itself more readily to poetry,—and Shina songs are sung by men who do not understand a word of that language.

Both Thums are still addressed as Soori, as a title of respect. This appears to be the same as *Sri*, an appellation of Lakshmi, the Hindoo goddess of wealth, commonly prefixed to the names of Hindoo princes in India, to denote their honour and prosperity. The Thum's wives are styled "*gánish*," which is almost identical with the original Sanscrit word for mother, and their sons are called "*gushpoor*." In cutting the throat of an animal for food, the people of Hunza make a practice of turning it towards the Thum's abode, even when many miles distant, instead of in the orthodox direction of Mecca.

Every village, according to its size, possesses one or more forts, sufficient to give shelter to the whole population. These are built of sun-dried bricks, with walls 15 feet high, and square towers at intervals of 20 yards. At night the whole population takes refuge within the walls. Similar forts exist in Gilgit, but under Cashmere rule they have fallen into disuse.

In Hunza there is a tradition preserved of the occurrence

[1] Animals not slaughtered according to the manner prescribed by Mahommedan law.

at some remote period of a Mongol invasion, but no clue exists to the approximate date. It is said to have taken place at a period before the separation of Hunza from Nager. In more recent times a prince of Nager is related to have visited Cashmere to seek assistance from Shah Jehan, which was granted, and the prince thereby enabled to expel his brother and make himself master of the country. Bernier mentions another prince from this neighbourhood, by name Bowali Khan, applying in a similar manner for assistance to Shah Jehan. This prince appears to have belonged to the family of the rulers of Iskardo or Shigar.

During the rule of Ghazanfur Khan, the father of the present Thum of Hunza, Nager was temporarily forced to give allegiance to the Hunza ruler, who had secured the active alliance of Suleiman Shah, of the Khushwakté family.

Returning into the Gilgit Valley, 19 miles above Gilgit, the Ponyal District is reached. This stretches for some 22 miles up to the Yassin frontier. Of old an appanage of Gilgit, Ponyal became in later times a bone of contention between the rulers of Yassin and Gilgit, who each possessed it in turn for a time, till it finally came into the possession of Cashmere in 1860. Soomalik, whose name will be found in the genealogy of the Gilgit Ras, is said to have given Ponyal as a dowry with his daughter to a prince of Chitral. At a later date it became an independent republic for a time, till a certain Shôt, a native of Darel, made himself Thum of Ponyal, but was shortly afterwards slain by Shah Pershah, of the Khushwakté family of Yassin, who established his son Booroosh as ruler. The present Ra of Ponyal, Akbar Khan, is a descendant of Booroosh, his father having been re-established and confirmed in his possession by the Cashmere Government in return for services rendered in the wars which finally established the Dogra rule on the right bank of the Indus. Cashmere troops garrison Ponyal, and grave cases are under the jurisdiction of the Gilgit officials, but no revenue is paid either to Cashmere or to Akbar Khan, who receives in lieu a fixed subsidy from the Maharajah, in consideration of which he is bound to maintain a certain number of men to guard the frontier posts in time of peace, and to render military service in war. But for this arrangement, Cashmere would hardly have been able to make good its footing west of the Indus, and its success in this matter may be said to be entirely owing to the father of Akbar Khan.

Great enmity exists between the people of Ponyal and those of Yassin and Chitral.

The principal place in Ponyal is Cher,[1] which has been corrupted into Sher by the Dogras. The people are, with few exceptions, Yeshkun or Boorish, but the language spoken is Shina. In religion they are mostly Maulais, a few Soonnees and Shiahs only being found amongst them. Ponyal contains about 2,000 inhabitants; the men are remarkable for their athletic figures. The soil, where cultivable at all, is fertile and yields two harvests in the year, but between the different patches of cultivation long stretches of sandy plain intervene, while at certain places the rocks close in on the river, which, for more than half the year, is an impassable torrent, so that the passage can be easily held by a few against superior numbers. In unsettled times guards are posted at these places to give the alarm by beacon fires.

At the western extremity of Ponyal is the fort and village of Gahkuch, which is the residence of the Rao Afiat Khan, a member of the Boorooshé family, who owns allegiance to Cashmere and receives a yearly subsidy in consideration of his holding this frontier post. Gahkuch is a place of some importance, as it commands the mouth of the Karoomber Valley as well as upper part of the main valley.

Opposite Gahkuch, the Karoomber Valley and river, running almost due south from the Hindoo Koosh, joins the main valley. Mr. Drew has described how this valley has during the last twenty years alternately belonged to Yassin and Gilgit. Nothing but extreme timidity or apathy can have induced the Cashmere Durbar to abandon it, as mentioned by Mr. Drew, for it is outside the natural boundary of Yassin, and could not have remained a portion of Yassin territory had the slightest disposition been evinced to retain it by the Dogras. For 25 miles the valley is broad and open, beyond that it contracts, and a road branches off past the village of Ishkaman or Ishkoman to the foot of the Durkot Pass. Continuing up the valley, which bends to the eastward, the Hindoo Koosh is crossed into the Oxus Valley by the Ishkoman Pass at a height of 12,000 feet. Formerly this road was a favourite one, but owing to recent physical changes it has now fallen into disuse.

The Karoomber Valley, which contains the ruins of several large villages, now supports only 300 souls. The former inhabitants are said to have been exposed to constant forays

[1] Meaning "an impregnable rock."

from the Wakhis and Sirikolis, but the wars of the Yassin rulers since the beginning of the century have been the most powerful agent in depopulating the country. The security given to inhabitants in one way has been accompanied by a fresh source of danger to them in another. More than once the glacier has temporarily dammed up the stream until sufficient water has accumulated to burst the barrier and carry destruction to the valley below. At Eemit there is a hot mineral spring.

CHAPTER III.

CASTES—ADMINISTRATION.

DR. LEITNER and Mr. Drew have already shown that the people of Gilgit and some of the adjacent valleys are divided into castes, which are governed by strict laws as to intermarriage. The distribution of the different castes, as shown roughly in the following table, may help to give some clue to their different origins :—

Table showing Distribution of Castes.

	Rono, Zundré or Haraiyo.	Shin.	Boorish or Yeshkun.	Krammin, Dom, Shoto, and Ustad.	Remarks.
Koli . . .	None	94½ per cent.	4 per cent.	1½ per cent.	Exclusive of Neemchas, but including under the head of Shins, Chiliss, Gabars, Mahrons, and Baterwaliks.
Palus . . .	Do.	50 ,,	40 ,,	10 ,,	
Puttun and Seo .	Do.	90 ,,	None	10 ,,	
Doobeyr and Kandia . . .	Do.	30 ,,	20 per cent.	50 ,,	
Herbund, Sazin .	Do.	64 ,,	3 ,,	33 ,,	Exclusive of Pathans and Goojurs.
Tangir . . .	Do.	60 ,,	25 ,,	15 ,,	
Darel . . .	Do.	25 ,,	50 ,,	25 ,,	
Chilas . . .	Do.	50 ,,	16 ,,	34 ,,	
Gor . . .	Do.	65 ,,	30 ,,	5 ,,	
Astor . . .	Do.	10 ,,	78 ,,	12 ,,	
Sai . . .	Do.	30 ,,	65 ,,	5 ,,	
Gilgit . . .	6 per cent.	35 ,,	55 ,,	4 ,,	Exclusive of Cashmeris and recent immigrants.
Nager . . .	5 ,,	20 ,,	60 ,,	15 ,,	
Hunza . . .	None	5 ,,	80 ,,	15 ,,	
Ponyal . . .	2 per cent.	30 ,,	55 ,,	13 ,,	
Woorshigoom .	A few families.	None	Greater part of the population.	A few families.	Exclusive of the ruling class.
Main valley above Ponyal to Chashi	None	55 per cent.	30 per cent.	15 per cent.	
Chitral Valley .	300 families	None	None	200 families	Exclusive of the regular population of Chitral.

At the risk of going over some ground that has already been traversed, a few remarks concerning them may not be out of place.

The most honoured caste is that of the Ronos, who rank next to the ruling family in every country in which they are found. The Wuzeers are generally, though not always, chosen from among the Rono families. They exist in small numbers in Nager, Gilgit, and Ponyal, gradually increasing in numbers as one travels westward through Yassin, Mastooch, and Chitral, in which places there are said to be altogether over 300 families. In Nager and Yassin they call themselves Hara and Haraiyo,[1] and in Chitral Zundra, but they claim to be all of the same stock. Some exist in Wakhan and Sirikol, where they are called Khaibar-khatar; and in Shighnan, where they are called Gaibalik-khatar. Wherever they exist they are held in great respect. They have two principal traditions concerning their origin, both of which may contain a germ of truth. One is that they are descended from three brothers, Zoon, Rono, and Harai, the sons of a certain Soomalik who ruled in Mastooch before the establishment of the Shahreis line. The other is that they are of Arab blood, and descended from Mahommed Hanifa, the son of Ali, the Prophet's son-in-law. Their small numbers, general distribution, and the universal estimation in which they are held, are evidence in favour of the first assertion, and it is possible that they may be descended from Arabs who settled in the upper part of the Chitral Valley at the time of the Arab conquest of Badakhshan, at the end of the seventh century. A claim to Arab descent is, however, very common among many sections of the inhabitants of these valleys, but it seems to rest on no real foundation. According to another version they came originally from Rajauri, near Poonch, and are descended from three brothers, Sirung, Sooroong, and Kunger Pùtool.

In appearance they are generally taller than the other inhabitants of the country, with rather high cheek bones, oval faces not thickly bearded, and fairly developed features. Some of them resemble in feature high-class Rajpoots. The esteem in which they are held is proved by the fact that they are able to give their daughters in marriage to the ruling families, and children born of such marriages are qualified to succeed to all the honours of the father's family, and intermarry with other ruling families. They also give daughters in marriage to Syuds, of whom there are a few scattered about the country, but not to the inferior castes. They, however, take daughters in marriage from both Shins and Yeshkuns. Children born of these unions rank as Ronos, and, if daughters, can, as above stated, intermarry with ruling families. The Zundré of Chitral do not refuse their daughters to the Afghans of Dir. Excep-

[1] This name recalls the Haroyu of the Zendavesta.

tional cases exist of Rono women being given to Shins and Yeshkuns when through immoral behaviour they cannot procure husbands of their own class. Rulers of Dard states give their daughters born of slaves or concubines to Ronos, but not those born of lawful wives.

Next to the Ronos, in order of consideration, come the Shins, who do not form the majority of the population anywhere except in Gor, Chilas, Tangir, the Indus Valley below Sazin, and the upper part of the Gilgit Valley above Ponyal, and are not found at all in the higher and less fertile parts, till one gets further up the Indus Valley beyond Haramosh. Although numerically inferior, they have established their language to the exclusion of others wherever they have penetrated, and there can be little doubt that they represent an alien race who at some time established themselves in the country by conquest. Amongst the many dialects of Shina now spoken, that of Gilgit, which was the seat of Shin rule, is still considered the most refined, but it is much mixed with Boorishki, and of late with Cashmeri owing to an immigration of Cashmeris which took place about a hundred years ago, at the same time as the formation of the Cashmeri colony in the Hodar Valley.

Shins give their daughters to Ronos and Syuds, but cannot marry the daughters of Ronos or Syuds in return. In the same way they marry Yeshkun women, but do not give their daughters to Yeshkuns in return. In the lower part of the Indus Valley they give daughters to the Neemchas. Owing to this system of mixed marriages they are, as Mr. Drew has pointed out, very far from being a pure race, and it is difficult to fix on any typical personal characteristics. The Shins of the Indus Valley below Sazin are small clean-limbed men, with dark complexion and eyes, and sharp features, of a type not uncommon in North-Western India. Above Sazin and about Gilgit they are of somewhat lighter complexion, but they do not show any marked type of feature.

There is a rare type, which I have only noticed among Shins, which may be characteristic of the race. These are small slight men, with thin sharp features, prominent noses and narrow chins. Mr. Drew also notices this type as prevailing in the side valleys of the Indus near Rondu and Iskardo. I am inclined to think, however, that the true Shin type is only to be found in the Indus Valley below Sazin, and that this small narrow-chinned race are merely a deteriorated type produced by long intermarriage within narrow limits.

Though their traditions as a separate race have long passed away, the Shins still look on themselves as the aristocracy of the country, and claim to be of a more honourable caste than others, without being able to show any foundation for this claim. A Shin considers it a disgrace to have to carry a load, and regards hunting and agriculture as the only honourable pursuits for a man. They are strictly confined to the Indus Valley and its affluents.

The Shins who are found in Baltistan do not, however, arrogate to themselves any superiority over their Tartar neighbours. On the contrary, the position they occupy towards the Tartars is similar to that of the Yeshkuns in Gilgit towards themselves. They are called by the Tartars, contemptuously, "Brokpas," or highlanders, from their cultivating the highest—that is, the least fertile—ground. The Baltis habitually mention this fact when speaking of the Brokpas or Dards of the Iskardo district, but do not try to account for it.

This, together with the difference of estimation in which the Shins are held in Gilgit and Iskardo, gives a valuable clue to changes which have taken place among the different races. It is evident that in Baltistan the Tartars, and not the Brokpas, are the last-comers.

As already mentioned, the part of the Indus Valley from below Gor to the Afghan limits near Ghorband is called Shinkari, and it is in the lower part of this that the purest Shin community is now probably to be found; but the name of Shinkari, which still exists in Pukli, where the population is now entirely Afghan, perhaps indicates that the original home of the Shins was in that valley.

The most remarkable peculiarity of the Shins is their feeling with regard to the cow, to which Mr. Drew has already directed attention. In spite of their conversion to Mahommedanism, the feeling is still maintained in Nager, Gilgit, Astor, and the Indus Valley above Boonji. In the Indus Valley below Astor the feeling has died out, but in the places mentioned, orthodox Shins will not eat beef, drink cow's milk, or touch a vessel containing it. A sucking calf, or any portion of a dead animal, is especially unclean, so that purification is necessary if even the garments should chance to touch them. It is not uncommon for a Shin to make over his cow and calf to a Yeshkun neighbour, to be restored to him when the calf is weaned. Shins also regard the domestic fowl as unclean, and in districts chiefly inhabited by them, not a single fowl is to be seen. These peculiarities are strictly confined to the Shin caste, and, together with other customs which will come under notice presently, afford good grounds for supposing that they were a race of Hindoos who came from the south, and, pressing up the Indus Valley, established a Hindoo state in these remote regions under the crest of the Hindoo Koosh.

The next in order and the most numerous caste are the Yeshkuns, who form the entire population of Hunza, Nager, and Ponyal, and nearly all the population of Yassin, besides being numerically superior in Gilgit, Sai, Darel, and Astor. In Hunza and Nager they do not call themselves Yeshkun, but Boorish ; and in Yassin, Woorshik and Boorisho. The language spoken, in slightly varying dialects, in these three states is known as Boorishki, Boorishaski, or Woorishki. The term "Khajoona," applied by the Gilgitis to the language as spoken in Nager, is never used in that country, and the old name also lingers in Yassin, which is still known as Woorshigoom. This language, of which an account is given in Appendix A, differs markedly from all languages in the neighbouring valleys. It has, I believe, been pronounced on good authority to belong to the Turanian family of languages.

In the colder climate of Hunza and Yassin, the people of this caste have ruddy complexions, and fair and even red hair is not uncommon. The Boorish of Nager show a somewhat different type. Many of them are short, thick-set men, with prominent cheek-bones, thick features, and thin beards. These characteristics, joined to their unwarlike nature, are probably due to an infusion of Tartar blood from Iskardo, gained during the time that Nager was subject to the Makpon ruler of Iskardo. If the Boorish are originally of Turanian origin, they have received at some time so large an infusion of Aryan blood as to have almost entirely swamped their original characteristics. Mr. Drew points out that the restrictions on their intermarriage with the Shins makes them the purer race of the two, and though these restrictions are not always closely observed, the Yeshkuns of Hunza and Nager would have little opportunity for profiting by their non-observance, so that their dash of Aryan blood must have been obtained before the appearance of the Shins. There does not appear to be any good foundation for Dr. Leitner's suggestion that the Yeshkuns are probably the product of intermarriage between the Shins and some aboriginal race. Considerable rivalry exists between the Shins and Yeshkuns, even in villages where they have lived side by side for generations.

Living among them, in varying numbers, are Syuds, Krammins, Doms, Shotos, and Goojurs. All of these occupy an inferior position except the Syuds, who relate that they first settled in the country in the time of Tamerlane. They are treated with the highest respect, and receive in marriage daughters from the ruling families, but without reciprocity, for a Syud's daughter is given only to a Syud. There are none in Hunza, but elsewhere they are scattered through the country in small numbers. There is seldom more than one Syud's house in each village.

The Krammins, who are millers and potters, are most numerous in Darel, and do not exist in Hunza or Nager. They do not intermarry with any other caste. Their name is probably derived from the Persian *kamin*, "mean," though Mr. Shaw, in his paper on "Stray Aryans in Thibet," suggests that the name is derived from *krum*, "work."

The Doms, who are musicians, blacksmiths, and leather-workers, are most numerous in Yassin, Nager, and Chilas, in which latter place they form a sixth of the population.

In Nager there is a caste called Shoto, which exists nowhere else; they work in leather, and rank below the Doms, who take daughters from them without giving in return.

Like the low caste of men of India, the men belonging to these inferior castes are of very dark complexion, coarse features, and inferior physique. Mr. Drew regards them as akin to the low castes of the Punjab, and accounts for their presence in these countries by suggesting that they are remnants of a pre-Aryan aboriginal race, who represent the earliest inhabitants of these valleys. I am more inclined to think that, like the Shins, they have come from the south to settle in these valleys. It is possible that they accompanied the Shins, or they may have followed them, gradually spreading under the protection of the Shin rule. Their status is only consistent with the existence of the Hindoo religion, which I believe to have been introduced by the Shins, and it is worthy of notice that they are not found in the upper part of the Chitral Valley.

In Gilgit itself there are a great number of Cashmeris, or, as they are called, Kashiroos, whose forefathers settled in the place in the time of Ahmed Shah Abdali, about 1760 A.D. They now form the largest section of the population, and the shrewdness which forms so distinctive a part of the character of the ordinary Cashmeri, has suffered little by transplanting. Some are said to have penetrated into Chitral, where they have since become merged in the regular population. Those in Gilgit are weavers and carpenters, and are regarded with some contempt both by Shins and Yeshkuns.

Their distinctive castes are Meer, Sheikh, Paiyr, Lon, Suniyar (goldsmiths), Dar, Rawut, But, and Tatchon (carpenters); all of which castes are also found in Cashmere. They are all tillers of the soil, and the trades at which they work occasionally, such as weaving, are irrespective of caste, with the exception of the goldsmiths and carpenters. They intermarry without restriction among themselves, except the Tatchon, who give daughters to the other castes, but do not receive from them in return. They occasionally give daughters to Shins and Yeshkuns without reciprocity. With the Krammins and Doms they do not marry at all. In spite of the small estimation in which they are held, they form the most thriving and energetic part of the population, while at the same time they have lost some of the worst characteristics of true Cashmeris.

In the valleys south of Gilgit, the Goojurs pasture their cattle on the high lands, not mixing with the people of the country in any way. In Tangir and Darel they are found in great numbers, and they count their herds by thousands. They attach themselves to no locality, though perhaps for a generation the same men frequent one pasture-ground, building rude hovels and making a poor pretence at cultivating small patches of ground; but a very small excuse seems to be sufficient to drive them, with their herds, in search of fresh pastures. A great number inhabit the upper part of the Dir and Swat Valleys, and a few have found their way into the Gilgit Valley. They all speak the dialect of Punjabi, peculiar to their caste. Like the Syuds, they must rank as a class rather than as a caste.

Vigne, speaking of the existence of caste in Baltistan, remarks that it may perhaps be considered as a proof of the Hindoo origin of the natives of that country. Though the Baltis have undoubtedly a considerable amount of Aryan blood in their veins, they must be classed as a Mongolian race; but the existence of a caste system among them, which will be mentioned further on, must be ascribed to Dard, or more particularly to Shin, influence; for it is to be noted that the caste distinctions above mentioned are only found in their strictly Hindoo form where the Shin element exists among the population. The class distinctions existing in Chitral are of a totally different nature, and the whole evidence seems to mark the Shins as having been a Brahminical race, who succeeded in imposing their language, and to a great extent their customs, on races to which they were numerically inferior.

The system of administration which existed under the old Shin rulers is still maintained by the Cashmere Government with slight modifications. The revenues of the Ra were derived as follows: From the land, a tax called "Koodkool" was paid on every crop, in kind, according to the quality of the land, which was regularly and apparently not heavily assessed. A pastoral tax of a sheep or goat, called "Ganoni mari," was paid by each household every alternate year. This might be commuted at the will of the payer for the sum of two shillings yearly. A tax called "Nyoori shairi," of four shillings a year, was paid by each water-mill, which was, however, exempted from payment the first year after construction. For washing gold-dust, in which a considerable number of people in certain villages find employment during the winter, a fixed tax of fifty-five pounds sterling, called "Ra-i-dillki," was paid yearly. In the autumn a grape tax, called "Jachai toni," was levied in kind on every vine according to its size; and when the wine-making began, a certain number of measures of grape juice, called "Rêkhoo," were also paid to the Ra. A money tax of sixteen shillings, called "Garé toloo," was levied on each marriage, for which the bridegroom was liable. Every weaver's house furnished eight yards of cotton cloth to the Ra, which was called "Buyetcho pâtchi." Silk also, which was produced by nearly every household, paid a tax called "Chooshi purtai," which consisted of as many cocoons as the Charboo could grasp in one hand, out of the heap collected by each family. Four villages, in which silk was not produced, paid a commutation of one fat sheep, valued at eight shillings, which was called "Chooshi mâri," per village.

Besides these, a curious tax, called "Cha etté goé," was paid by the villages of Burmess, Khomer, and Naupoor only, which consisted of all the milk and butter produced by one cow from each house in those villages between the Ganoni and Chili festivals,—that is, from the middle of May to the end of October. These three villages also gave the Ra one small kid yearly from each house. This impost was called

"Cheloo." No reason is assigned for the origin of these peculiar taxes, which are said to have been instituted by Queen Jowari. No Shin ruler would have received cow's milk. Another local tax, called "Satêgi," was paid by the village of Bagrot. This originated in a visit paid by Habbi Khan when a boy, during the reign of his mother Jowari, on which occasion the village community made him a grant of a piece of land. It was, however, found inconvenient to cultivate it under the same system as the other crown lands, so it was, shortly afterwards, resumed by the village, on an agreement to pay a tax of thirteen taraks of wheat, equal to five and a half quarters, yearly.

Every trader who entered the country paid a duty, "Masool," of one roll of cloth out of each load, or two per cent. of live-stock, or the equivalent in other goods. At the time of sheep-slaughtering at the winter solstice, one hind quarter was furnished by each house, out of which a certain number went to each of the minor officials, and the head and hind quarters of all game killed was the perquisite of the Ra.

Money payments were made in gold-dust, which is still largely used as a circulating medium. An amount of the value of eight shillings is called "Baghaloo."

The Yerfah, or Ra's steward, was responsible for the collection of the land revenue; but special men called "Burro" were appointed to collect the other dues.

In addition to these sources of revenue, the Ra owned tracts of land in each of the larger villages, the cultivation of which was managed by the Yerfah. In each of the villages a certain number of families called "Wairêtché" were responsible for the ploughing, sowing, and irrigation of the Ra's lands under the management of the Yerfah, in return for which they were exempt from all other payments. The harvesting and winnowing were done by the whole village, who combined on certain days for the purpose. The "Wairêtché" of Gilgit, who numbered twenty families as against six or seven in other villages, were also bound to furnish a load of wood from each family daily during the winter, for the use of the Ra's household, and one load of torchwood a year. Certain families in Gilgit also held the hereditary office of cooks to the Ra, for which they were exempt from all taxes. There are still four families who claim that their ancestors cooked for Shiri Buddutt, and who take no part in the Taleni festival, which celebrates his death, but shut themselves up in their houses, and regard it as a time of mourning. These are apart from several other families of hereditary cooks to the later rulers, who still render service to the present Ra of Gilgit.

The country was divided into districts, for each of which a Wuzeer was responsible. Wuzeers were obliged to be of good family, and are still chosen only from the three principal castes, *viz.*, Rono, Shin, or Yeshkun. The office was not hereditary, but was held for life. On the appointment of a Wuzeer, three pieces of land were taken from among the peasants' holdings, and assigned to him in addition to his own family possessions. Four families were appointed to manage the whole cultivation of his land and furnish him with one household servant, in return for which they were exempt from all dues of personal service to the Ra. The Wuzeer was responsible for the peace and welfare of his district, and for leading the men of it in war. When the population was called to arms, the Wuzeer had the right of releasing one man in each fortified village from military service, in return for which he received from the man so released two "baghaloos" of gold-dust on the return of the army. If, however, the expedition returned without having fought, only half the fee was paid. On the occasion of a marriage taking place, a cake of leavened bread was sent to the Wuzeer of the district by the father of the bride.

In each village was a "Tarangfah" appointed by the Ra, who acted under the orders of the Wuzeer within his own limits. In time of war he had the right to release three men of his village from military service, from whom he received the same dues as the Wuzeer. He also received a fee of three shillings on each marriage taking place in his village, and had three families assigned to him for service, who were exempt from all other tax or service. He further received sixteen yards of cotton cloth yearly from the village weavers, and was especially charged with the management and preservation of the irrigation arrangements.

The dues paid to all officials are called " Luspik."

Next in rank to the Tarangfah, but with totally different duties, came the Yerfah, who had charge of all the private lands of the Ra, to whom he filled the office of steward. He was responsible for everything connected with the cultivation of the Ra's lands in each district, and received six kharwars of grain out of each crop. As *luspik*, four families in Gilgit, and one in each outlying village in which the Ra owned land, were assigned to him, whose duty it was to furnish him each with a yoke of oxen for ploughing his own lands. This service he could commute if he pleased for one baghaloo of gold for each yoke of oxen. He was also responsible for the collection of the "Koodkool" tax, but no authority could be exercised over him by the Wuzeers or Tarangfahs.

Next to the Tarangfah among the district officials was the Charboo, who acted as an assistant to the Tarangfah in each village. His *luspik* consisted in exemption from all taxes, and two of the ruler's fees on marriage a year; it being part of his duty to collect the "Garé toloo" tax. He also received a certain amount of the meat tribute. To help him in his work he was allowed four men called "Zeytoo," who only served for a year as peons to the Charboo, and were paid by an impost of 12 lbs. of grain from each house, which was divided among them.

Dr. Leitner suggests that these names of officials are of Tartar origin. None of them now exist in Baltistan except Wuzeer and Trangpah (Tarangfah). If it be the case that they are originally Tartar titles, it may be taken as a proof of the influence which the Iskardo rulers once exercised in Dardistan.

Justice was administered by the Wuzeers in their own districts. Cases which principally arose out of disputes about land were generally settled by a fine of cattle, sheep, or gold-dust. Any case involving a larger fine than one baghaloo of gold-dust was heard by the Ra. Serious crimes, such as murder or treason, were punished by the destruction of the whole family of the offender. His house was razed to the ground, and his relations reduced to slavery, and sold or distributed according to the will of the Ra.

The dues above mentioned are still paid, some of them to the Cashmere Government, and some to the present Ra of Gilgit.

The same system exists in Hunza and Nager, and in some respects in Wakhan. The following measures are in common use; in some cases they differ only in name, in others they differ slightly in amount :—

Dry measure.

1 haiy	=	$2\frac{1}{2}$ lbs. English . . .	Shina.
6 haiy	=	1 kot	Shina.
1 heejootee	=	3 double handfuls, about 2 lbs. .	Boorish.
8 heejootee	=	1 heechok	Boorish.

Gold-dust measure.

2 surkhoo	=	1 rut.
2 ruts	=	1 baghaloo (Shina), or Khur (Boorish).
2 baghaloo	=	1 toloo (Shina), or Bai (Boorish).

The hollow formed between the thumb and the back of the hand, placed palm downwards with the fingers extended, was the old measure of a Baghaloo.

Land measure.

1 chookili	=	the amount it takes 6 kots of wheat to sow.
2 chookili	=	1 chooni.
2 chooni	=	1 makhmi.

Long measure.

A span is called Ditt (Shina), or Tishti (Boorish).
2 spans = 1 hutt (Shina), or khash (Boorish).

CHAPTER IV.

BALTISTAN—THE BROKPAS.

A SURVEY of the Dard tribes of the Indus Valley would not be complete without a brief excursion into Baltistan.

Returning to the Indus Valley, the small district of Haramosh above Boonji calls for little remark. The inhabitants are principally Yeshkuns, and speak the Gilgiti dialect of Shina. Above Haramosh a complete change takes place in the population, which thence upwards is almost entirely Balti,—that is, of Tartar blood,—and the language spoken is a dialect of Thibetan. Dwelling among the Baltis, in small numbers in the Rondu and Iskardo districts, and in a larger proportion in Khurmang and Himbaps,[1] are, as is shown in the accompanying table, Shins, Yeshkuns, and Doms who speak Shina.

	Rono.	Shin (Rom).	Yeshkun.	Dom.	Balti.
Haramosh	None	8 per cent.	84 per cent.	8 per cent.	None.
Rondu	None	1 ,,	12 ,,	1·5 ,,	85·5 per cent.
Iskardo	None	6·5 ,,	1·5 ,,	A few houses	92 ,,
Khurmang.	None	23 ,,	12 ,,	5 per cent.	60 ,,
Himbaps . . .	None	52 ,,	13 ,,	1 ,,	34 ,,

But it must be noted that the dialect of Shina spoken in Rondu[2] and Iskardo is the Astori, while in the Khurmang and Himbaps districts that of Chilas-Darel is in use. These people hold a position in the community inferior to that of the Baltis, who call them Brokpas, "highlanders," from the circumstance of their cultivating the higher and less fertile ground in the lateral valleys and on the mountain sides, while the lower—that is, the best—ground is in the hands of Baltis. Mr. Drew, who overlooked this fact, accounts for the name

[1] The district drained by the Shingo River is included in the Khurmang district, and is chiefly inhabited by Brokpas. Himbaps is the name given by the Baltis to the Dras district, which by the Brokpas is called Hoomuss.

[2] The village of Doro is the only one in the Rondu district in which the Gilgit dialect of Shina is spoken.

and their presence in Baltistan by suggesting that they came over the passes from Nager and settled among the Baltis;[1] but there are no Shins in Nager, nor is the Shina language spoken there. The account given of themselves by the Brokpas is no doubt the true one. About the beginning or middle of the seventeenth century the Makpon[2] ruler of Iskardo was Ahmed Shah, who had four sons. The eldest of these succeeded him as Prince of Iskardo, and by the aid of his brothers subdued the country to the westward as far as Chitral. The three younger brothers were eventually established in Khurmang, Rondu, and Astor, and founded the families which ruled in those places with more or less independence till the conquest of the country by the Dogras. The Brokpas say that in the course of the different warlike expeditions of the four brothers, they were carried off from their own countries, Astor and Chilas, and forcibly settled in the places in which we now find them. This is borne out, not only by different dialects of Shina spoken among them, but by the fact that no Brokpas are to be found in Shigar and Khapalor, the princes of which places do not belong to the Makpon family. Had they found their way into Baltistan by the route suggested by Mr. Drew, Shigar is the district in which they would now be most numerous.

Towards the Brokpas the Baltis occupy the same position of a superior and privileged class, as the Shins occupy towards the Yeshkuns elsewhere. Notwithstanding their inferior position, the Brokpas maintain their caste system among themselves. The distinctive term of Shin is rarely used, probably on account of the terms Shiné and Shinalok being applied indiscriminately to all classes of Brokpas by the Baltis. The name by which the Shins of Baltistan prefer to call themselves is Rom, which must not cause them to be confused with the Rono caste previously mentioned. They acknowledge themselves to belong to the Shin caste of Gilgit, Astor, &c., but divide themselves into four sub-castes—

1. Sharsing,	3. Doro,
2. Gaboor,	4. Yoodey,

—who intermarry freely and are in all respects equal amongst themselves. This probably represents a state of things which once existed in the Shin countries further west. It is perhaps worth noting that the term Rom is the one applied to them-

[1] Drew's *Jummoo and Cashmere*, page 433.

[2] Makpon is the family name of the princes of Iskardo, Rondu, Astor, and Khurmang.

selves by our English gipsies; it would be curious if any connection could be traced between them and the Shins.

The Roms refuse to intermarry with the Yeshkuns, who, in Khurmang and Himbaps, are also called Broosha. This is almost the same name as that by which the Yeshkun caste still call themselves, as already mentioned, in Hunza and Nager.

Greatly as the Baltis differ in physical appearance from the Dards, they differ equally from their brethren the Ladakh Tartars. Mr. Drew notices this, and ascribes their thicker beards, better-cut features, and taller stature, to the fact of their being Mahommedans and to climatic influences.[1] But a difference of religion could scarcely produce such physical changes, and modifications of feature caused by the influence of local circumstances must require a great number of generations to show any marked result. The difference is undoubtedly due to their having been Aryanised by a mixture of Dard blood. It requires but a very superficial observation to see that the Baltis are a mixed race possessing no distinctive type of their own. I have seen Baltis who in personal appearance could not be distinguished from Dards, while others only require a pigtail and a sheepskin coat to pass for Ladakhis, and Mr. Drew has remarked the same fact :—

"In one or two higher valleys of Baltistan I have noticed a difference in the people, as compared with the ordinary Balti, which may perhaps be due to some admixture of Dard blood, although the fact is not noticed or known by the people themselves. Thus, at Pakora in Braldu, the men were much better-looking than the ordinary Baltis; they had well-shaped features and a manly bearing. I noted this at a time when I knew less about the Dards than afterwards; now it seems to me likely that some of that race came over the difficult passes from Nager and made a settlement among the Baltis. Again, in the Turmik Valley many villagers have a high and broad forehead and hooked nose, though they call themselves Balti. I have little doubt that here, too, is Dard blood, the immigrating Dards having become absorbed into the community of Baltis, but still making a mark."[2]

The Baltis of Shigar generally, and the higher classes of Baltis everywhere, show the greatest amount of Aryan blood in their features. Cunningham says the Shigar Baltis show the greatest amount of Kirghiz blood, and are much shorter than those of Iskardo: he was probably referring to the people of the upper part of the Shigar Valley, who show less Aryan blood than their neighbours. Strongly-marked Dard features among the Baltis are invariably coupled with inferior muscular

[1] Drew's *Jummoo and Cashmere*, page 356. [2] *Ibid*, page 433.

development—a point in which the ordinary Ladakh Tartar will compare favourably with any race.

I quite agree with Mr. Drew as to the means by which the Baltistan Tartars have improved their not very classical features, but I should strongly doubt Shin immigrants intermarrying willingly with them; considering the caste prejudices which still exist among the Shins further west, they are not likely to have consented to free intermarriage till they had been reduced to the position of a conquered race.

The actual facts tend to show that at some period a wave of Tartar conquest flowed down the Indus Valley from the eastward, absorbing an Aryan race who were the prior occupants, and was not checked till it reached Rondu. Both in Iskardo and Rondu the tradition survives that the former inhabitants of the country were Dards, or, as the Baltis call them, "Bloyil," the name they now apply to the people of Gilgit, Astor, &c. It is said that when the Makpons first came to Baltistan the country was under Bloyil rulers; but that Tartars had already begun to settle there. The Brokpas are universally recognised as recent arrivals, and not as the descendants of the former inhabitants. The result of this mixture of Aryan and Mongolian blood is decidedly good. Without losing the patient, industrious habits of the Tartar, the Balti has acquired a keener intelligence and a more enterprising spirit,[1] which qualities, though latent in the Dard, are of little benefit to him owing to his want of energy and dislike of steady work.

No more flourishing community is to be found in the North-Western Himalayas than that of Baltistan. Wherever there is water, the hill sides are terraced and cultivated with the greatest care, but the increasing population is overflowing its limits, and bids fair, under the protection of Cashmere rule, to extend itself into districts hitherto considered exclusively Dard.

Intermarriage between the Brokpas and Baltis, though practised, is not common. The children are called according to the father's race, but the two races live alongside each other with little intermixing. Nevertheless it is evident that the Baltis have at some time been strongly influenced by Dard customs. It is not my intention to enter into any detailed account of the Baltis, but a brief acquaintance with them is sufficient to show that they are far more deeply imbued with Dard customs than casual intermarriage with the present Brokpas would account for.

[1] Drew's *Jummoo and Cashmere*, pages 357-8.

Amongst other peculiarities, they have adopted caste distinctions which are unknown among Ladakh Tartars. The Balti castes are—

1. Wuzeer.
2. Riboo Trakchos.
3. Shali Trakchos.
4. Plamopa.
5. Mon.

The Wuzeer caste is again divided into twelve sub-castes, who intermarry on equal terms. They are—

1. Wullipa.
2. Aphatpa.
3. Yoostrumpa.
4. Kanapa.
5. Isgownpapa.
6. Koorsoopa.
7. Boropa.
8. Shagirpa.
9. Mooradpa.
10. Shatoosenpa.
11. Guchapa.
12. Chukutpa.

As mentioned by Mr. Drew, the Wuzeer caste shows the largest admission of Dard blood. It is a matter for speculation whether this is the cause or the effect of the superior position they hold. They take daughters from the caste next below them, but do not give daughters in return. The next three castes intermarry on equal terms, but the Riboo Trakchos rank highest. The Plamopa are the most numerous, and form the great body of the population. The Mons are musicians, and answer in every respect to the Doms of Gilgit. They do not intermarry with the other castes, who do not even take daughters from them, and they are held in small estimation.

It is naturally a matter of great interest to know what was the Aryan race that preceded the Tartars in Baltistan, and a clue may still be found. In the Indus Valley above Khurmang, Mr. Drew gives the names of ten villages of Buddhist Dards. I have not had an opportunity of visiting these villages, and most of the information I have concerning them is gathered from Mr. Drew's work and from Mr. Shaw's paper.[1] From the specimens of their language given by Messrs. Drew and Shaw, it is evident that they speak a dialect of Shina, which, however, differs so much from that spoken by the Baltistan Brokpas, that the latter are obliged to use the Balti language in conversing with them.

The following extracts from Mr. Shaw's paper will show the chief points of interest concerning them as compared with other Dard communities:—

"While isolated among strangers they have preserved themselves

[1] Stray Aryans in Thibet, *Journal, Ben. Asiat. Socy.*, 1878.

with a caste-like feeling from amalgamating with them, and seem to have only recently and very superficially accepted the religious beliefs of their neighbours. The greater part of the tribe is thus nominally Buddhist, while two or three of their north-western villages bordering on Baltistan have become Mussalman."

* * * * * *

"Foremost among their tenets is the abhorrence of the cow. This is an essentially Dard peculiarity, though not universal among them. Unlike Hindus, they consider that animal's touch contamination, and though they are obliged to use bullocks in ploughing, they scarcely handle them at all. Calves they seem to hold aloof from still more. They use a forked stick to put them to, or remove them from, the mother. They will not drink cow's milk (or touch any of its products in any form); and it is only recently that they have overcome their repugnance to using shoes made of the skin of the animal they so contemn. When asked whether their abstaining from drinking the milk and eating the flesh of cows is due to reverence such as that of the Hindus, they say that their feeling is quite the reverse. The cow is looked upon as bad, not good, and if one of them drank its milk, they would not admit him into their houses."

* * * * * *

"Thus, although the Brokpas of Dah-Hanu are nominally Buddhists, yet their real worship is that of local spirits or demons, like the Lha-mo (goddess) of Dah. Her name is Shiring-mo.[1] A certain family in the village supplies the hereditary officiating priest. This person has to purify himself for the annual ceremony by washings and fastings for the space of seven days, during which he sits apart, not even members of his own family being allowed to approach him, although they are compelled during the same period to abstain from onions, salt, chang (a sort of beer), and other unholy food. At the end of this period he goes up alone, on to the rocky point before mentioned, above the village, and after worshipping in the name of the community the deity who dwells there in a small cairn, he renews the branches of the "Shukpa" (*Juniperus excelsa*) which were placed there the previous year, the old branches being carefully stowed away under a rock and covered up with stones."

* * * * * *

"In each house the fireplace consists of three upright stones, of which the one at the back of the hearth is the largest, 18 inches or 2 feet in height. On this stone they place an offering for the Lha-mo from every dish cooked there, before they eat of it. They also place there the first-fruits of the harvest. Such is their household worship.

"Besides this spirit-worship, which is their tribal religion, they have a superficial coating of Buddhism. They say that three or four cycles,—that is, forty or fifty years ago,—after a war between Shigar and Ladakh, when their country was occupied by the Ladakh army, the Lamas converted them. The head Lama at the monastery of Skirbuchan, further up the river, told me, however, that it was only some twelve or fifteen years ago that the Brokpas were converted by Lamas from his monas-

[1] The *Shiri* in this name is worthy of note.

tery, who went on begging tours amongst them. But this may have been a mere revival. At any rate, there is a remarkable absence in the Dah-Hanu country of those Buddhist monuments (long stone dykes covered with inscriptions, and tall structures surmounted by obelisks and containing relics, called respectively Mané and Chorten), which form such a conspicuous feature along the roads and in the villages of Thibet."

* * * * * *

"Mr. Drew, who has given a most interesting short account of these Brokpas in his 'Jummoo and Kashmir' is, I think, mistaken in supposing that they have no caste as the other Dards have. I have heard of at least three caste-like divisions, which we may call those of priests, cultivators, and artizans. The priestly families (called Lhabdak, *Thib.*) form the highest division in each village. Although men of the next caste are allowed to come into their houses, yet it is only on condition of washing their hands and faces before so doing, especially if they have recently been among the Gentiles (Thibetans, &c.)—a precaution that does not seem to be considered necessary on other occasions by the Brokpas, who are a very dirty people. This next caste which forms the bulk of the people is called Rüshens. The younger branches of the priestly families become Rüshens, since there can only be one priest of a Lhabdak family in each village.

"Besides these, there is a lower caste consisting, in the village of Dah, of only five families. They were originally blacksmiths, it is said, but no longer carry on the ancestral calling. They are called Ruzmet (*Thib.*), or Gargyut. Their women are not allowed to approach the cooking-hearths of the higher caste, nor are the Rüzmet men, excepting after a purification similar to that of the Rüshen on going into the houses of the priests. The higher caste will not eat what is cooked by them.

"Reversing the custom of the Hindus in the matter of marriage, the lower caste may take wives from the higher, but not *vice versâ* (except in the case of the priests, who, I gather, can marry Rüshen women). Probably as a consequence of this, a married daughter is never allowed to re-enter the house of her parents, and may not touch anything belonging to them. After three generations of marriages with the higher caste, the progeny are admitted into it.

"Polyandry is the rule in Dah-Hanu."

* * * * * *

"It is not only in marriage that they keep themselves apart from their neighbours. They will not eat with the Thibetan Buddhists or Mussalmans or other outsiders, nor will they allow these to come near their cooking places. The caste prejudice seems to originate on the side of the Brokpa, for their neighbours often eat in their houses; only separate dishes are given them, which are afterwards purified by burning juniper. No Brokpa will eat in the house or from the dishes of a Thibetan; nor will he eat fish or birds, or (of course) cow's flesh. Formerly, if they had been among the Thibetans, they would purify themselves with the smoke of the "Shukpa" before entering their houses again."

* * * * * *

"The people of each group consider themselves to be one community. The Dah people reckon from seven ancestors, who first colonised their villages, and of whom they give the names, *viz.*, Lalüsho (from whom the Lhabdaks, or priests, spring); Zoné, Dákré, Gachaghé (these three are the ancestors of the Rüshen caste); Düsé, Gabüré, and Tukshüré (these are the fathers of the Rüzmet caste). The land of Dah is still divided according to these families, though some of it has changed hands."

*　　*　　*　　*　　*　　*

"So much for the (so-called) Buddhist Brokpas. But the villages of the same tribe which lie exposed to Mussalman influences down the Indus on the two roads leading north-west and south-west respectively, have all been converted to Islam. Of the settlements on the former road—that down the Indus—and in side valleys near it, the village of Ganok is entirely inhabited by Mussalman Brokpas, while those of Dangel, Marul, Chulichan, and Singkarmon are inhabited partly by Mussulman (Shiah) Brokpas, and partly by Baltis (Thibetan Mussulman) of the same sect. Below this the population is entirely Balti. On the other road, that across a low pass south-westward to Kargil, the villages of Tsirmo and Lalung are also inhabited partly by Mussulman Brokpas and partly by Mussulman Thibetans from the adjoining district of Purik. These Mussulman Brokpas on both roads speak the Dah dialect, and dress like the Dah people, and keep apart from the Mussulman Thibetans, both in matter of marriage and eating. But they have no caste inequalities amongst them like their non-Mussulman kinsmen, and generally they do not object to drinking milk, though at Tsirmo there seems to be a relic of the Brokpa prejudice against the cow, in the fact that their women do not touch that animal."

The intensity of their feeling with regard to the cow and domestic fowl shows their kinship with the Shins of Gilgit, and the fact that that feeling is one of aversion, and not of reverence, is sufficient to show that in the case of the latter it has not sprung into existence since their conversion to the faith of Islam, but is an ancient tradition of the race. The form of spirit-worship, the traces of which are preserved among them, appears to be identical with that of which the traditions still linger in Gilgit, and the reverence shown for the cedar and its purifying properties links the Dah-Hanu Dards still closer to the Shins of Gilgit. Buddhism, having been recently introduced among them, has penetrated only skin-deep, and their practices in these matters are probably little changed from their pre-Buddhistic state, proving what can otherwise only be a matter of inference and conjecture, that the religion of the Gilgit Shins previous to the introduction of Islam was not Buddhism. The existence of a strict caste system among them mentioned by Mr. Shaw is particularly noteworthy, though the reversal of the system by which higher castes take wives from the lower without exchange is especially curious. The maintenance of the custom of not eating with outsiders, even of their own religion, is most remarkable, and shows the former prevalence among the Shins of some type of Brahminism. Mr. Shaw speaks of them as Brokpas, but I did not hear that name applied to them, either by Baltis or by the Brokpas of Dras. I was told that they call themselves Árderkaro, and by the Baltis they are named Kyango. The latter recognise them to be of the same stock as the other Brokpas, though these do not acknowledge them as kinsmen.

Mr. Drew mentions a tradition existing among them that they came from the westward, and suggests that they belong to an earlier immigration. I believe that we may see in them the relics of the race which once occupied the whole Indus Valley between Leh and Gilgit, and to which the Baltis of the present day are indebted for their infusion of Aryan blood.

CHAPTER V.

YASSIN—CHITRAL.

FOUR miles above Gahkuch, the frontier fort of Ponyal, the valley contracts to a narrow defile, and travelling becomes exceedingly difficult for a distance of 9 miles. In the course of this defile there are two points, about 4 miles apart, at which the passage can literally be barred by a single man, the precipitous rocks on either side making it impossible for the most expert cragsman to find a way, except along the narrow path beside the river. These two points are situated on the respective frontiers of Ponyal and Yassin, and a small guard is maintained on either side of them; the 4 miles of debateable ground between them being claimed by neither state. Passing into Yassin territory, the valley slightly opens out, the hills on both sides rising to a great height in fantastic pinnacles and castle-like crags with perpendicular scarps. Sixteen miles from the Ponyal frontier the mouth of the Woorshigoom Valley is reached, and 10 miles beyond the junction is the village of Yassin, or Yessen, at an elevation of 7,800 feet. The valley here opens out to more than a mile in width, and the mountains on both sides lose their precipitous appearance. Ten miles further on the valley again contracts, and at about 25 miles from Yassin the foot of the Durkot Pass is reached, whence Surhad on the right bank of the Oxus is at a distance of only two days' journey. For about four months in the year horses are unable to traverse this pass, but men on foot can find a passage at all times, except for about two months in the depth of winter. The height of the summit of the pass is probably about 14,000 feet. The village of Durkot at its foot is memorable for the treacherous murder, in 1870, of Mr. Hayward, the first Englishman who visited Yassin.

The people of Woorshigoom, as already mentioned, belong to the Boorish stock, and speak the same language as that spoken in Hunza and Nager, with only slight variations of dialect. This applies only to the main body of the tillers of the soil, and not to the ruler or the ruling class, who threaten in time to efface the original inhabitants. By them the local name of Boorishé has been converted into Woorshik, from which also the valley takes its name. I am unable to say to what language the term *goom* belongs, but it evidently means either "valley" or "country," as there are several instances of its application to signify the place inhabited by certain people, as Kalashgoom, the country of the Kalash. In Hunza, Nager, and Gilgit, Yassin is sometimes called Azair, which may be the ancient name of the valley, but is more likely a corruption of the name Ghizr, a district of some importance further to the westward. The people of both Yassin and Chitral are also sometimes styled by their eastern neighbours Poré, and their country Poriaki, from *boor*, "the west." The fixed population of Woorshigoom is, owing to oppression and misgovernment, very small, probably not exceeding 3,000 souls. The soil is particularly rich and fertile, though the climate will not permit of its yielding more than one crop in the year. The ruling family are styled Khushwakté, from an ancestor named Khushwakt, and the title assumed is the Persian one of "Mihter." Reminiscences of the more ancient rulers exist in the names of certain spots, such as *Thum rai*, "the Thum's seat." The present Mihter, Gholam Mohi-oodeen, is better known by his nickname of Peihlowan Bahadoor. He is a young man of twenty-nine years of age, and of manly and energetic character, inherited from his father, Gohr Aman, whose cruelties in Gilgit have been related by Mr. Drew, but who with all his cruelty of disposition was undoubtedly an able and energetic soldier. Peihlowan Bahadoor succeeded his brother Meer Wulli, when the latter was forced to fly from the country after the murder of Mr. Hayward. The princes of the Khushwakté family rule over a considerable part of Upper Chitral as well as Yassin, but generally prefer the latter as their place of residence.

From Yassin two roads lead to the Chitral Valley. By the Toowi Pass, Mastooch can be reached in five days: this route, however, can only be used in summer, when it is the one most frequented, as by it the numerous river-crossings, which constitute the chief difficulty to be encountered, are avoided. The pass is a high one, probably not less than 16,000 feet, and a difficult piece of glacier has to be traversed. The second and easier, though longer, route is by Ghizr and Laspoor.

This road runs from the mouth of the Woorshigoom Valley

along the bank of what I will still call the Gilgit river,[1] though the name is not properly applied to it in the upper part. Forty-three miles from the Ponyal frontier the village of Chashi is reached.

General Cunningham and Pundit Munphool give the name of Parasot to this branch of the river; but, though I have questioned many people on the spot, I have not found any to whom the name is known. This strip of valley is called Kho; it is thinly populated, and very narrow. More than half the population are Shins, who here reach their most westerly limit, and the language spoken is Shina. In the Battigah or Battiret Valley there is a considerable colony of Goojurs.

In the Woorshigoom and Kho Valleys, a number of remarkable stone tables of great antiquity are found. They are about 30 feet in diameter, and are formed of huge boulders, arranged with great precision with a flat side outwards, so placed as to form a perfect circle about 3½ feet high. On these are placed a number of flattish boulders of nearly equal size, projecting a few inches beyond the edge of the circle all round. The centre is filled with small stones and rubbish, which may or may not have been as originally intended. The labour of transporting and placing in position such huge blocks must have been immense. The local tradition is that they were the work of giants in old days. At Chashi and Yassin there are collections of several of these tables placed close together, and in several places between these points and the upper part of the Woorshigoom Valley there are single tables scattered about.

In none of the neighbouring valleys have I found traces of similar erections, nor have I heard of their being found elsewhere in Dardistan. Under the title of "Prehistoric Remains in Central India"[2] Mr. Rivett-Carnac has described a number of circular grave mounds, which would seem from the description to resemble these stone-circles in Yassin. It is strange that they should exist in this valley only, for, when once made, they must be practicably indestructible; but owing to its physical features, Yassin is well adapted to have become the refuge of an isolated race unable to maintain itself on equal terms against warlike neighbours. The circle in most

[1] The river, from its source in the Karoomber Valley to the Indus, is sometimes called *Anisari*, from *anisar*, which, in the Khowar language, signifies a mountain lake,—referring to the lake formed by glaciers in the Karoomber Valley. This may have been the *Riwansar* of the Ramayana. The name indicates that the Kho race formerly extended further to the east than at present.

[2] *Journal, Bengal Asiatic Society*, 1879.

perfect preservation is situated on the tongue of land formed by the junction of the rivers near Goopis. Vigne mentions having been told of these circles when at Astor. They are in all probability funeral mounds.

Circular stone sepulchral mound at Chashi.

At Chashi the road leaves the main valley, which above that place becomes still more narrow and precipitous, and rises suddenly among the rounded hills to open Pamir-like ground past the Pandar Lake. This lake is $2\frac{1}{2}$ miles long and half a mile broad, and is situated at an elevation of 9,400 feet. It is said to have been formed by a landslip about seventy years ago, and is now gradually drying up. Eleven miles beyond Chashi the large straggling village of Ghizr (called by the Shins Shevare) is reached, which gives its name to the whole district. At Ghizr a considerable stream joins the main stream from the south, by which a good road leads into the head of the Swat Valley. At Chashi the Shina language is not spoken, and we come in contact with the Kho race, who have crossed the watershed from the Kashkar Valley and settled in the Ghizr district, from which they have expelled the Shins. Close above Ghizr the valley contracts for a few miles, then curving round to the south opens out again to a breadth of a mile and a half, gradually contracting again to its source in the mountains at the head of the Swat Valley. This is the most western source of the Gilgit River, the different branches of which, as will be seen from the map, drain an enormous tract of country. The number of large streams rising on the north side of the mountains at the head of the Swat Valley, appears to indicate the existence there of snow-fields and glaciers of great extent.

Thirteen miles above Ghizr the road leaves the valley, and ascends for 3 miles through broad grassy slopes to the Shandur plateau, which, at the height of about 12,000 feet, is about 5 miles in breadth and perfectly level. There

Zincographed at the Surveyor General's Office, Calcutta

TIRICHMIR FROM MASTOOCH.

are two pieces of water on it, the largest of which is $2\frac{1}{2}$ miles long and three quarters of a mile broad. There is no surface drainage from either lake. Across the Shandur plateau lies the principal thoroughfare between the Kashkar Valley and the valleys to the eastward, and it is open to traffic of all kinds throughout the year. The peaks overlooking it on the north and south rise to a height of some 2,000 feet above the level of the plateau. On the western side the descent is somewhat abrupt into the narrow but fertile Laspoor Valley. The stream forming this valley takes its rise in the mountains at the head of the Panjkora Valley, and 15 miles from the foot of the Shandur plateau joins the Kashkar Valley at Mastooch at an elevation of 7,500 feet. The valley above Mastooch to the foot of the Baroghil Pass is called Yarkhoon, or, "the friend's murder," from the fatal termination of a quarrel between two fellow-travellers which once occurred in it. Below Mastooch it is called Kho, the whole being known as part of Kashkar Bala, and forming an important part of the possessions of the Khushwakté family, who, however, prefer Yassin as a residence. Mastooch is capable of supporting a considerable population, and the valley for many miles averages from three quarters of a mile to a mile in breadth. Looking down the valley from Mastooch, the magnificent mountain of Tirich Mir[1] fills the whole view. Looking up the valley from Chitral, it occupies the whole landscape in the same way, and it is said to be equally conspicuous from Zebak in the Oxus Valley. It is visible also from many points in Kaffiristan, where it is called Meysurmoon. Many wonderful tales are related about this mountain, one of which is, that in a deep glen high up on its snow-clad sides is a large tank of great beauty lined with blocks of white marble.

From the foot of Tirich Mir the Tirich Valley runs northwards for over 60 miles, gradually curving round to the eastward till it joins the Toorikho Valley, and the two streams combined, after a further course of nearly 40 miles in a southerly direction through the Moolkho Valley, join the Kho Valley 25 miles below Mastooch. These valleys form the region known as Kashkar Bala, the whole of which,

[1] Sir H. Rawlinson (in his Monograph on the Oxus, *Royal Geo. Socy. Journal*), in discussing the etymology of the word Pamir, has suggested the connection of the second syllable with our English word "mere," but in Tirich Mir and Dyemir (Nanga Parbat), not to mention Mount Meru of the Brahmins, there is nothing to connect the word "Mir" specially with the idea of a lake country.

In Baber's Memoirs (page 313) it is especially mentioned that *Mir* means a hill, but it is not specified in what language. The pronunciation appears to be properly "Mer," and not "Mîr."

with the exception of Yarkhoon and the portion of the main valley already mentioned, belongs to Chitral. The Toorikho Valley runs north-east and south-west parallel with the Yarkhoon Valley for over 60 miles to its junction with the Tirich Valley. All the three valleys, Moolkho, Toorikho, and Tirich, are extremely fertile and populous; the cultivation is continuous, instead of being in patches, as is the case in all the valleys hitherto mentioned. The soil is mostly clay and gravel, the hill sides are bare with gentle slopes, and there are no pine forests, the only trees being cedars. The villages extend high up the mountain sides, independent of the main stream, and are supported by innumerable springs which gush out everywhere. Toorikho is generally selected as the residence of the heir-apparent of the Chitral ruler. A route from the Baroghil Pass to Chitral, after crossing the Shajanalli spur, lies down the Toorikho and Moolkho Valleys, and is the one generally used in summer, owing to the difficulty experienced, at that time of year, by horses in traversing that by the Yarkhoon Valley. In Kashkar Bala ingenious wicker-work footbridges are made of plaited osiers. They are called "*chipul.*" Their vibration is very great, and they must be crossed cautiously by the most experienced. Owing to this, persons have to cross by them singly, and horses cannot use them.

Below the converging point of the valleys of Kashkar Bala, the main valley again contracts, and the Kashkar River flowing between precipitous rocks has a depth which varies in places 20 feet between its summer and winter levels. The land, where cultivable, is rich and fertile; the villages are large and populous, and the neat cultivation gives evidence of a considerable amount of prosperity. On the right bank the whole country belongs to Chitral; on the left the land, to within 20 miles of Chitral itself, belongs to Yassin. The rocks become more precipitous and the channel narrower and more tortuous, till bursting through a rock-bound gorge the Kashkar River receives the Ludkho or Injigan stream. The valley then suddenly widens, its whole character changes, and at 4 miles below the junction Chitral is reached. The hills, no longer rocky and bare, slope back gradually into grassy rounded tops with sides thickly clad with pine forest, and the distant peaks on either hand are hidden by the lower intervening hills. The climate, too, is changed, and instead of the arid, rainless character peculiar to the valleys hitherto described, it becomes like that of Cashmere, with heavy and frequent rainfalls. Further to the south the population increases in density. Forty miles below Chitral a route leads from the main valley past Ashuret over the Lowri Pass to the Afghan state of Dir. Twenty miles lower down, at Birkot, is the mouth of the valley inhabited by the Siah Posh of the Bushgali tribe, the upper end of which is entered from the Dorah Pass. Several smaller valleys are inhabited by Siah Posh, who have lost their independence, and at Bailam the southernmost Kashkar village is passed, and the Afghan state of Asmar is reached. The boundary between Kashkar and Asmar is marked by a wall built across the valley on the right bank between Bailam and Nawakali, and on the left bank by the small stream below Saoo. The valley for many miles above the boundary is reputed to be extraordinarily fertile.

Chitral, which is the seat of the ruler of Kashkar, comprises six large villages, which extend for 3 miles along both sides of the river at an elevation of about 4,000 feet. Its name has gradually come to be applied to the whole country. On the right bank is the fort in which the Mihter, or Badshah,—for he is known by both titles,—resides. Half a mile above the fort is an excellent wooden bridge protected by a stone tower at each end. All the forts in Kashkar differ in construction from those inhabited by the Shin and Boorish races, having inordinately high towers rising 18 feet above the ramparts, which are themselves 30 feet high. Their distribution also gives evidence of a more secure state of society. Instead of every village having one, and sometimes two, forts sufficient to hold all the inhabitants, as is the case in the valleys draining directly into the Indus, the only forts in Kashkar are the abodes of rulers of districts, or persons nearly related to the ruler.

The ruling family are styled Katooré, from Shah Katoor, brother of Shah Khushwakt, the ancestor of the reigning family of Yassin; but the name Kator seems to have been applied to the country in former times, before the existence of the present dynasty of rulers. The present Mihter, Aman-ool-Mulk, is about 58 years of age, and notorious for his astute and deceitful character. The number of the population he rules over can only be roughly computed, and probably amounts to less than 200,000 souls. These numbers would appear scanty for so large an extent of country, but the population is wholly agricultural, and, as in all these very mountainous countries, the habitations are, with few exceptions, confined to a narrow strip along the sides of streams.

This estimate does not include the tributary tribe of Bushgali Kaffirs, or the subjects of the Yassin ruler, who is independent of Chitral, though the close relationship existing between the two families causes them to act in concert in all important matters. Both rulers pay a tribute of horses, hawks, and hounds to the Maharajah of Cashmere, to whom they acknowledge allegiance. Iron, copper, and orpiment of superior quality are found in Kashkar. Cotton carpets of an inferior kind, which have the peculiarity of being alike on both sides, are made for local use, and Chitral daggers and sword-hilts are in great demand in the neighbouring valleys. Amongst the people of Kashkar, Chitral is constantly pronounced and written Chitrar and Chitlal. This seems to arise from a curious inability[1] to distinguish between the letters *r* and *l*; in this way Koonur becomes Koonul, Punjkorah Punjkolah, the Lowri Pass the Rowli Pass, &c.

The population of Chitral is a curious and intricate ethnological puzzle. The largest section of the population are the Kho, who inhabit the whole of Kashkar Bala, the Ludkho and Arkari Valleys, and the main valley down to Darosh, and have penetrated across the watershed as far as Chashi. They call the country also Kho, dividing it into different sections under the names *Toori*kho (*Upper*), *Mool*kho (*Middle*), and *Lud*kho (*Great*), and their language Khowar. This is the language given by Dr. Leitner under the name of Arnyia, by which it is known to the Shins of Gilgit, who style the Yassin portion of Kashkar Bala Arinah. In sound it is soft and musical.[2] Unlike the Shins and other cognate tribes hitherto mentioned, the existence of these people in the localities in which we now find them appears to date from so far back as virtually to entitle them to be considered aboriginal. They may have once occupied a wider extent of country, but there is no trace of their having conquered or displaced any previous race of inhabitants. They were undoubtedly the owners of the country until a period not very remote, and they have succeeded in imposing their language on the present ruling class, who style them contemptuously "Fakir Mushkin." They are divided into classes of which a few are Toryié, Shiré, Darkhané, and Shohané. No caste distinctions exist among them.

Above them is a large privileged class, which is divided into clans like the Afghan Khels, and spread all over Kashkar.

[1] The *l* and *r* are scarcely distinguishable in the old Persian.—*Rawlinson's Ancient Monarchies*, Vol. III, p. 110.

[2] See Appendix H.

First in rank comes the Sangallié, Rezaé, Mahomed Begé, and Khush Amadé, who are descended from the common ancestor and founder of the Katooré and Khushwakté families. They are generally spoken of as Shah Sangallié.[1] Next to them come the Zundré, or Ronos, of whom mention has already been made.[2] They are most numerous about Oyon. Below the Zundré comes a large class styled "Ashimadek." Their clans are—

Kashé.	Shaooké.
Atambegé.	Baiyeké.
Dushmunné.	Shighnié.
Ludimé.	Borshintek.
Bairambegé.	Majé.
Koshialbegé.	Jikané.

The term Ashimadek, which signifies "food-givers," is applied to all of these on account of their being bound to supply the ruler and his retainers with food to the extent of eight sheep and eight kherwars of wheat from each house, whenever he passes through their villages. This is the only revenue of any description paid by them to the ruler, and those living in the more remote villages often remain for several years exempt from even this impost. The Shah Sangallié and Zundré are altogether exempt,—the former on account of their relationship to the present ruling family, and the latter because they are descended from a former race of rulers.

Among the Ashimadek, the Shighnié and Kashé claim respectively to come from Shighnan and Kash (Kishm?), a village close to Jirm, in Badakhshan. The names of many of the others show that they trace their descent from some individual, and there appears little doubt that they are the descendants of Tajiks from Badakhshan, who settled in Chitral at the time of the establishment of the present ruling dynasty, about the beginning of the seventeenth century, whose founder they probably accompanied and aided. Their present position is not, however, due to conquest, but they appear to have gradually grown up as a large privileged class. They speak the Khowar language and form the most warlike part of the population.

In the upper part of the Ludkho Valley, above Drooshp, is a race who occupy the same position with regard to the Ashimadek as the Kho do in Kashkar Bala, and who are also styled

[1] See Katooré Genealogy. [2] See page 34.

"fakir mushkin." They are a portion of the race which occupies Munjan on the northern side of the Hindoo Koosh, and they speak the same language, with slight variation in dialect. They claim to have migrated from Munjan seven generations ago, in consequence of an invasion of that district by the ruler of Badakhshan, in which the Meer of Munjan was slain. They number about a thousand families, and, like the Munjanis, all belong to the Maulai sect. In Ludkho they call themselves Yidghâh,[1] and give the name of Yidokh to the whole valley with all its branches from the Hindoo Koosh to the Chitral river.

By the people of Badakhshan and the Oxus Valley north of the Hindoo Koosh the valley is called Injigan. The principal place is Drooshp. At Ludkho in the Tirich Valley there are a few families who speak a different language from their neighbours; but it appears doubtful whether it is a purely separate language, or only a mixture of the dialects spoken around them.

Below Chitral the mixture of tribes becomes still more puzzling. On the western side are the two small valleys of Kalashgoom and Bidir, inhabited by Kalash Kaffirs, who have long been subject to Chitral. The villages of Jinjuret, Loi, Sawair, Nager, and Shishi are also inhabited by Siah Posh, who have become Mahommedans, though in other respects they adhere to their ancient customs. They speak the Kalash language.[2]

Tradition relates that the whole Chitral Valley was once occupied by Kaffirs; but it is impossible to say whether by this term a tribe of the Siah Posh is indicated, or merely that the people in question were not Mahommedans. At Madaglusht is a small Badakhshi colony who speak Persian. Ashuret, Beorai, Poorgal, and Kalkatak[3] are inhabited by a tribe, said to speak a language cognate with Shina, who are still styled Dangariks by their neighbours, though they have long ago embraced Islam. The term Dangarik would seem to show that they were Hindoos before being converted. The villages of Pasinger, Birkote, Langorbat, Gud, Narisat, Maimena, Sukai, Nawakali, and Choondak are inhabited by a tribe who call themselves Gubber, but are called by their neighbours Narisati.[4] Their name would seem to connect them with the Gabaré of the

[1] See Appendix J.
[2] An account of the Kalash language is given in Dr. Leitner's work.
[3] This is evidently the Calcutta of Vigne.
[4] See Appendix G.

Indus Valley, but their language differs a good deal. The Chitralis always speak of them as a bald race, and the few individuals I have seen had very scanty beards. The splendid flowing locks of the Kho would make them term bald any race less liberallv endowed by nature than themselves. They are no doubt the Gebrek of Baber's Memoirs. Their language seems to link them with the Bushgalis on one side, and the tribes at the head of the Swat and Panjkorah Valleys on the other; but further examination may show that they have only borrowed words from their neighbours' languages. Several small valleys on the western side below Birkot are inhabited by Siah Posh of the Bushgali tribe, who retain their own religion and customs, though they have long been subject to Chitral. These broken tribes all belong to the "Fakir Mushkin" class. In Bailam, or, as they style it, Bargam, are a few Afghan families.

The origin of many of these tribes can be at present only a matter of conjecture, but it can hardly be doubted that this mixture of broken fragments could only have been produced by pressure from the south. The frequent occurrence of the names of Shoghoor, Shoogram, and Shogot, seems to point to the prevalence once of Shivaism, but there are no relics of ancient customs still existing to bear out the presumption that it was practised by any of the tribes now to be found in the valley. A tradition exists that the valley about Mastooch was at one time ruled over by Dangariks, who most probably were Shins from the Gilgit Valley, but there is nothing to show what religion was professed by the Kho before they embraced Islam.

As in the valleys to the eastward, manufactures are less esteemed than agriculture. In the valley below Chitral, scattered among the villages, a number of the meaner castes are found, as in the Gilgit and Indus Valleys. They are called *Ustâds*, "artificers," and are divided into *Dertoché*, "carpenters," *Dergeré*, "wooden bowl makers," *Koolalé*, "potters," *Doms*, "musicians," and *Mochis*, "blacksmiths." The two latter only intermarry among themselves, and are looked down upon by all other castes and classes. The other three castes intermarry without restriction among themselves, and occasionally give daughters to the Fakir Mushkins, who are all agriculturists. No Ustâds are found in Kashkar Bala or in Ludkho. The ruling class recognise certain restrictions on intermarriages among themselves. The Shah Sangallié marry amongst themselves, and take daughters from the

Zundré and Ashimadek, but do not give daughters in return, except to the Zundré, who, being descended from a former dynasty of rulers of the country, are regarded as of royal blood. All the rest, including the Zundré, intermarry without restriction, but never with the Fakir Mushkin class, from whom, however, they take daughters as concubines.

The regular revenue of the country is paid solely by the "Fakir Mushkin" class. Those who live by agriculture are assessed at a tenth of all produce, one sheep, one blanket, and 20 lbs. of honey from each house yearly. The pastoral community is assessed at four sheep, three woollen robes, and 30 lbs. of butter from each house yearly. A few villages, which are almost entirely employed in mining, pay 16 lbs. of mine produce yearly for each house. There is, however, very little regularity observed in collecting these imposts, and, in practice, as much is wrung from the subject population as possible. Considerable dues are collected from the merchants who trade between Badakhshan and the Punjab, and the Chitral ruler's revenue is further increased by the sale of hawks and falcons, of which great numbers are captured every year and sold to merchants, who take them to the Punjab.

The administration of justice is practically the will of the ruler, though nominally the precepts of the Sharyat are observed. In some cases the intervention of the Moollahs is useful. In one case which came to my knowledge they intervened to save the life of a condemned man who had murdered a favourite follower of the Mihter, by pointing out that the Mihter's injustice in permitting his favourite to forcibly abduct the man's wife had led to the murder. Small cases are settled by the district Ataliks.

A somewhat elaborate administrative machinery exists which was probably instituted by, or borrowed from, the Shin Ras of Gilgit. The names of many of the officials are the same, though their functions differ, and the presence of extra officials with Usbek titles shows that a new system has been grafted on the old one.

The country is divided into eight districts. At the head of each is an Atalik, whose duty it is to collect the revenue of his district and to command the men of it in war. Like the Wuzeers of districts in Gilgit, he has the right of releasing one man in each village from military service. Out of the revenue of his district he receives 12 sheep, 12 measures of butter, 20 measures of wheat, and a proportion of the produce of any mines. His land is exempt from taxes, and ten families are assigned to him as labourers. He also receives a fee of one tilla, equal to 10 shillings, on each marriage. Next to the Atalik is the Charwêlo, who has charge of a group of villages. The country being much intersected by side valleys branching out of the main valley, the whole population of each of these is generally under one Charwêlo. He is directly responsible to the Atalik of his district, and has four families allotted to him for service. His "ishpin" is eight of each kind of produce. With a few exceptions the office is confined to the Ashimadek class.

Below the Charwêlo is the Baramoosh, or head of the village. He is particularly charged with the maintenance of roads, forts, and bridges, for which he receives a yearly "ishpin" of 10 sheep, 10 measures of butter, 10 measures of wheat, and a proportion of the produce of any mines with which he is connected. His land also is free from payment of taxes, and he has the right of releasing ten men of his village from military service.

To assist him he has an attendant "Charboo," whose duties are the same as those of the Zeytoo in Gilgit. He receives a woollen robe and five sheep yearly, and his land is exempt from taxation.

In Yassin territory, both on the Chitral and Woorshigoom sides, the system and titles of officials are the same as in Chitral, showing, perhaps more strongly, the mixture of two systems.

About the person of the Mihter are five Wuzeers, who, with the exception of the Chief Wuzeer, have no fixed functions. The Chief Wuzeer is also styled Diwanbegi, and is the Mihter's slave agent. The practice of selling their own subjects has gained the rulers of Chitral and Yassin an unenviable notoriety, even among people who have not yet learned to regard slavery with the detestation in which it is held in Europe. The beauty of the Chitral (Kho) women has long been proverbial in Peshawur, Cabul, and Badakhshan, and female slaves still form not the least acceptable portion of the presents given by Chitral rulers to neighbouring princes. Chitral, therefore, has always been a favourite resort for slave-dealers from neighbouring countries, and a system grew up under which the rulers of Kashkar came to regard the sale of their subjects as a legitimate and ordinary way of eking out a scanty revenue. All who in any way fell under the displeasure of the Mihter, were consigned to the Diwanbegi, and his agents were always on the look-out for victims whose conduct might have furnished a pretext for their being sold. Failing an excuse of this sort, the requisite number was made up by forcible seizure. Of late years the market for the disposal of slaves has become circumscribed, and in Chitral the system is now limited to little more than the selling or giving away of female children to supply the harems of Cabul, Badakhshan, and Yaghestan. In Chitral the Ashimadek class can hold slaves without special permission, but none of the "Fakir Mushkin" are allowed to do so.

The weights and measures in use are—

Dry measure.

4 cheiraks = 1 batti.
2 battis = 1 mun.
3 muns = 1 bel.

A cheirak equals about 1¼ lb. English.

Long measure.

A span = 1 eisht.
2 dishts = 1 host.
2 hosts = 1 gaz.

Land measure.

2 choorums = 1 chakwarum.
4 chakwarums = 1 tukt.

A choorum is the extent of land which it takes three battis, or about 15 lbs., of wheat to sow. The money in use is the Cabul coinage.

CHAPTER VI.

TORWAL AND BUSHKAR.

IN the Punjkorah and Swat Valleys are two communities, Torwal and Bushkar, whose people can claim a close relationship with the tribes already mentioned, especially with those of the Indus Valley. The more considerable of the two are the Torwalik in the Swat Valley, who occupy the main valley for about 60 miles from Araneh to Chiroleh, and the Chahil Durrah, the habitable part of which is about 20 miles long. Within these limits there are nine fortified villages, the largest of which are Chahil, containing 1,000 families, Branihal, 800 families, and Ramet, 600 families. The whole community numbers upwards of 20,000 souls. In appearance they do not differ from the tribes of the Indus Valley, and there can be little doubt that the Chiliss are an offshoot of the Torwalik, and take their name from Chahil, the principal village of Torwal. I have not seen a sufficient number of the Torwalik to ascertain whether any tradition exists among them as to their having formerly occupied any other locality, and neither tribe seems to have retained any tradition of connection with the other, but the tradition[1] still extant among the Chiliss evidently supplies the correct clue to their former history. The separation of the two portions of the tribe has, however, produced considerable differences in the dialects now spoken.[2]

The large number of the Torwalik, as compared with most of the other Dard tribes, indicates that they must have once occupied some extensive valley like Boneyr, from whence they, like the rest, have been expelled and thrust up into the more mountainous tracts by the aggressive Afghans. By the Afghans they are called Kohistanis, a name given everywhere by Pathans to Mussulmans of Indic descent, living in the Hindoo Koosh Valleys. The never-ceasing encroachment from the south is gradually pushing the Torwalik further north. Their most southern village, Chiroleh, has a mixed population of Afghans and Kohistanis, from which the latter

[1] See page 10. [2] See Appendix D.

will no doubt before long be eliminated. Greatly as they dislike the Afghans, their hostility seldom rises to active opposition, their usual attitude being one of passive resistance. The Afghan, on his part, penetrates fearlessly into the Kohistan for purposes of trade, disregarding black looks and cold welcome so long as he can discern a profit to be made. Many of the villages have Pushtoo as well as local names. The Torwal country is rich and fertile, yielding below Chodgram two crops of great abundance yearly. This would show that the elevation of Chodgram is about 7,000 feet. The people own enormous flocks of sheep, goats, and cattle, yielding great quantities of butter, much of which finds its way into the Peshawur market by the hands of Afghan traders. Iron also is found in Torwal.

The Torwalik have been too long converted to Islam and exposed to the preaching of Swat Moollahs to have retained any customs connected with other religions. Like most of the other Dard tribes, they have retained their national dances.

Bushkar is the name given to the community which inhabit the upper part of the Punjkorah Valley, whence they have overflowed into the upper part of the Swat Valley, and occupied the three large villages of Otrote, Ushoo, and Kalam. They live on good terms with their Torwal neighbours, and number altogether from 12,000 to 15,000 souls. Their principal villages are Tull and Kalkot in the Punjkorah Valley, containing respectively 1,500 families. They are the most degraded of all the Dard tribes, and, in spite of a fertile soil and abundant flocks and herds, live in great squalor. Amongst themselves they are exceedingly quarrelsome, and are adepts in the use of the sling, by means of which they hurl stones with great force and precision. Exposed as they are to raids from every side, they seem unable to offer any resistance; and, notwithstanding a payment of yearly tribute, they are subjected to frequent attacks for the sake of wringing additional payments from them. The three villages in the Swat Valley pay tribute to Yassin, and the three northernmost villages in the Punjkorah Valley pay a double tribute to Yassin and Chitral. Birkot, Biar, and Rashkot pay a double tribute to Chitral and Dir, and the five Bushkar villages below Rashkot pay tribute solely to Dir. Rashkot is better known under its Pushtoo name of Patrak. There is also a large Goojur population, which pays tribute to Dir. In recent years a considerable migration of Kho has taken place from Ghizr to Ushoo, where Khowar is in consequence beginning to be spoken. The Bushkarik proper are divided into three clans, the Moolanor, Kootchkhor, and Joghior. They say that they have been Mussulmans for nine generations, and the peculiar customs still common among the Shins do not exist among them. Till somewhat recently they used to expose their dead in coffins on the tops of hills. The Bushkar dialect[1] approaches more nearly to modern Punjabi than any other of the Dard languages; but in some respects seems to show some affinity to the dialects of the Siah Posh.

The Bushkarik intermarry with the Torwalik, but not with their other neighbours. Forts are not in use among them, but their villages are built in a peculiar fashion for safety. A hill side with a suitable slope is selected, against which the houses are built in a succession of terraces rising one above the other, so that the flat roof of each house is on a level with the floor of the one above it. The whole are connected by an outer wall, within the confines of which is a labyrinth of passages, and the site is often selected so that a stream of water runs through the mass of buildings. All the houses are built of wood, and those on the outside of the village have no parapets. Bushkar is said to be very thickly wooded, and the trees are said to grow to an unusual size.

[1] See Appendix E.

CHAPTER VII.

HABITS AND CUSTOMS.

NOTWITHSTANDING original tribal differences, the Shin rule in Gilgit and the surrounding valleys practically welded both conquerors and conquered into one people, distinguished only by caste divisions; and, though Mahommedanism has in some instances modified and in others abolished old customs, many of great interest still remain. Many of these, though originating in religious rites and beliefs, have now lost all connection with them in the minds of those who still practise them. It is difficult, almost impossible, now to distinguish between those which were introduced by the Shins, and those which were adopted by them from the original inhabitants; but fairly correct conjectures concerning the origin of some of them may be formed. Hunza is the country least affected by external influences, and in which the laxest form of Mahommedanism now exists, but there is scarcely any custom or observance maintained there which has not its counterpart still existing, or which till lately existed in the neighbouring valleys. In Chitral and some of the valleys to the westward, many customs seem to have partly disappeared. This may, not improbably, be due to the inhabitants having been earlier converts to Islam, or more exposed to external influences. In the valleys to the southward, like Chilas and Darel, the want of a single ruler and the stricter tenets of Soonnee Mahommedanism have contributed to cause many old customs and festivals to fall into disuse. In spite, however, of local differences, enough remains to show that a strong bond of kinship exists between all the Dard and Ghalchah tribes.

In appearance the men are light, active figures, averaging from 5 feet 5 inches to 5 feet 8 inches in height. Though well made, they are not, as a rule, remarkable for muscular development, presenting in this respect a marked contrast to the Tartar races. Notwithstanding their hardy, simple lives, they seem unequal to any prolonged physical effort. In travelling and shooting I have constantly found them knock up before natives of other parts. Their constitutions also seem to want stamina, and they succumb easily to disease or change of climate. This want of physical energy and enterprise is most strongly marked in the Shin caste. They consider husbandry the only honourable employment for men, and so averse are they to labour, that the poorest of them employ Baltis in their agriculture, which is of a rude and slovenly kind. Numbers of Baltis come yearly into the Gilgit district to serve for hire; they receive 6 lbs. of grain for a day's labour.

In disposition they are tractable, good-tempered, fond of rejoicing and merry-making, neither cruel nor quarrelsome, and they submit readily to constituted authority. The worst cruelties perpetrated in the wars between Yassin and Cashmere are distinctly attributable to the Ashimadek class of Yassin and Chitral, who compare unfavourably with the older tribes in this respect. In all the accounts of the Kunjooti depredations on caravans, and of wars in which the people of Hunza and Nager were concerned, there are no records of wanton cruelty or of the exercise of torture. The women are pleasing-looking when young, but are not particularly handsome. Exception must be made in favour of the Khos of the "Fakir Mushkin" class in Chitral, who show certain physical peculiarities not shared by the other Dard tribes. In person they are Indo-Aryans of a high type, not unlike the Shins of the Indus Valley about Koli, but more handsome, with oval faces and finely-cut features, which would compare favourably with the highest types of beauty in Europe. The most striking feature about them, and one which distinguishes them from all other Dard tribes, is their large and beautiful eyes, which remind one of English gypsies, with whom they share the reputation of being expert thieves. They have also unusually fine hair, of which they are very proud. The women of Chitral were formerly sought out for their beauty in the slave markets of Cabul, Peshawur, and Badakhshan. The fairest complexions are to be seen among the Boorish of Hunza and Yassin, where individuals may be found who would pass for Europeans. Among them red hair is not uncommon.

In dress there is little variety. The loose woollen robe described by Mr. Drew is worn also in Sirikol, Wakhan, Zebak, Chitral, Yassin, Hunza, Nager, and the Yaghestan Valleys. Those who can afford it substitute in summer a cotton robe of the same cut, with quilted edges, worked round the neck and front with silk embroidery. When first put on, the sleeves, which are very full, are crimped in minute folds right up to the neck, giving the wearer a clerical appearance. In the Indus Valley about Shinkari, the men wear turbans and tight-fitting clothes, and retain the curious leather leg wrappings called "*Towti*," mentioned by Mr. Drew, which are peculiar to the Shina-speaking tribes, and the Torwal and Bushkar tribes of the Swat Kohistan. They are often called "towti-bads" or "towtching" in consequence, by their neighbours. In Chitral, boots of soft leather are worn. The women wear wide trowsers, over which is a loose chemise of coarse-coloured cotton stuff, fastening in the middle at the throat, and coming down to the knees. The opening is held together by a circular buckle, from which hangs a curious triangular silver ornament called "Peshawez," that varies in size according to the circumstances of the wearer. Round the neck are generally one or two necklaces of amber and coloured beads. The wealthier wear necklaces of silver beads with oval silver medallions, and a piece of cornelian or turquoise set in them. In Chitral, Wakhan, and Sirikol the men wear very small scanty turbans. In Gilgit, Astor, and the greater part of Yaghestan the rolled woollen cap mentioned by Mr. Drew is commonly worn. The women also wear a loose woollen cap, generally of dark colour. In the Shin caste unmarried women are distinguished by a white cap, which is never worn by married Shin women. Both men and women wear numbers of charms, sewn in bright-coloured silk, and suspended from the cap or dress by small circular brass buckles. Some of the buckles are very tastefully worked. A curious kind of cloth is sometimes woven out of bird's down. That of wild fowl and of the great vulture (*G. himalayensis*) is most generally used. The down is twisted into coarse thread, which is then woven like ordinary cloth. Robes made of it are very warm, but always have a fluffy uncomfortable look, suggestive of dirt. They are only made in the houses of those in good circumstances. The pushm of the Ibex is also in great demand for warm clothing, but it never seems to lose its strong goaty smell.

The men when young shave the whole top of the head from the forehead to the nape of the neck; the hair on both sides is allowed to grow long, and is gathered into a single large curl on each side of the neck, and the beard is kept shorn. This fashion has also been adopted by the Baltis from the Dards. Young men of the better class only shave

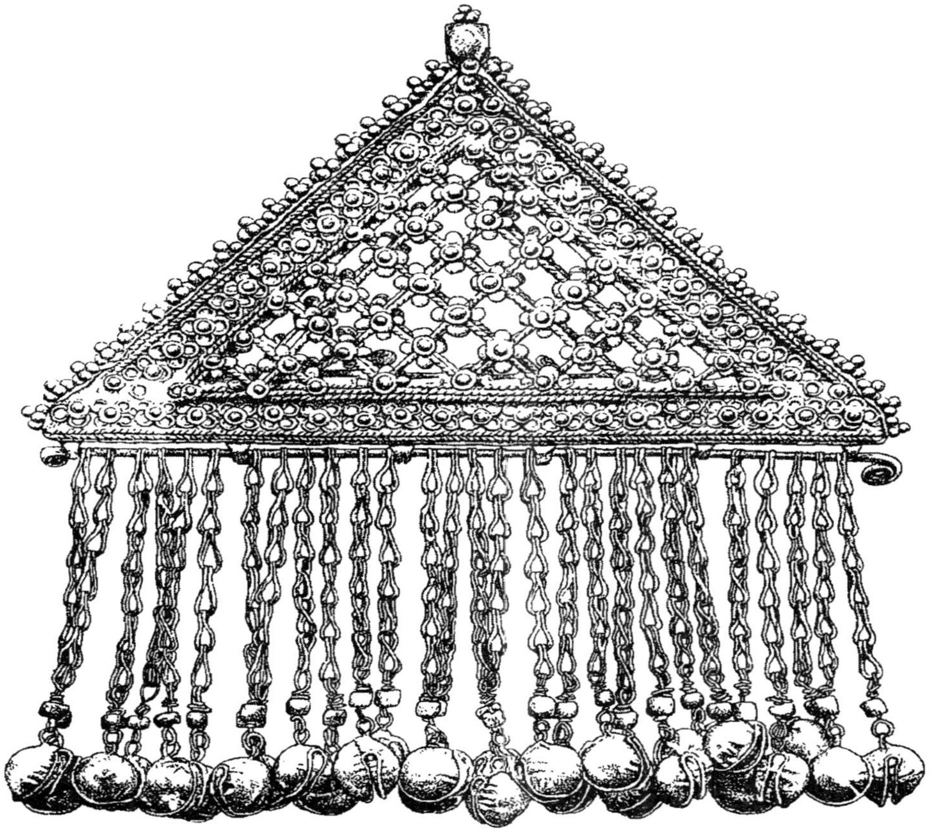

PESHAWEZ

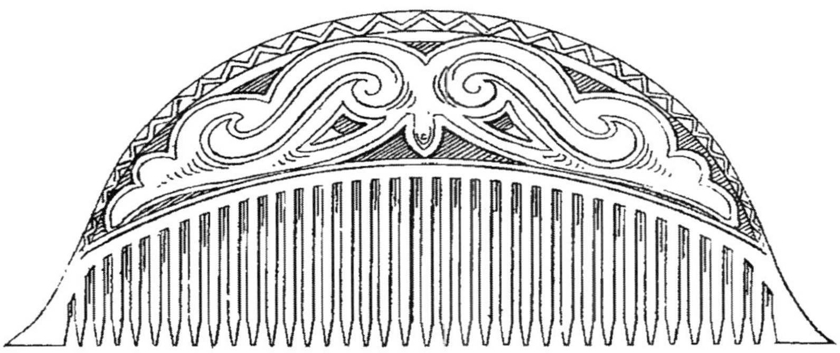

CHITRAL COMB

the top of the head for a space 2 inches broad in front, tapering to half an inch behind. Those who cannot boast of long locks, dress their hair into numerous small cork-screw ringlets all round the head.[1] On the approach of middle age the whole head is shaved, according to the orthodox Mahommedan fashion, and the beard is allowed to grow. In Chitral the effect of the long-flowing locks reaching to the waist is often extremely picturesque.

The mode of salutation between equals, on meeting after a prolonged absence, is graceful and pleasing. After clasping each other, first on one side then on the other, hands are joined, and each person in turn kisses the hand of the other. Superiors are greeted either by kissing the hand or touching the foot, both at meeting and parting. In Chitral, when the meeting is between two of unequal rank, the inferior kisses the hand of the superior, who in return kisses the former on the cheek. A similar practice is said to have existed among the ancient Persians.[2]

On the occasion of the visit of one chief to another, a rather curious ceremony called "Kobah" takes place. On arrival, the visitor is conducted to the Shawaran,[3] and the followers of both chiefs show their dexterity in firing at a mark set up on a tall pole, from horseback while galloping at speed. After this a bullock is led out before the guest, who draws his sword and does his best to cut its head off at a single blow, or deputes one of his followers to do so, and the carcase is given to his retinue. The custom exists in Shighnan, Badakhshan, Wakhan, Chitral, Yassin, Gilgit, Hunza, and Nager. In the latter place it is customary to slay the bullock with bow and arrow. Of late years the practice has become somewhat modified owing to the strict observance of Mahommedan customs, and it is more usual to give over the bullock alive to the guest, so that its throat may be cut in a more orthodox fashion; but occasionally a chief wishing to show off the strength of his arm and the temper of his blade, will adhere to the old custom.

Polygamy is of course practised, and the right of divorce is somewhat wantonly exercised. The marriage of very young children is not common, though occasionally practised. Girls are generally married between the ages of ten and four-

[1] Rawlinson mentions this as an ancient Persian fashion.—*Ancient Monarchies*, Vol. IV.

[2] Strabo Book XV., Chapter 3, Section 20.

[3] The Shawaran answers all the purposes of the village green in England, being used for all gatherings and games.

teen. Wives are regarded as the absolute property of the husband and his heirs. On a man's death his brother can claim to marry all his widows, and no widow can marry again without the consent of her husband's brothers. Frequently, if a man leaves several widows as well as several brothers, the latter apportion the former among themselves. So strictly is the rule observed that, should there be only one surviving brother and he an infant, the widow cannot remarry elsewhere till he is old enough to say whether he will marry her or not; On the other hand, it is considered disgraceful to refuse to marry a brother's widow, so that it is not uncommon for a boy of ten years old to marry a woman more than twice his age. So absolute is the custom, that a woman cannot refuse to marry her deceased husband's brother, and her own parents have no voice in the matter. This often leads to two sisters being wives to the same man simultaneously, though the practice is forbidden by Mahommedan law. In Chitral, marriage with a husband's brother, though common, is not compulsory on the woman. Among the Afghans of Dir, if a widow should refuse to marry her husband's brother, he has the power of selling her, as she is regarded in the light of family property, which has been purchased and paid for. Among the Shin caste the marriage of first cousins or other relations within that degree (such as uncle and niece) is strictly prohibited, though allowed by Mahommedan law. In Torwal and Bushkar the marriage of first cousins is allowed, but marriages such as of uncle and niece or niece's daughter are forbidden.

In none of the Dard languages are there terms distinctive of polygamous relationship. All wives are of equal rank, priority of marriage not conferring any claim. In the Shina and Boorishki languages, uncles on the father's side are styled "great father" or "little father," according to their age in comparison with that of the speaker's father; but there is a distinct term for an uncle on the mother's side. In the same way the term "aunt" is only applied to those on the father's side, the mother's sisters being all styled "mother." There is no specific term either for nephew and niece, who are styled "son" and "daughter." In the same way cousins are styled "brother" or "sister." This would seem to point to the former existence of communal marriage, such as still exists in some parts of India. In the Khowar language the term "uncle" is applied to the brothers of both father and mother without distinction; but aunts on the mother's side are styled "mother," which would point to polygamy, and not to communal marriage, as an ancient institution in the Chitral Valley. In the Bushkarik language the terms point towards polyandry.

Cases of infidelity are extremely common, and the men show none of the jealousy of their wives usual in older Mahommedan communities. In cases of adultery the injured husband has the right to slay the guilty couple when he finds them together; but should he slay one and not the other, he is held guilty of murder. This practice is followed in Sirikol and Wakhan as well as south of the Hindoo Koosh. It is said that the Afghans of Swat, Dir, and Asmar take no notice of a wife's infidelity if, when it comes to their knowledge, they are able to disguise the knowledge from others; but should they learn it through a third person, a bloody vengeance is inflicted. In cases where conclusive proof is wanting, and which are brought for settlement before the ruler or Wuzeer, guarantee is taken for the future by the accused placing his lips to the woman's breast. She thenceforth is regarded as his foster-mother, and no other relations but those of mother and son can exist between them. So sacred is the tie thus established esteemed, that it has never been known to be broken, and the most jealous husband ceases to suspect even though a confession of previous guilt may have been made. In such a case a sheep and a toloo of gold are placed at the feet of the husband by the offender, who humbly sues for forgiveness.

It would appear that morals were more lax formerly than they are now. In Hunza, where the community approaches most nearly to its pre-Mahommedan state, infidelity is not regarded as an offence, and custom requires that a man shall place his wife at his guest's disposal, as in Hazara. The *droit de seigneur* was exercised by the father of the present ruler, and though the custom has been allowed to fall into disuse, it is evident from the accounts given of weekly orgies held by Ghazan Khan that the right is only held in abeyance and not formally renounced. In Nager things are but slightly better, and a man considers himself highly honoured if his wife attracts the attention of the Thum. Islam has not yet brought about the seclusion of the women, who mix freely with the men on all occasions Young men and maidens of different families eat and converse together without restraint, and great liberty is allowed to young women, with frequent evil results. Infanticide arising from illicit connections is common, and is not considered a crime.

Marriage is the occasion for much ceremony, which differs slightly in each locality. Though the young people often arrange a marriage between themselves, it is more usual for the match to be arranged by the parents. After determining by private negotiation the conditions of the match, the bridegroom's father proceeds to make a formal proposal. Dressed in his gayest clothes, and accompanied by his friend, he visits the bride's family, who are assembled to meet him, taking with him certain presents, such as a cow or sheep, beads, clothes, and a sword or gun. The formal demand for the bride having been made and assented to, an interchange of presents takes place. In Chitral, Wakhan, and Sirikol the bride has a bracelet of beads placed on her arm by the bridegroom's father. In Gilgit, cedar branches are burnt, and the bride's parents are presented with a knife, a rope, a few yards of cloth, and a leather bag for holding grain; the bridegroom's father receives in return some wool and a gourd. This interchange of gifts is apparently emblematical. In Torwal the price of the bride is paid over at this time, and the bridegroom's father is accompanied by men dressed as women, who dance and sport to the assembled company. In some places it is not etiquette for the bridegroom to be present. The betrothal being completed, the marriage may not follow for some time, but it generally takes place within the following year. For convenience marriages generally take place in January and February. There is then no agricultural work to occupy the men, and the houses are well stored with meat. So firmly established is the custom in Nager, that a heavy fine is inflicted on marriages held at any other season.

The fixing of the day for the marriage now rests with the bridegroom's parents. After giving private notice, a smartly-dressed friend of the bridegroom is sent to announce formally that he will arrive on a certain day to claim his bride. Certain prescribed presents are interchanged on the occasion. On the appointed day the bridegroom, surrounded by his friends and equipped with bow, arrows, and battle axe, sets out for the bride's house. The bride remains in the inner apartments, dressed in her gayest clothes with a fillet of cowrie shells bound on her head. This decoration is said to have been introduced by the Shins, and is obligatory among them. On entering the house branches of cedar are burned in an iron dish and waved about over the bridegroom's head, and the party is sprinkled with flour. In Wakhan and Sirikol the bridegroom is met and sprinkled with flour at some distance from the bride's house. All being seated, a large platter full of bread is presented to the bridegroom, who distributes it to all the company, after which he places his gun or sword on the platter and it becomes the perquisite of the dish-bearer. In Gilgit two of the bride's and two of the bridegroom's friends are seated face to face, and a cake of bread is passed across; each of the bride's friends breaks off a piece, which is left in the dish, and the bridegroom's men place their turbans or caps in it as a token that their heads are at the bride's disposal. The dish is carried in to the bride, who sends back the turbans. In former days the eating of bread together, at this stage, by the bride and bridegroom, was considered to complete the marriage. The idea was that, whoever managed first to eat a morsel would have the mastery in wedded life, and this always caused a scramble. At every stage a prescribed interchange of presents, which have all been carefully stipulated for beforehand, takes place. Meanwhile the friends of both families have been spending the day outside the house in singing and dancing, and this is kept up all night also. The price of the bride, and the presents agreed upon, having been made over to her family, the Moollah appears and reads the marriage service according to the Sharyat. In Chitral the bridegroom then starts for his home with his bride. In Wakhan and Sirikol he is conducted to the bride, and does not take her away till next day; the women of her family resist his entering the room in which she is until he pacifies them with presents. In Gilgit the two still remain apart, and next day the "Kalak Malak," which is peculiar to Gilgit, takes place. This constitutes the ratification of the marriage, and is the assessment of all the presents given from first to last. Two friends of each side meet and appraise all the presents given by the bridegroom. Three toloos of gold-dust, equal to twenty-four rupees, represent the price of the bride herself. Her father then produces a large cooking-pot, a bed, jewels, clothes, dishes, and other articles needful for setting up house. The bride is summoned and allowed to select any two of the articles, which are given with her free. The assessors then price the rest, not forgetting to value the presents given and received since the betrothal, and the price of the balance is paid over at once by the bridegroom or his father.

All being satisfactorily settled, preparations are made for bringing out the bride. The bridegroom and his friends stand round the door, and everybody is sprinkled with flour. In Chitral the bride is led out by her mother, who hands her over to the bridegroom, receiving a present in exchange. In Gilgit the women of the bride's family follow the party, assailing the bridegroom with abuse and pelting him with mud and filth, feigning anger. After going a mile in this way, the bridegroom gives a present to the bride's mother, and is then allowed to depart in peace. This is no doubt a relic of the practice of marriage by capture. Sometimes on leaving the house a goat is slaughtered in front of the couple. The flour-sprinkling is practised everywhere and at different stages, but I cannot ascertain what the custom denotes. In Gilgit it is called Doobun.

After a few days it is customary for the bride's parents to visit the newly-married couple, when they are received with flour-sprinkling, which is repeated on the first occasion of the bride revisiting her father's house. In some places it is customary for the couple to go and stay for several months with the bride's parents soon after marriage.

In Wakhan and Chitral, after leading out the bride the bridegroom returns alone and deposits a present of a gun or a sword on the hearth. In Munjan and Ludkho the couple are accompanied to their homes by all the women of the villages, dancing and singing. They are left alone in the house for seven days, during which food is conveyed to them, but nobody enters, nor are they allowed to leave.

In Torwal the bridegroom's party is accompanied by men dressed as women, who dance and jest, and the whole village take part in the entertainment of the bridegroom's friends. The day after marriage the bride is visited by the women of her husband's family, to whom she must show proofs of her not having brought "a cracked teacup" into the family. She is then congratulated and praised; but should she fail to show the requisite proofs, she is ever after treated with contempt.

In Baltistan, according to Vigne, the husband goes in person to see the bride instead of sending a friend or relation to do so, and if he please he may refuse her, and on the marriage day the bride comes to his house instead of his going to fetch her.

Though the young people often arrange a marriage among themselves before asking the consent of their parents, they are not allowed to meet after it has been agreed upon. Should they meet out of doors by accident, etiquette demands that they should pass with averted eyes and without speaking.

In Gor, rings are exchanged at marriage. In the ruling families of Hunza and Nager, it is the custom, when a daughter is married, for the bridegroom to present her at betrothal with a gold and silver needle. In Yassin, when, as not unfrequently happens, the bridegroom is too poor to pay the required price, the young couple elope, with the consent of the bride's parents. At the end of ten days the bridegroom comes to them and asks forgiveness, promising to pay the required sum by degrees. A little scene is acted, forgiveness is granted, the neighbours are summoned to the feast which has been already prepared, and the wedding is celebrated. This is to save the credit of the bride's family in not having received a sufficient price for her.

The old marriage barriers between the castes are beginning to be broken down under the levelling influence of Mahommedanism, and in a few generations will probably disappear altogether. The birth of a son is always a matter of general rejoicing. The friends of the happy father at once make it an excuse to stop work for the day, and seizing their matchlocks keep up a general *feu-de-joie* till their powder flasks are empty. The village band is summoned, and dancing kept up round the door for the rest of the day. No notice is taken of the birth of daughters. In the Oxus Valley and in Sirikol, when a son is born, all the father's friends hang their weapons on the walls of his house, so as to accustom the infant to martial sights. After seven days the weapons are returned to the owners, except those belonging to near relations, who receive special presents in exchange.

After the birth of a child a woman is esteemed unclean, and no one will eat from her hand for seven days. North of the Hindoo Koosh this period is extended to forty days, and for the first seven the infant is not allowed to suckle its mother.

I have elsewhere discussed the old custom of disposing of the dead by burning. Now the common form of Mussulman interment is used. A small flat slab of earth about two feet long is neatly plastered over the graves, and a light is kept burning at night by newly-made graves, under the pretence of keeping away wild beasts till the earth has hardened; but, as Mr. Drew has remarked, this is more probably a relic of the old practice of cremation. No attention or care is paid to old graves, which constantly present a most unpleasant appearance, owing to the falling-in of the arched roof. I remarked in Sirikol the same want of attention to old graves as exists south of the Hindoo Koosh, and Wood remarked the same in Kundooz. In Darel and Tangir a piece of roughly-carved wood is placed at each end of the grave, which is neatly plaistered over, and small pieces of white spar are placed along the ridges between the pieces of wood, which are about 8 feet apart. In Chitral, instead of wood, flat pieces of stone or slate, 3 or 4 feet long, are used.

All that concerns the division and inheritance of land is naturally of great consequence among a people who live almost entirely by agriculture. In Gilgit and the adjacent valleys, on a man's death his land is not divided equally among his sons, as is prescribed in the Sharyat, but in equal portions between his wives' families; for instance, should a man leave one son by one wife and three by another, the one son inherits half land, and the other three the other half, which again is sub-divided between them. Should one wife have sons, and the other only daughters, the land is divided among the former, the daughters being only entitled to a marriage-portion out of the land. Should a man die leaving only daughters, the land goes to the nearest male heir of the deceased; but a curious exception is made in the case of a man leaving only a single daughter, who is allowed to take the whole land as her marriage-portion. The practice is always spoken of as a favour, and not a right, but it seems to be a relic of a custom by which the succession of women was once recognised. The history of these countries shows several instances of the succession of female rulers in default of male heirs. In Wakhan and Sirikol daughters share equally in everything except land, which is divided among the sons. In Chitral and the Swat Valley the law of the Sharyat, by which all sons have equal shares, is followed. Daughters are entitled to a dowry out of the paternal land on marriage. In Torwal, women inherit the father's land in equal shares with the sons.

The custom of foster relationship is maintained among all the ruling families, and its ties seem more stringent than those of blood kinship. On the occasion of a son or daughter being born, the child is assigned to a foster-mother, in whose house it is brought up, so that frequently the father does not see his children till they are six or seven years old, and the whole family of the nurse place themselves at the disposal of their foster-child, with whom, for the rest of their lives, their fortunes are unalterably bound up. Whatever are a man's misfortunes or crimes in after-life, his good and bad fortunes are equally shared. Should exile be his lot, his foster kindred accompany him. On the other hand, if he rises to influence, his foster-father is generally his most confidential adviser, and his foster-brothers are employed on the most important missions.

The custom of cementing friendship by the milk connection seems a favourite one. Should a woman dream that she has adopted any person as a son, or should any man dream that he has been adopted by a certain woman, the connection is carried out in the same way as the forced adoption before mentioned, and nobody would think of refusing to recognise it. The practice is now falling somewhat into disuse, but it was extremely common not many years ago. Milk from a woman's breast is esteemed a sovereign remedy for cataract and other eye-diseases. A resort to it also establishes the milk-tie for ever afterwards.

It is sometimes customary for a young couple, at the time of marriage, to induce a mutual friend to become their foster-father. The tie is ratified at the time of eating bread together. Bride and bridegroom being seated opposite to one another, the foster-father elect seats himself between them, and taking a piece of bread in each hand crosses his arms, observing to keep the right one uppermost, and puts the bread into their mouths. From that time he is regarded as their father.

The foster relationship is regarded as so close, that marriage between foster relations would be looked upon as incestuous, and, in spite of the precepts of the Koran, it would be impossible for a man to marry the widow of his foster-son.

The formation of these ties is practised in a peculiar way among the Ashimadek clans of Chitral. It is customary for every infant to be suckled in turn by every nursing mother of the clan; consequently there is a constant interchange of infants going on among the mothers, for the purpose of strengthening tribal unity.

The Shins are noted for their miserly habits, which they sometimes carry to great extremes. Every man has a secret hiding place in the mountains, where he conceals his money, metal pots, wife's jewels, and all his most valuable property. Occasional stealthy visits are paid to the treasure, which is never taken out for use except on festive occasions. No feeling of honour seems to exist as to the appropriation of another's treasure should it by chance be discovered, and frequent quarrels arise from this cause. Treasures are frequently lost altogether by the sudden death of the owner, before he has had time to confide the secret of their hiding place to his son. The practice is entirely confined to the Shins, who have many legends of lost treasures which have fallen under the guardianship of demons.

In both Chilas and Darel, a practice exists of storing clarified butter in cellars for a great number of years. It turns deep red and keeps for more than a hundred years, when it is much prized. A tree is sometimes planted over the cellar to ensure its not being disturbed, and wealth is computed by the amount of butter stored up. On one occasion a deputation came to me from Darel to ask that some run-away slaves should be compelled to say where they had buried their master's butter, as they alone knew the secret.

Wine, which at one time was universally drunk, is also placed in flagged underground cellars to ripen in large earthen jars, but is never kept more than a year. In digging the foundations of my house at Gilgit, I came on one of these old cellars with two large jars in it, which had evidently been undisturbed for many years. The drinking of wine has much diminished under Islam, and where still practised is concealed as much as possible, except in Hunza and Ponyal, where public jollifications are not uncommon. The Maulai sect make no secret of the practice, and on my visit to Hunza, in 1876, a bottle of Scotch whiskey made Ghazan Khan so gloriously drunk that all Hunza spoke of it with admiration.

Polo-playing, of which so complete an account has been given by Mr. Drew, is the national game. Dardistan play, however, lacks the neatness of the Munnipoori game; but what is wanting in style is quite made up in enthusiasm, old men joining in the game as long as they are able to sit on a horse. Matches are generally played for some small stake, and the conquerors exact all the rights of victory by taunting their beaten opponents. In Chitral the game, which is called "ghal," is played somewhat differently from the way described by Mr. Drew. Aman-ool-mulk, the present ruler of Chitral, was said to be the best player in the country when a young man.

The game is quite unknown in Badakhshan, where "buzkushi," or "goat-snatching," is the favourite amusement. The following description of this game as played by the Kirghiz is given by Shaw, [1] under the name of "Ooghlak:—"

"The headless body of a goat is thrown on the ground, and every one tries to pick it up without leaving the saddle. The press is tremen-

[1] Shaw's High Tartary, Yarkand and Kashgar.

dous, as, with one foot and one hand on the saddle, they stretch down the other hand to the ground. Presently one succeeds, and is off, swinging himself back into the saddle as he goes. He is chased by the rest, doubling and turning to avoid them. At last, another and another gets a hold of the goat. The first man throws his leg over the body to tighten his hold, and away they go across country till their horses diverge, and all but one lose their grasp. He is again caught, but throws the goat on the opposite side. The others wrestle with him as they gallop three or four abreast, the outermost riders almost leaving their horses as they stretch their whole bodies across their neighbours."

A similar amusement is described by Vambéry[1] as one of the marriage ceremonies of the Turkomans, called by them Kokbüri (green wolf). In this the bride carries on her lap the carcase of a lamb or goat, and setting off at full gallop, is pursued by the bridegroom and other young men of the party, also on horseback.

Firing at a mark from horseback is another favourite pastime. The mark is a gourd filled with ashes, or a small ball, hung from a pole about 30 feet high. The marksmen gallop at full speed and fire as they pass underneath. Every successful shot is marked by a shower of ashes, and they do not desist till every particle of the gourd is shot away. Considering the clumsiness of the weapons used, the shooting is sometimes remarkably good.

As polo is the national game, so dancing is the national amusement, and no description of these people would be complete without mention of it. Feast-days, births, weddings, any occasion of a gathering, serves as an excuse for dancing, and the end of a game of polo is always signalised by a dance on the Shawaran. The spectators form a ring, inside which the musicians are seated, opposite the principal personage present. The instruments tune up, and a murmur goes round the circle as to who will dance. Soon a name is called out, or a volunteer steps into the ring, and, with a word to the band, commences. Several different steps are in vogue, each of which has its special air, the Dunni, Soz, Balôs (Iskardo), Tuppnutt, Tajwer (Badakhshan or Tajik), Sirikoli, and Cashmeri. Almost all of these commence slowly, increasing in pace till the performer is bounding round the circle at top speed. As soon as one is tired, fresh dancers are always ready to come forward, and hours are often passed without either performers or spectators seeming to weary. The dancing is sometimes really graceful and interesting to watch, and forms a great contrast to the terrible monotony of an

[1] Vambery's Travels in Central Asia.

Indian nautch. In Hunza a very spirited sword-dance is performed. Sometimes two or three dancers enter the circle together, one acting as leader to the others. At weddings ten or twelve join in, each holding sword or battle-axe in hand. The public dancing of women, mixed with men, is now only practised in Hunza. In Bushkar dances of women take place on feast days, but men are not allowed to be present. In Chitral and Yassin the Ashimadek class affect to despise dancing, and seldom join in it, but the rulers of those countries keep dancing-boys for their amusement. In Yassin, on one occasion, I witnessed some of their performances by torchlight, which made a very picturesque scene.

The music consists of a double-headed drum beaten with sticks, two or three pairs of small metal kettle-drums, and two or three clarionets made of apricot wood. Special airs are reserved for the ruler and different officials. The musicians are Doms, and every man of any consideration has his own band, which attends him whenever he moves. Every village also has its band. The singing is of a less pleasing nature, but it is interesting, as being one of the methods by which old historical traditions are preserved. In Gilgit singing by individuals is not common, the usual practice being to form large chorus parties, which chaunt the deeds of former kings. Generally the singers form into two parties, each of ten or a dozen, and sing alternate verses. The end of the verse is emphasized by a simultaneous step or bound forward, or sideways, which causes jostling and somewhat mars the effect.

Considerable difference exists in the nature of the songs of the different countries. In Gilgit, Hunza, and Nager, the songs are, with few exceptions, of a warlike nature, and celebrate the achievements of different princes. In Hunza and Nager, where the language spoken is Boorishki, the songs are in Shina, as the native language does not readily lend itself to poetry. Shina songs are harsh, and the words present a few striking images which want connection, and which are often repeated with wearisome iteration. The Khowar songs are mostly of an amatory nature, seldom treating of warlike subjects, and give evidence of a more cultivated taste than those in Shina, while the musical nature of the language and the better rhythm of the verse entitle them to the first place in Dard poetry. Generally two performers stand a little distance apart and sing in strophe and antistrophe to each other: a chorus stand by who do not repeat the words, but give emphasis to the periods by a loud *Ah Ha* and by stamping.

The following examples will give a good idea of the different styles :—

SHINA.

I.

Loh wâto, Soori Gowrithum, loh wâto,
Bùtîgá birdi loh wâto, dùnya sung tarêgo.
Loh wâto, sâjo Malika, loh wâto,
Bùtîgá birdi loh wâto, dùnyá sung tarêgo.
Nê loh wâto, Soori Habbi Khan, loh wâto,
Bùtîgá birdi loh wâto, dùnyá sung tarêgo.
Tai zùzi sîgá bùdik té allah in Sargin goomêchorê
Loh wâto, sâjo Malika, loh wâto.
Tai zùzi sîgá bùdik té allah in Sargin goomêchorê.

Translation.

Dawn has come, Soori Gowrithum, dawn has come.
To the whole earth dawn has come, the world is lighted up.
Dawn has come, grandson of Malika, dawn has come.
To the whole earth dawn has come, the world is lighted up.
Again dawn has come, Soori Habbi Khan, dawn has come.
To the whole earth dawn has come, the world is lighted up.
Thy mother, too, in her wisdom cherished us in Sargin.
Dawn has come, grandson of Malika, dawn has come.
Thy mother, too, in her wisdom cherished us in Sargin.

II.

The forest serpent, Soori Mahommed Khan.
The forest serpent rouses himself.
Beyond Sharot he will brandish his sabre.
The forest serpent of the race of Malika.
The forest serpent rouses himself.
Beyond Sharot he will brandish his sabre.

KHOWAR.

I.

Hazâra Beg ispah petch,
Chitrâreté bissé ketch,
Chitrâroh Mihter ispah ghetch,
Khooshâné korùm jânooṇ.

Má Mihter yoh nisai,
Pinjâreshoh muss nisai,
Muss nisioh doko prai.
Khooshâné korùm jânooṇ.

Eh ! Gohr Khùdaiyâr,
Shah Mohturrum jânooyâr,
Má Mihteroh bol Khatâr,
Mastoochoh koyun shotâr.
Khooshâné korùm jânooṇ.

Kai Khowas Khan Doorâni,
Tùl nîzoh ai gunné,
Kohi Taoosum maidâni.
Khooshâni korùm jânooṇ.

Maiyá Mihter chaiyak hoyi,
Jân tanârı joodá hoyi,
Nissá Mihter tuzzá hoyi,
Khùdai mutté rezá hoyi.
Khooshâné korùm jânooṇ.

Yeri Mihter purri prai,
Purri Gohr jâni prai,
Khùdai Mihteroté prai.
Khooshâné korùm jânooṇ.

TRANSLATION.

Huzara Beg is our heart's friend.
We will go with your family to Chitral.
The prince of Chitral is our eye.
Oh my life we will make him happy.

My prince came out,
The full moon shone out.
The moon shone out and set again.
Oh my life we will make him happy.

Oh Gohı Good-bye to you,
My life's friend Shah Mohturrum (comes),
My prince's army is terrible,
He will subdue Mastooch.
Oh my life we will make him happy.

Kai Khowas Khan (brave as) a Doorani,
With a broad spear in his hand,
Will ride on the Taoos maidan.
Oh my life we will make him happy.

My prince became ill,
Life nearly left my body,
Again my prince became well,
God filled me with joy.
Oh my life we will make him happy.

My prince crossed over (the river),
Gohr on the other side was ready to die,
God gave victory to my prince,
Oh my life we will make him happy.

The above refers to an incident in the life of Badshah, son of Suleiman Shah, Khushwaktia.

II.

Bulbul komistai jung joyer ogoté,
Jirêko no bom drùng bom jung goloté,
Heh má jân, jâné tutté guroom.

Bulbul komistai tungázá chágoté,
Awá tá treshtoo anzowá dágoté,
Heh má jân, jâné tutté guroom.

Bulbul shariki tá jâná koh kyah sher,
Má jân tutté mâloom funná láki sher,
Heh má jân, jâné tutte guroom.

Awá brîyoomun tutté hyah paichâni,
Idi ai koré bilaur ghetchâni,
Heh má jân, jâné tutté guroom.

Buttun má buttun sirgushtá kussi maiṇ,
Koh kyah jum ánùs tum mokoh pushimaiṇ,
Heh má jân, jâné tutté guroom.

Daiyùs gerduni chirgùlah buss boyê,
Goyá ki chirosori muggus doyê,
Heh má jân, jâné tutté guroom.

TRANSLATION.

A bulbul has alighted to drink at the fountain,
I cannot restrain myself from clasping her neck.
Oh my life, I will give my life for you!

A bulbul has alighted on the turf for shade,
I am ready to be cooked like an onion for you.
Oh my life, I will give my life for you!

Oh bulbul, oh mynah, what is in your heart?
You know my life is placed in my hand for you,
Oh my life, I will give my life for you!

Let it not be concealed, I am dying for love of you,
Give me one glance with your crystal eye.
Oh my life, I will give my life for you!

Forgetting my country I am distracted and wander,
On what joyful day shall I see your face?
Oh my life, I will give my life for you!

Your cuckoldy husband touching your milk-white neck
Is like a fly defiling cream.
Oh my life, I will give my life for you!

III.

I roam on the mountains as if I trod on hot ashes,
The sword of love has stricken me; I made of myself a shield of two bones.
Oh Yoormun Hamin!

Oh Fairy I swear by God after seeing you there is no light,
Night and day are alike dark to me, no dawn comes to me.
Oh Yoormun Hamin!

The curls of my bulbul are like rosebuds and maiden hair fern,
Come sit by me and sing like a mynah or a bulbul.
Oh Yoormun Hamin!

Still I look at you; you turn away and look elsewhere,
My life is yours, why do you look at my enemies?
Oh Yoormun Hamin!

Your long ringlets and your well-curled hair are like bedmushk,
You bind up your locks to slay this lad.
Oh Yoormun Hamin!

I sigh day and night for the bulbul,
I kiss your pearly ringlets in my dreams.
Oh Yoormun Hamin!

This is a very favourite song in Upper Chitral, where the grave of Yoormun Hamin is still to be seen. A romantic story is attached to her memory.

The above songs must not be studied as examples of the language: they contain many inflexions which are not found

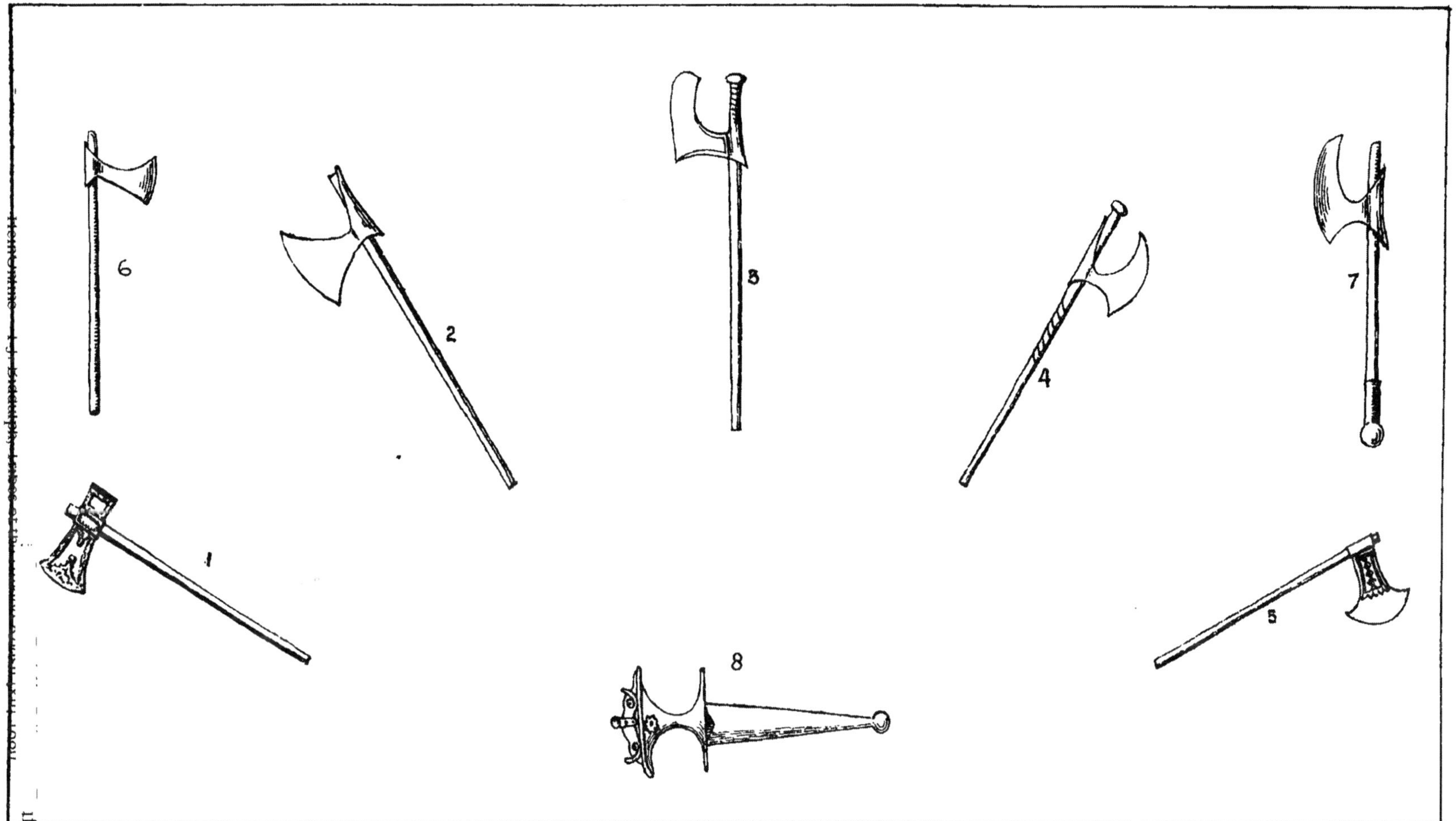

Photo mezzographed at the Surveyor General's Office Calcutta.

1. BATTLE AXE OF BADAKHSHAN, INLAID WITH SILVER.
2. HUNZA, NAGER, AND GILGIT BATTLE AXE.
3. BALTISTAN BATTLE AXE.
4. CHITRAL BATTLE AXE
5. BATTLE AXE OF THE INDUS VALLEY BELOW SAZIN.
6. BATTLE AXE OF THE KALASH KAFFIRS.
7. BALTISTAN BATTLE AXE (KHURMANG).
8. DAGGER OF THE SIAH-POSH KAFFIRS.

in the colloquial. Dr. Leitner has collected a large number of Shina songs.

Oral traditions and genealogies are also preserved in families to whom this duty is assigned, and carefully handed down from father to son.

The ancient weapons were bow and arrows, battle-axe and round leather shield. Those able to afford it also wore a shirt of mail and a steel cap. The bow and battle-axe have been replaced by matchlock and sword, but are not yet quite obsolete. Though powder is easily made, the tribes have to depend on Cashmere and Badakhshan for matchlock barrels, so Robin Hood's weapon is still used in the chase. The bows are made of strips of ibex horn, softened in water and bound together, and are very tough, powerful weapons. The battle-axes are of different shapes, according to locality, some of them being inlaid with silver, or having engraved patterns on them. The old weapons are carefully preserved and produced on the occasion of weddings, which would not be thought complete without them. A bridegroom presenting himself at the house of his father-in-law elect without a battle-axe would be sent away to get one, and if unable to do so would have to make an extra payment. In the present day the men of Chitral are noted for their swordsmanship, which has gained many a victory over matchlocks. In 1852 a regiment of Goorkhas in the Maharajah of Cashmere's service were cut to pieces by Chitral and Yassin swordsmen within 3 miles of Gilgit, though they formed square, and tried to reach the fort from which they had been cut off, in that formation.

Dard warfare is, however, seldom of a very resolute nature, and their records are full of accounts in which two or three days' skirmishing has led to the defeat of one party or the other with the loss of a few men only. Every village has one or more forts according to the number of inhabitants, in which all can take refuge in case of need. Owing to the easily defensible nature of the country, surprise is absolutely necessary to success. An attack having been determined on, every effort is made to throw the enemy off his guard, and then, by a succession of forced marches, possession is gained of the pass or the narrow part of the valley which forms the key of his country. Should these be gained, the inhabitants of the invaded country take refuge in their forts. Their defence then depends almost entirely on the state of their supplies. Sometimes their water-supply is cut off or their stores fail, and they are obliged to make terms. On the other hand, if they are well supplied, the invader gets tired after a short time and retires. If they feel strong and confident, the garrison sallies out to offer battle outside the walls, but the taking of a fort by assault is unknown. On account of the supplies it is usual to plan an attack for the time when the standing crops in the invaded country are just ripe.[1] The store in the fort is then at its lowest, and the invader finds no difficulty in subsistence.

Though Islam has introduced the inconvenient Mahommedan calendar, the ancient method of computation by the sun is still in use. In Gilgit and the valleys to the south the months are now distinguished by the Arabic names of the zodiacal signs. In Hunza and Nager a more ancient nomenclature still exists, as it did till lately in Gilgit, though most of the names in the latter place are now lost. The year is divided into two seasons, from solstice to solstice, called "yôl" (Boorish) and "hallôl" (Shina). The season commencing at the winter solstice is called "baiy," and the one commencing at the summer solstice "shini." Each season is divided into six months, the names of which are repeated in each season in a different order; the second season beginning with the first month, and then the other names being taken backwards. The months are named from certain objects or fancied resemblances on the horizon behind which the sun sets at certain dates, as seen from the gate of the ruler's castle, so that each place has a different set of names for the month. The calendar as it still exists in Nager will give a sufficiently good idea of the system.

The months are as follows, commencing with the winter solstice:—

1. Baiy Isha.
2. ,, Gamoosa (*ice-sun,* the sun sets behind a glacier).
3. ,, Tikkidir, (*earth line,* the sun sets behind a level space).
4. ,, Kabula, (*kebla,* the direction of Mecca).
5. ,, Hingbalter (*door-way,* from a rock resembling a gateway).
6. ,, Booye (*shoulder-blade,* from a rock resembling the blade bone of a sheep).
7. Shini Isha (commencing with the summer solstice).
8. ,, Booye.
9. ,, Hingbalter.
10. ,, Kabula.
11. ,, Tikkidir.
12. ,, Gamoosa.

[1] "The time that kings go out to battle," 1 Chron., XX, 1.

Isha literally means a mill-pond, but in this case it is not meant to represent a mark on the horizon, but to signify a receptacle, the place beyond which there is no going. The Kebla month is no doubt a name of modern introduction. In ancient times computation seems to have been by these seasons. The term "yôl" has now come to be used for the whole year, and the half year is called "yôl trang," but a man of forty when asked his age will often say that he is eighty "yôl-trang." According to Mr. Schuyler, the Kirghiz make the same computation. The half-month is called *toonts* (Boorish), and *putch* (Shina), and no smaller division of days is recognised, though in Shina there are but seven names of days, which closely resemble the Sanscrit days of the week, thus—

Sunday . .	Adit	*in Sanscrit*	Aditya bar.
Monday . .	Tsundora	,,	Sambar.
Tuesday . .	Ungaroo	,,	Mangal bar.
Wednesday . .	Bodo	,,	Budh bar.
Thursday . .	Bressput	,,	Brihaspati bar.
Friday . .	Shooker	,,	Suka bar.
Saturday . .	Shimshere	,,	Sanischar bar.

These names are used in Gilgit, Hunza, and Nager, and were most probably introduced by the Shins, as they were in use long before the Sikh power was felt across the Indus. It would seem as if the Shins, while introducing the Hindoo days of the week, adopted in other respects the mode of computing time already existing in the country.

In Chitral the calendar is computed by the solar year commencing with the winter solstice; but the months take their names from peculiarities of season or agricultural operations, not from local land marks. They are—

1. Toongshal (*long nights*).
2. Phutting (*Extreme cold*).
3. Aryan (*Wild ducks*).
4. Shadakh (*Black mark*, in allusion to the black appearance of the earth when the snow melts).
5. Boi (*Sparrows*).
6. Ronzuk (*Trembling*, in allusion to the waving appearance of the growing corn).
7. Yogh (*Full*).
8. Mooj (*Middle*, alluding to summer being half over)
9. Poiyanaso (*The end*).
10. Kolkomi (*Threshing*).
11. Kirman (*Sowing*).
12. Chunchoori (*Leaf falling*).

The ordinary Mahommedan calendar is, however, coming into use, especially among the Ashimadek class. The days of the week are named according to the Mahommedan calendar, except that Friday is named Adinna.

In Bushkar and Torwal, the Mahommedan calendar is followed. In the latter place the ordinary names are preserved, in the former the months are named—

Hussan Hoosein.
Safar.
Purum ishpo (*First sister*).
Dowim ishpo (*Second sister*).
Tlooi ishpo (*Third sister*):
Chot ishpo (*Fourth sister*).
Sooepi (*Great month*).
Shokudder.
Roz.
Lokyül (*Small festival*).
Miâna (*Intervening*).
Gânyül (*Great festival*).

The constellation of the Great Bear is called "the maiden's corpse," the four corner stars being supposed to represent a bier: the small star above the middle star of the tail is called the "star of life," as it is supposed to be invisible to a person forty days before death. The pleiades are called the flock of sheep; a comet, "the star with a tail," is supposed to portend the death of a king. The milky way is called the "track of the cow and horse," the tradition being that in the broad part about the middle the horse fell down from going too fast, while the cow travelled safely. The world is supposed to rest on the horns of a cow, which shakes its head occasionally at the sins of the inhabitants, and so causes earthquakes.

The west and south are always spoken of as up, and the north and east as down. A man going west or south to a place talks of going up to it. Fairies and demons that live in caves among the mountains or in desert places, have a prominent place in the belief of the Dards. Dr. Leitner has already given an account of the Yetch and its female counterpart the Rooé. In Boorishki they are known as Phoot and Billuss. Madness is supposed to be caused by a demon casting its shadow over a person, while the shadow of a fairy confers the gift of prophecy. Demons assume the appearance of human beings to lure men to destruction, but they are recognisable by their feet being turned backwards.

In Gilgit, Hunza, and Nager the ruler's family is supposed to be specially under the protection of a guardian fairy called Yoodeni. A drum, called the Yoodeni drum, is always kept on the top of the ruler's castle. When it is heard to sound at certain festivals and at critical times it presages good fortune. Nobody must try to see the Yoodeni, or look in that direction when the drum is heard; if he did so, some evil would be certain to happen to the daring individual, the least he could expect would be that his head would be twisted round to his back, and remain so for the rest of his life. A warlike expedition undertaken without the sounding of the Yoodeni drum would certainly end in disaster.

Trial by appeal to the ordeal of fire is still practised. Seven paces are measured, and a red-hot axe-head is placed on the open palm of the accused, on which a green leaf has first been spread. He must then deposit the hot iron at the spot appointed seven paces distant, and should any mark of a burn remain on his hand, it is a proof of guilt. The Vakeel of the Thum of Hunza on one occasion offered to subject himself to the ordeal before me, in order to clear his master of a false accusation.

Magic has a prominent place in Dard ideas, and many individuals are credited with the power of exercising magical arts. The rulers of Hunza and Nager are credited by their subjects with the power of producing rain. During a very severe winter I captured a full-grown markhor, which had wandered during the night into the cultivated land. The occurrence being unusual, the animal was at once regarded as a *jin*, and a deputation came to me shortly after it was captured, asking me to release it lest it should bring misfortune on the place. The death of the Wuzeer, which happened unexpectedly a few days afterwards, is still ascribed to the occurrence. Written charms are in great request, and every person wears one or more suspended to different parts of the dress by circular brass buckles. Those most in demand are charms conferring invulnerability and courage on the wearer. Charms are also attached to the mane and forelock of favourite horses. Certain springs are supposed to have the power of causing tempests if anything impure, such as a cowskin, is placed in them. This seems to have been an old and widely-spread superstition. Baber mentions it in his memoirs. "Some books mention that in Ghazni there is a fountain, into which if any filth or ordure be thrown, immediately there rises a tempest and hurricane with snow and rain."[1] The same is mentioned by another writer.[2] "Many days elapsed without the opponents having engaged each other, when it was mentioned to Mahmood that in the camp of Jeipal was a spring into which if a mixture of ordure should be thrown, the sky would immediately become overcast, and a dreadful

[1] Baber's Memoirs by Erskine, p. 149. [2] Brigg's Ferishta, Vol. I, p. 16.

storm of hail and wind arise. Mahmood having caused this to be done, the effects became visible; for, instantly the sky lowered, and thunder, lightning, wind, and hail succeeded, turning the day into night, and spreading horror and destruction around."

Divination is still practised, in spite of the conversion of the country to Mahommedanism. The Dainyals, or diviners, who are of both sexes but are more frequently women, are supposed to receive the gift of second sight by the shadow of a Barai, or fairy, having fallen on them in sleep. Dr. Leitner speaks of the gift as being supposed to be hereditary, but this is not the case, though the daughters of Dainyals often become Dainyals also. Dainyals are said to be only found among the shepherd population, and it is easy to understand how a solitary life among the wild crags of the Hindoo Koosh should encourage a belief in the power of intercourse with the unseen world. Quite young people become Dainyals, and the spirit of prophecy is supposed to remain with them for life.

The first intimation of the gift to the friends of the recipient is conveyed by their finding him or her in a deep trance. The requisite music is brought, flageolets being substituted for the ordinary clarionets, and softly modulated airs are played close to the ear of the entranced. Gradually he moves and begins to show signs of life, on which a goat is brought and decapitated, and the bleeding neck presented to the Dainyal novice. This is the test of a true Dainyal. If the gift of divination has really come to him, he seizes the bleeding neck, and sucks the blood. Some find this too much for them, and refusing to suck the blood are looked on afterwards as only feebly gifted with the spirit of prophecy. The idea of imposture never seems to be entertained by these simple-minded people. The recognised Dainyals are consulted on all special occasions, such as the yearly festivals in summer, or the declaration of war with a neighbouring state. The spirit of divination is supposed to lie dormant in winter, and to be strong in proportion to the heat of the weather.

On the first occasion of my witnessing an incantation, two Dainyals were brought from a considerable distance to prophesy at the Ganoni festival in June. They were both women, one of about twenty-five and the other about forty years of age, who showed by their wild and haggard looks the strain of the often-practised ceremony on their faculties. A circle being formed round which the spectators seated themselves, a bunch of cedar twigs was placed on a flat stone and set on fire, and while two or three men vigorously blew up the flame, the Dainyal with a cloth over her head inhaled the thick pungent smoke which curled round her head, while the music played softly. In a few minutes she became violently agitated, her hands were convulsively clasped over her head, and her whole body was shaken with uncontrollable muscular motion, till, dashing the burning branches aside, she fell prostrate at the feet of the musicians, grasping the drum with her hands, and violently throwing her head backwards and forwards in a way that threatened dislocation. At length, overcome by the violence of her exertions, she fell apparently senseless on the ground. The spectators shouted long and loud at this triumphant manifestation of the fairy's presence, and the music played its loudest. Then the second Dainyal entered the circle, and in a few minutes was also lying motionless. The music now changed to a harsh cadence, and soon one, and then the other, rose and staggered round the circle in a rude attempt at stepping in time to the music. With their long hair floating loose, half-closed eyes, drunk with the fumes of the cedar smoke, and occasionally coming into collision, they formed a most weird and somewhat painful spectacle, while the shouts of the spectators rose and fell at each uncouth gesture, varied by shrill whistles that would have done credit to the gallery of a popular London theatre. The violent exertion soon produced fatigue, while the worst effects of the cedar smoke seemed to disappear and the prophesying began. While the music played softly, the two witches reduced their movements to a sort of aimless walk round the circle, with fixed and vacant gaze, occasionally one would stop and place her head close to the flutes or the drum as if listening to a language that others could not hear, and then again resume the weary round. Sometimes, during one of these pauses, one would, after listening, raise a shrill chaunt which was attentively listened to by the musicians, and after being repeated once or twice was caught up by them and loudly chaunted to the audience, while murmurs of surprise or congratulation ran round the circle.

This, varied with intervals of leaping and dancing which seemed to excite both themselves and the spectators to the highest pitch, lasted for about an hour, when the palpable exhaustion of the Dainyals made it necessary to close the meeting. A man going into the circle gave a back, as at leapfrog, and one of the women, taking a flying leap on to his shoulders, was carried out of the ring, the second Dainyal following in like fashion on another back being offered, and the meeting broke up. No attempt is made to direct the prophecy to any topic by hint or question, and the Dainyal is always free to give, as the communication of the fairy, whatever comes into her head. Considerable freedom of speech is gained in this way, and an unpopular ruler often gets a broad hint given him. Dainyals only exist now in Gilgit, Hunza, and Nager, the stricter Mahommedanism of the neighbouring valleys having disestablished them. Circumstances point to this mode of divination being of Shin introduction, the majority of Dainyals being of that caste. Stronger evidence is afforded by the fact that it is incumbent upon a Dainyal, of whatever caste, to refrain from cow's milk, like the most orthodox Shin.

During the ceremony the witches attempt, occasionally, to rush out of the circle, but are thrust back by the spectators, the idea being that they are forced to prophecy against their will. Occasionally, too, they affect to become excited by the sight of certain persons, bright colours, dogs, &c., and rush at and try to tear them, but are repelled by the spectators, and so are forced to content themselves with hurling stones at the object of aversion.

According to Elphinstone's account of the Siah Posh Kaffirs, something of the same kind exists among them. He says: "They have also persons who can procure an inspiration of some superior being, by holding their heads over the smoke of a sacrifice; but these are held in no particular reverence." Moorcroft mentions mountain witches at Nadaun who were called *Dain*, and a form of divination called *Dewalla* is still practised in some parts of the Punjab.

Serious crimes, such as murder, are rare. In Wakhan murder is punished by a fine of six horses, six guns, and thirty woollen robes; should the murderer be unable to pay the fine, he is forced to give up a son or daughter as a slave to the family of the murdered person. Theft is punished by a fourfold restoration of the stolen property, and the thief is bound to a tree and beaten. Grave disturbances, in which deadly weapons are used, are punished by heavy fines, and an offender is not pardoned till he succeeds in bringing a live hare to the Meer, which at certain seasons is a matter of difficulty.

Though bloodshed is rare among the Dards as compared with the Afghans, brutal murders are sometimes committed on travellers. On one occasion that came to my knowledge, it was ascertained that a Goojur travelling through Darel had a small packet in his waist—band which was supposed to contain gold-dust. Two men waylaid him, and shot him down at a narrow place in the road. On opening the packet it was found to contain snuff.

Though now used by all classes without distinction where the population is mixed, the difference between the Shin and Yeshkun nomenclature is great. Of the Shin names a great number have the suffix of *Sing*, which is retained in spite of the conversion of the people to Mahommedanism. These names are never found among the purely Boorish population of Hunza and Nager, but it is to be noted that the suffix *Sing* is found among the earlier Makpon Kings of Iskardo. The Yeshkun names have reference to animals or some familiar object, and are not always of a complimentary nature. When one or two children in a family die, it is the custom to give the next born a mean name, such as, "the unclean," "old rags," in order to avert misfortune.

Shin Names.

Men.

Moosing.	Hubba Sing.	Ram Sing.
Kummoosing.	Gissing.	Pooṇyâr Sing.
Melsing.	Chumâr Sing.	Singoo.
Demsing.	Booṇyâl Sing.	Dingoo.
Hinnasing.	Gelsing.	

Women.

Sheli Bai.	Sookoomull.	Rozi Bai.
Shubibi.	Bibi.	Shermull.
Shoosha Bai.	Bai.	

Yeshkun Names.

Shooṇ	Dog.	Girkis	Mouse.
Jakooṇ	Ass.	Ooshato	Unclean.
Butt	Stone.	Tonker	Grasshopper.
Yechilo	Mad man.	Ghoko	Ass foal.
Rajo	Snake.	Kootooro	Puppy.
Chooto	Rags.	Bosero	Calf.
Barai	Fairy.	Itch	Bear.
Kurâto	Basket.	Shen	Bed.
Boodulo	Old clothes.	Buck	Cheese.

CHAPTER VIII.

FESTIVALS.

IN spite of the general conversion of the tribes to Mahommedanism, ancient semi-religious festivals, mostly connected with agriculture, are still observed by them more or less in accordance with ancient customs. About Gilgit, where Mahommedan ways of thought have as yet only penetrated skin-deep, the festivals are still observed with little less ceremony than formerly, and are called "Shiné baradesi," or "Great days of the Shins," which would appear to show that they are mainly of Shin introduction. The dates of the festivals connected with ploughing, sowing, and reaping, differ slightly according to the proper seasons for those operations in different places.

The first festival is that of *Nôs*, at the time of the winter solstice in celebration of the beginning of the new year, which, according to ancient computation, commenced then. The name *Nôs* means "fattening," and alludes to the slaughtering of cattle which takes place. The first day is one of work, and is devoted in every household to dressing and storing the carcases of bullocks, sheep, and goats slaughtered a few days previously. This is done by drying them in a particular way, so that they remain fit for food for several months. This is necessary because the pastures have become covered with snow, and only sufficient fodder is stored to keep a few animals alive through the winter.[1] The next morning, two hours before day-light, the *Taleni*[2] celebration takes place. Bonfires are lighted, and everybody flocks to the Shawaran, torch in hand. The drums sound summoning all laggards, and as the first streaks of day-light appear, the torches are thrown in the direction of Gilgit, or in that place are scattered about at pleasure. Singing, dancing, and polo go on through the day, and are continued at intervals daily for a whole month.

[1] A similar process of storing meat is practised in Cabul.

[2] *Taleni* is the name given to a bundle of strips of wood bound together and used as a torch.

This festival is celebrated in Yassin, Ponyal, Gilgit, Hunza, Nager, Astor, and Gor. In Hunza and Nager the bonfire portion is called *Tùm shelling*, "tree-scattering," and in Astor, *Lomi*. It is said to commemorate the death of a ruler who once tyrannised over Gilgit; but there seems good reason for supposing that it is a relic of fire-worship. In Chitral the festival is celebrated under the name of *Dushti*, without the bonfires, as also in Chilas and Darel, where it is called *Daiko*. In the villages of the tract of valley between Ponyal and Ghizr, where the population is almost entirely Shin, no language but Shina is allowed to be spoken on the day of the Nôs festival, and a sort of demonstration is made against the neighbouring Kho and Woorshik communities. Each family makes a bonfire of cedar wood on its own land, and a cry is raised, "To-day let all our enemies in the upper country remain above, and those in the lower country remain below. Let those who wear the 'kori' (the leather boots worn by the Kho people) perish, and let all who wear the 'towti' (the leather leg-wrappings worn by the Shins) increase and prosper." Any man who speaks Khowar or Woorshiki in the village on that day is beaten and ill-treated.

The next festival is the *Bazono*, which celebrates the beginning of spring and the appearance of the first green shoots of corn. On the occasion of this festival the people assemble on the Shawaran, and a lean miserable sheep is brought. It must not be a good one. The Tarangfah sacrifices it, and the blood is sprinkled on everybody's polo stick. The Tarangfah on horseback trundles the head along the ground for a short distance with his stick. Doms then tie a rope to the horns and drag the head along the whole length of the ground, taking the carcase as their perquisite. Polo and dancing conclude the day. In Hunza and Nager the ceremony of the sheep sacrifice is performed at the same time as the *Thumer Bopow* mentioned further on.

Bazono literally means "leanness," referring to the miserable state of the cattle at the end of the winter. This festival is peculiar to Gilgit.

After the Bazono was a festival called Aiboi, which took place during the first week in March, but which is now no longer observed. This appears also to have been confined to Gilgit.

The evening before the festival a peculiar kind of plum-cake, called Jutchbut, was baked and eaten in every house. The gates of the fort were closed, and all probable absentees, such as traders and travellers, were put under surveillance. The next morning a party was sent round by the Ra to bring every man in the place inside the fort. Some would make a pretence of hiding, but in time all were hunted out and brought in. The women of the place had meanwhile assembled and formed a double line from the inner castle to the outer gate of the fort, each being provided with a stout willow stick. When all was ready, the Ra rode out, as if to leave the fort. On arriving at the head of the line, a cry was raised for a present, which he promptly complied with and then rode on between the lines. All the men were then bound to follow him, one by one. The Wuzeers and members of the Ra's family were allowed to ransom themselves like the Ra, but the rest had to run the gauntlet and get through as best they might. The women plied their sticks with hearty good will, and unpopular members of society came off badly.

On the following day the men again assembled in the fort, and formed themselves into two parties, one under the Ra inside the castle, and the other under the Wuzeer in the outer fort. Both sides were provided with wood-ashes and dust which had previously been collected for the occasion, and a sham fight ensued. The Wuzeer's party tried to storm the castle, while the Ra's men showered earth and ashes on them. Sometimes the assailants were successful, and the Ra was made a prisoner in his own castle. After an hour or two he consented to pay a ransom, which was fixed at a bullock and three sheep for the victors, and a robe of honour for their leader. If, on the contrary, the Wuzeer's party were defeated, every man had to give a present to the Ra. The parts of both days not occupied in the performances were spent in feasting, polo, dancing, and consulting the Dainyals.

This curious festival, which was said to mark the time for pruning vines and the first budding of the apricot trees, was discontinued when the advent of Sikh troops introduced a stricter observance of Mahommedan forms,[1] and forced women to remain in greater seclusion. A trace of it still exists in Ponyal, where the women are privileged on that day to address abusive remarks, in jest, to the Ra when he first comes out of his house. The whole festival appears to show some connection with that of the Holi, which takes place in India about the same time.

[1] The first Governor appointed under the Sikhs was a Mahommedan, who did much towards introducing a more orthodox type of the faith.

Next to the Aiboi came the *Ganoni* feast, which celebrated the commencement of the wheat harvest. It is still kept up in Gilgit and all the neighbouring valleys. The day having been fixed with reference to the state of the crop, the last hour of day-light for the preceding ten days is spent in dancing on the Shawaran. At dusk on the evening before the festival, a member of every household gathers a handful of ears of corn. This is supposed to be done secretly. A few of the ears are hung over the door of the house, and the rest are roasted next morning and eaten steeped in milk. The day is passed in the usual rejoicings, and on the following day harvest operations are commenced. As some crops are always more forward than others, and ready to be reaped before the appointed day, no restriction is placed on their being cut; but to eat of the grain before the Ganoni would provoke ill-luck and misfortune. The festival is observed in Sirikol and Wakhan; in the latter place it is called *Shagit*. In Chitral it is called *Phindik*. The tribes in Torwal, Bushkar, and in the Indus Valley below Sazin do not observe it.

The next festival is the *Domenika*, "smoke-making," which celebrates the completion of the harvest. When the last crop of the autumn has been gathered, it is necessary to drive away evil spirits from the granaries. A kind of porridge called "mool" is eaten, and the head of the household takes his matchlock and fires it into the floor. Then, going outside, he sets to work loading and firing till his powder horn is exhausted, all his neighbours being similarly employed. The next day is spent in the usual rejoicings, part of which consists in firing at a sheep's head set up as a mark. In Chitral this festival is called *Justundikaik*, "devil-driving."

The last festival in the year, and the most important of all, is the *Chili*, which formerly celebrated the worship of the Chili tree (*Juniperus excelsa*), and marked the commencement of wheat-sowing. Within the last sixty years the rites connected with tree-worship have ceased, but the ceremonies connected with sowing are still maintained. The feast now lasts two days, beginning on the first day of the sun entering the sign of the Scorpion. The first is called the Ra's day, the second the people's day. The evening before the first day a procession goes to the Ra's granary, from which they receive between twenty and thirty pounds of the best wheat, which is placed in a skin mixed with sprigs of the sacred *chili* tree. A large bonfire of the sacred cedar wood is lighted, and the quantity of wheat to be used in the next day's sowing is held over the smoke. The rest is ground and made into a large cake about 2 feet in diameter, which is baked on the same fire and then placed in a secure place for the night, a man being specially placed on guard over it. The musicians have meanwhile been hard at work, and dancing is kept up by the firelight till a late hour. Next day the people having assembled on the Ra's land, the Ra rides out from his castle attended by all his family and retainers. Before him is borne in procession the large cake of leavened bread, on which wheat is heaped up, and a pomegranate, with a sprig of cedar stuck in it, placed on the top. This is carried by a man with his face smeared with flour, who is called Dono. The crowd having gathered round the Ra in a ring, the Yerfah approaches, holding two or three handfuls of the smoked wheat in the skirt of his robe, into which the Ra empties a small quantity of gold-dust. Then with a loud voice the Yerfah cries out: "Oh people, be ready, the Ra has mixed the gold and will scatter the seed; may your fortune be good!" Then the Ra, taking the mixed wheat and gold, throws it among the people, who scramble to catch it in their skirts. More wheat and gold-dust are then poured into the Yerfah's skirt and scattered, the ceremony being repeated four times, to the north, south, east, and west. Those to whom it has once been thrown are not allowed to shift their places so as to get more. Then a yoke of oxen is brought to the Ra, who takes the plough handle and ploughs two furrows, eastwards and westwards, scattering seed; he then returns to the castle, after making over the large cake to his ploughmen, whose perquisite it is. After this the *Râtch Mooger*, or, "the Ra's he-goat," is taken up to the tower of the castle and sacrificed by a Rono; one of this caste alone being permitted to officiate. Cutting off the head and feet, the officiating Rono holds them up in view of the assembled people, and all the drums strike up. The carcase of the goat is made over to those whose perquisite it is. In Gilgit it is the perquisite of the men of the village of Boormuss, who are Shins, and whose privilege it is to carry the Ra's standard in war, for which they receive a goat a day while in the field. Then, while the people stand expectant, the *Yoodeni durrung*, "the fairy's drum," is heard to sound. All faces are averted to prevent the evil that would surely happen to him who should catch sight of the performer, and the *Yoodeni-ai*, or, "fairy's she-goat," is brought and sacrificed. Some of the blood is sprinked on the fairy's drum, and the carcase is given to the Dom musicians, whose perquisite it is. This ends the ceremony, and the day is wound up with archery, dancing, singing, and polo. The mark for the bowmen is a block of wood, with a small wedge of silver, given by the Ra, beaten into it, which becomes the prize of the most skilful marskman.

On the second, or people's day, feasting and dancing go on almost the whole day. They visit one another's houses, being expected to eat something in each house. A few yards of ploughing are commenced as a matter of form by every land-holder, for without this a good crop could not be expected.

In Hunza and Nager this festival is called *Thumer Bopow*, or, "the Thum's sowing," and is celebrated in exactly the same way, but it does not take place till spring owing to the difference of climate. A somewhat similar festival takes place in Yassin and Chitral, where it is called *Binisik*, "seed-sowing;" but the ruler does not take part in it, the present ruling class in Yassin and Chitral having never identified themselves with their humbler subjects. In Yassin the festival is accompanied by a curious custom. The Tarangfah is mounted on a good horse and clad in a robe of honour given him by the Mihter. In this way he is conducted to the polo ground, where all seat themselves while the music strikes up and the Tarangfah gallops twice up and down the ground. Should any accident happen to him, such as either himself or his horse falling, it is regarded as a presage of misfortune to the whole community, and of speedy death to himself. In order to avert evil, he and his family observe the day as a solemn fast.

In Wakhan no public ceremony takes place, but the first seed-sowing is a time of festivity in every household. A bowl of grain, half of which has been roasted, is carried out and scattered round the house. Then the goodman starts for his ploughing, but returning clambers up to his house-top and scatters seed through the central sky-hole which gives light and ventilation to the house. Then, proceeding to his field, he traces a circular furrow twice round it, scatters a little seed, and returns home, where he finds the door barred against him, and he is not admitted by the women till after much entreaty. The next morning he rises before daylight and drives an ass into the house, giving occasion for much fun and joking, after which the ass is sprinkled with flour and driven out again.

I think there can be little doubt that in this festival we see a relic of the Hindoo Dussehra. A native gentleman has obliged me with the following note on the subject:—

"The chief Hindoo festival connected with agriculture was Dussehra, the 10th day of Asru Sukla, when the previous nine days have been spent in worshipping the goddess Doorga, barley being sown near the place of worship it is given to the Raja by the Brahmins as an emblem of success, and after that the sowing of spring crops commences. The Raja going through the form of ploughing and sowing was, in ancient days, considered to take away the sin which tilling land is supposed to convey, and the Raja being the master of the land must take the first and principal part in the operation before his subjects would consent to plough. I can find only one instance of the Raja being obliged to plough in person. It is in the Ramayana. Raja Janak, the father of Sita, the wife of Rama, when there was a drought of twelve years in his kingdom, was solicited by the people and Brahmins to plough in person. He did plough, and there was plenty of rain, and Sita was born."

The ceremonial of the cedar worship in Gilgit was as follows:—

For three days previously, three chosen unmarried youths underwent daily washing and purification. On the fourth day they started for the mountain, provided with wine, oil, bread, and fruit of every kind. Having found a suitable tree they chose a branch, on which the wine and oil were sprinkled, while the bread and fruit were eaten as a sacrificial feast. The branch was then cut off and carried to the village. At its entrance the party were met by all the people in holiday attire and conducted to the appointed place with music and rejoicing, where the branch of cedar was placed on a large stone by the side of running water. A goat was then sacrificed, its blood poured over the cedar branch, and a wild dance took place, in which weapons were brandished about, and the head of the slaughtered goat was borne aloft, after which it was set up as a mark for arrows and bullet-practice. Every good shot was rewarded with a gourd full of wine and some of the flesh of the goat. When the flesh was finished, the bones were thrown into the stream, and a general ablution took place, after which every man went to his house, taking with him a spray of the cedar. On arrival at his house he found the door shut in his face, and on his knocking for admission, his wife asked, "What have you brought?" to which he answered, "If you want children, I have brought them to you; if you want food, I have brought it; if you want cattle, I have brought them; whatever you want, I have it." The door was then opened and he entered with his cedar spray. The wife then took some of the leaves, and pouring wine and water on them placed them on the fire, and the rest were sprinkled with flour and suspended from the ceiling. She then sprinkled flour on her husband's head and shoulders, and addressed him thus :—"Ai Shiri Bagerthum, son of the fairies, you have come from far!" *Shiri Bagerthum*, "the dreadful king," being the form of address to the cedar when praying for wants to be fulfilled. The next day the wife baked a number of cakes, and, taking them with her, drove the family goats to the Chili stone. When they were collected round the stone, she began to pelt them with pebbles, invoking the Chili at the same time. According to the direction in which the goats ran off, omens were drawn as to the number and sex of the kids expected during the ensuing year. Walnuts and pomegranates were then placed on the Chili stone, the cakes were distributed and eaten, and the goats followed to pasture in whatever direction they showed a disposition to go. For five days afterwards this song was sung in all the houses :—

Dread Fairy King, I sacrifice before you,
How nobly do you stand! you have filled up my house,
You have brought me a wife when I had not one,
Instead of daughters you have given me sons.
You have shown me the ways of right,
You have given me many children,
You have made me like the mountain,
I have brought the family of the mountain tops,
I have gone to Sargin Gilit,
That I might see the people.
You slay many wild goats,
You with the gun on your shoulder,
Oh you with the sword in your hand!
Oh you riding upon a horse!
Oh you clothed in a fine robe!
Dread king, I will slay you a ram.
Oh you that have come from the mountain,
I will rub your feet with butter.
Oh you that have come from below,
I will anoint you with oil.
I have been to the wide plain,
They have slain you a fine he-goat,
A ram has been slain, I have honoured you to-day,
To-morrow you will depart.
Go, dread Fairy King, I salute you,
You have given me prosperity,
How shall I let you depart!

The Chili stone is still to be seen at the entrance of every Shin village.

CHAPTER IX.

PAST AND PRESENT RELIGIONS.

MR. DREW has shown that the stricter observance of Mahommedan customs in Gilgit dates from a very recent period, and though the tenets of Islam, owing to local circumstances, have taken firmer root in some valleys of Dardistan than in others, there are no positive records or traditions to indicate the nature of the religion which they supplanted. Circumstantial evidence, however, enables some opinion to be formed on the subject, and each religion that has in turn prevailed in these valleys has left some trace of its existence.

The Oxus Valley having been the cradle of the religion of Zoroaster, the valleys south of the Hindoo Koosh are not likely to have escaped its influence. In Wakhan there are many towers and structures which are still ascribed to the worshippers of fire, and the tradition of this worship still lingers in Yassin. The secluded easily defensible valleys of Yassin and Gilgit are so eminently suited to afford shelter from persecution to the followers of a dying faith, that fire-worship probably existed in them long after it had been driven out of neighbouring, more accessible, valleys. In the "Taleni" portion of the Nôs festival, of which mention has already been made, we probably see the last surviving relic of Magian worship in these countries.

Richardson, in his Dissertation, says, speaking of the ancient fire-worshippers—

"In December, on the shortest night of the year, was the anniversary of the great festival of fire, called *Shub Sadah* (شب سادہ), when their temples were illuminated, and large piles of fire blazed all over the kingdom; round which the people entertained themselves all night with choral dances, and various amusements peculiar to the season."

He also says that the festival was instituted to commemorate a popular tradition—

"In the time of King Hushang (about 860 years before the Christian era) a monstrous dragon infesting the country, the king himself attacked him with stones, when one of them falling with prodigious force upon

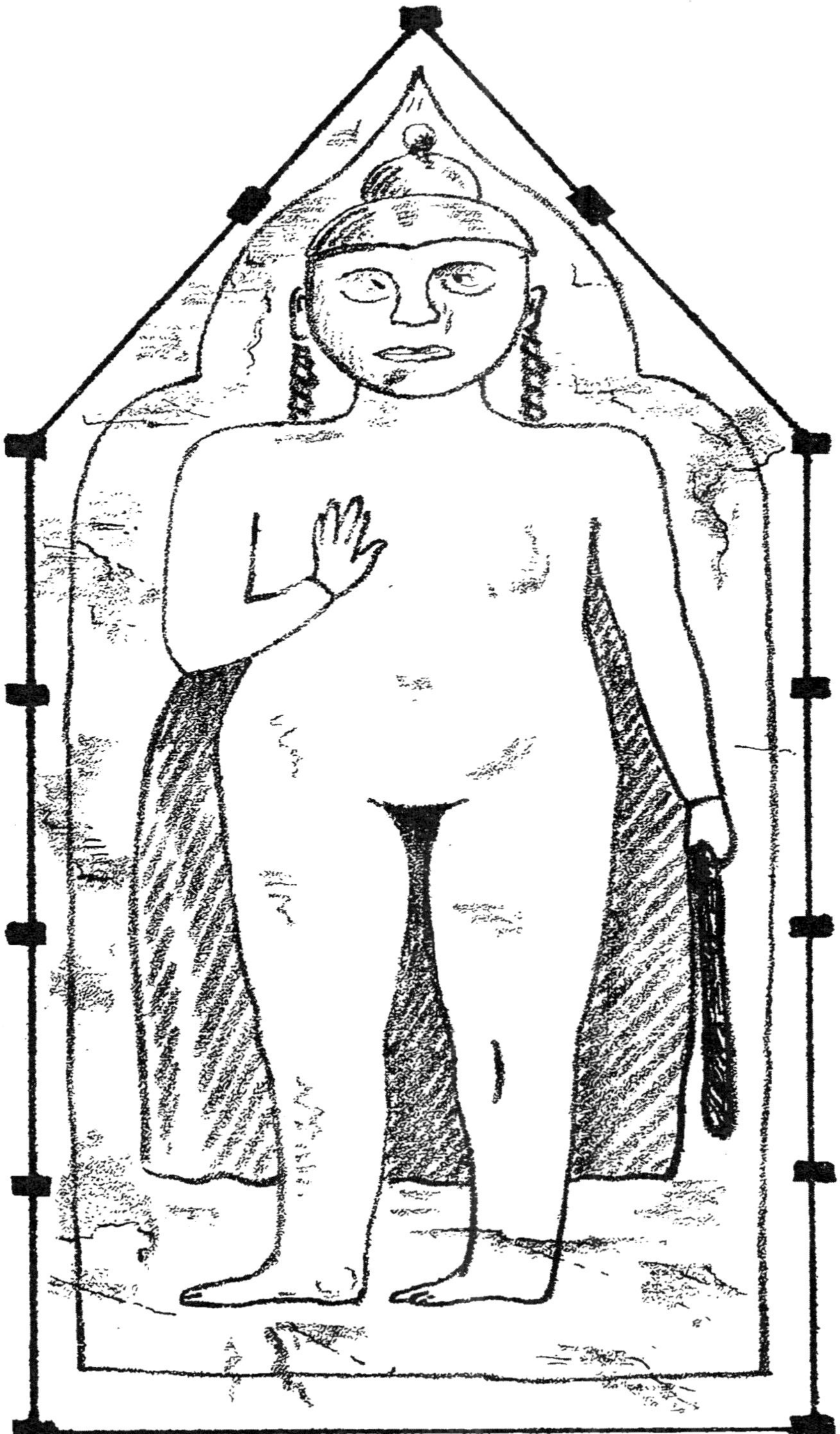

Zincographed at the Surveyor General's Office, Calcutta.

ROCK-CUT FIGURE OF BUDDHA
NEAR GILGIT.

another, struck fire, set the herbage and surrounding trees in a blaze, and consumed the dragon in the flames."

The resemblance of this legend to the Gilgit legend, which the Taleni festival is said to commemorate, is noteworthy. Under the story of the tyrant Shiri Buddutt devouring his subjects is probably concealed an ancient sun-myth. Long after the original meaning of the celebration had been forgotten, the custom no doubt survived; and advantage may have been taken of the festival to get rid of an unpopular ruler. In the legend of Shiri Buddutt it is represented that his life could not resist fire, and he is still fabled as dwelling in a place surrounded by glaciers, from which he attempts to issue yearly at the time of the winter solstice, but is driven back by the Taleni.

Later, when Buddhism was the prevailing religion on both sides of the Hindoo Koosh, this religion doubtless established itself as strongly in the southern valleys as it did in the lateral valleys of Badakhshan. Scattered through the Gilgit and Astor Valleys are a number of remains of Buddhistic stone altars, similar to those which are so common in Ladakh. The name "Munni," which is still applied to them, sufficiently attests their origin, though the natives attempt to account for them by saying that they have been made for the convenience of people carrying loads to rest their burdens upon. Their size, position, and the labour that has evidently been expended on them, however, forbid the acceptance of the reason assigned. They are sometimes also called "Thalli."

Both in the Sai and Gilgit Valleys there are several remains of Buddhist Chogtens, whose forms can still be distinctly traced. Those in best preservation are about 3 miles from Gilgit, near the village of Nowpoor, where there are four Chogtens close together in line. The remains of a large one also exist in the Chitral Valley, on a conspicuous point near the road not far from the valley of Koosht, and are still spoken of as "the idol." Closer research would no doubt discover many others.

Near the village of Nowpoor,[1] not far from Gilgit, is a large rock-cut figure of Buddha. The angle of the fork of two ravines is formed by an abrupt perpendicular rock several hundred feet high. In the very point of the angle the rock has split, so as to leave a broad smooth surface 50 feet from the ground. On this a deep slot has been cut in

[1] Nowpoor would appear to have been formerly the more important place of the two. Its ancient name was Amsar.

the form of a pentagon, within which the figure has been cut in intaglio. The face is exactly as represented on well-known figures of Buddha, with ear ornaments and head-dress, thick compressed lips, smooth face, and impassive countenance. The figure is erect, and is about 9 feet high. The upper part, which is in excellent preservation, is well finished, the lower part is not so well executed. The right arm is held across the body with the hand open, palm outwards; the left hand hangs by the side, and holds a staff or some kind of weapon. The whole figure is exposed, but the edge of a robe or some hanging drapery is portrayed, which, with the smooth face, has given rise to the modern belief that it is intended for a female figure. The lines of the pentacle are accurately drawn and deeply cut. On the edge are deep square niches, cut at regular intervals, which may have been used to hold timber supports of a frame to protect the figure from injury. The feet of the figure are upwards of 30 feet from the ground, and it must have been a matter of considerable difficulty to execute the work in such a position.

It is probable, however, that the level of the soil below the figure was formerly higher than it is at present, for there are signs close by of the existence of an old watercourse for purposes of irrigation, part of which appears to have been carried for a considerable distance along the face of the rock in a wooden trough. This watercourse has been rendered useless by the sinking of the water-levels, probably accompanied by a sinking of the level of the adjacent soil; and, this being the case, it appears likely that, at the time at which the figure was cut, no very high platform was necessary to enable the cutters to reach the proper position. The cutting both of the figure and of the sockets, which appear to have been used for the supports of the watercourse, show a knowledge of stone-cutting quite beyond the power of the present inhabitants of the country.

Were it not for the difference in size, I should be inclined to regard this as the figure of Buddha mentioned by the Chinese traveller Fah-Hian, who visited India about A.D. 400. According to him the figure was 94 feet high, and the length of one foot 9 feet 4 inches. His route as far as Khoten is traced without difficulty, and To-li, or Tha-li-lo, must certainly be Darel or Gilgit; but the route followed between these two points is less easily identified. General Cunningham has given strong reasons for identifying Kiech-ha with Leh, thus making Fah-Hian's route to have been along the course of the Indus from Leh to Darel; but the narrative shows that the great mountain range was not crossed till after leaving Kiech-ha, which must therefore have been on the north side of the mountains. Also it is scarcely possible that the travellers should have journeyed for a month along the bank of Indus, from Leh to Darel, without making mention of the river, and the first mention of it is not made till after passing To-li. Moreover, the route down the Indus Valley from Leh would necessitate frequent crossings and recrossings of the river, which would scarcely have escaped mention, and is so difficult, even in the present day, as to be only accessible to practised mountaineers, so it is not likely to have ever been used by ordinary travellers. Had Fah Hian passed through Leh on his way to India, he would naturally have continued by the route in present use through Cashmere, which he certainly did not visit. Beal identifies Kiech-ha with Karchoo, which has lately been re-discovered by Shaw; but the elevation of Karchoo is not sufficient to justify the statement that no grain except corn ever ripened there, or to procure for the inhabitants the title of "Men of the snowy mountains." Beal identifies Tsu-ho with Yarkund, while Cunningham, following Klaproth, would identify it with Cogiar. The balance of evidence is certainly in favour of Beal's view. Cogiar has not advantages sufficient ever to have made it so important a place as Tsu-ho seems to have been, and it is situated immediately at the foot of the mountains, which would be entered by the travellers on the first march after leaving the place. But the narrative states that they did not enter the mountains till four days after leaving Tsu-ho, and this would correspond well with the position of Yarkund. The twenty-five days occupied by the travellers on the road between Khoten and Yarkund gives a fair idea of their general rate of march. I should be disposed to identify Kiech-ha either with Sirikol, which in spite of its elevation was certainly an important place in those days, or with Raskum, which, though now deserted, is said to have once been the centre of a flourishing community. Each of these places would answer fairly well to Kiechha. The distances, however, judging by the number of days taken by the travellers, agree best with Sirikol, in which, therefore, I would recognise Kiech-ha. From Yarkund the travellers must have reached Sirikol by the Koosherab route, and the Yu-hwui must have been nomad tribes, answering to the Kirghiz of the present day. From Sirikol Fah-

Hian and his companions must have travelled either through Hunza down to Gilgit, and so on to Darel, or, more probably, across the Pamir, which would account for the mention of their route proceeding westward from Sirikol, and into the Gilgit Valley by the Durkot Pass, as suggested by Beal. From the Gilgit Valley they would naturally take the route to Darel up the Kergah Valley, at the mouth of which is the rock figure in question. This would certainly have been their most direct route to the Punjab. Striking the Indus (Sin-to) at the mouth of the Darel Valley, they must have followed the course of the river for several days, and reached Swat (Su-ho-to) by one of the lateral routes, such as that by Ghorbund.

Whether or not this be the actual figure mentioned by Fah-Hian, his account enables the date of the introduction of Buddhism into these valleys to be approximately fixed at about 150 B. C., or three hundred years after the Nirvana of Buddha.

The account now given of the figure is, that in ancient times a *Deonee*, or female demon who preyed on men, lived in the ravine, from which she sallied forth to seize passers-by; her custom being to devour only half of her prey, that is, if she seized two men, she devoured one and left the other; if she seized one, she only ate half of her victim. One day a holy man arrived who undertook to free the country of the demon. The Deonee sallied out as usual to seize him, but by the power of the holy man was turned into stone, and fixed to the rock. Being soon after desirous of leaving the country, the holy man told the people that, to ensure the continuance of the spell by which the demon had been rendered powerless, it was necessary that at his death he should be buried at the foot of the rock, and stringently charged them to be careful to bring back his body for the purpose from whatever place in which he might chance to die.

The people of Gilgit, according to the account of their descendants, took a very practical view of the case. They said that they could not be at the trouble of searching for, and bringing back, his body from any distant place he might chance to die in, with the risk of the demon being restored to life in case of failure, so they chopped off his head there and then, and buried him as directed. At the foot of the rock is a tomb which is pointed out as that of the unlucky saint.

Buddhism was no doubt the religion of the country at the time of the Shin invasion. There seem, however, to be

16 Inches high.
11 Inches long.
9 Inches broad

14 Inches long.
8 Inches broad.
$5\frac{1}{2}$ Inches deep outside.

COFFINS

Lithographed at the Surveyor General's Office, Calcutta, April 1880.

good grounds for supposing that the religion of the Shins was of the Brahminical type.

Mention has already been made of the curious fact of the cow being esteemed unclean. Mr. Shaw has shown how the feeling among the Shins of Dah Hanu is one of aversion, and not of reverence, and Mr. Drew remarks that anything more opposed to modern Hindooism cannot be imagined. But the most orthodox Brahmin would consider himself defiled by touching leather, or any part of a dead cow, so that there does not appear to be anything in the present practice directly opposed to modern Hindooism, but rather a perverted feeling that has grown out of it.

This peculiarity of the ruling race led to the appellation of Dangariké,[1] *i. e.*, "cow-people," being conferred on them by their neighbours, who apply the term to all the Shina-speaking people. Though this can hardly be cited as a proof in itself of the Hindoo origin of the Shins, I think that, when considered in connection with other points, it forms a strong argument. The feeling of the Shins with regard to the domestic fowl is shared with them by Hindoos all over India.

This feeling regarding the cow and domestic fowls is not shared by any other tribe in the Hindoo Koosh, except by a small one in Chitral, to whom the name of Dangariké is also applied by their neighbours, and by the Kalash Kaffirs, who dwell close to them. I have not been able to obtain the language of the Chitral Dangariké, but there seems to be no reason to suppose that they have any connection with the Shins of Gilgit.

Till a very recent period burning the dead was practised, the burning places being still called Jaiṇ, which would appear to be identical with Châni, the name by which burning places are called in some parts of the Punjab. The ashes were carefully collected and buried in rude wooden boxes, sometimes carved out of a solid block, or in round earthen jars. I have dug up several of both kinds. The bones are neatly packed in the boxes, which have previously been lined with birch bark. In one or two I found pieces of check cotton cloths, of a kind not now known in the country, with pieces of brass chains and other ornaments. Women's urns are readily distinguished by a number of wooden spindle whorls, mixed with the bones.

[1] Cunningham met with the term in Baltistan, and speaks of Gilgit being inhabited by Dangariks, and of the Dangri language, as if it was the name of a tribe. The now well-known term of Dard has no doubt come to be applied in the same manner.

It is also a matter of accepted tradition in Gilgit, Gor, Hunza, and Nager, that suttee was formerly practised. The dead man, with his finest clothes and his weapons girded on him was placed on the pyre, and as the fire burnt up, the woman, arrayed in her jewellery and her richest clothes, leaped into the flames.

The burning of the dead ceased to be practised more than sixty years ago. One or two old men have told me that they could remember hearing it mentioned, as a not uncommon occurrence, in their youth, but none could recollect having witnessed any actual instance. So lately as in 1877, a very old man in Darel scandalised his neighbours by calling his sons to him on his death bed, and after having his arms and valuables brought to him, desiring to be burnt with them when dead. His wish, however, was not carried out. He and a man of Gor, who died twenty years ago, are known to have always refused to be circumcised, or to call themselves Mahommedans. They were probably the very last Hindoos in Dangaristan. Suttee was abolished earlier, and has certainly not been practised in Dangaristan for the last hundred years.

It is to be remarked that none of these customs, which savour so strongly of modern Hindooism, are to be found, either as now existing or as resting on former tradition, in any of the valleys to which the Shin rule did not extend; nor is the term Dangarik applied in any cases except those mentioned. The difference between some types of Hindooism and Buddhism is not necessarily very great, but the existence of customs among them, not shared by their neighbours, the establishment of a caste system, the use of the title of Ra for their rulers, and the common suffix of *Sing* to their own names, with the frequent use of Sanscrit terms, show that considerable differences exist between the Shins and their neighbours of the Swat, Punjkorah, and Chitral Valleys, with whose language their own has so much in common.

In spite of the more severe type of Mahommedanism which prevails, and which gathers strength year by year, idolatrous customs still survive. In every village in which Shins are in the majority, there is a large stone, which is still more or less the object of reverence. Each village has its own name for this stone, but an oath taken or an engagement made over it, is often held more binding than where the Koran is used. In several villages goats are still annually sacrificed beside the stone, which is sprinkled with blood, and in other places the practice has only lately been discontinued. Though the religion introduced by the Shins would appear to have been of a Brahminical type, it must have contained also a considerable amount of demon worship, as is shown by Mr. Shaw in his account of the Hanu Dards.

I have been told that when the Cashmere troops first occupied Gilgit, there was in the fort a slab of stone about 3 feet long, bearing a Sanscrit inscription. My informant told me that he had made out the words, "Ishwar ling murti," or, "the Lingum incarnation of Shiva," but that the rest of the inscription was illegible. In 1871 the fort was destroyed by an earthquake which exploded the powder magazine and reduced the whole to ruins. The present fort was erected on the same site, and the stone was doubtless built into the foundations. The names of many of the rulers and of a number of places, not only in the Indus and Gilgit Valleys, but also in the Chitral Valley, point to a Brahminical origin. Amongst the names of places may be mentioned *Seo* (Siva, *or* Mahadeo), *Shogram* (Siva's village), *Shogoor* (Siva's priest), and *Swami*. In the Hunza and Nager genealogies we find the names of *Lullithum* (the beautiful Thum), *Hurrithum*,[1] and *Bookhatthum*,[2] and one of the last independent Ras of Gilgit, Suleiman Khan, is best known by the name of *Gowrithum*.[3]

With all this evidence it can scarcely be doubted that some form of Brahminism was introduced by the Shins into the Gilgit Valley, and, to a greater or less degree, wherever their rule extended. In valleys in which they were out-numbered by the former inhabitants, the result was, doubtless, a mixture of Buddhism and Hindooism, grafted on a form of demon-worship already existing in the country. The religious practices of the Hanu Dards described by Mr. Shaw, probably approach most nearly to those which formerly existed in Gilgit and the neighbouring valleys, when under Shin rule.

The Shins seem to have introduced, along with their form of Hindooism, a piece of tree-worship, which has been already described. Though no longer an object of public worship, supplications are still addressed to the *Chili*, especially by women desirous of children, by burning its branches, and it is still regarded as possessing special powers of puri-

[1] From Huri, a name for Mahadeo.

[2] Probably a corruption of *Mookhatthum*, referring to *Mookhat* "the final transmigration."

[3] From Gowri, the wife of Mahadeo.

fication. It plays a conspicuous part in the incantations of the Dainyals, and on a great man entering a Shin village a pan of burning Chili branches is waved before him. On certain occasions both men and women saturate themselves with the smoke, which is of a particularly pungent nature.

The custom of Chili worship does not appear to have penetrated to Hunza or Nager, nor is any trace of it to be found in the Oxus Valley, in Chitral, or among the tribes of the Swat Valley; but among the Siah-Posh it seems to exist in almost the same form as it did among the Shins. Chili wood, or Padam, is still taken down to the Punjab to be used in Hindoo ceremonials. According to Colonel Prejevalski, the same tree is also held sacred by the Mongols and Tangutans, who burn the branches for incense during prayer time. At Hemis Shukpa, within 20 miles of Leh, a few trees of great age exist, and are held in much veneration by the Tartars of the village, though the tree is not generally an object of Tartar respect.[1] It may be that the feeling of veneration was imbibed from the Shins, whose influence must have extended nearly to Leh. It is still usual in Gilgit to sprinkle goat's blood on a tree of any kind before cutting it down.

The religion of the whole country is now some form of Mahommedanism, and in the immense knot of mountains of which Yassin forms the centre, three different types of the same religion have met, and are now striving for the mastery. From the south, Soonnee Moollahs have carried their tenets up the different valleys with more or less success. From the eastward a current of Shiah doctrines has set in from Iskardo; and from the westward the curious Maulai, or Muglee,[2] tenets have found their way up the Oxus Valley. It is to be noticed that the subversion of Hindooism by Mahommedanism in the remoter valleys seems to have been extremely gradual, and to have been more owing to gradual conversion than to persecution.

The genealogical tables of the present ruling families of Hunza, Nager, and Gilgit, enable a fair idea to be formed of the date of the introduction of Islam into the country. Tradition records the death of the Gilgit Ra with the non-Mussulman name of Shiri Buddutt,[3] at the hands of a stranger bearing the Mussulman name of Azru, or Azor, from whom the present Ra of Gilgit, and the Thums of Hunza and Nager, trace

[1] Henderson's *Lahore to Yarkund*, page 51.
[2] The common uneducated pronunciation.
[3] The meaning of the name is perhaps "Given by Sri Buddha."—*Sri Buddha Datta*.

their descent. Allowing twenty-five years for each generation, this would place the first appearance of Mahommedanism in Gilgit at about the end of the thirteenth, or the beginning of the fourteenth century—a time when that faith had already spread over the more accessible parts of Central Asia. It is to be noted that this exactly corresponds with the time when Islam was first introduced into Cashmere, which, according to Ferishta, happened between A. D. 1315 and 1326. General Cunningham, by computing thirty years for each generation, and fifteen for the reign of each ruler, places the introduction of Mahommedanism into Khapolor about a century later.[1] According to one tradition Azor came from Iskardo, and in the genealogy of the Makpon princes, a Mahommedan adventurer is shown to have established himself in that place at exactly the same time, if the same computation be allowed for the duration of a generation.

It is not, however, probable that the usurper would have been in a position to attempt the forcible conversion of his new subjects; and it may be presumed that, for a long period, his descendants contented themselves with practising their own faith, with, no doubt, greatly relaxed stringency, without interfering with that of their subjects. It is not till eight generations of rulers later, which would represent a period of two centuries, that we meet with a Mussulman Thum in the neighbouring state of Nager. There was, probably, a fresh impulse given to Mahommedanism about the end of the sixteenth century, for it was at about that period that a Persian adventurer, the founder of the present ruling families of Chitral and Yassin, established himself in Kashkar. The names of those whose kingdom he usurped are lost, the only record being that they were of the Shahreis family, which is the name by which the Gilgit rulers previous to the time of Azor were known, and which was retained by the descendants of the usurper for four generations. The Emperor Baber, writing in the early part of the sixteenth century, speaks of Chitral as forming part of Kafiristan, "in the hill-country to the north-east lies Kafiristan, such as Kattor and Gebrek."[2] But on several occasions he distinguishes this Kafiristan from Kafiristan Pich (which is still a Kafir country), as if some difference existed between the two. It is probable, therefore, that though the faith of Islam was introduced into the country mentioned about the beginning of the fourteenth century, it was long confined to

[1] Cunningham's Ladakh.
[2] Erskine's Memoirs of Baber, page 140.

a limited number of the inhabitants, and did not become general till the middle or end of the sixteenth century. Even then its acceptance was so irregular that it is not surprising that Hindooism has lingered on, and has only become extinct in the present day.

The tribes of the Indus Valley were exposed earlier to the fervid preaching of the Moollahs of Swat and Boneyr, and this has led to the adoption by them of the Soonnee tenets. The people of Chilas, who were always a less tractable race than their neighbours, make it their boast that, though travellers and traders are safe in their country, no Shiah ever escapes out of their hands. At Gor, also, a few miles above Chilas, the people are all Soonnees, but a looser type of Mahommedanism prevails, and prayers were till recently addressed to the god Taiban, whose horse is sculptured on the rock near the village.

In Gilgit the population is now three-fourths Soonnee and the rest Shiah, but at the commencement of the Sikh occupation, the greater proportion were Shiahs or Maulais, and it is related that any Soonnee falling into their hands was branded with a hot iron unless he consented to become a proselyte. Those who now still adhere to the Maulai tenets, are mostly old men, who keep the fact concealed as far as possible, and call themselves Shiahs. At Soomma, a secluded village in Yassin, the people, though professed Mussulmans, still make offerings to the god Shaitum. In several other places the names of local deities are still preserved, and objects, such as a peculiar-shaped rock near a village, are still regarded with veneration, and invoked in the registration of solemn covenants.

The influence of the Iskardo Princes introduced Shiah tenets into the north-eastern part of Dardistan, while the tenets of the Maulais have made their way from the Oxus Valley across the passes of the Hindoo Koosh. In Nager the entire population are Shiahs of the orthodox type, and so are two-thirds of the people of Baltistan; the rest belong to the Noor Buksh sect. In Hunza, till a few years ago, Shiah tenets found many followers; now the Meer and the whole population are Maulais.

The Shiahs in these countries lament the martyrdom of the sons of Ali twice a year; once at the usual time according to the Mahommedan calendar, and again in the month of August, the season at which they say the martyrdom actually occurred.

Wherever Soonnees and Shiahs are found living together, they seem to practise a mutual tolerance rare in other purely Mahommedan communities. Intermarriage between the sects is so common as not to excite remark.

The whole of the people of Hunza, Ponyal, Zebak, Shighnan, Roshan, Munjan, Kolab, and Darwaz, more than half the people of Sirikol, Wakhan, Yassin, and the greater number of the inhabitants of the Ludkho Valley in Chitral, belong to the Maulai sect. A few Maulais are said to exist in Khokand, Karategin, and Badakhshan, among the poorest of the people, and in one district near Balkh, they are known as the disciples of Syud Jaffer Khan. Some are also to be found in Afghanistan, where they are known as Muftadis. A few may possibly exist in Bokhara and Khorasan, but in a fanatical country they would probably pass themselves off as Shiahs.

The head of this sect is Agha Khan, the acknowledged spiritual chief of the Khojas of India and Persia, a gentleman of Khorasan, who came to India in 1840 for political reasons, and who has resided in Bombay ever since.

The countries inhabited by the Maulais are roughly divided among a number of Pirs, who are treated by their disciples with extraordinary respect, but residence does not give the Pir authority over the whole of any special district. The office is hereditary, and Maulai families transfer their spiritual obedience from father to son, regardless of changes of residence. For instance, Shah Abdul Rahim of Zebak, who is honoured and respected as being next in rank to Agha Khan himself, has disciples in Sirikol, Kunjoot, Zebak, Yassin, and Badakhshan, but other Pirs also have disciples in those places. The respect paid to the Pirs by their disciples is unbounded; nothing is refused them. If they ask for a son or a daughter of any house, no refusal is dreamt of. One of them once said to me, "If I ordered a father to kill his own son, he dare not refuse." Whenever they move about, they are attended by a large number of followers, who are fed and maintained out of their superfluities, and they live entirely on the offerings of their disciples. Presents of horses, cattle, clothes, fruit, wheat, &c., are continually being made them, and the best of everything a Maulai possesses is given to his Pir. A portion of these offerings is converted into coin and sent yearly to Agha Khan, and agents travel yearly from these remote parts to Bombay solely for the purpose of conveying these contributions to him.

Next in rank to the Pirs are Caliphas, whose duty consists in little more than the collection of offerings. The Pirs each correspond direct with Agha Khan.

The Maulais must not be confounded with the Maulavi sect of dancing Darweshes, with whom they have nothing in common. They assert that their sect was founded by the Imam Jaffer Ali Sadik (the just), a descendant of Ali, by the daughter of the Prophet, who died A.H. 148. Aboo Mahommed Hussain, however, writing in the *Zubdat-ool-akhbar*, says, that Mahommed, surnamed Mahdi, who claimed to be sixth in descent from the Imam Jaffer Ali Sadik, founded the sect, who were first known as Ismailyas,[1] in Egypt in the year A.H. 299. His followers recognised him as the twelfth Imam, and quoted a supposed saying of the Prophet Mahommed that every 300 years the sun would rise in the west, explaining that Mahommed Mahdi's preaching 300 years after the Hijra was a fulfilment of the prophecy. Aboo Yezid, a Moolla who questioned Mahommed Mahdi's descent from Jaffer Ali Sadik, on the plea that Ismail's only son had died childless, was proclaimed to be Dejjal (Antichrist). The conquest of Egypt by Sultan Sala-oo-deen Yusuf destroyed the temporal power of the sect in that country. They were, at that time, ruled by Azid, a descendant of Mahommed Mahdi. Meanwhile, the tenets of the sect had been brought to Persia by Hassan-i-Sabbah, an Arab of the tribe of Himyar in Yemen, who established himself later in Alamot, where his grandson, on the seventh day of the Ramazan, A.H. 555, publicly proclaimed that fasting and other observances of the Sharyat were no longer obligatory.

Colonel Yule, in his notes on the Travels of Marco Polo, has given an interesting account of the "old man of the mountain," whose representative he recognises in Agha Khan. On this supposition the Maulais of the Hindoo Koosh and Oxus Valley belong to the sect of assassins, and are an offshoot of the sect to which the Druses of the Lebanon belong. They call themselves Muglees, Maulais, or Mawallis indifferently. Mr. Drew suggests that the name is derived from Maula, an Arabic name for God. The appellation may equally claim to be a corruption of Muwahideen, the name by which the Druses still call themselves, or Mulahidah, from *Mulhed*, "an infidel," the name given to the sect in old times.

[1] So named from Ismail, son of Imam Jaffer.

The precepts and observances of the sect are difficult to ascertain, one of their sayings being that "a man should conceal his faith and his women;" and the little I have been able to ascertain is from Maulais who have proselytized, and those only men of no education.

Soonnees speak of them as "Kaffirs" and "Rafizi," but they themselves do not refuse to pray or eat with Soonnees. They are sometimes accused of worshipping Ali, the son-in-law of the Prophet, and accordingly styled "Ali-purust," and they undoubtedly esteem Ali, who, they say, was born of Light as superior to the Prophet Mahommed, and an incarnation of the deity. They reject the idea of a future state, believing in the transmigration of souls. Evil deeds are punished by the spirit being translated into a dog or other mean animal. Good actions are rewarded by a future incarnation as a great or holy man. They claim little in common with other sects of Mahommedans, saying, the Soonnee is a dog and the Shiah is an ass. They question the divine character of the Koran, though they say that it was entrusted to the Angel Gabriel to give to Ali, but that he gave it by mistake to Mahommed.

They use in place of the Koran a book called the Kalam-i-Pir, a Persian work, which is shown to none but men of their faith. The precept most commonly quoted by them is, that a man should blind himself, so that he should not be moved with envy at sight of his neighbour's prosperity; he should weaken his hands, so that they can grasp nothing belonging to others; and lame himself, that he may be unable to disobey the commands of his Pir. Cattle that have strayed into standing crops are not to be driven out till they have satisfied themselves. A good Maulai is already as one dead, prayers therefore are unnecessary, as also is fasting. If any forcible attempt should be made to cause a Maulai to fast, he should resist it by devouring a pinch of dust. The only pilgrimage enjoined is to the living head of their faith, who is styled the Imam-i-Zeman, or Sahib-i-Zeman. Marriage can be performed by any man whose beard is white. Seating himself with the bridegroom on his right hand and the bride on his left, he takes a few pieces of roasted sheep's liver in both hands, and crossing his arms gives them to the man with his left hand and to the woman with his right. Then taking a cup of water he gives half to the woman, and after he has said a few words out of the Kalam-i-Pir, the ceremony is completed. The form of the Maulai Kalima is changed yearly in accordance with instructions from their spiritual head.

The following is a favourite poem recited in praise of the Imam-i-zeman:—

HELP! OH ALI.

Oh amulet of life, thou glory, Sahib-i-zeman,
Speak thy praise incessantly,
Sahib-i-zeman.

Sultan of both worlds from east to west,
All kings are beggars compared to you,
Sahib-i-zeman.

The sun of heaven shines by your beauty,
Sun and moon by your light,
Sahib-i-zeman.

When shall peace be from evil and strife of Dejjal,
Except it be your pleasure,
Sahib-i-zeman.

I hope that my heart may be lighted up
One day under the dust of your feet,
Sahib-i-zeman.

There will be a day with my last breath,
I shall speak your praises,
Sahib-i-zeman.

It is time that the sound of your trumpet
Be heard through the world,
Sahib-i-zeman.

From Kaf to Kaf take the whole world
In your world-conquering hand,
Sahib-i-zeman.

The time is come for the faithful to gird
Their loins and follow you,
Sahib-i-zeman.

Jesus will come down from the fourth heaven
To imitate you,
Sahib-i-zeman.

Nobody will worship or pay respect to God
Without worshipping also you,
Sahib-i-zeman.

Others go their own way
But I am faithful to you,
Sahib-i-zeman.

I, Suleem, the distracted in mind,
Have seized the skirts of your bounty,
Sahib-i-zeman.

Wine is drunk by the Maulais without concealment, and they do not strictly abstain from eating the flesh of animals not killed in the orthodox manner. Being absolved from the constraints of prayer and fasting, the practical religion of the uneducated consists of little more than obeying the commands of their Caliphas and Pirs, and making offerings freely through them to their spiritual chief. They are by no means intolerant, and, where permitted, live on good terms with Soonnees and Shiahs, with whom they intermarry without restraint. The only cases I have known of ill-feeling between the sects have been caused in the first instance by Soonnees from other places. From Shiahs they seldom meet with hostility, owing probably to the respect they show to Ali ; though they do not celebrate the martyrdom of Hassan and Hoossain.

On the death of a Maulai the choicest articles of his portable property are set aside for the Imam-i-zeman. No food is cooked in the house, for from three to eight days, according to the rank of the deceased, and the family subsist on food cooked elsewhere. Food is also placed on trees and exposed places for birds to eat. On the evening of the appointed day a Calipha comes to the house, and food is cooked and offered to him. He eats a mouthful and places a piece of bread in the mouth of the dead man's heir, after which the rest of the family partake. The lamp is then lighted (from which the ceremony is called "Chiragh roshan"), and a six-stringed guitar called "gherba" being produced, singing is kept up for the whole night.

I have sometimes shown the portrait of Agha Khan in Yule's Marco Palo to Maulais. They pass their fingers lightly over it and then touch their eyes and lips.

The Noor Buksh sect, which has been before referred to, is peculiar to Baltistan, where it numbers over twenty thousands followers, most of whom are to be found in Shigar and Khapolor. It is apparently an attempt to form a *viâ media* between Shiah and Soonnee doctrines. Mahommedanism is said to have been first introduced into Baltistan according to Soonnee tenets by Syud Ali Hamadani. Later, a certain

Syud Mahommed Noor Buksh, a native of Samarcand, resided for some time in Baltistan on his way to Hindostan. He was succeeded by Syud Shums-oo-deen Iraki, the disciple of Shah Kasim Faiz Buksh, who was the son of Syud Mahommed Noor Buksh, and he tried to convert the Baltis to Shiah tenets. Only partially succeeding, he planned to gain his object by fraud. He drew up the book which afterwards became the foundation of the Noor Buksh sect, and secretly placed it under the bark of a tree. At the end of a year, when the tree had assumed a natural appearance, he announced that Syud Noor Buksh had appeared to him in a dream and directed him to cut down and search a certain tree, and that by this means of reconciling all doubts would be found. So miraculous a thing as a book imbedded in a tree proved sufficient to convince the most unbelieving, and those who had before refused to adopt Shiah tenets, hastened to enroll themselves as members of the new sect.

Such is the account of the origin of the sect now given in Baltistan. Other accounts differ somewhat. According to the Zuffer Namah—

"In the reign of Futteh Shah, King of Cashmere, one Shums-oo-deen arrived from Irak, and began to disseminate doctrines different from those of any other sect. His followers assumed the title of Noor Buksh (Illuminati), but the holy men of the Mahommedan faith succeeded in putting down these sectarians. The King of Little Thibet, contiguous to Cashmere, is so prejudiced in favour of Shiahs, that he allows no man of any other faith to enter his towns. The tribe of Chuk in Cashmere contends that Meer Shums-oo-deen of Irak was a Shiah, and that he converted many thousands of people, after which he was crowned in the name of the twelve Imams; and that the Ahowita, the book containing the tenets of the Noor Buksh religion, is not the composition of that venerable personage, but the production of some ignorant infidel."

Ferishta writes—

"About this time (A.D. 1496) one Meer Shums-oo-deen, a disciple of Shah Kasim Anwur, the son of Syud Mahomed Noor Buksh, arrived in Kashmir from Irak. Futteh Khan made over to this holy personage all the confiscated lands which had lately fallen to the Crown; and his disciples went forth destroying the temples of the idolaters, in which they met with the support of the Government, so that no one dared to oppose them. In a short time many of the Cashmeris, particularly those of the tribe of Chuk, became converts to the Noor Buksh tenets."[1]

The book, which is written in Arabic, is called the *Fikr Ahwat.* The distinctive religious forms to which both Shiah and Soonee attach so much importance are mixed together

[1] Brigg's Mahommedan Power in India.

in a strange medley. In winter the Noor Bukshis pray with folded arms, like the Soonnees, in summer with the hands hanging down like the Shiahs. Like the Soonnees they pray together and observe Friday prayers, but they do not wash their feet before praying, and only perform the "masak" like Shiahs. In doctrine they give the first place to the Prophet and the second to Ali, but they observe the Mohurrum mourning for the martyred sons of Ali. From the Mohurrum observances arises one of their chief causes of quarrel with the Shiahs. The Noor Bukshis maintain that the mourning should take place in the musjids, which the Shiahs do not allow to be proper, and occasional disturbances are the result. The Noor Buksh call to prayers is *Ali yun Wali Ullah* instead of the *Ali yun Wasir Russool Allah* of the Shiahs.

Vigne mentions the sect under the name of Keluncheh, and states that at some time about the middle of the 18th century, they temporarily usurped the throne of Iskardo. A few of the sect are now to be found in Kishtwar, to which place they were deported by Golab Sing when he conquered Baltistan.

The graves of Meer Mooktar and Meer Yahya, sons of Shums-oo-deen, are still to be seen in Kiris and Shigar, and it is probable that the complete establishment of the Noor Buksh tenets in Baltistan is to a great degree due to them.

CHAPTER X.

THE SIAH POSH.

BETWEEN Chitral, Afghanistan, and the Hindoo Koosh, the maps show a large tract of unknown country under the name of Kaffiristan, concerning whose inhabitants the wildest conjectures have been formed. The fact that while surrounded on all sides by fanatical Mahommedans, with whom they are in a chronic state of war, they have been able in spite of all attacks to preserve both their independence and their faith intact, and that their customs and traditions, which differ from those of their neighbours, furnish some grounds for the assumption that they at one time enjoyed a higher state of civilisation than they do at present, has been sufficient to stimulate the curiosity of travellers and ethnologists. Conjectures have been hazarded that the Siah Posh people are of Greek descent, while a recent Russian author[1] has confidently asserted that they are incontestibly of Slav origin, and the natural subjects of the Czar. A closer acquaintance with them will probably show that their relationship with neighbouring tribes is not so distant as either of these two theories would make out.

During my visit to Chitral, in 1878, two deputations of Siah Posh tribes came to meet me and invited me into their country; an invitation of which I was unfortunately unable to avail myself. Besides the opportunities then afforded me of seeing some of these interesting people, I have frequently conversed with men who have visited different parts of Kaffiristan. So far from the Siah Posh being one people, as is ordinarily supposed, they are in fact composed of a number of tribes speaking a diversity of languages and dialects, who, though undoubtedly of cognate origin, recognize no common tie among themselves. Their manners and customs, and their form of religion, are generally similar; but many of the tribes are unable to converse with each other, and they carry on an unceasing and deadly intertribal warfare, compared with which

[1] Terentieff.

their encounters with their Mussulman neighbours are desultory and harmless. There can be little doubt that they are a number of Aryan tribes who, from the force of circumstances, are living now in the same primitive state that they probably enjoyed long before the commencement of the Christian era.

As far as can be ascertained, they are separable into three main tribes, conforming to the natural divisions of the country. These are—(I) the Rumgalis, or Lumgalis, who inhabit the upper parts of the valleys which run down from the Hindoo Koosh in a south-westerly direction, where they come into contact with the Afghans of Cabul. This tribe also extends, apparently, to the north side of the mountains. The people of Lughman are probably of this stock converted to Islam in comparatively recent times. (II) The Waigalis, who inhabit the valleys extending south-east from the Hindoo Koosh, which join the Kooner Valley at Chaghan Serai; and (III) the Bushgalis, who inhabit the valleys extending from further north in a south-south-easterly direction, and joining the Kooner Valley at Birkot. These, again, are sub-divided into smaller clans, of which the Waigalis alone furnish eighteen. In the Darah-i-Noor and other valleys joining that of Kooner from the north below Chaghan Serai, are portions of the Waigali tribe who have been recently converted to Islam. Many of these still retain the distinctive black garments.

Besides these main tribes, there are several broken or detached clans, such as the Kalashis, who are subject to Chitral, but are claimed by the Bushgalis as their slaves, and the Kittigalis or Wirigalis, a small tribe who dwell either on the north side of the Hindoo Koosh, or in the northernmost part of the Wai country on the south side, and are subject to Munjan, a small mountain state of the Oxus Valley, concerning which less is known than of the Siah Posh themselves. This last clan is called Sufeid Posh, from their wearing white garments, and the race is said to be very small.

The principal tribe of the Bushgali country is divided into Kamoz (Upper Kam) and Kamtoz (Lower Kam). The termination *gal* means "country" in the Bushgali tongue, and is apparently the same as we find in *Doongagali*, *Nuttiagali*, and other well-known *galis* near Murree. The Siah Posh employ these names amongst themselves when speaking of a tribe as the people inhabiting such and such a country, and employ the clan names when closer specification is necessary, but there is no recognised term known amongst them to distinguish the Kaffirs collectively, as opposed to their Mussulman neighbours. When pushed to use some such distinctive term, the only one they employ is "Kappra," which is only a corruption of the abusive name given them by Mahommedans. They include in the term all who shave the head in Siah Posh fashion, but not those who have turned Mussulman.

In feature they are pure Aryans of a high type, and I was much struck by the amiable looks and finely-chiselled features of a grey-headed Siah Posh Chief, whose acquaintance I made. His appearance, however, contrasted strangely with his language, while he pleaded his unwillingness to part with his dagger on account of the unusual number of enemies (upwards of forty) whom he had despatched with it. The men are well-made, muscular fellows, but incorrigibly lazy. War and hunting are regarded as the only legitimate occupations for a man, and almost the whole work of agriculture is done by women, who are even yoked alongside of oxen to the plough; for this purpose they have yokes specially constructed. They differ considerably in complexion, some of those living at high elevations being very fair. This seems to be especially the case with those living on the higher slopes of the Hindoo Koosh to the westward, who consequently go by the name of Red Kaffirs. The black garments which have given a distinctive name to the race, apparently differ in different tribes. Those on the Cabul side wear entire goatskins with the hair on. The Bushgalis wear tunics, with sleeves not reaching to the elbow, of woven black goat's hair reaching nearly to the knee, gathered in at the waist with a leather belt, from which hangs a dagger, and with a broad red edging along the bottom. The Kalash Kaffirs wear similar tunics, but they are gradually adopting coarse cotton garments, the material of which is brought by pedlers from Peshawur. The Waigalis of the Darah-i-noor and other valleys south of Chigan Serai are said to have entirely adopted cotton clothes, though some of the recent converts to Islam still adhere to the black garments. On their feet they wear rude sandals made of the skin of the wild goat, with a tuft of hair on the instep as a decoration. The women wear long sack-like garments of black woven goat's hair, with long loose sleeves, reaching to the ankles, and gathered in loosely at the waist, with a coloured cotton scarf tightly bound over the shoulders.

The men shave the whole of the head, except a circular patch of about 3 inches in diameter on the crown, where the hair is allowed to grow long and hangs down behind, often to the waist. They never wear any head-covering. The women wear their hair plaited in a number of thin long plaits, which are coiled away under the head-dress, one plait being exactly over the middle of the forehead. The Bushgali women wear a curious head-dress, consisting of a sort of black cap with lappets, and two horns about a foot long, made of wood wrapped round with black cloth and fixed to the cap. This curious fashion does not seem to have been always confined to these tribes, or it may be that they were more widely spread than at present. The Chinese traveller Sung-Yun writing in about 520 A.D. of the Ye-tha, who must have been the people of Sirikol or Hunza, says—

"The ladies cover their heads, using horns, from which hang down veils all round."[1]

Hwen Thsang, who travelled through Badakhshan about 630 A.D., in writing of Himatala, which name he applies apparently to the country about Kundooz, says—

"Les femmes mariées portent sur leur bonnet une corne haute d'environ trois pieds, garnie en avant de deux pointes qui désignent le père et la mère du mari; celle d'en haute se rapporte au père et celle d'en bas à la mère. Si l'un des deux meurt avant l'autre, on retranche la pointe qui le désignait; mais lorsque le beau-père et la belle-mère sont morts, on supprime complètement ce genre de bonnet."[2]

The Kalash women do not wear this head-dress, but simply wear on their heads a sort of broad cap thickly covered with cowrie shells, with lappets which hang down behind, not unlike the head-dresses of the Tartar women in Ladakh.

The intercourse between the Siah Posh and their Mussulman neighbours is not so restricted, at least on the eastern side, as is generally supposed. Though any stranger entering their country without warning is certain to be attacked, they receive visitors freely when passed into the country by one of themselves. In this way pedlers with cheap wares from Peshawur penetrate into the country and dispose of their goods, and I have been told by several persons that they have visited the country for sport and to enjoy the hospitality for which the Siah Posh are famous. Treachery under such circumstances is unknown.

The valleys on the eastern side are described as thickly wooded and very fertile. The Siah Posh breeds of hounds, cattle, sheep, and fowls, and all their agricultural products, are

[1] Beal's Travels of Buddhist Pilgrims.
[2] Histoire de la vie de Hiouen-Thsang, par Stanislas Julien.

celebrated for their fine quality, and are much sought after by their neighbours. The cattle, which in appearance and size compare favourably with English breeds, are parti-coloured, with large humps. Those in the neighbouring valleys are small and humpless. Their houses, which generally consist of more than one story, are remarkable both inside and out for neatness and cleanness. These characteristics, however, are not shared by the Kalash Kaffirs, who are a very degraded race. Villages of sufficient importance are surrounded by timber stockades about 10 feet in height, but forts are unknown. The well-known practice of the Siah Posh of using stools to sit upon, instead of seating themselves on the ground, is perhaps the most curious point of distinction between them and other Asiatic races. The arms of the Siah Posh warrior are bow and arrows, battleaxe and dagger. The bows are small and weak, made of wood, and about 4½ feet long, far less powerful weapons than the horn bows of Hunza and Nager. It is said that they discarded horn bows some twenty years ago on account of their liability to break unexpectedly. The arrows are of reed with heavy iron heads, hardly 2 feet long. They are carried in a leather quiver slung at the back. Notwithstanding their feeble appearance, I have seen practice made with them up to sixty yards with considerable force and accuracy. The daggers are of capital workmanship, with deep double cross, handles of iron, ornamented with brass studs, carried in a triangular iron sheath hung from the girdle. Battle-axes are beginning to give place to swords, and do not appear at any time to have been favourite weapons. Matchlocks of rude make are now beginning to come into use. Each clan manages its own affairs regardless of its neighbours, and is directed by the elders of villages, who are styled Jusht. This is apparently the same title as the Jushtero of the Shinkari republics.

There seem to be grounds for supposing that the religion of the Siah Posh is a crude form of the ancient Vedic. One Supreme Being is worshipped under the name of Imbra, and next to Imbra in importance is the Prophet Mani. He is called the son of Imbra, and once lived on earth, and he mediates with Imbra on behalf of men. Stones are set up as emblems of Imbra, but carved idols are not used. These two names cannot but suggest the Indra and Manu of the Brahmins. Below them in rank are a whole host of deities, whose number is stated at 18,000, evidently an arbitrary number. Some of these have particular functions, as in Greek mythology, but they are acknowledged to have once been mortals, who were deified after death. First in importance is Gej, who is spoken of as a great chief who fought with the Prophet Ali and commenced the feud between the Siah Posh and the Mahommedans, which has continued ever since. Next comes Bagej, the god of rivers, who also has power over flocks and herds. Sacrifices to Bagej are made by the water-side, and the heads of the victims after being burnt with fire are thrown into the stream. Of the others, the most important are Proozi, Dooji, Poorateh (Parbati ?), Arum, Marer, Disni, Kroomai, Saranji, and Witr. It is probable that the names of these inferior deities differ among the different tribes, and many of them must be tribal heroes only recognised by particular tribes.

To all the deities cows are sacrificed, and cedar branches are burned ; on all occasions of slaughtering an animal for food the name of some deity is invoked, and sacrificial ceremonies are observed. The mode of sacrifice was shown to me by the Bushgalis, who killed a goat for the purpose. A small fire is lighted, and a number of cedar branches prepared. The officiating priest bares his feet, while one of his attendants holds a bowl of water with a piece of butter in it. The priest, after washing his hands, sprinkles water on the animal and on the fire, muttering some words of invocation. Then taking a branch of cedar he places it on the fire. He then sprinkles the animal several times with water, uttering each time the word "sooch," to which the by-standers answer "hêmach." This is repeated till the animal shakes itself, which is the sign of its having been accepted by the deity. To ensure this, water is thrown into the animal's ear, which speedily has the desired effect. Then all join in the cry "sooch hêmach" several times, and the cedar branches are placed on the fire, on which also butter is thrown ; after this the animal is thrown down and its throat is cut. The priest catches some of the blood in his hand and sprinkles it on the fire, the head of the animal is severed and placed on the fire for a few moments, and the ceremony ends.[1]

The tradition of the Siah Posh concerning their origin is that they are descended from one of three brothers, two of whom became Mahommedans, while the third, their progenitor, refused to do so. This may show that they recognise them-

[1] It was not till after carefully noting this procedure that I read the excellent account of the Siah Posh mode of sacrifice in Elphinstone's *Cabul*. There is a slight difference in some of the details recorded.

selves to be of cognate origin with their Mussulman neighbours. They say that the name of this progenitor was Koorshye, which has helped to spread the idea among Mahommedans that they are of the Arab tribe of Koresh, and has probably led western writers to seek some connection between the Siah Posh and the Greeks who followed the conqueror of Bactria. Neither theory seems to rest on any adequate foundations. The Siah Posh traditions, however, point to their having been driven into their present narrow limits from a much wider extent of country than they now occupy, and they say that the art of writing was once known among them. There seems to be no doubt that the Kalash tribe of the Siah Posh once occupied the south part of the Kashkar Valley about Asmar, and the upper part as far as the junction of the Moolkho Valley.

Up to the present no forcible entrance into the Siah Posh country has been made through either of the great valleys which join the Kooner, owing to the tangled thickets which cover the junctions and materially assist the defenders. Owing to the same cause solitary travellers and traders run some risk in passing these places. Some twenty years ago a large party of Afghans from Asmar made a sudden raid and surprised several villages, but they were waylaid on their return and cut off almost to a man. Within the last twenty years, part of the Kamoz clan of the Bushgalis has become tributary to the Chitral ruler, whose forces find an entrance through the Kalash country from Bimboret over a steep pass, and periodical raids, together with interference invited by the clan in their internal quarrels, have led to their acknowledging Chitral supremacy. They now pay an annual tribute of several hundredweights of butter and honey, of which latter their country is said to produce enormous quantities, besides cattle, female slaves, silver cups and necklaces, and a great quantity of woollen blankets. Their chief village is called Bragamatal, meaning "the houses on the hill," but by the Chitralis it is called Luddeh, or "the great village."

The Kalash Kaffirs are entirely subject to Chitral, and have been so apparently for some time. They were formerly subject to the Bushgalis, who still speak of them as their slaves. A Kam Kaffir, on his way to Chitral, walks into a Kalash village and claims to have his wants satisfied without fear of refusal or opposition. Half of the Kalash are now Mahommedans, but there seems to be no attempt at forcible conversion. They refuse to eat domestic fowls or their eggs, both of which they regard as unclean, nor will they touch beef, cow's milk, or butter made from it. These prejudices are not shared by other Siah Posh tribes.

There is also a small slave population existing among the Bushgalis, who speak their language and seem to differ from them in no respect except in social position. They are called Patsas, and are probably descendants of captives taken from other tribes in war. They bear arms, and identify themselves in every way with their masters in all contests with external enemies. They are distinguished by their tunics having no sleeves, very narrow edgings, and a coloured badge sown on to the back. Their women are not allowed to wear the head-dress with horns, like the other Bushgali women.

The Siah Posh are exceedingly fond of dancing, but their mode differs considerably from that of the tribes to the eastward. Instead of only one or two performers, everybody present, women as well as men, join in the dance together. A village dance was held before me—a wild and strange exhibition—the men brandished axes, clubs, and guns which they fired off at intervals, amidst a chorus of whoops and shrill whistles. At times the whole would lock arms by pairs and revolve backwards and forwards in a grotesque waltz, or following in order wind round and round in figures of 8. Sometimes all would break off and dance singly, setting first to one and then to another in a sort of wild jig, or, forming in lines with locked arms, advance and retreat in steps like the Koles of Chota Nagpore. The music consisted of two drums and a feeble flute made of bamboo. On the death of a man, his corpse is carried round the village in procession for several days before being finally disposed of, the attendants dancing around it. According to some accounts polygamy is not practised, but the balance of evidence tends to show that each man is allowed to have as many wives as he can maintain, and four or five is not an uncommon number. The women are very immoral, and marital jealousy is satisfied with a slight fine. On discovering his wife's infidelity, a Siah Posh contents himself with giving her a few blows and taking in compensation something of small value, such as a turban, or a robe, from the male offender, should he be a stranger; if he is one of the tribe, he has generally to give a cow as compensation. Female children are freely sold by their fathers to their Mussulman neighbours, and the Chitral ruler receives an annual tribute of children of both sexes.

CHAPTER XI.

THE GILGIT PRINCES.

THE history of the Gilgit rulers rests only on oral tradition and popular songs connected with the names of different princes. Did more trustworthy records exist, they would probably contain little of real interest. The genealogies of their respective families, which were supplied to me independently by the present representatives of the Trakhané, Moghloté, and Ayeshé families, correspond well with each other in the number of generations, and are probably correct, or very nearly so. In the *Historical Legend of Gilgit*, Dr. Leitner has given an account of the earliest occurrence in the tangible history of the country. Several versions of the legend are extant, but the historical outline in all is the same. Stripped of all supernatural additions, the facts related are, that Gilgit was the abode of a prince of the name of Shiri Buddutt, whose rule extended over Hunza, Nager, Darel, Chilas, Astor, Haramosh, Gurais, Yassin, and Chitral. Many of these places were no doubt governed by inferior princes who acknowledged allegiance to Gilgit. The people, suffering under the oppression of Shiri Buddutt, were induced by an adventurer of the name of Azor, who is represented as having come from the direction of Iskardo, and, according to some versions, as being the brother of the Iskardo ruler, to rise and put him to death. Having slain the tyrant, Azor espoused his daughter, established himself on his throne, and founded a line of Ras who bear Mahommedan names. In spite of the supernatural attributes now assigned to him, there can be no doubt that Shiri Buddutt was a real personage; the term Shiri is doubtless the title of respect still given to Hindoo princes.

Allowing 25 years to each generation, the usurpation by Azor must have occurred about the commencement of the 14th century, and there can be little doubt that it marks the extinction of the Shin princes, and the introduction of Mahommedanism into the valley. It is worthy of note that the genealogy of the Makpons of Iskardo[1] shows exactly the same number of

[1] See page 145.

GENEALOGY OF THE TRAKHANÉ (GILGIT), THE MOGHLOTÉ (NAGER), AND AYESHÉ (HUNZA) FAMILIES.

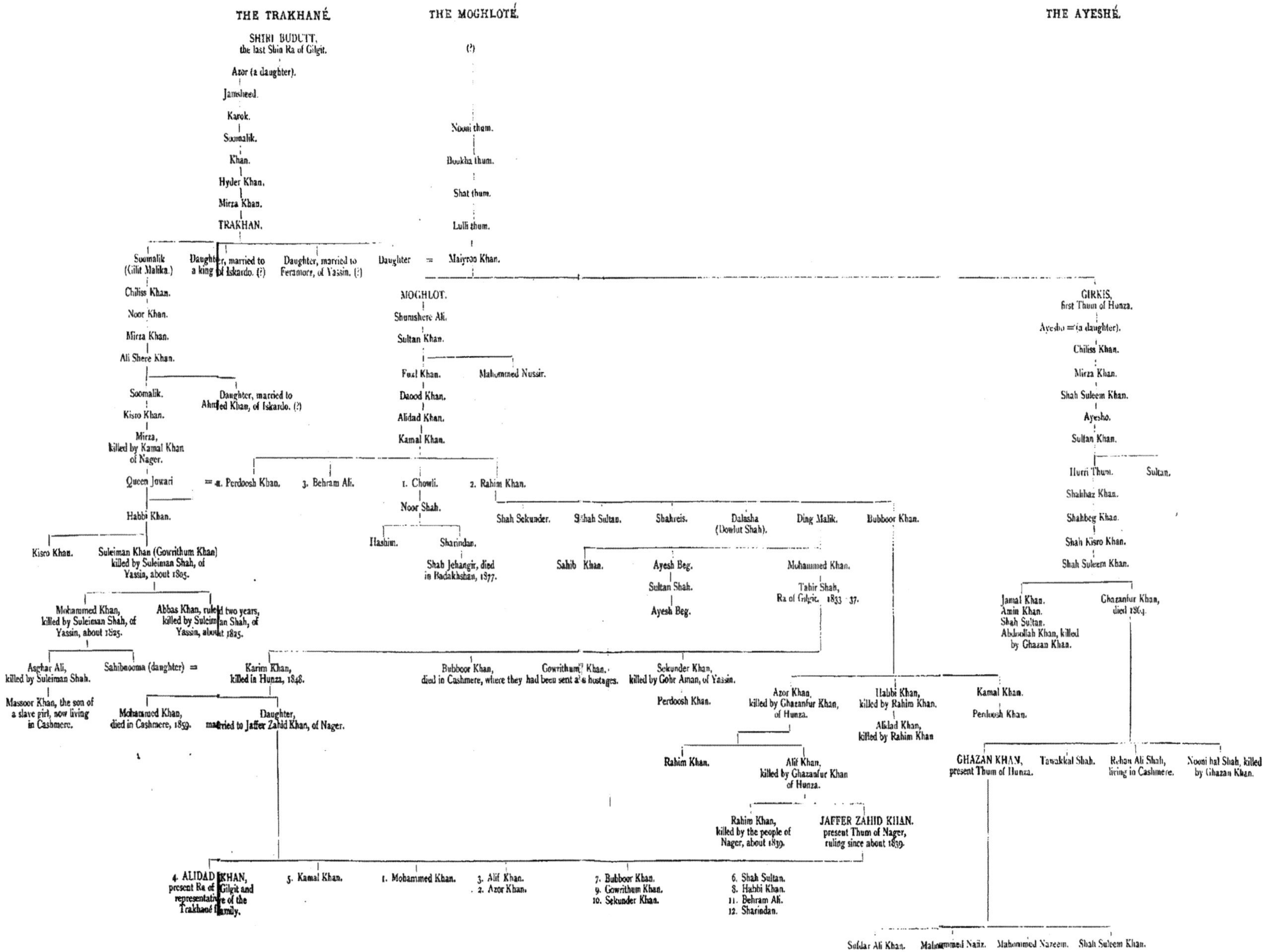

generations from their founder as that of the Trakhané. From this it may be inferred that the introduction of Islam into Baltistan and Gilgit was simultaneous, and in both cases owing to the same cause. General Cunningham, by allowing 30 years to a generation, places it a century earlier than the date I have mentioned.

Under the Shin rule Hunza and Nager appear to have been under one prince, whose capital was Nager. His allegiance was no doubt transferred to Shiri Buddutt's successor, but it is not till eight generations later, or about the beginning of the 16th century, that we find a Nager ruler with a Mahommedan name. This prince married a daughter of the Gilgit ruler, and became the father of the twins Moghlot and Girkis, the latter of whom founded the principality of Hunza.

Mirza Khan, the sixth in succession from Azor, is celebrated in song and story as the most warlike of the older Ras of Gilgit. He is said to have been poisoned by his own wife, in revenge for the death of her seven brothers who had opposed Mirza Khan in the field. From Trakhan, his successor, the present Ra's family, derive their name. This would seem to point to a break in the direct line of descent, were it not that in the genealogies of Iskardo, Chitral, Yassin, Hunza, and Nager we also find the present ruling families taking their names, not from the reputed founder of their line, but from some intermediate ancestor. Trakhan is said to have been a posthumous child of Mirza Khan, and it is related that he was set afloat in a box on the river by his mother. At Hudar he was rescued by a poor man who brought him up among his own children, and he was eventually acknowledged as the rightful Ra of Gilgit.

Soomalik, the son of Trakhan, who is sometimes also called Gilit Malika, is related to have been taken prisoner and carried into Badakhshan, where he remained, unable to escape, for several years. Many wonderful stories are told of his imprisonment and escape, in which a fabulous horse, Asp Tulfar,[1] plays a conspicuous part. He is said to have had three sisters, one of whom married Maiyroo Khan of Nager, the second married Feramorz, a prince of Yassin, and the third married a prince of Iskardo. There would, however, appear to be some confusion between this Soomalik and the Ra of the same name five generations later. The Gilgit and Nager genealogies agree so exactly as to the number of generations,

[1] "Asp Tulfar" is a very small horse, possessing extraordinary powers of endurance, supposed to be the offspring of a horse and mare, which have both reached maturity at one year old. It plays a conspicuous part in Usbek tales.

as to leave no doubt that the sister of Soomalik who married Maiyroo Khan, was the sister of the first Ra of this name. But the same tradition also states most positively that the sister who married the Makpon prince of Iskardo was the mother of the three warlike brothers, Shere Shah, Ali Shah, and Shah Murad, who aided Soomalik in his wars against Yassin. Now, General Cunningham fixes the date of these brothers at about A.D. 1600, and this, compared with the number of generations accounted for in the various genealogies, shows that their mother must have been sister to the second Soomalik, the son of Ali Shere Khan. The Yassin prince who is said to have married Soomalik's second sister, cannot be identified in the Khushwakté genealogy, but the name given is common in that family, which was not founded till after the time of the first Soomalik.

During the lifetime of the three Makpon brothers above mentioned, Gilgit was apparently tributary to them, or more especially to Ali Shah, the founder of the Rondu family.

Mirza, the grandson of the second Soomalik, and his daughter Jowari, are still favourite subjects for Gilgit songs. Under Mirza a successful raid was made on Gurais, which would appear, before that time, to have slipped from the grasp of the Gilgit Ras, and there are many indications that their power steadily decreased, in spite of temporary triumphs, from the day of the extinction of the Shin dynasty. While on a friendly visit to Nager, Mirza was treacherously slain by Kamal Khan, and as he left no sons, an attempt was apparently made to establish a prince of the Moghloté family in Gilgit. Jowari, who, having married an Iskardo ruler, had been left a widow and childless, consented to marry Perdoosh, of Nager, to whom she bore Habbi Khan. It is related that when Habbi Khan was twelve years old Perdoosh was publicly told that Jowari had only consented to marry him to secure the succession of the Trakhané, and that now the sooner he returned to Nager the better it would be for him—a hint which he was not slow to take. Jowari then abdicated in favour of her son, who in time became the father of Suleiman Khan, the last Ra of Gilgit who maintained anything approaching to the power of his predecessors. Suleiman Khan, who is better known under his assumed name of Gowrithum[1] Khan, is said to have ruled fifty-three years, and was in the end mur-

[1] The use of the name of Gowri, the wife of Mahadeo, shows how long the traces of Hindooism lingered after the first conversion to Islam, while the strength of the **Boorish or Yeshkun element in the population is shown by the use of the title Thum.**

dered about A.D. 1803, by the Khushwakté Prince Suleiman Shah, who had sought refuge in Gilgit from the enmity of his own brother. A rumour of a threatened attack from Hunza had drawn away most of his attendants, and as the aged Ra sat in his garden he was slain, together with his Wuzeer, by the man to whom he had given protection.

From this time the prosperity of Gilgit seems to have rapidly declined, and it became the prey of rival families whose wars almost depopulated the valley, until the firm establishment of Dogra rule gave the country what may be hoped in time to become a fresh lease of prosperity. Suleiman Shah fled to Tangir after the murder without attempting to establish himself in Gowrithum Khan's seat, which was occupied by Mahommed Khan, the rightful heir. In 1804 Moolk Aman of the Khushwakté family died, and was succeeded in Yassin by his brother Kuwat Khan, who gave Ponyal, which seems to have come into the possession of the Yassin rulers about A.D. 1780, to his brother Shere Shah. Kuwat Khan had hardly taken possession when Mahommed Khan invaded Ponyal, but was repulsed. The two brothers following up their advantage too hastily were entrapped in some broken ground and killed. Mahommed Khan's triumph was of short duration. His victory had the effect of making his enemy, Suleiman Shah, ruler of Yassin. Suleiman Shah seems to have been a man of considerable ability, and in less than a year he had re-conquered the greater part of Ponyal. In the following year he invaded and took Gilgit and carried Mahommed Khan a prisoner to Yassin, leaving in Gilgit Abbas Khan, a younger son of Gowrithum Khan, who swore allegiance to him. Abbas Khan soon tried to renounce his allegiance, and in 1819 Suleiman Shah again invaded and took Gilgit and put to death both Mahommed Khan and Abbas Khan. Asghar Ali, the son of Mahommed Khan, fled to Nager, but Suleiman Shah's influence was sufficient to procure his being put to death, and the sole remaining representative of the Trakhané was an infant daughter of Mahommed Khan, through whom the line is now perpetuated. Suleiman Shah then formed the idea of incorporating Gilgit with Yassin, and made the former his chief place of residence. In 1827 Suleiman Shah, being engaged in an invasion of Chitral, placed Azad Khan of the Boorooshé family, in Drasun with a garrison of Gilgitis. Taking advantage of the opportunity, Azad Khan prevailed on the garrison to espouse his cause, abandoned his post, and hastened to Gilgit, where he was accepted by the people as their Ra. The people soon found that Azad Khan's rule was not less tyrannical than that of Suleiman Shah, and again sought a change of oppressors. The Trakhané family was virtually extinct, but the Moghloté family had been connected with it for so many generations that they were looked on as the natural heirs to the principality. Consequently, Tahir Shah, a younger son of the Moghloté, was induced to accept the Ra-ship of Gilgit, and on his arrival accompanied by a small force from Hunza, Azad Khan was at once seized and put to death in 1833.

After a short reign of between three and four years, Tahir Shah died and was succeeded by his younger son Sekunder Khan, in whose favour Karim Khan, who was a man of weak character, had been set aside. His rule was short and troubled. Immediately after Tahir Shah's death the Gurais maliks made an unexpected raid on Gilgit, and succeeded in gaining possession of the fort by surprise, with the exception of the inner redoubt. This held out long enough to allow of the people assembling to the Ra's assistance, and the invaders were slain to a man. Hardly had this danger been surmounted, when Gilgit was invaded by Gohr Aman, who had lately succeeded to the throne of Yassin. Sekunder Khan, being able to offer but a feeble resistance, contented himself by occupying a strong position which could only be assaulted on one side. After a blockade which lasted many months, he was taken prisoner and put to death in 1841. Karim Khan then sought refuge in Cashmere, while Gohr Aman established himself in Gilgit. Like many of the Khushwakté family, he seems to have possessed considerable energy and ability, but his blood-thirsty cruelty, which seemed to be directed especially against the people of Gilgit, threatened to depopulate the country. Whole villages were driven into slavery, and whole districts ruined, apparently to gratify his resentment. The misery inflicted by this man is almost beyond belief, and his name is still never mentioned without horror. A certain Syud in Badakhshan is still known by the nickname of *Syud Sud Burdai*, in consequence of his having accepted a present of a hundred Gilgiti slaves from Gohr Aman. Numbers of Gilgitis are still living in slavery in Badakhshan, Bokhara, Khokand, and other neighbouring countries. Every year stragglers of different ages find their way back, after slavery and wanderings of the greater part of a lifetime, from Yarkund, Samarcand, and other parts of Central Asia. It was, therefore, with much gratitude that the people welcomed a Sikh force, whose aid Karim Khan had secured, and which had been despatched by the Governor of Cashmere. They were at first repulsed, but advancing a second time they defeated Gohr Aman and installed Karim Khan as Ra of Gilgit under their protection in September 1842. Six years later Karim Khan was slain, together with the Sikh Governor, while invading Hunza. Eleven years later again his son Mahommed Khan dying childless, the nominal, as well as the actual, ownership of Glgit devolved on the Dogras, who had succeeded the Sikhis in Cashmere. Not wishing to leave Gilgit without a nominal Ra, the Cashmere Government summoned from Nager the present Ra, Alidad Khan, the infant son of the Nager ruler, who, through his mother, was still held to represent the Trakhané line, and installed him when only one year old. A son of Asghar Ali is still living in Cashmere, but, being born of a slave mother, he was held incapable of succeeding.

Mr. Drew has given a succinct account of the events which led to the consolidation of the Hindoo power on the right bank of the Indus. Whatever the faults and shortcomings of Cashmere rule may be when judged by a European standard, it has undoubtedly conferred on this part of the country an amount of prosperity and security which could not have been attained under the Khushwakté family, in whose grasp it would otherwise have remained. Freedom from the liability to be sold as slaves alone outweighs the disadvantage of being ruled by men of a different faith. It is scarcely an exaggeration to say that, of the inhabitants of Gilgit over 40 years of age, nearly half have passed some portion of their lives in slavery. There is not a family of which one or more of their members have not been lost in this way. The stories of their wanderings told by many are full of interest, and many curious scenes occur on occasions of their return. On one occasion a young man arrived, who had been carried off when a child in arms. From his companions in slavery he had learned his name and that of his father, who received him with open arms; but, having been all the time at Seo, where the Shina language is not spoken, he could not converse with his father for several weeks except through an interpreter. On another occasion a "claimant" appeared from Badakhshan, avowing himself to be the brother of the Wuzeer, whose mother and brother had been sold into slavery thirty years before. His coming being notified beforehand, the fatted calf was killed, and great preparations made to receive him by his aged mother, who had herself been redeemed from slavery only two years before.

Throwing herself on his neck she welcomed back the wanderer; but then being struck with suspicion, she looked steadily at him for a moment, pushed the hair off his temples to look for a scar remembered only by herself, and declared that he was not her son. The man protested vehemently that he was, till at last, overcome with confusion by the woman's positive manner, he confessed that he was not the man he pretended to represent, but his foster-brother. The two had lived as slaves under the same master till the death of the Wuzeer's son had suggested the possibility of the imposture on his regaining his freedom.

The following story, given me by one who was better able than most to give a connected account of his adventures, is a fair sample of the history of hundreds :—

THE STORY OF BIRA KHAN.

"I was born at Minawur, near Gilgit. My father died when I was a boy, and Suleiman Shah killed my grandfather in Cher. When I was about sixteen years old, Suleiman Shah sent me with a hundred others of my family and village to Yassin as slaves. At the end of three years I escaped back to Gilgit. Azad Khan was then ruling there. After a time Azad Khan was killed by Tahir Shah of Nager, who ruled in Gilgit about three years and then died. He was succeeded by his son Sekunder, who ruled for about six years. When Gohr Aman invaded the country, Sekunder came from Bagrot to meet him, and a fight took place at Gilgit, on the left bank of the river, in which Sekunder was killed. At the end of a year Gohr Aman returned to Yassin, taking with him 500 Gilgitis, among whom were my brotherand myself, and gave us both to Ibrahim Khan, the son of his cousin Kuwat Khan, who took us to Yarkhoon. At the end of four months we two and another Gilgiti escaped by night. We reached the top of the mountain of Kut, on which was much snow, by morning. We descended into the valley of Toorikho, near three small villages. The people of Toorikho cultivate the hill-side in the same manner as is done in the Sai Valley (*i.e.*, in terraces rising above the road on both sides). Between Mastooch and Toorikho is a pass; the distance is three ordinary days' journey. To the west of Mastooch are Sonoghor, Awi, and Booni. Beyond Booni is Reshan. I once went as far as this before I escaped, but on this occasion I did not get beyond Shogram, where I was seized by the people of Aman-ool-Mulk who happened to be there at the time. By his order I was taken to Wakhan and given to Meer Futteh Ali Shah. In three days we arrived at Surhad-i-Wakhan. Between Toorikho and Surhad is a pass which has snow on it in summer, and part of it is difficult to travel over. At Punja I was sold by Futteh Ali Shah, in exchange for merchandise, to a merchant of Zebak, named Erbabak, who took me to Yarkund by way of Sirikol. We went in six days from Wakhan to Sirikol with a caravan of merchants. From Sirikol we went to Yarkund by the Koosherab road. As far as Koosherab the people are

Mugli (*i.e.*, Sirikolis). From Koosherab we arrived at Yarkund in six easy marches. In Yarkund Erbabak sold me to a widow for one yamboo and ten tangas in copper (about £17). This woman, who kept a shop, employed me for a year in carrying wood and water, and then sold me for the same money to Mir Rahim Bai, an Andijani merchant. This Mir Rahim Bai was the owner of much land, on which he employed fifteen slaves. Five other slaves were employed in his house. My business was to ride in attendance on him when he went out. At that time the Chinese ruled the country. Though they were not Mussulmans, except a few who were called Tungas (Tunganis), the call to prayers was not forbidden, and the precepts of the Sharyat were observed. No duties were levied, and if a man went on pilgrimage, assistance was given him. A youth at that time, in Yarkund, would fetch as a slave two yamboos, and a young man about the price I was sold for. A handsome young woman would sell for three yamboos (about £50). At the end of two years, with nine other slaves I escaped from Yarkund, trying to reach Gilgit by way of Cogiar. We had a supply of baked bread with us, and only travelled by night, avoiding all habitations. We reached Cogiar after fifteen days, and had nearly arrived at the top of the range, when a fall of snow obliged us to halt in a valley. Here fifteen men on horseback overtook us, and as we had only one sword among us, we could not beat them off. I killed one man with the sword, and taking his gun shot another; one of our number also was killed, and the rest of us taken back to Yarkund. The journey back only took five days, and had we known the road at first, we should not have been taken. On our return we were taken before the Chinese Governor, who, however, did not punish us, but gave us back to our former masters. Mir Rahim Bai imprisoned me for one month, with a plank of wood fitted over my neck, and then made me work with chains on for a year, when he sold me to another Andijani merchant named Mahommed Yonas Bai, for the same price he had given for me. My employment with Mahommed Yonas Bai was to carry his loads of merchandise. At the end of two years I again escaped with four men and two women. In twelve days' travelling by night we reached Cogiar, and in six days more Urduksaldi, where we found some Kirghiz. From this we travelled by night for two days towards Muztagh and Shigar with a kafila of Baltis, when we were attacked in a camping place by a band of Kunjootis, who took us and also ten Baltis, and plundered the caravan; the rest of the Baltis escaped back to Yarkund. In four days we were taken to Shimshal, which is in the Hunza country. The road was difficult and mountainous. Horses cannot travel by it. There are two mountains covered with snow to be crossed, and it is uninhabited. The distance is about the same as from Gilgit to Astor. Shimshal is a small place with about forty houses; the village is on a plateau 300 feet above the river. From Shimshal to Meerkoon is two marches; the road is only fit for men on foot, but there is no snow in summer, and only a little in winter. There are ten houses and a small fort at Meerkoon. Between Meerkoon and Girtchah two small but steep mountains have to be crossed. The road is closed by snow for two months. At Girtchah is a small fort with twelve houses. Beyond Girtchah is Soostee. At Soostee I was imprisoned for a year, and then was sold for two horses to Mahommed Alim Khan, brother of the Meer Futteh Ali Shah of Wakhan. At that time Ghazanfur Khan was ruler of Hunza. From Soostee people go to Poosee, from Poosee to Goolkun, and thence to Hunza on the third day. I did not see the road, but was told it was mountainous and covered with snow. From Soostee I was taken to Chopoostee, which contains twelve houses; the distance is about 12 miles. From Chopoostee I was taken to Babagoondi, where there is a ziarat, but no habitations. The road is difficult, and there is much snow in winter. Horses travel the road with difficulty. From Babagoondi, crossing the mountain, we reached Surhad in Wakhan; the distance is as that from Gilgit to Sai. When I arrived at Punja, Futteh Ali Shah did not recognise me. Many merchants came, but none bought me. At last Futteh Ali Shah recognised me. I said to him, 'Oh Ameer, men do but kill a sheep once; you kill me twice.' I related to him the history of my being sold by him to Erbabak, and what had happened since. He said, 'This time I have nothing to do with you, you are in the hands of my brother Mahommed Alim Khan.' After some time Mahommed Alim Khan sold me to Sekunder Shah, the Wazeer of the Hakim of Jirm. At that time Mir Shah was ruler of Badakhshan. I remained in Jirm one winter, then I was sold to Nasroollah Bai of Salolah, about 10 miles from Jirm. There are about thirty houses in Salolah, and the people are Soonnees, as at Jirm. At New Jirm, close to Jirm, they are Maulai Syuds. After two years I escaped from Salolah, and wandered in the mountains for three days, but could find no road, so returned to near Jirm, where I lay hid for three days in the house of a man who was friendly to me. On the fourth day he showed me the way to escape, and I arrived at Zebak in four stages, travelling only by night. On the way I crossed a high mountain, and avoiding Zebak in three stages more I reached Injigan, where there is a small fort. There ten men seized me and wanted to send me back to Badakhshan, but they could not agree among themselves. I told them that I was a servant of Adam Khor, who had lately visited Badakhshan, and that when he had left I was ill and could not travel with him. They believed me and showed me the road over the bridge opposite the fort. From there I travelled eastward up a valley, but found much snow and no way out, so turning back I followed a valley to the right, and at midday reached a great lake. From the lake I reached the top of a steep mountain. In winter nobody travels this road, but in summer very rarely and on urgent occasions men travel by it. Horses cannot use it. From the top of the mountain two roads go—one on the right, very narrow and bad, goes into the country of the Bushgali Kaffirs, the other, by the Ludkho Valley, leads to Chitral. I travelled by this road to Shoghor. From Ludkho to Shoghoor is one long day's journey. Here I found a small fort belonging to Adam Khor, and no one lived here except his family. From Shoghoor I arrived at Chitral in two days. I stayed there three months, and when Adam Khor, having made war against his father Shah Afzul, was defeated and fled to Dir, I accompanied him. At that time Ghazan Khan was the ruler of Dir. I remained there two months and then went to Swat, by the country of the Sultan Khel. I reached Sedoo, where the Akhoond lives, and stayed there three days, after which I went by Murdan to Peshawur. Thence I travelled through Hazara and Mozufferabad to Cashmere, where I lived for a year, and then at last was able to return to Gilgit."

The story of Bira Khan is a fair sample of the history of scores of men and women in the Gilgit district. I have not chosen it for any special points, but Bira Khan, being a man of intelligence, is able to give a more connected narrative than most of the others I have spoken to. I have written down his tale exactly as he related it. In spite of some mistakes, his recollection of the places he visited in his wanderings is excellent.

CHAPTER XII.

THE BALTISTAN PRINCES.

A NOTICE of the Baltistan princes scarcely comes within the scope of a sketch of the Hindoo Koosh tribes, but their genealogy is worth attention, as it helps to throw light upon the different changes which have taken place in the valleys further westward.

As has already been pointed out, the introduction of Islam into Gilgit and Baltistan seems to have been simultaneous. The genealogy of the Makpons shows that at the same time that Azor established himself in Gilgit, which according to General Cunningham's computation must have been in the early part of the 13th century, a Mahommedan adventurer named Ibrahim Shah usurped the sovereignty of Baltistan, and founded the Makpon family. The written records of the Makpons were unfortunately destroyed when Iskardo was taken by the Sikhs, but tradition relates that Ibrahim Shah came originally from Egypt by way of Hindustan, and that Buddhism was at that time the religion of the country. The term *Makpon* means, in Thibetan, "Commander-in-chief," thus appearing to be nearly identical with the Chinese *Tung*, of which Thum is probably a corruption.[1] The name was, however, apparently not applied to the family till nine generations later. The accompanying genealogy of the Iskardo princes was given to me by Ali Shah, the present head of the Makpons. The names of the seven princes succeeding Ibrahim Shah are not Mahommedan, and afford a clue to the race which reigned in Baltistan previous to his advent. The first four have the suffix of *singeh* to their names, which is the same as the suffix *sing* still used by the Shins in Gilgit, as already mentioned.[2] Taking this with the fact of the existence of the Shin colony of Dah Hanu, it is allowable to infer that the race formerly ruling in Iskardo were Shins.

The next two princes bear the Boorish title of Gowrithum, which may denote the temporary ascendancy of Boorish princes; but as the title has been in use till recently among

[1] Sec page 24 [2] See page 99.

GENEALOGY OF THE MAKPONS OF ISKARDO.

IBRAHIM SHAH,
an Egyptian adventurer.
|
Istak Singeh.
|
Brook Singeh.
|
Zik Singeh.
|
Sik Singeh.
|
Snum Gowrithum.
|
Sah Gowrithum.
|
Ghotachoh.
|
Behram Shah.
|
Makpon Bokha,
about A. D. 1500 according to Cunningham.
|
Shere.
|
Ghazi.
|
Ali Shere Khan.
|
Ahmed Khan.

Shah Murad.	Ali Shah, founder of the Makpons of Rondu.	Shere Shah, founder of the Makpons of Khurmang.	Shah Sultan, founder of the Makpons of Astor.

Shah Murad.
|
Rafi Khan.
|
Sultan Murad.
|
Zuffer Khan, Ghazi.
|
Ali Shere Khan.
|
Ahmed Shah.
|
Mahmood Shah.
|
ALI SHAH,
the present Choh.
|
Shah Abbas,
æt 20, A.D. 1879.

TABLE OF THE AMACHAH PRINCES.

	Name.	Probable date.
		A.D.
1	Amáchah	1440
2	Châh-thum	1455
3	Chama-thum	1470
4	Yaksir Gao-thum	1485
5	Khomulgo-thum	1500
6	Gobálgo-thum	1515
7	Khan	1530
8	Makhan	1545
9	Ram	1560
10	Rahmûm	1575
11	Daolat Shah	1590
12	Haripal Marchak	1605
13	Ambarat	1620
14	Ghazi Mir	1635
15	Ali Mir	1650
16	Amachan Dé	1665
17	Ghir-ze	1680
18	Haidar Khan	1695
19	Hasan Khan	1710
20	Imam Kuli Khan	1725
21	Kuli Khan	1740
22	Azem Khan	1755
23	Ali Khan	1770
24	Husen Khan	1785
25	Mohammed Khan	1800
26	Kuli Khan	1815
27	Sulimán Khan	1830

the non-Boorish princes of Gilgit, no great stress can be laid on the circumstance. The mixture of names from Ibrahim Shah to Makpon Bokha would seem to point to a broken succession, rather than to a regular descent from father to son, and it is not improbable that Iskardo fell temporarily under the rule of princes of the Shigar family.

The title by which Baltistan princes are addressed is Choh, which forms part of the name of the seventh in succession from Ibrahim Shah.

Ahmed Khan, who was ruler of Iskardo towards the end of the 16th century, had four sons whose warlike efforts forced all the surrounding country to acknowledge allegiance to Iskardo, and from three of them are descended the present Makpon princes of Rondu, Khurmang, and Astor. It was in the course of their wars, which General Cunningham fixes at about A.D. 1600, that the ancestors of the present Brokpas were brought into Baltistan. The most powerful was Ali Shah, the founder of the Rondu family, who conquered the country to the westward as far as Chitral, in which place he ruled for twelve years. The bridge over the river at Chitral is said to have been constructed by him, and a plane tree of his planting is still pointed out. A level piece of ground at the mouth of the Gilgit Valley is still called Makpon Shawaran, "the Polo ground of the Makpons." Cunningham writes by mistake Makpon-i-Shangrong. It is evident, however, that the Makpons held a superior position among all the surrounding families of rulers even before the days of Ahmed Khan. The mother of the four warlike brothers was of the Trakhané family, and there are several similar instances mentioned of daughters of the Trakhané being given to Makpons, while there is not a single instance recorded of a Trakhané prince receiving a Makpon wife. At the present time the four Makpon families receive daughters from the Ayeshé, Moghloté, Trakhané, &c., but only give daughters to a Makpon. From the earliest times Iskardo was probably the seat of wealthier and more powerful princes than Gilgit, owing to its natural advantages.

The Shigar princes, to whom allusion has already been made, bear the family name of Amachah from their founder, who is related to have been of unknown parentage, rescued as a child from the nest of an eagle, which had carried him off. The accompanying table of the Shigar princes, extracted from General Cunningham's work, is interesting, as it shows the frequent use of the title Thum. In appearance the present representatives of the Amachah are of extremely fair complexion, with high caste features, such as are seen only among Brahmins in Hindustan. General Cunningham in this case only allows fifteen years to each ruler, but does not say on what the calculation is based. The Shigar princes, though subordinate to the Makpons, seems, in spite of their proximity to Iskardo, to have been sufficiently strong to resist total extinction.

From their peculiar appearance and the number of rulers given, I should be inclined to look upon the Amachahs as the representatives of Shin princes who once ruled in Iskardo, and who, after expulsion by Ibrahim Shah, established themselves in Shigar.

There can be, I think, little doubt that it is to Iskardo we must look for the centre of the ancient kingdom of Bolor, as suggested by General Cunningham. In Gilgit, Hunza, Nager, and all the valleys to the westward, the name Iskardo is almost unknown, and the place is called "Palor," "Balors," or "Balornts." The Iskardo people ignore this name altogether, and say that the place was founded by Alexander, who named it Iskanderia, from which it was converted to its present form. It was probably this tradition that led Vigne to identify Iskardo with Aornos, but it is impossible that Alexander's army should ever have marched through the Indus Valley.

In connection with this, it may not be out of place to remark that various travellers and writers have mentioned the claim of the rulers of different states, both north and south of the Hindoo Koosh, to be descended from Alexander the Great. This claim, however, seems always to be urged at second-hand, and is so passed on from one race to another that the descendants of the Macedonian conqueror still elude identification. In the Punjab the distinguished honour is claimed for the Gilgit princes, in Gilgit the Wakhan princes are said to be entitled to it, in Wakhan the Chitral rulers are named as the real descendants, and in Chitral the distinction is assigned to the Darwaz rulers. Baber also mentions in his Memoirs that the princes of Darwaz are descended from Alexander. With the exception of these latter, with whom I have not yet become acquainted, all disclaim the honour for themselves and pass it on to their neighbours. The claim is probably equally shadowy in all cases, but it is interesting to note how deep an impression was made on a rude and illiterate people by the brief and wonderful career of the great conqueror. Whether it is a ruined tower, whose history is buried in oblivion, or a trace of a higher civilisation than now exists, the great name of Alexander is invoked to supply the gap in local tradition. In spite of the twenty-two centuries that have elapsed, and the many storms of conquest that since his time have swept over Asia, the invasion of the Oxus States by the son of Philip is still the great historical landmark in the mind of every man.

It would seem that in their progress up the Indus Valley, the Shins founded, in Baltistan, a principality which overshadowed that of Gilgit, and commanded the allegiance of the valleys to the westward as far as Chitral. Mr Shaw discovered that the name Bolor is still applied to Chitral by the Kirghiz. Chitral, being the principal highway from the Upper Oxus to the Punjab, was necessarily the country south of the Hindoo Koosh, best known to those dwelling north of the range, and there is nothing strange in the name of the whole country being applied by strangers and travellers to what was only a part. The Bolor of Marco Polo was probably Sirikol, which, no doubt, formed part of the Baltistan kingdom.

CHAPTER XIII.

THE YASSIN AND CHITRAL PRINCES.

THE family name of the rulers of Chitral is Katooré. The name Kator seems to have been applied to the country in early times, before the present Katooré family was founded. Baber writes in his Memoirs :—

"In the hill country to the north-east (of Cabul) lies Kafferistan, such as Kattor and Gebrek."

Going further back, General Cunningham identifies the name Katoor with Kitolo, the king of the Great Yuechi, who, in the beginning of the 5th century, conquered Balkh and Gandhara, and whose son established the kingdom of the Little Yuechi at Peshawur.

Later, the name appears in the *Tarikh-i-Binakiti* and the *Jami-ul-Tawarikh*.

"In the list of the Turk dynasty of Cabul kings, who preceded the Ghuznevides, the last is called Katoran, King of the Kators."

* * * * * *

"And Kank returned to his country and he was the last of the Kataurman kings."[1]

According to the line of reasoning followed by General Cunningham, it would appear that a dynasty of Indo-Scythic kings who established themselves temporarily in Cabul, derived their name of Katoor from their having come from Chitral, that is to say, that the name Katoor belonged to Chitral at an altogether earlier date. Nothing is more probable than that a line of rulers of Yuechi blood established themselves at one time in Chitral, but I do not see what evidence there is to show that the name Katoor was not introduced by them, and did not belong to the country previously. This presumption is borne out by General Cunningham's identification of the Katâr tribe, now located east of the Indus in the neighbourhood of Hussan Abdal, as descendants of the Yuechi. The Yuechi occupation of Chitral was cer-

[1] Elliot's Ancient Historians of India.
Journal of Royal Asiatic Soc., Vol. IX. Paper by E. Thomas, on the Coins of the dynasty of the Hindoo Kings of Cabul.

tainly most superficial, for there is no tribe mentioned in this work which shows all the characteristics of an Aryan race of pure blood in a higher degree than the poorer population of that state.

Opposite the village of Barenis, 20 miles above Chitral, is a figure with an inscription in ancient Sanscrit rudely cut upon a rock. General Cunningham has kindly favoured me with the following reading of the inscription: *Deva dharm-maya Raja Jiva Pâla*—"The pious gift of Raja Jiva Pâla." This inscription refers, in all probability, to a building, of which the figure is a facsimile, erected somewhere near. General Cunningham tells me that from the character used, it cannot belong to an earlier period than the 3rd century A.D., and the date of it is probably a good deal later. The name Jiva Pâla is, no doubt, the Jeipal of early Mahommedan writers. According to Al-Biruni, the fourth King of Cabul, who succeeded Kank, whose period was about A.D. 900, was named Jeipal, and his rule may have extended to Chitral. The figure is Buddhistic, and is interesting, as helping to show that Buddhism existed in Chitral before Mahommedanism.[1]

The earliest traditions now existing of the Chitral Valley relate to a certain king Bahman,[2] an idolater whose rule extended eastward as far as Puttun, in the Indus Valley, and who dwelt at Mushgool in the Moolkho Valley. During his reign an Arab army conquered Badakhshan, slew Zungibar[3] the ruler of Wakhan, and invaded Chitral by the Yarkhoon Valley, where they were met by Bahman. Among the invaders were two champions, named Saifnosh and Istiftanosh, who challenged individuals in the Chitral army to a trial of strength. King Bahman, who was famed for his skill in martial exercises, accepted the challenge in person, and for a whole day wrestled with one of the champions in view of both armies, without either gaining the advantage. On the second day, when Bahman offered himself to renew the contest, the other Arab champion was substituted without his knowledge, and, exhausted by his struggles of the previous day, he was vanquished, and carried bound to the Arab Chief, who, by a curious anachronism, is said to have been Hemza, the uncle of the Prophet.[4] Bahman, consenting to render

[1] See also page 109.

[2] The name sometimes given by the Siah Posh to their country is Wamastan, which may have some connection with this name.

[3] The name is still found in Wakhan, where a ruined fort, called Kila Zanguebar, is pointed out. See Wood's Oxus, page 218.

[4] Hemza, the Prophet's uncle, was slain at the battle of Ohod A.D. 625, but the first Arab invasion of Badakhshan did not take place till the middle of the 7th century.

allegiance, was released, and the Arab Chief retired to Madaian in Persia. After a few years Bahman, by renouncing his allegiance, invoked a second invasion, which also terminated in his submission, but on his rebelling yet again he was put to death.

Later, the country was ruled by a succession of princes styled Reis, the name which is also given to Gilgit rulers of Shiri Buddutt's line. They are sometimes said to have belonged to the Makpon family of Iskardo. Their names have not been preserved, but it is related that during the rule of one of them, a Calmak (Chinese) army, in alliance with a prince of Badakhshan, invaded and subdued the country. This is spoken of as occurring after the death of Abdoollah Khan, the Usbek. During the Chinese occupation, a Chitrali ravished a female slave of the Chinese leader, and a general slaughter of the inhabitants was in consequence ordered. For three days the massacre proceeded, after which the survivors were seized and carried off to Badakhshan. To test the completeness of the depopulation, a whip was left hanging on a tree in a conspicuous place, and, after inscribing their achievements on a stone, the invaders departed. After a year a messenger was sent to bring the whip, which he found untouched, and returning to Badakhshan he reported that he had not seen a living soul in the country. On receipt of this report a fresh hide was spread in front of the door of the fort, in which the Chitrali prisoners were confined, and they were made to pass out over it one by one. When a sufficient number had passed out to wear a hole in the hide, they were allowed to depart to their own country, and those who remained were put to death.

Towards the end of the sixteenth or beginning of the seventeenth century, Chitral was ruled by a Reis who is said to have been of the same family as the rulers of Gilgit before the introduction of Mahommedanism. His name has not been preserved, but he was apparently a Mahommedan, as his tomb is still preserved in Chitral. There is some reason for supposing that he belonged to the Makpon (Iskardo) family, as some branches of the Makpon family still speak of him as an ancestor. He was childless, but adopted as his son a certain Baba Eyoub, said to have been of a noble Khorasan family, who had settled in Chitral and ingratiated himself with the ruler. On the Reis' death he was accepted by the people as their prince and assumed the title of Mihter, which his descendants still retain. The third in succession from him was

GENEALOGY OF THE KATOORÉ OF CHITRAL.

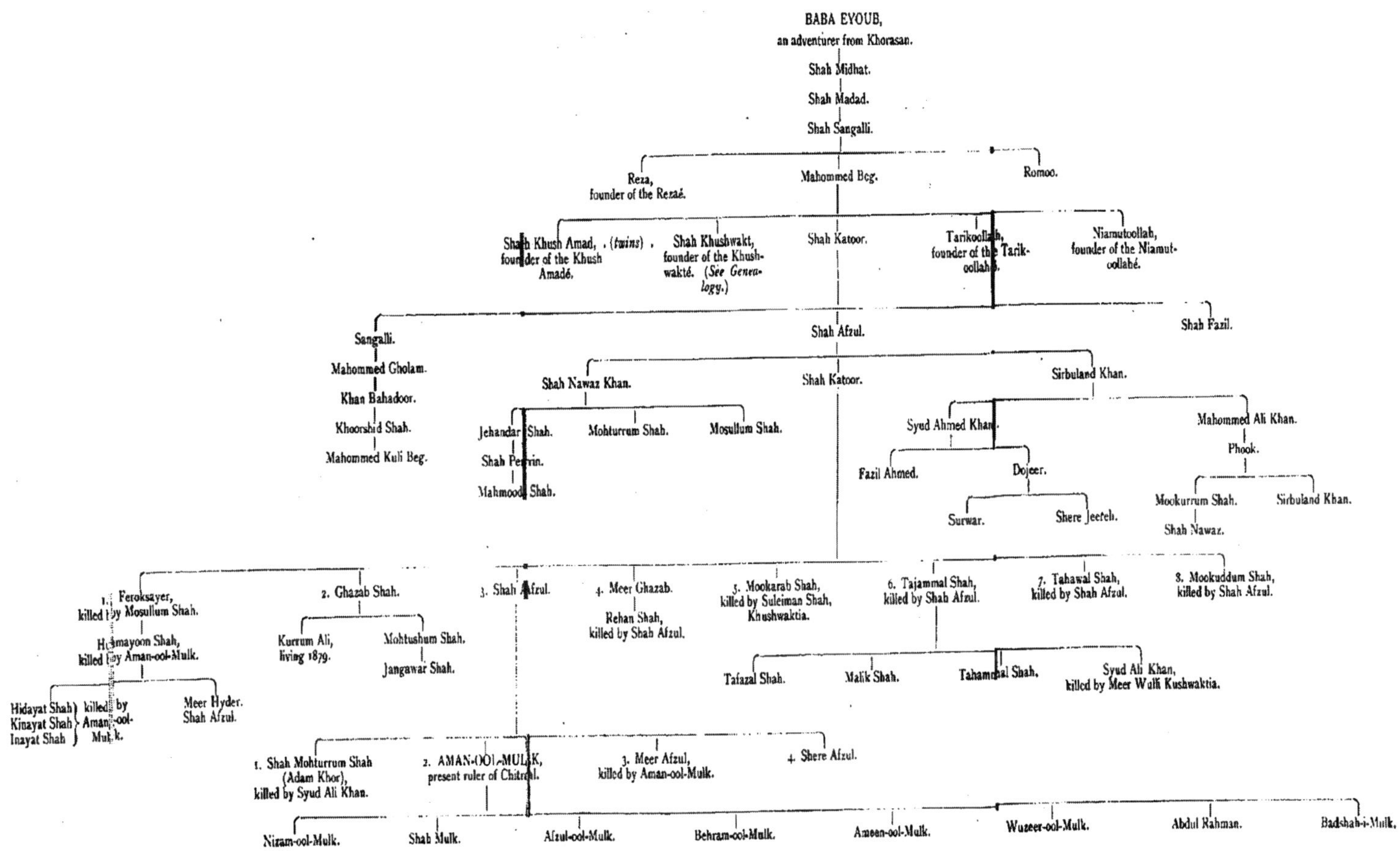

Shah Sangalli, who, being the first of the family to establish a reputation for warlike prowess, is often spoken of as the founder of the family. To his son Mahommed Beg were born twins, happily named Khush Amad and Khush Wakt. The former was, however, wanting in ability, and was set aside in favour of another son Katoor, from whom the present Katooré family are descended. Khush Wakt was established in Mastooch as a semi-independent ruler, and became the founder of the Khush Wakté branch. It is uncertain whether Yassin at this time belonged to one of the Chitral family or to the Gilgit rulers, but it probably belonged to the latter. In the next generation the extension of the Khush Wakté family, which was only arrested by the intervention of the Sikhs, seems to have begun.

Khush Wakt is said to have been slain by the Chinese at Koghoozi, near Chitral, but the details have not been preserved. Though the Chinese figure in many episodes of Chitral history, no tradition exists of the country having been permanently tributary to them. Khush Wakt's son, Feramorz, was a notable warrior, whose exploits are still spoken of with enthusiasm. He conquered Yassin, forced his cousins of Chitral to give allegiance to him, and made himself master of the valley down to Chaghan Serai, besides subduing the Punjkorah Valley and part of Swat. His nephew Khush Amad, the second of the name, was ruling in Mastooch when Chitral was invaded by a Chinese army in concert with the ruler of Badakhshan, Meer Sultan Shah. The Chitralis, unable to offer any effective resistance, fled to Mastooch, which was shortly invested by the invaders. The fort was strong, and Khush Amad, who belonged to the Maulai sect, followed the advice of his Caliphas, who counselled him to content himself with a passive resistance, and not to offer battle in the field. The besiegers, trusting to starvation to give them possession of the fort, were satisfied with establishing a blockade. They were, meanwhile, harassed by Khush Amad's partizans outside the fort, who inflicted some loss on them by feigning submission and leading them into an ambush among the mountains. At the end of seven months, both parties being willing to make terms, an envoy from the besiegers was admitted into the fort, and several tricks were played on both sides to give an impression of their readiness to continue the war. On the envoy entering the fort, he was made to wait some time, in order that the reason of his coming might be explained to the Mihter, who was still unaware that his fort was being besieged. The envoy on his part, while awaiting an audience, distributed powder and lead to any of the garrison who chose to take it, by way of showing the super-abundance of warlike stores in the besiegers' camp. On being admitted he was invited to partake of the meal which the Mihter's attendants shared with him daily. Double the usual amount of food was brought for consumption, and served out by a man whose hands were clotted with blood, as if he had not cleansed them since the fray of the day before. No remark was made, and each devoured his portion, as if the taste of an enemy's blood was no new thing to them, which caused the astonished envoy to regard them as cannibals. Terms were ultimately agreed to, and the invaders retired, taking with them four hostages. As they passed Brep, in Yarkhoon, each man of the invading army cast down a stone to show their numbers. The great heap thus formed is still pointed out. Very shortly after this Khush Amad died.

This tradition is interesting, as helping to identify Chitral with the Bolor of Chinese records; the following account of Bolor is translated by M. Klaproth from the Chinese Imperial Geography, published in 1790:—[1]

Bolor.

"Ce pays est situé au sud-ouest de *Yarkiang* et à l'orient de Badakhchân. Le chemin par lequel son tribut arrive à Péking est le même que celui des autres pays Mahométans. Sous les Han, le *Bolor* faisait partie d'*Ou tchha,* sous les Goei, c'était le royaume d'*A Keou khiang*.

"En 1749, son prince, *Chakhou Chamed* (peut-être *Chakou Chah Amed*) se soumit aux Chinois, et son pays fut enclavé dans les limites. L'année suivante, il envoya *Chah bek* comme ambassadeur à l'empereur, qui le reçut avee bienveillance l'invita à un festin et lui fit remettre un diplôme pour son maître.

"En 1763, un autre ambassade apporta le tribut consistant en sabres et haches d'armes. L'annèe après ce pays fut envahi par *Sultan-chah* de Badakhchân; alors le prince de Bolor demanda du secours au général chinois qui commandait à Yarkiang. Celui-ci enjoignit à Sultan-chah d'évacuer le Bolor et de faire cesser les hostilités. Le roi de Badakhchân se conforma à cet ordre, et *Chakhou Chamed* écrivit une lettre de remercîment. Les deux adversaires envoyèrent des ambassades et le tribut à l'empereur, consistant en poignards, qui sont d'excellente qualitité chez eux.

"En 1769 un nouveau tribut de pierre de *yu* et en poignards arriva de Bolor, et depuis ce temps il a toujours été offert à l'époque prescrite."

Consanguinity did not prevent constant wars between the rulers of Chitral and Yassin, but the records of these wars contain little worthy of notice. The Khush Wakté seem to have

[1] Maasin Asiatique, Vol. I, page 96.

GENEALOGY OF THE KHUSHWAKTÉ (YASSIN) AND THE BOOROOSHÉ (PONYAL).

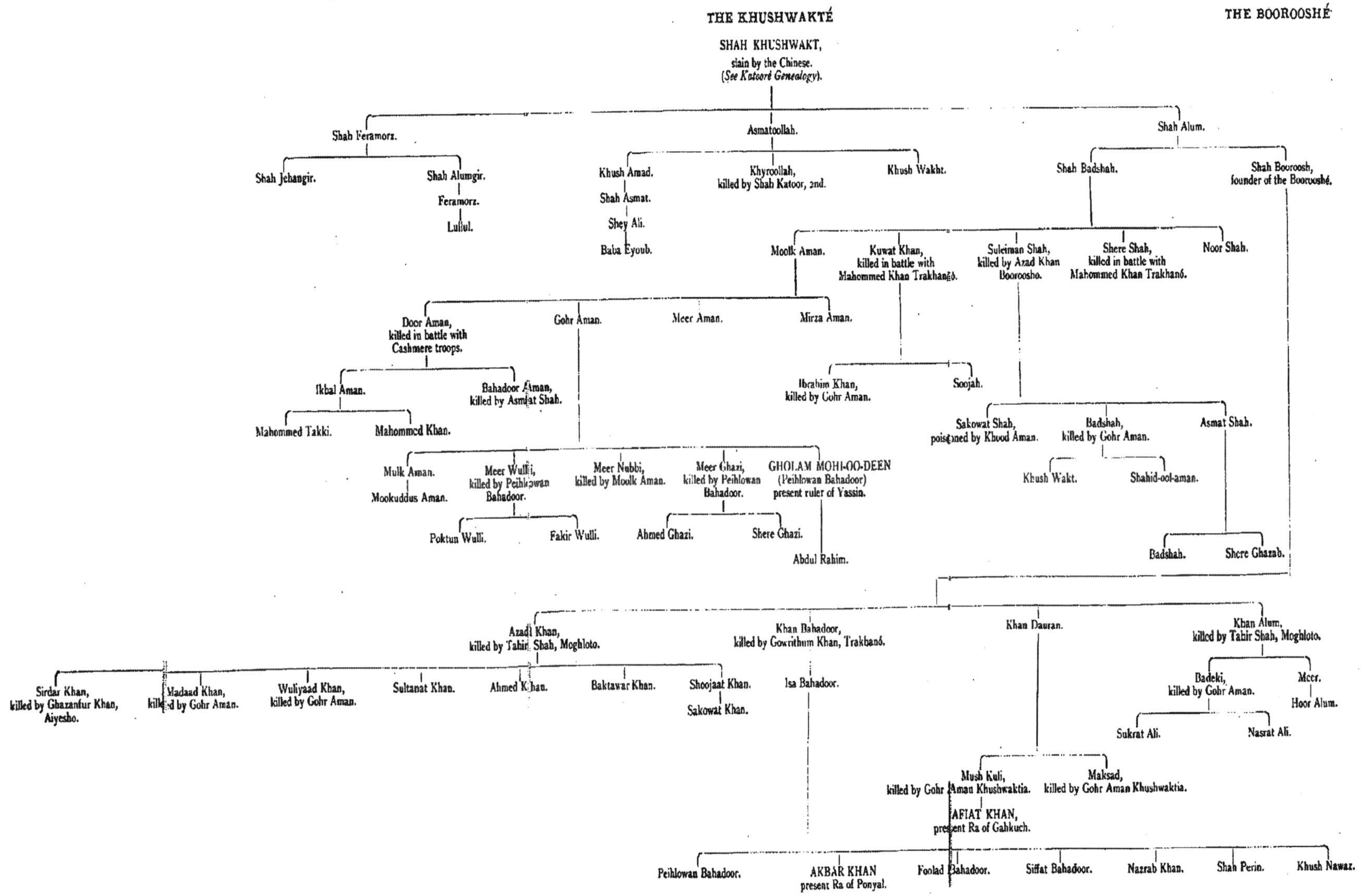

shown the greater warlike skill, but this advantage was balanced by the superior wealth and population of Chitral. Suleiman Shah, whose conquest of Gilgit has been already mentioned,[1] for a short time bid fair to found a considerable principality, but the incapacity for organisation, which seems to form so essential a part of all minds thoroughly imbued with Mahommedan tenets, prevented him from making any adequate use of his victories. Eastward he made himself master of the right bank of the Indus as far as Haramosh, and forced Ahmed Shah of Iskardo to acknowledge his supremacy. Boonji, which was then a flourishing place and formed part of the Iskardo domains, was twice besieged by him, the first time unsuccessfully, the second time it fell after a siege of eleven months, during which Shah Katoor of Chitral, taking advantage of Suleiman's absence, laid siege to Mastooch. Suleiman Shah, by a masterly march through the mountains, seized Drasun, cutting off Shah Katoor from his capital, and forced him to fight at a disadvantage a series of actions in which he was defeated, and his son Mookarab Shah slain. Being without resources, Shah Katoor threw himself on the mercy of his victorious foe. Taking with him his wife, a sister of his conqueror, he made his way on foot and unattended to the camp of Suleiman Shah, who received him generously and allowed him to return to Chitral after swearing friendship.

During his residence in Gilgit, which lasted seven years, Suleiman Shah, in concert with Ghazanfur Khan of Hunza, invaded Nager and made himself master of the whole country, with the exception of a single fort. During the siege, a false alarm one night caused a disastrous loss of men, who fell by the hands of their own comrades, and the siege was abandoned next day.

After the loss of Gilgit[2] his power rapidly waned. A severe earthquake levelled his fort of Mastooch, and this mishap was at once taken advantage of by Shah Katoor. The Yassin force under Sakowat Shah, eldest son of Suleiman Shah, was defeated at Gusht in the Laspoor Valley, and Sakowat Shah himself was treacherously murdered by his cousin Khood Aman, who introduced poison into a wound received by him in the fight. Shah Katoor followed up his advantage by invading Yassin, and was aided in the invasion by a Badakhshan or Wakhan force under Kokan Beg. Suleiman

[1] See page 137. [2] See page 138.

Shah was, however, able to sow dissension between the allies who retired to Chitral, and there Shah Katoor put Kokan Beg to death by casting him from a high rock into the foaming river and disarmed his followers.

Suleiman Shah was, however, doomed to fall by treachery equal to that which he had himself so freely employed. Rahmat-oollah Khan, his half-brother, born of a slave mother, conspired with Azad Khan and introduced a Gilgiti force into the castle of Cher, in Ponyal, where Suleiman Shah was residing. After defending himself for two days in a tower of the fort with no aid but that of his sons and a few servants, Suleiman Shah surrendered, and after a month's imprisonment, was put to death by Azad Khan. He was succeeded by Meer Aman, who ruled in Yassin for nearly eleven years, till he was ousted in 1840 by his brother Gohr Aman, whose wars against the Sikhs and Dogras have been already related by Mr. Drew and Dr. Leitner.

The annals of the Katooré branch of the family are of even less interest than those of the Khush Wakté. They seem to have produced no warrior or administrator of any pretensions, while their records abound in treachery and murder committed by son against father, and brother against brother. No attempt seems to have been made to weld the whole of the Katooré possessions into one principality, but each ruler in turn, by dividing the country during his lifetime among his sons, has directly encouraged the continuance of the family quarrels and intrigues.

CHAPTER XIV.

DARDISTAN.

IN the Appendix I have given lists of words of ten languages spoken in the country lying south of the Hindoo Koosh, which has been included in the general name of Dardistan. With three of these vocabularies, I have endeavoured to give sketches of the grammar of three languages, which appear to me to represent three different types. These, from the circumstances under which I gathered the information, and from the fact that I have refrained from giving any forms of which I could not be tolerably certain, are necessarily incomplete; but, in the hands of a skilled philologist, they will probably help to throw light on the ethnological affinities of the different tribes mentioned in this volume. Those alone who have made the experiment can fully realise the difficulty of extracting the grammatical forms of a strange language from uneducated men, frequently through the medium of an interpreter who is himself ignorant of grammar.

It may be well here to mention a few of the most obvious features in the languages given.

The Yidghâh language,[1] spoken in the Ludkho Valley, is simply a dialect of the Munjan language, which, I believe, has never yet been published. Its grammatical construction is identical with that of the Ghalchah languages, the grammar of which has been already given to the world by Mr. Shaw.[2] Like those, the Yidghâh differs from the Dand languages in its frequent use of the letter *v*, and in having only one tense to express both the present and the future.

The Khowar or Chitral language, which I believe further research will show to be typical of the Siah Posh languages, resembles the Ghalchah languages in having no inflexions distinctive of gender; but in other respects it approximates rather to the Dard languages, except that it has a larger amount of Persian roots. The passive voice is formed by the use of the auxiliary verb " to become."

[1] Appendix J. [2] Journal of the Bengal Asiatic Society, 1876.

The grammar of the Shina[1] language may be taken as fairly typical of that of the languages spoken by the broken tribes in the Indus, Swat, Kooner, and Punjkorah Valleys. Though differing slightly among themselves, these all grade into one another, and into Punjabi, and a closer examination will probably show that they have some affinity with Cashmeri. As in Punjabi and Hindustani, distinctions of gender are preserved in nouns and verbs, and the use of the cerebral *n* and the soft *j* is very common. In Shina, Torwalik, and Bushkarik[2] the passive voice is formed by the use of the auxiliary verb "to go," as in Punjabi and Hindustani.

The verbs of the two latter languages of the Swat Valley differ from those of Shina in having only one masculine and one feminine form in the singular, and a different single form for the plural, while the Gowro and Chiliss[3] differ in having the same form both in the singular and plural.

The most singular and interesting language of all is the Boorishki,[4] spoken in Hunza, Nager, and Yassin. It stands by itself and cannot be classed with any other Dard language. The foundation of this language has been identified as of Turanian origin; but, as far as I am able to judge, it has little or no claim to be classed as a Toork language, and it has forms which are only found among the most primitive races. Besides this, it has at some period borrowed largely from some Aryan language, many of the gramatical forms of which it has adopted. While preserving distinctions of gender, both in verbs and nouns, it uses them in a totally different manner from any of the Dard languages. The use of the celebral *n* is rare, and the verbs have no passive voice, though in the active voice they have the same tenses as exist in Khowar, Shina, and other Dard languages.

Under the convenient term of Dardistan have been included the whole of the valleys lying between the Western Punjab and the Hindoo Koosh, which are inhabited by a number of tribes mostly of Aryan origin. The greater part of these tribes appear to have been gradually crowded up into the less accessible and desirable localities, by external pressure. The circumstances which have caused them to quit their former homes have not, apparently, been simultaneous, or even of the same nature in all cases.

The name "Dard" is not acknowledged by any section of the tribes to whom it has been so sweepingly applied. In a single instance, the term is applied by one tribe to some of

[1] Appendix B. [2] Appendices D & E. [3] Appendices F and C. [4] Appendix A.

their neighbours.[1] Though the Dards are frequently mentioned by ancient writers, it is difficult now to identify with certainty the exact locality of the tribes referred to under that name. In the Vishnu Purana they are thus mentioned among other tribes, " also Sudras, Abhiras, Daradas, Kasmiras, with Pattis, Khasiras, Antacharas, or borderers, Pahnaras, and dwellers in mountain caves." Some of these names evidently refer to castes rather than to ethnological divisions. Arrian speaks of " the Derdai, who inhabit the mountains on the eastern borders ; " but this would hardly apply to tribes inhabiting the present limits of Dardistan. Pliny's description, " Fertilissimi sunt auri Dardœ," might apply to tribes dwelling in many parts of the Indus Valley, as far eastward as the Thok Jalung gold-fields in Long. 81.° Ptolemy also speaks of the race, as living at the sources of the Indus: "Sub fontibus vero Indi Daradræ, et horum montana superemi-nent." Thus it is evident that the tribes referred to under the name of " Dard " must formerly have stretched very much further to the eastward than those now so called. I think the name must have been given, in a general way, to all mountain tribes living in the Indus Valley, by the less warlike people of the plains and the effeminate Cashmeris, and that the legend grew up concerning them, not an uncommon one in wild countries, that they were descended from wild beasts. " Why do you call me Dardoo ? " is the question most commonly asked by the Gilgitis who visit Cashmere. " Because your grandfather was a bear," is the not infrequent answer. Thus from the Persian دد *dud*, "a beast of prey," or from درنده *darenda*, " fierce," the name Dard may have come to be used as an ethnological term in the same way as *dahyu*, "a robber," gave its name to Dahistan and the Dahœ tribe, as shown by General Cunningham,[2] and as Kaffir, Cossack, and Kirghiz are now applied to different Asiatic Tribes. The term Dard is not known in Chitral.

Mr. Shaw, in treating of the Ghalchah languages, is inclined to look upon the tribes north and south of the Hindoo Koosh as forming one group, whose linguistic differences are due to the interposition of the great mountain barrier,' but whose present position is the same as it always has been since the first separation. Closer examination will, I believe, show that the Hindoo Koosh tribes are divisible into several well-defined groups. The difference between the Ghalchahs

[1] See page 12.   [2] Archæological Report, Vol. II, pages 47-48.

and the tribes to whom the name of Dard has more especially been applied cannot be satisfactorily accounted for by the intervention of a mountain range, which has been crossed by emigrants on a smaller scale more than once since the first wave of Aryan migration swept southwards, while the differences existing between the Dardistan tribes themselves is, in some cases, greater still.

In the first group I would place the Sirikolis, Wakhis, Shighnis, the people of Munjan, and the upper part of the Ludkho Valley, and the Wooditsai, or people of Sanglich and Ishkashim. The people of Hissar, Darwaz, and Karategin, north of the Oxus, may probably claim close relationship with this group, though they now speak Persian or Toorki, and, in some places, have received a considerable infusion of Usbeg blood. The process of the disappearance of a language seems to be that the tribe first becomes bi-lingual, as is the case at present in Shighnan, Wakhan, and Sirikol, where almost every man speaks Persian in addition to his native language, and in the Swat, Kooner, and Punjkorah Valleys, where many of the Dard tribes speak Pushtoo in addition to their own dialects. In the course of time, increased intercourse with the outer world causes the more widely-spread of the two languages to be preferred, and finally altogether adopted, to the exclusion of the native tongue, which falls into disuse. Such a process must be accelerated by the absence of writing.

The people of Pakpooh and Shakshooh, in the valley of the Yarkund River, probably also belong to this group, and remnants of other tribes belonging to it may possibly still exist in the Kokcha and other valleys to the westward.

In the second group I would class the Kho of Chitral and the Siah-Posh tribes; further research will perhaps show that the tribes of the Nijrao, Panjsher, and Ghorbund Valleys in Afghanistan also belong to this group.

In the third group I would class the Shins, the Gowro, Chiliss, and other broken tribes of the Indus Valley, the Bushkarik and Torwalik of the Swat and Punjkorah Valleys, and the broken tribes of the Kooner Valley between Chitral and Kooner. Sufficient is not known of the Maiyoṇ tribe of Kandia, Doobeyr, and Seo to determine with certainty whether they belong to this group, but it is probable that they do.

One point which is worthy of note in regard to the languages of these three groups is, that while those spoken by the Ghalchah tribes, that is, those belonging to the first group, appear to be sprung from ancient Persian (Zend), those of the third group show greater affinity with the Sanscrit. But Zend and Sanscrit being sister languages,[1] a relationship is shown to exist between the two groups. The Khowar language, as has already been mentioned, shows affinities with those of both groups, and will be found, I believe, to constitute an intermediate link between the two.

The Yeshkuns, or Boorish, of Hunza, Nager, &c., must be classed separately from all the three groups, though they have now, perhaps, nearly as much Aryan as Turanian blood in their veins.

Conjecture is permissible as to the events which brought these tribes into their present localities, although the actual facts must remain unknown. Some idea also may be formed as to the order in which these events happened, but anything approaching to exact chronology is utterly unattainable.

It is generally agreed that Badakhshan and the upper part of the Oxus Valley was one of the earliest homes of the Aryan race. Their progress southwards was probably gradual, and at first more due to natural expansion than to any desire for conquest. As they came to occupy localities of greater fertility in a more genial climate, their number would naturally increase more rapidly. Warlike expeditions on a large scale would become possible, and each step in advance would be taken with greater confidence. In the tribes of the first, or Ghalchah, group may probably be recognised the descendants of those who remained settled in their original locality, and who, in latter times, were gradually driven up into the narrow valleys where they are now found. In some instances, as in the Ludkho Valley, they crossed the great range and settled on the south side of it at a comparatively recent date.

The tribes of the second and third groups I take to represent those who migrated southwards at the earliest period. Of these a certain number must have settled in the ground first occupied by the emigrants, leaving the more energetic to push on further south. In the Kho and the Siah-Posh, I would recognise the descendants of these first settlers who, after crossing the Hindoo Koosh and exterminating or driving before them the aboriginal inhabitants, remained in occupation of the hill country down to an elevation of about 2,500

[1] Muir's Sanscrit Texts, Vol. II. page 266.

feet, and probably spread along the hills for a considerable distance to the eastward.

In the tribes of the third group I would recognise the descendants of those who settled in the fertile valleys among the lower hills. In the course of generations considerable differences would naturally arise between the three groups, living under different conditions, and acted on by different circumstances, and in time all community of feeling would disappear. The first great change to occur must have been the intrusion of the Boorish. I believe that in them we see the descendants of the Yuechi, who conquered Bactria about 120 B.C. In the term Yeshkun, applied to them by their neighbours, the old name perhaps survives, and the name *Boorish*, by which they still call themselves, is perhaps traceable in "Pooroosha," the ancient name of Peshawur, which was the seat of the Indo-Scythic kingdom founded by the son of Kitolo, of the Little Yuechi tribe, who conquered Gandhara and Ariana in the beginning of the fifth century A. D. They probably once occupied the Shigar Valley, and all the affluents of the Indus, together with the Indus Valley itself, down to about Jalkot. In the process of occupation of this country, they must have subdued the Aryan (Siah Posh) inhabitants, whose women were probably not less sought after for their beauty then than at the present day, and in this way, and by absorbing the tribes already occupying the ground, they gained a sufficient infusion of Aryan blood to alter their type of feature and their general characteristics. It is no doubt to them that Abu Rihan, who wrote in the beginning of the eleventh century, refers in his description of the course of the Indus—

"In two days' journey you arrive at another part of Turkestan, where the Bhotyas and Dyan dwell. Their king is called Bhot Shah, and their cities are Gilgit, Asurah (Hasora or Astor), Salsas (Chilas), and their language is Turki. The inhabitants of Cashmere suffer greatly from their encroachments and depredations."

In another place he styles them :

"The Bhotyawari Turks, from whose encroachments the Cashmerians suffer great distress."[1]

The next event of importance in the shifting of tribes was probably the movement of the Shins northward, which may have happened about the time of, and was possibly occasioned by, the irruption of the Mahommedans into India; but I should be inclined to assign an earlier date to it. It is to be

[1] Elliot's Ancient Historians of India.

noted that the northward impulse appears to have been given to them under somewhat different conditions, and at a considerably earlier period than it was imparted to cognate tribes in other valleys. That their religion was a form of Hindooism, and not of Buddhism, I think there can be little doubt. The preservation of a caste system, and their feeling for the cow, which has procured them a distinctive name among their neighbours, point to this conclusion, while no tradition or reverence survives for the Buddhistic remains still to be found in their country. Leaving their home in Pukli they must have pressed up the Indus Valley, founding a number of small principalities, the most important of which were Gilgit and Baltistan, and extended almost as far as Leh. The rock-carved Hindoo idols still to be met with in Western Ladakh, some of which show the Brahminical thread, were no doubt their work. The conquerors naturally settled in the most fertile parts where the climate was least severe, forcing the original occupants to take refuge in the wilder, colder, and more mountainous districts, where some of them were perhaps enabled to preserve a semi-independence. As time elapsed, in the parts where both races continued to live side by side, the language of the conquerors would be imposed on the conquered. The strict caste habits of the Shins would, however, prevent a thorough blending of the two races, so that, long after their relative positions of conquerors and conquered were lost sight of, a rigid line of separation was maintained between them. Had the Shins come into the country by mere immigration, without conquest, they could hardly have imposed their language on, and assumed a position of superiority over, a people who out-numbered them.

Now, if things had happened as I have suggested, we should naturally search in the difficult fastnesses of Hunza for the original race in its greatest purity, and that is what is actually found. In Nager also, a country not quite so impregnable as Hunza, but sufficiently so to make it difficult of conquest, the population is entirely Boorish. At the villages of Myoon and Hini, or Hindi, in Hunza, a few Shins are found. Below Hini on both sides of the valley they form an increasing proportion of the population as Gilgit is approached. Below Myoon the Boorish language is not spoken. At Chaprot, however, there are plenty of Shins, and the nature of the ground is such that the possession of Chaprot secures the command of the upper valley. It is, therefore, allowable to suppose that much the same state of things existed in the days of the Shin rule as now, that is, that while Hunza was nominally obedient to Gilgit, there was little intercourse between the two states.

Turning westward to Yassin, we again find the Boorish, or Woorshik, forming the population of the upper valley in which the Boorish language is spoken. Here, again, the language boundary nearly corresponds with the present political boundary, and here again, as on the Hunza side, physical difficulties form a natural barrier between the upper and lower valley, though the Shins have extended along the main valley west of its junction with the Woorshigoom Valley. Below Gahkuch, and as far as the Indus, the Shins are found in increasing numbers, though still in the minority. The language, however, is Shina. As the table already given[1] has shown, the proportion of Yeshkuns to other races decreases steadily the further south one goes, and the Shins preponderate in the more fertile valleys till the Pathan population is reached, the single exception to this rule being the community of Palus. Now, how else, I would ask, except by this theory of conquest, is it possible to account for this wedge of a strange language driven in between countries like Yassin and Hunza divided from each other by lofty mountains, which stops short at the natural frontiers?

The next event must have been the movement of the Tartars from the eastward along the Indus Valley. The period of the establishment of their power in Iskardo is perhaps marked by the appearance of the name Ghotachoh in the Makpon genealogy. There was, no doubt, at the time a Yeshkun population living mixed with the Shins, and owing to the absence of caste prejudices, they would be the first to be absorbed by intermarriage with the conquerors. In the people of Dah-Hanu, we see the only remaining relics of the former Shin inhabitants of Baltistan, and here again the preservation of their languages and themselves as a separate community appears to be due to the isolation caused by the physical difficulties of the spot which they inhabit.

Mr. Shaw, describing the localities, says :—

"In a wild gorge, through which the narrow Indus rushes, and where the grand masses of granite seemingly piled in confusion on both banks scarcely leave room for the passage of the river, and conceal the mountains behind them, my camp was pitched. Close by, the Hanu ravine, which in its upper part expands into a wide inhabited valley, escapes through a rocky chasm into the Indus. My next day's march led through similar scenery, the path now rising up the side of

[1] See page 35.

the cliff, supported on frail-looking scaffoldings of tree trunks, resting on projecting rocks or on wooden trestles, now plunging precipitously down to the river side, where a stone could be thrown to strike the opposite cliff across the Indus. The village of Darchik, likewise, is cut off from the lower course of the valley by a vertical cliff, the escarpment of the plateau on which it stands. There are only two ways of approach—one high up and away from the river, is guarded by a fortified communal dwelling; the other, near the river, consists of a rugged narrow staircase, constructed in the face of the cliff and closed by a gateway at the top."

In each case it is apparent how much concern the physical conformation of the country has with the preservation of ethnological divisions.

The movement of the smaller tribes was no doubt due to the increasing pressure of the Afghans in the sixteenth and seventeenth centuries, gradually pushing before them a less warlike people who lacked cohesion. The Gawaré of the Indus Valley, and the Gubbers of the Kooner Valley about Narisat, must be looked upon as separated branches of one tribe, and are, no doubt, the Gourœi of ancient geographers, whose former abode was in the Punjkorah Valley, if that river has been correctly identified with the Garæus of the ancients. Their name has certainly nothing to do with fire-worship, for in the Kooner Valley it is only used among themselves, and not by their neighbours of Chitral, who call them Narisatis. The Torwalik of the Swat Kohistan, and the Chiliss of the Indus Valley, apparently were also formerly one tribe, and according to the Chiliss tradition came from Boneyr.

The Kho would seem to have once spread over a much greater extent of country than they now occupy. Their name appears in the ancient Khophen (the Cabul River), the Choaspes (the Kooner River), the Choes (the combined Swat and Punjkorah Rivers), and in the name of the Comedæ mountains, which must have been those at the head of the Swat Valley. They were, no doubt, the Khasiras of the Vishnu Purana, and perhaps the Cosyri of Pliny; and in the name of And-Kho, 350 miles to the westward, we may perhaps see traces of them.

The number and diversity of the dialects spoken among the Siah Posh points to their having occupied a more extended area, from which they have been dislodged and driven into their present narrow limits, and the conversion of the surrounding tribes, first to Buddhism and later to Mahommedanism, has isolated them from their neighbours. But while their enmity with their Afghan neighbours to the west is deadly and unceasing, their relations with their eastern neighbours admit of friendly intercourse in spite of occasional raids.

It is impossible to view the so-called Dards closely without recognising that they are a decadent race. From the south and west the Pathan, from the east the Tartar, and in a less degree the Cashmeri, and from the north the Tajik, are steadily pressing upon and supplanting them. In the Swat, Punjkorah, and Indus Valleys their attitude is one of passive resistance, which always yields when the pressure reaches a certain point. Their want of energy and adaptability, their unwillingness to employ themselves except in agriculture, or to strike out new modes of life, their slow numerical increases, and their want of cohesion among themselves, seem to show that they are doomed to be absorbed by more vigorous races. Men of other races settle among them and grow rich and numerous, while the owners of the soil remain contented with the same poverty that satisfied their forefathers, unmoved by the contrast presented between their own state and the increasing prosperity of those who settle among them. In the Neemchas of the Indus Valley, we may witness the commencement of the process by which all the Dards as a race are destined in time to disappear.

FINIS.

APPENDICES.

EXPLANATORY NOTE.

As the following languages are not found in a written form, transliteration is not possible: they are, therefore, written according to simple English pronunciation, eked out with signs :—

a *unaccented* to be pronounced as in "have."
á or *ah* as the short *a* in "America."
â as in "dark."
e *unaccented* as in "shell."
é or *eh* as in the French "était."
è as the first *e* in "where."
ê or *ey* as the *a* in "way."
i *unaccented* as in "kill."
î as the *ee* in "feet."
o *unaccented* as in the French "votre."
ò as in "knot."
ō as in "for."
ô as in "hole."
ö as in the German "schön."
u *unaccented* as in "gun."
ù as in "full."
ü as in the French "mieux."
ai as the *y* in "my."
th and *ph* as in "Trentham," and "up-hold," not as the Greek θ and φ.
gh and *kh* are pronounced much less gutturally than in Persian, excepting in the language given in Appendix J.
ṇ and g *with a dot underneath*, cerebrally as in the French "non," "long."
j *with a dot underneath*, soft as in the French "jamais."
ñ as in the Spanish "señor."

APPENDIX A.

BOORISHKI

(Nager dialect)

Spoken in Hunza, Nager, and Yassin.

[This is the language called Khajuna by Dr. Leitner.]

SKETCH OF GRAMMAR.

THE SUBSTANTIVE.

Substantives are either masculine or feminine, as are also the first three numerals, which have masculine and feminine forms.

The genders of nouns expressing human beings are according to sex; all other living creatures, irrespective of sex, are masculine. All things made of wood are masculine, and all metals or things made of metal are feminine, except *jamé* "a bow," which is feminine; and *toomák* "a gun," *deedoo* "a bullet," *chŭr* "a knife," and "coined money," which are masculine. Things made of cloth of any kind are feminine, with some exceptions. All trees, plants, and grains are feminine, with one or two exceptions; and fruits are masculine, except *gaing* "a grape," which is feminine. All liquids are feminine.

The relations of substantives are expressed by the application of postpositions, which are alike both in the singular and plural.

	Singular.		*Plural.*	
Nom.	a man . . .	siss.	men . . .	siss.
Gen.	of a man . .	siss-é.	of men . . .	siss-é.
Dat.	to a man . .	siss-er.	to men . . .	siss-er.
Acc.	a man . . .	siss.	men . . .	siss.
Abl.	on a man . .	siss-etté.	on men . . .	siss-etté.
	in a man . .	siss-é-ùloo.	in men . . .	siss-é-ùloo.
	with a man . .	siss-é-kât.	with men . .	siss-é-kât.
	for a man . .	siss-é-gunné.	for men . . .	siss-é-gunné.
	by *or* from a man	siss-tsùm.	by *or* from men .	siss-tsùm.
Voc.	oh man . . .	leh sîss.	oh men . . .	leh sîss.

The *é* interposed between the noun and postposition in the ablative is only for the sake of euphony, and is often omitted. All nouns, both masculine and feminine, are declined like SISS, except feminine nouns relating to human beings, as:

	Singular.		*Plural.*	
Nom.	(thy) wife	gùs.	(thy) wives	gùs-hiunts.
Gen.	of (thy) wife	gùs-moh.	of (thy) wives	gùs-hiunts-é.
Dat.	to (thy) wife	gùs-mor.	to (thy) wives	gùs-hiunts-er.
Acc.	(thy) wife	gùs.	(thy) wives	gùs-hiunts.
Abl.	on (thy) wife	gùs-moy-etté.	on (thy) wives	gùs-hiunts-etté.
	in (thy) wife	gùs-mo-loo.	in (thy) wives	gùs-hiunts-moloo.
	with (thy) wife	gùs-mo-kât.	with ,,	gùs-hiunts-kât.
	for (thy) wife	gùs-mo-gunné.	for ,,	gùs-hiunts-gunné.
	by *or* from (thy) wife.	gùs-mo-tsùm.	by from *or* (thy) wives.	gùs-hiunts-tsùm.
Voc.	oh wife	wah gùs.	oh wives	wah gùshiunts.

The vocative exclamation differs according to the relationship between the persons. Men say *leh* to one another, and *wâh* to all women except their own wives. To their wives they use the exclamation *seh*, which is also used by women to one another.

The noun in the genitive is placed before the governing noun, as: *Sissé* hághoor "The man's horse;" *Sissé toomáké* deedoo "The man's gun's bullet."

Every substantive and adjective has a suffixed termination both in the singular and plural, which is used somewhat as an indefinite or definite article, and is interposed between the substantive and the postposition. This termination is always *un* or *wun* in the singular, but varies considerably in the plural, the commonest forms being *ing*, *isho*, *ùts*, *ik*, and *unts*. It is not necessarily discarded when used with a numeral, as: *Oomé bérùmân siss*-ik *yotsùmâ* "How many men did you see?" *Jáh hin siss*-un *yetsum* "I saw one man." *Jeh siss*-un-*kât niyum* "I went with the man."

The termination is never used in the singular with both adjective and substantive, but is suffixed to whichever comes last in the sentence, as:

A strong man	Shatillo siss-*un*.
That man is very strong	Iné sis bùt shatillo-*wun* bai.

The rule, however, does not always hold good in the plural, where the termination can be used at pleasure, either with both substantive and adjective, or only with one; but it is more correct to use it only as in the singular, as:

Strong men	Shatillo siss-*ik*.
Those men are very strong	Ooé siss-*ik* bùt shatill-*joko* bán.
Ten swift horses	Toromo hùmalkùm-isho hághoor.

THE ADJECTIVES.

The adjective precedes the substantive, as shown above.

PRONOMINAL SUBSTANTIVES AND ADJECTIVES.

A number of substantives and adjectives have pronominal prefixes, without which they are never used, and which are employed according to the relation of the noun to which they are prefixed. Each has seven forms; thus, to express "head" it is necessary to say "my head," "your head," &c.; but there is no word for "head" in the abstract. For instance:

my head . . .	ai-*yetis*.	her head . . .	moo-*yetis*.
thy head . . .	go-*yetis*.	our head . . .	mi-*yetis*.
his head . . .	i-*yetis*.	your head . . .	mai-*yetis*.
their head	oo-*yetis*.		

When applied to animals or objects, the forms of the third persons singular and plural are used. The prefix is nearly the same in all pronominal words, both substantive and adjective.

The use of the regular pronouns is not obviated by these prefixes, but they are employed in addition; nor are the plural terminations discarded, as:

My head aches	Jâ ai*yetis ákholjibi*.
What is thy name?	Oomé goo-ik *bessun dila?*
She had (*lit.*, saw) a dream . .	Kiné mooljî-un *yétsoobo*.
Your tongues speak	Ma mow-*músho gharichibiún*.
Their brothers have gone . . .	Ooé o*chookón nibán*.

These substantives all denote objects or attributes which belong to a single individual, possession of which cannot be shared, such as "head," "dream," "temper," "father," "wife," &c.

The pronominal adjectives are compounds formed from the above substantives, as, *es*-shokùm "generous," from *es* (pronom. subs.) "heart," and *shokùm* "wide," the prefix being changed either according to the person of the verb it governs or is governed by, and denoting qualities which cannot be shared, as:

I became independent	Jeh *ás*-goorùmuṇ manâm.
His father is brave	Iné yoo *es*-dághânusun bai.
My wife is timid	Jâ ows *moos*-goosâsun bo.
We are clever	Miṇ *mil*-chikoyo baṇ.

The following list comprises nearly all the pronominal substantives:—

	SINGULAR.				PLURAL.		
	1st. Pers.	*2nd Pers.*	*3rd Pers. Mas.*	*3rd Pers. Fem.*	*1st Pers.*	*2nd Pers.*	*3rd Pers.*
Anger	ámoskish	goomoskish	imoskish	moomoskish	mimoskish	mámoskish	oomoskish.
Arm	áshuck	gooshuck	ishuck	mooshuck	mishuck	máshuck	ooshuck.
Aunt	ántsoo	goontsoo	intsoo	moontsoo	mintsoo	mántsoo	oontsoo.
Back	áwuldus	goowuldus	iwuldus	moowuldus	miwuldus	máwuldus	oowuldus.
Beard	aiṇgyi	gooṇgyi	iṇgyi	mooṇgyi	miṇgyi	maiṇgyi	ooṇgyi.
Belly	owl	gool	yool	mool	miyool	mowl	ool.
Body	ádim	goodim	idim	moodim	midim	mádim	oodim.
Bone	áltin	gooltin	iltin	mooltin	miltin	máltin	ooltin.
Brother	áchoo	gochoo	echoo	mochoo	mechoo	máchoo	ochoo.
Cheek	ámookùsh	goomookùsh	imookùsh	moomookùsh	mimookùsh	mámookùsh	oomookùsh.
Chin	ásun	goosun	isun	moosun	misun	másun	oosun.
Daughter	aiy	goy	êy	moy	mêy	maiy	oyi.
Daughter-in-law	ákhâkin	gookhâkin	ikhâkin	mookhâkin	mikhâkin	mákhâkin	ookhâkin.
Dream	owljî	gooljî	yooljî	mooljî	mîljî	máljî	oljî.
Ear	áltùmál	gooltùmál	iltùmál	mooltùmál	miltùmál	máltùmál	ooltùmál.
Elbow	ásùsùn	goosùsùn	isùsùn	moosùsùn	misùsùn	másùsùn	oosùsùn.
Eye	álchin	goolchin	ilchin	moolchin	milchin	málchin	oolchin.
Eyebrow	áltâns	gooltâns	iltâns	mooltâns	miltâns	máltâns	ooltâns.
Eyelash	árpùr	goorpùr	irpùr	moorpùr	mirpùr	márpùr	oorpùr.
Face	áshkil	gooshkil	ishkil	mooshkil	mishkil	máshkil	ooshkil.
Father	ow	goow	yoow	moow	myoow	mow	oow.
Finger	ámish	gomish	emish	momish	memish	mámish	oomish.
Foot	owtis	gootis	yootis	mootis	myootis	mowtis	ootis.
Grandfather } Grandmother }	ápi	gopi	epi	mopi	mepi	mápi	opi.
Hair	ágoyiung	gogoyiung	igoyiung	moogoyiung	migoyiung	mágoyiung	oogoyiung.
Hand	árîng	goorîng	irîng	moorîng	mirîng	mârîng	oorîng.
Head	aiyetis	goyetis	iyetis	mooyetis	miyetis	maiyetis	ooyetis.
Heart	ás	gùs	es	moos	mes	más	oos.
Heel	ághân	googhân	ighân	mooghân	meghân	mághân	ooghân.

Husband	owyer	gooyer	——	mooyer	myooyer	moyer	ooyer.
Knee	ádoomùs	goodoomùs	idoomùs	moodoomùs	midoomùs	mádoomùs	oodoomùs.
Lip	aiyl	goyl	îyl	moyl	mîyl	maiyl	ooyl.
Liver	aikin	gookin	ekin	mookin	mekin	maikin	okin.
Loins	áshting	goshting	eshting	moshting	meshting	máshting	oshting.
Mother	ámi	goomi	imi	moomi	mimi	mámi	oomi.
Mouth	âkhát	gookhát	ikhát	mookhát	mikhát	mâkhát	ookhát.
Nail	owrî	goorî	yoorî	moorî	myoorî	mowrî	oorî.
Name	aik	gooik	îk	mooîk	mîk	maik	ooik.
Neck	ush	gosh	esh	mosh	mesh	másh	osh.
Nose	ámoopùsh	goomoopùsh	imoopùsh	moomoopùsh	mimoopùsh	mámoopùsh	oomoopùsh.
Palm of the hand	âtuttus	gootuttus	ituttus	mootuttus	mituttus	mâtuttus	ootuttus.
Shoulder	ápoing	gooping	ipoing	mopoing	mipoing	mápoing	oopoing.
Sister	aiyus	gooyus	iyus	mooyus	miyus	maiyus	ooyus.
Son	aiyî	gooyî	îyì	mooyî	mîyî	maîyî	ooyî.
Son-in-law	árer	gorer	erer	morer	merer	márer	orer.
Temper	átsir	gootsir	itsir	mootsir	mitsir	mátsir	ootsir.
Toe	ámish	gomish	emish	momish	memish	mámish	omish.
Tongue	owmùs	goomùs	yoomùs	moomùs	myoomùs	mowmùs	oomùs.
Tooth	ámé	goomé	imé	moomé	mimé	mámé	oomé.
Uncle	ángoo	goongoo	ingoo	moongoo	mingoo	mungoo	oongoo.
Wife	ows	goos	yoos	——	myoos	mows	oos.

The pronominal adjectives are very few :—

Angry	ámos	goomos	imos	moomos	mimos	mámos	oomos.
Brave	ás-dághânùs	gùs-dághânùs	es-dághânùs	moos-dághânús	mes-dághânùs	más-dághânùs	oos-dághânùs.
Clever	álchikooin	goolchikooin	ilchikooin	moolchikooin	milchikooin	málchikooin	oolchikoin
Generous	ás-shokùm	goos-shokùm	es-shokùm	moos-shokùm	mes-shokùm	más-shokùm	oos-shokùm.
Independent	ás-goorùm	goos-goorùm	es-goorùm	moos-goorum	mes-goorùm	más-goorùm	oos-goorùm.
Miserly / Quick-tempered	ás-chedùm	goos-chedùm	es-chedùm	moos-chedùm	mes-chedùm	más-chedùm	oos-chedùm.
Timid	ás-goosâs	goos-goosâs	es-goosâs	moos-goosâs	mes-goosâs	más-goosâs	oos-goosâs.

PRONOUNS.

The personal and demonstrative pronouns are declined as follows :—

The *locative* and *ablative* are formed as in the noun.

	Nom.	*Gen.*	*Dat.*	*Acc.*					
I (*trans.*)	jáh	jâ	jâr	jeh	jâ- *etté*	jâ- *ùloo*	jâ- *kát*	jâ- *gunné*	jâ- *tsùm*
I (*intrans.*) . . .	jeh								
Thou	oom	oomé	oomer	oom	oomé-	oomé-	oomé-	oomé-	oom-
He (*this one*) . . .	kin	kiné	kiner	kin	kiné-	kiné-	kiné-	kiné-	kin-
He (*that one*) . . .	in	iné	iner	in	iné-	iné-	iné-	iné-	in-
She (*this one*) . . .	kin	kinmoh	kinmor	kin	kinmoh-	kinmoh-	kinmoh-	kinmoh-	kinmoh-
She (*that one*) . . .	in	inmoh	inmor	in	inmoh-	inmoh-	inmoh-	inmoh-	inmoh-
We	miṇ	mîṇ	mîṇmer,	miṇ	mîṇ-	mîṇ-	mîṇ-	mîṇ-	mîṇmé-
You	máh	mâ	mámer	máh	mâ-	mâ-	mâ-	mâ-	mâmá-
They (*these*) . . .	koo	kooé	kooer	koo	koo-	koo-	koo-	koo-	koo-
They (*those*) . . .	oo	ooé	ooer	oo	oo-	oo-	oo-	oo-	oo-

In the nominative singular a difference is made between a transitive and intransitive verb, by adding *é* when the former is employed, except in the first person, when a slightly different form is used, as shown above. No difference is made in the first and second persons plural: *é* is added to the third person sometimes, but is not obligatory:

I went	*Jeh* niyum.
I saw the man	*Jáh* sissun yétsum.
Thou sawest the man	*Oomé* siss-un yétsooma.
She went	*Kin* nimo.
He saw the man	*Iné* sissum yétsimi.
They will come	*Koo* joochen.
They saw me	*Ooé* jeh aiyétsoomun.

When reference is made to objects or animals, the following forms, which are not applicable to human beings, are used:—

this	*khos*, masc. *khot*, fem.	That	*ess*, masc. *et*, fem.
of this	*khosé*, masc. *khoté*, fem.	Of that	*essé*, masc. *eté*, fem.
these	*khots.*	Those	*ets*
of these	*khotsé.*	Of those	*etsé.*

This is the horse	*Khos* hághoor bi.
This water is good	*Khot* tsil tultus dila.
This is better than that	*Khos essé*-tsùm tultus bi.

REFLECTIVE PRONOUNS.

The reflective pronoun is formed by a reduplication of the personal pronoun:

I myself	*Jeh jé.*	we ourselves	*min min.*
thou thyself	*oom gooí* or *goo gooí.*	you yourselves	*máh maiyí.*
he himself	*in í.*	they themselves	*oo ooí.*
she herself	*in mooí.*	they themselves *(objects)*	*ets í.*
it itself (*masc.*)	*ess í.*		
it itself (*fem.*)	*et í.*		

The genitive is formed by using the personal and possessive pronouns together,—*jáh jehimoh, oomé gooimoh, iné íyimoh,* &c.:

Dative.	Accusative.
ákherer.	Same as nominative.
gookherer.	
ikherer.	
mookherer.	
mikherer.	
mákherer.	
ookherer.	

POSSESSIVE PRONOUNS.

The possessive is also indicated by the following form:—

mine	*jehimoh.*	her	*mooyimoh.*
thine	*gooimoh.*	ours	*míyimoh.*
mis	*íyimoh.*	yours.	*maiyimoh.*
theirs	*ooyimoh.*		

Examples.

My house	*jehimoh* háh.
Her horse	*mooyimoh* hághoor.
His mother's head . . .	iné *imimoh mooyimoh* mooyetis.
I wish you to teach me your language; in return I will teach you mine.	jáh ruck echabá *gooimoh* bâsh aikin ; etté budul *jehimoh* bâsh oomer goykyum.
The cows which you saw were ours	boouns be yotsoomá etsé *mīyimoh* bíùn.

INTERROGATIVE PRONOUNS.

The interrogative pronoun is expressed by *ámin* or *menun* when relating to human beings, and *ámis* (masc.) and *ámit* (fem.) when relating to animals or objects, as :

Which horse is this? . . .	Khos *ámis* hághoor bi.
Which milk is best? . . .	*Ámit* mámoo tultus dila.
Whose horse is this? . . .	Khos hághoor *áminé* bi.
Whose house did you enter? .	Oom *mené* hâhlé nibum.
Whose is this?	Khos *áminé* bi.

RELATIVE PRONOUNS.

The relative is expressed by using *be* with the personal pronoun, as :

I who went	Jéh *be* niyum.
I who saw the man . . .	Jáh *be* sissun yétsum.
This is the man who went .	*Be* nimi iné siss bai.
The horse which I saw . .	Hághoor *be* yétsum.
This is the man I saw . .	Jáh *be* yétsum iné siss bai.

INDEFINITE PRONOUNS.

Kúts and *men* are used in the sense that *wallah* is employed in Hindoostani, but are not used to make into verbal substantives as in that language, as :

A person of Hunza . . .	Hunzoo *kúts*un.
Nager people	Náger *kúts*ik.
Somebody must go . . .	*Menun* niyuss áwâji.

PREPOSITIONS.

Besides *kât* "with" and *yer* "before," which are suffixed to the noun they govern, certain prepositions have pronominal forms—

	ME.	THEE.	HIM.	HER.	US.	YOU.	THEM.
near	ápuch	goopuch	ipuch	moopuch	mipuch	mápuch	oopuch
behind	álji	goolji	ilji	moolji	milji	málji	oolji
accompanying . . .	ákât	gokât	ékât	mookât	mîkât	mâkât	ookât
before	aiyer	gooyer	îyer	mooyer	miyer	maiyer	ooyer
preceding	ángi	gùṇgi	iṇgi	mooṇgi	miṇgi	máṇgi	ùṇgi
like	áshâski	gúshaski	ishâski	múshaski	mishaski	máshâski	ooshâski

Example.

"He was standing in front of me; when I began to go, he went behind my brother."	In jâ *aiyer* tsut diebum; jeh niyumúloo jâ áchoo *ilji* nimi.

THE NEGATIVE.

The simple negative "no" is expressed by *bé*. "Not" is expressed by *ápi*, which is apparently a compound of the word *bi* "is," with the negative *a* affixed. For human beings *ápai* is used in the masculine and *ápo* in the feminine, as:

Have you seen him? No	Oomé in yétsoomá? *Bé.*
This is not your gun	Khos oomé toomák *ápi.*
He is not here	In kohlé *ápai.*
The Queen is not in the house	Gánish háhlé *ápo.*

A negative form is given to the verb by affixing *ai, á, ow.* In compound verbs the negative is interposed, as:

I will not do (it)	Jáh *ai*yechum.
I do not know	Jáh *á*keyum.
I am unable	Jáh *ow*leyum.
I will not forget	Jeh till-*ai*-âljum.
I have not forgotten	Jeh till-*ai*-âlum.

If the verb already begins with *ai,* Á is interposed, as: *aikenuss* "to teach me," *ai-*Á*-kenuss* "not to teach me."

If the verb already begins with Á, *ai* is prefixed, as: *áruss* "to send me," Ai-*áruss* "not to send me."

THE VERB.

The verb is generally very regular with terminations expressing tense and person. The infinitive always ends in *áss*, *ess* or *uss*.

A great number of verbs form the past participle irregularly, and certain of them conjugate the past participle as a tense. Among the latter are—

to do *or* to make	etuss.	to see	yétsuss.
to bring	ditthuss.	to come	jooyess.
to ask	doghârùsuss.	to go	niyuss.
to sleep	gùchêyuss.		

Jooyess also forms three of its tenses irregularly.

All tenses, except in the imperative mood, have different terminations of the 3rd person singular to express different genders of nouns or of persons.

The imperfect tense in the 1st person singular and plural, and the pluperfect in the 1st person singular, have two forms, which are used at pleasure without changing the meaning.

By the use of *úloo* and *etté* with the perfect tense a gerund in the form of a tense is produced.

The conditional or potential mood is formed by the suffix *ábé* "or not" to all tenses of the indicative mood.

A verbal substantive is formed by adding postpositions to the infinitive, as:

in the going	niyuss-*úloo.*	for the going	niyuss-*gunné.*
on the going	niyuss-*etté.*	from the going	niyuss-*tsúm.*
with the going	niyuss-*kât.*		

THE VERB.

Conjugation of the verb "To Go."

Infinitive Mood.

Present.		*Future.*	
to go . . .	niyuss.	to be about to go.	niyuss niyuss.

Past.

to have gone . . . niyuss dilùm.

Participles.

Present.		*Future.*	
going . . .	nichoomé.	being about to go . .	niyussé.

Past.

Singular.		*Plural.*	
I having gone . . .	ná.	we having gone . .	nimen.
thou having gone . .	nokô.	you having gone . .	námâ.
he *or* it having gone . .	nî.	they having gone . .	noo.
she *or* it having gone . .	nomo.	they having gone (*objects*) (*fem.*)	nî.

Gerunds.

in my having gone	jeh niyum-ùloo.	in our having gone	min nim-ùloo.
in thy having gone	oom nim-ùloo.	in your having gone	máh nim-ùloo.
in his, her, its having gone.	in nim-ùloo.	in their having gone	oo nim-ùloo.

In the same way *jeh niyum-etté* "on *or* by my having gone, &c."

Supines.

possibly to go . .	niyuss-ábé.	must go . . .	niyuss-awájé.
meet to go . .	niyuss-maiymi.	ought to go . .	niyuss-dila.

Indicative Mood.

Present.

Singular.		*Plural.*	
I am going . .	nichabá.	we are going . .	nichabân.
thou art going . .	nichoobá.	you are going . .	nichoobân.
he is going . .	nichoobai.	they (*human beings*) are going.	nichoobân.
she is going . .	nichoobo.	they (*objects*) are going (*mas.*)	nichooibiùn.
it is going (*mas.*) .	nichibi.	they (*objects*) are going (*fem.*)	nichoobitsun.
it is going (*fem.*) .	nichimdila.		

Imperfect.

I was going . .	nichabum *or* nichabaiyum.	we were going.	nichabum *or* nichabaiyum.
thou wast going .	nichoobum.	you were going .	nichoobum.
he was going . .	nichoobum.	they (*human beings*) were going.	nichoobum.
she was going . .	nichoobom.	they (*objects*) were going (*mas.*)	nichoobiùm.
it was going (*mas.*) .	nichibim.	they (*objects*) were going (*fem.*)	nichoobitsùm.
it was going (*fem.*)	nichim dilùm.		

Pluperfect.

Singular.		*Plural.*	
I had gone	niyabum *or* niyabaiyum.	we had gone	nibum.
thou hadst gone	nibum.	you had gone	nibum.
he had gone	nibum.	they (*human beings*) had gone.	nibum.
she had gone	nibom.	they (*objects*) had gone (*mas.*)	nibiùm.
it had gone (*mas.*)	nibim.	they (*objects*) had gone (*fem.*)	nibitsùm.
it had gone (*fem.*)	nimdilùm.		

Perfect.

I went	niyum.	we went	nimen.
thou wentest	nima.	you went	nimen.
he *or* it went	nimi.	they (*human beings*) went.	nimen.
she went	nimo.	they went (*objects*) (*mas.*)	nimiun.
		they went (*objects*) (*fem.*)	nimi.

The perfect also acts as a future præterite, as "I shall have gone, &c., niyum."

Præterite.

Singular.		*Plural.*	
I have gone	niyabá.	we have gone	nibân.
thou hast gone	nibá.	you have gone	nibân.
he has gone	nibai.	they (*human beings*) have gone.	nibân.
she has gone	nibo.	they (*objects*) have gone (*mas.*)	nibiùn.
it has gone (*mas.*)	nibi.	they (*objects*) have gone (*fem.*)	nibitsun.
it has gone (*fem.*)	nimdila.		

Future.

I will go	nichum.	we will go	nichun.
thou wilt go	nichoomá.	you will go	nichoomun.
he *or* it will go	nichi.	they (*human beings*) will go.	nichen.
she will go	nicho.	they (*objects*) will go (*mas.*)	nichoomiùn.
		they (*objects*) will go (*fem.*)	nichimi.

IMPERATIVE.

let me go	nisha.	let us go	nishen.
go thou	ni.	go you	nîn.
let him, her, *or* it go	nish.	let them go	nishen.

CONDITIONAL MOOD.

Present.		*Perfect.*	
I may be going, &c.	nichaba-ábé.	I might have gone, &c.	niyum-ábé.
Imperfect.		*Præterite.*	
I may have been going, &c.	nichabum-ábé.	I should have gone, &c.	niyabá-ábé.
Pluperfect.		*Future.*	
I may *or* would have gone, &c.	niyabum-ábé.	I may go	nichum-ábé.

A future form is given to the verb in all its tenses, either by reduplication, as:

I am about to go	niyuss nichaba.	I was about to go	niyuss nichabum.

or by using the verb *manáss* "to become," as:

I am about to go	niyuss maiyaba.

A verbal substantive is formed by adding the terminations *un* in the singular and *ik, oyki,* &c., in the plural to the infinitive, as:

one who goes	niyuss-*un*.	one who strikes	delluss-*un*.
those who go	niyuss-*ik*.	those who strike	delluss-*shoyhi*.

also in an alternative sense, as:

something to eat	shiyuss-*un*.	something to do	etuss-*un*.

PRONOMINAL VERBS.

A number of verbs have pronominal affixes, without which they cannot be employed, and may be divided into two classes:

CLASS I.

Verbs which change the pronominal affix according to the agent.

	1st pers. sing. I.	2nd pers. sing. THOU.	3rd pers. sing. masc. HE.	3rd pers. sing. fem. SHE.	1st pers. plur. WE.	2nd pers. plur. YOU.	3rd pers. plur. THEY.
to arrive	dushkultuss	dokushkultuss	deshkultuss	doomùshkultuss	dimishkultuss	dámáshkultuss	dùshkultuss.
,, be angry	ámos-manâss	goomos-manâss	imos-manâss	moomos-manâss	mimos-manâss	mámos-manâss	oomos-manâss.
,, be born	dumunuss	dokomunuss	dîmunuss	doomoomunuss	dimêmunuss	dámomunuss	doomunuss.
,, burn (*trans.*)	áskolâss	gooskolâss	eskolâss	mooskolâss	meskolâss	máskolass	ooskolâss.
,, die	aiyruss	gooyruss	îyruss	mooyruss	mîyruss	maiyruss	ooyruss.
,, fall	áwulluss	goowulluss	iwulluss	moowulluss	miwullus	máwulluss	oowullus.
,, be fatigued	áwáruss	goowáruss	iwáruss	moowáruss	miwáruss	máwáruss	oowáruss.
,, fear	ás-goosâss	goos-goosâss	es-goosâss	moos-goosâss	mes-goosâss	más-goosâss	oos-goosâss.
,, forget	till-âluss	till-goluss	till-êluss	till-moluss	till-mêluss	till-mâluss	till-ôluss.
,, be happy	ás-goorâss	goos-goorâss	es-goorâss	moos-goorâss	mes-goorâss	más-goorâss	oos-goorâss.
,, near	daíyaluss	dokoyaluss	dêyaluss	domoyaluss	dimîyaluss	dámaiyaluss	doyaluss.
,, be hurt	ákoluss	gookoluss	ikoluss	mookoluss	mikoluss	mákoluss	ookoluss.
,, receive	áyêyess	gooyêyess	iyêyess	mooyêyess	myêyess	moyêyess	ooyêyess.
,, recognize	aiyênuss	gooyênuss	iyênuss	mooyênuss	miyênuss	maiyênuss	ooyênuss.
,, remember	áset-gunuss	gooset-gunuss	eset-gunuss	mooset-gunuss	meset-gunuss	máset-gunuss	ooset-gunuss.
,, try *or* to see	ásaluss	gosaluss	esaluss	mosaluss	mesaluss	másaluss	osaluss.

cum multis aliis.

A tense of one of these verbs is conjugated as follows:

Singular.			*Plural.*		
I am dying	(jeh)	aiyrichabá.	we are dying	(min)	mîyrichoobân.
thou art dying	(oom)	gooyrichabá.	you are dying	(máh)	maiyrichoobân.
he is dying	(in)	iyrichoobai.	they are dying	(oo)	ooyrichoobân.
she is dying	(in)	mooyrichoobo.			

CLASS II.

Verbs which change the pronominal form according to the object. These verbs supply the place of the passive voice, which is not directly expressed.

	1st pers. sing. ME.	*2nd pers. sing.* THEE.	*3rd pers. sing. masc.* HIM.	*3rd pers. sing. fem.* HER.	*1st pers. plur.* US.	*2nd pers. plur.* YOU.	*3rd pers. plur.* THEM.
to ask	dághârùsuss	dokoghârùsuss	dighârùsuss	domoghârùsuss	dimighârùsuss	dámághârùsuss	doghârùsuss.
,, beat	ádelluss	goodelluss	idelluss	moodelluss	midelluss	mádelluss	oodelluss.
,, buy *or* sell	gushátuss	gushgotuss	gushetuss	gushmootuss	gushmetuss	gushmátuss	gushotuss.
,, count	átsenuss	gootsenuss	itsenuss	mootsenuss	mitsenuss	mátsenuss	ootsenuss.
,, deceive	áfilenuss	goofilenuss	efilenuss	moofilenuss	mifilenuss	máfilenuss	oofilenuss.
,, feed	owshiyess	gooshiyess	yooshiyess	mooshiyess	myooshiyess	mowshiyess	ooshiyess.
,, finish *or* kill	phushátuss	phush-gotuss	phush-etuss	phush-motuss	phush-metuss	phush-mátuss	phush-ôtuss.
,, give	jôyess	gooyess	yooyess	mooyess	myooyess	môyess	ooyess.
,, kill	áskanuss	gooskanuss	eskanuss	mooskanuss	meskanuss	máskanuss	ooskanuss.
,, make	átuss	gôtuss	etuss	mootuss	metuss	mátuss	ôtuss.
,, penetrate	âluss	gôluss	êluss	moluss	myoluss	mowluss	oluss.
,, pull	jáshátuss	jáshgôtuss	jáshetuss	jáshmootuss	jáshmetuss	jáshmátuss	jáshôtuss.
,, search for	áyegooyess	gooye gooyess	iyegooyess	mooyegooyess	miyegooyess	máyegooyess	ooyegooyess.
,, see	áyétsuss	gooyétsuss	iyétsuss	moyétsuss	miyétsuss	máyétsuss	ooyétsuss.
,, send	âruss	gôruss	êruss	môruss	mêruss	mâruss	ôruss.
,, shut up	áfoosuss	goofoosuss	ifoosuss	moofoosuss	mifoosuss	máfoosuss	oofoosuss.
,, cause to sit	owrootuss.	gorootuss	erootuss	morootuss	mirootuss	mowrootuss	orootuss.
,, summon	dâruss	dokoruss	deruss	doomooruss	dimiruss	dámâruss	doruss.
,, take away	átsooyess	gootsooyess	itsooyess	mootsooyess	mitsooyess	mátsooyess	ootsooyess.
,, take out	dáoosuss	dookoosuss	diyoosuss.	doomoosuss	dimyoosuss	dámâ-oosuss	doosuss.
,, take up	áyenuss	gooyenuss	iyenuss	mooyenuss	mîyenuss	máyenuss	ooyenuss.
,, teach	aikinuss	goykinuss	ékinuss	moykinuss	mêkinuss	maiykinuss.	oikinuss.

A tense of one of these verbs is conjugated as follows :—

Singular.

I am teaching thee	(jáh oom) gokyum.
I am teaching him	(jáh in) êkyum.
I am teaching her	(jáh in) moykyum.
I am teaching you	(jáh mâ) maikyum.
I am teaching them	(jáh oo) oykyum.
thou art teaching me . . .	(oomé jeh) aikimá.
thou art teaching him . . .	(oomé in) êkimá.
thou art teaching her . . .	(oomé in) moykimá.
thou art teaching us	(oomé miṇ) mêkimá.
thou art teaching them . . .	(oomé oo) oykimá.
he is teaching me	(iné jeh) aikîmi.
he is teaching thee	(iné oom) goykîmi.
he is teaching her	(iné moy) moykîmi.
he is teaching us	(iné miṇ) mêkîmi.
he is teaching you	(iné mâ) maikîmi.
he is teaching them	(iné oo) oykîmi.
she is teaching me	(iné jeh) aikîmo.
she is teaching thee	(iné oom) goykîmo.
she is teaching him	(iné in) êkimo.
she is teaching us	(iné miṇ) mêkîmo.
she is teaching you	(iné mâ) maikîmo.
she is teaching them	(iné oo) oykîmo.

Plural.

we are teaching thee	(miṇ oom) goykéyun.
we are teaching him	(miṇ in) êkéyun.
we are teaching her	(miṇ in) moykéyun.
we are teaching you	(miṇ mâ) maikéyun.
we are teaching them	(miṇ oo) oykéyun.
you are teaching me	(máh jeh) aikéymun.
you are teaching him	(máh in) êkéymun.
you are teaching her	(máh in) moykéymun.
you are teaching us	(máh miṇ) mêkéymun.
you are teaching them	(máh oo) oykéymun.
they are teaching me	(oo jeh) aikéymun.
they are teaching thee	(oo oom) goykéymun.
they are teaching him	(oo in) êkéymun.
they are teaching her	(oo in) moykéymun.
they are teaching us	(oo miṇ) mêkéymun.
they are teaching you	(oo mâ) maikéymun.

The reflective form "I am teaching myself, &c.," is never used.

A few verbs, such as *delluss* "to strike," are also used in an abstract sense or as compounds, without the pronominal prefix.

A few, such as *yegooyess* "to search for," only employ the prefix when referring to human beings.

NUMERAL VERBS.

A number of verbs have two forms according to the number of the object, as:

to bring (one) .	dit-thuss.
to bring (many) .	doot-thuss.
to count (one) .	itsenuss.
to count (many) .	ootsenuss.
to eat (one) . .	shiyuss.
to eat (many) .	shooyuss.
to finish (one) .	phush-etuss.
to finish (many) .	phush-otuss.
to join (one) .	desmâss.
to join (many) .	dùsmâss.
to make (one) .	etuss.
to make (many) .	otuss.
to open (one) .	dinseruss.
to open (many) .	doonserus.
to play upon (one) instrument.	egaruss.
to play upon (many) instruments.	ogaruss.
to produce (one) .	desmenuss.
to produce (many)	doosmenuss.
to pull (one) .	jashetuss.
to pull (many) .	jashotuss.
to summon (one) .	yegooyess.
to summon (many)	ooyegooyess.
to see (one) .	yétsuss.
to see (many) .	yotsuss.
to cause (one) to sit	erootuss.
to cause (many) to sit	orootuss.
to strike (one) .	delluss.
to strike (many) .	dôluss.
to take up (one) .	yenuss.
to take up (many) .	ooyenuss.
to teach (one) .	ékinuss.
to teach (many) .	oykinuss.
to throw (one) .	phull-etuss.
to throw (many) .	phull-otuss.

and all compounds of *etuss* "to make."

Examples.

I have eaten one apple	Jáh hun báltun *shiyum.*
I have eaten five apples	Jáh tsùndo bálting *shooyum.*

A comparison of the above lists will show that several verbs, such as "to count," "to teach," are both numeral and pronominal.

GENERIC VERBS.

A few verbs have different forms according to the gender of the object, as:

	Masculine form.	*Feminine form.*
to bring	dit-thuss.	doosooyuss.
to eat	shiyuss.	sheyuss.
to take up . . .	yenuss.	gunuss.

Examples.

I took up the gun	Jáh toomákun yenum.
I took up the sword	Jáh guttunchun gunum.
I brought bread	Jáh shùro ditsum.
I brought water	Jáh tsil doosooyum.

THE VERB "TO BE."

The Verb To Be is defective, the only parts being—

Indicative Mood.

Present.

	Singular.	*Plural.*
1.	bâ	bân.
2.	bâ	bân.
3.	bai *mas.*, bo *fem.* } *for human beings.*	bân (*for human beings*).
	bi *mas.*, dila *fem.* } *for animals and objects.*	biùn *mas.*, bitsun *fem.* } *for animals and objects*

Past.

Singular.		*Plural.*	
1.	baiyum.	1.	bum.
2.	bum.	2.	bum.
3.	bum *mas.* } *for human beings.*	3.	bum (*for human beings*).
	bom *fem.* }		biùn *mas.* (*for animals and objects*).
	bim (*for animals and objects*).		dilùm *fem.*

The conditional is formed by the suffix of *ábé,* as in the verb "To Go."

GERUNDS.

baiyum-ùloo	*speaking of oneself*	in my being.
baiyum-etté		on my being.
bumùloo	*speaking of others*	in his, her, *or* their being.
bum-etté		on his, her *or* their being.

The verb MANASS "to become" is used to supply the deficiencies of the above verb.

Both are employed to express possession as in Latin, there being no verb "to have."

I have a good horse	Jâ ápuch tultus hághoorun bi.
My father had a good sword . . .	Jâ ow ipuché tultus guttunchun maim-dilùm.

THE VERB "TO BECOME."

INFINITIVE MOOD.

Present.		*Past.*	
to become . . .	manâss.	to have become . .	manâss dilùm.

Future.

to be about to become . manâss manâss.

PARTICIPLES.

Present.		*Past.*	
becoming . . .	maiyimé.	having become . .	nùmun. / nùma.

Future.

being about to become manâss nùmun.

SUPINES.

possibly to become .	manâss ábé.	must become . .	manâss-awájé.
meet to become .	manâss-maiymi.	ought to become .	manâss-dila.

INDICATIVE MOOD.

Present.

Singular.			*Plural.*		
I am becoming . . .		maiyâba.	we are becoming . .		maiyâbân.
thou art becoming .		maiba.	you are becoming . .		maibân.
he, she, it is becoming	*for human beings* *m.*	maibai.	they are becoming.	*for human beings*	maibân.
	f.	maibo.			
	for animals and objects *m.*	maibi.		*for animals and objects* *m.*	maibiùn.
	f.	maiymdila.		*f.*	maibitsun.

Imperfect.

Singular.		*Plural.*	
I was becoming	maiyâbum.	we were becoming	maiyâbum.
thou wast becoming	maibum.	you were becoming	maibum.
he, she, it was becoming — *for human beings* — *m.*	maibum.	they were becoming — *for human beings*	maibum.
f.	maibom.		
for animals and objects — *m.*	maibim.	*for animals and objects* — *m.*	maibiùm.
f.	maiymdilùm.	*f.*	maiymbitsùm.

Pluperfect.

Singular.		*Plural.*	
I had become	manâbum.	we had become	manoobum.
thou hadst become	manoobum.	you had become	manoobum.
he, she, it had become — *for human beings* — *m.*	manoobum.	they had become — *for human beings*	manoobum
f.	manoobôm.		
for animals and objects — *m.*	manibim.	*for animals and objects* — *m.*	manibiùm.
f.	manùmdilum.	*f.*	manoobitsùm.

Perfect.

Singular.		*Plural.*	
I became	manâm.	we became	manoomun.
thou becamest	manooma.	you became	manoomun.
he, she, it became — *for human beings* — *m.*	manimi.	they became — *for human beings*	manoomun.
f.	manoomo.		
for animals and objects — *m*	manibi.	*for animals and objects* — *m.*	manibiùn.
f.	manimdila.	*f.*	manibitsun.

There is also a pronominal form of the perfect—

Singular.		*Plural.*	
I became	amanum.	we became	mimanoomun.
thou becamest	goomanooma.	you became	mámanoonum.
he, she, it became — *for human beings* — *m.*	imanimi.	they became — *for human beings*	oomanoomun.
f.	moomanoomo.		
for animals and objects — *m.*	imanibi.	*for animals and objects* — *m.*	oomanibiùn.
f.	maním dilùm.	*f.*	oomanoobitsun.

Præterite.

Singular.		*Plural.*	
I have become	manâba.	we have become	manoobân.
thou hast become	manooba.	you have become	manoobân.
he, she, it has become — *for human beings* — *m.*	manoobai.	they have become — *for human beings*	manoobân.
f.	manoobo.		
for animals and objects — *m.*	manibi.	*for animals and objects* — *m.*	manibiùn.
f.	manimdila.	*f.*	manibitsun.

Future.

Singular.		*Plural.*	
I will become	maiyâm.	we will become	maiyân.
thou wilt become	maiyma.	you will become	maimen.
he, she, it will become — *for human beings* — *m.*	maiyimi.	they will become — *for human beings*	maimen.
f.	maiyimo.		
for animals and objects	maiyimi.	*for animals and objects* — *m.*	maiy miùn.
		f.	maiy imi.

Imperative Mood.

become thou	mané.	become ye	manin.
let him, her, it become	manísh.	let them become	manishen.

There is also a pronominal form—

Singular.		*Plural.*	
let me become	amanish.	let us become	mimanishen.
let thyself become	goomanish.	let yourselves become	mámanooshen.
let him, her, it become — *m.*	imanish.	let them become	oomanishen.
f.	moomanish.		

The conditional mood is formed as in the verb NIYUSS "to go" by adding *ábé* to all forms of the indicative.

THE INTERROGATIVE.

The interrogative is formed by adding *á* or by laying a stronger accent on the final syllable of the verb, if it already terminates in *a*, as:

Singular.		*Plural.*	
is he bringing? . . .	dishoobaiy*a*.	are they drinking? . .	mibân*a*.
hast thou brought? . .	dithoom*á*.	were we drinking? . .	miabum*a*.

ADVERBS.

There are a few regular adverbs, such as *áshingai* "carelessly," *tullán* "slowly," &c., but the more usual form is to employ the adjective without adding the termination *un*, or to use *né* or *nùmun* the past participles of the verbs ETUSS "to do" or MANÂSS "to become" with the termination, as:

He came quickly, and proudly (and) bravely drew his sword.	In hùmalkùm dîmi, dâ muchârun *númun* es-dághânùsun *né* guttunch dyoosimi.

Lit. "He quick came, and proud having become, brave having done, sword drew.[1]"

EXAMPLES.

I.

Iron is hard	Chîmer dungun dila.
Lead is heavy	Nâng tsoomun dila.
Gold is heavier than silver . . .	Genish boorî tsùm tsoomun dila.
My horse is swifter than my brother's	Jâ hághoor jâ achooé hághoor tsùm hùmalkùmun bi.
Who is that man?	Iné ámin bai?
Your horse is lame	Oomé hághoor gowoo bi.
I forgot to get it shod	Sârpomùts efoosuss tillàlum.
Remember to do it tomorrow . .	Gosùloo gun chimden iner etuss.
How far is it from here to Nager? .	Bérùmân muttun dila kolêmoo Nagerer.
I went to Bassin to play polo, but when I arrived at the Shawaran I was ill, so I returned.	Jeh Bassiner niyum bùlla delluss gunné, umma, shawârun dushkultum atôloo gális amanum, etté gunné ilji talinum.
I am hungry; give me something to eat	Chumini bâ jâr shiyussun jowoo.
Here are ten water melons . .	Koleh toromo booerisho biùn.
They are too acid to eat. . . .	Shooyesser bùt shùkoorùmisho biùn.
I saw some fine fruit in my brother's garden.	Jâ achooé bussîloo tultus phámùlishoik yotsum.
Have you forgotten to ask him? . .	Oomé iner doghârùsuss tillgoloomâ?
I will beat you if you do not remember.	Akanâ oomé gùsetté owgunoomáké jáh oom goodejum.

You must go there . . . . . Oom eué niyuss áwâjé.

I want to go, but I am too busy. . Niyuss dila, akoorùmunké dùrô bùt dila.

will send my foster brother in my place. Ooshum achoowun jâ bâgo erchum seyabá.

Yesterday one man "a hawk on a walnut tree is perched" (*lit.* fallen) said then I went and there two men caused to sit. Night to become till they sat, afterwards they came, and to sleep time on its becoming light having taken I went with me six men I took. Gently making near it we went, long time we sat. Time from one I sent, that man near it having gone carelessly rose. On his rising that hawk alert made to so much (that) having flown he went. I to the boy "a torch should be, (that) having looked if elsewhere where on the trees (it) has perched," said. Those lads "a torch is not" said, on that silently having come (home) I slept.

Sáboor hiné bashân tillyetté wullibi senimi, etôloo jeh niyum nâ elleh altun siss orootum. Shâm manâss kâshinger hrootoomun, itsyeté doomun, dâ gùchêyuss ken manâssùloo gâring nookun niyum ákhât mishindoowân siss ootsooyum. Jool echoomé ipuch nimen, tooshâr kenum hrootoomun. Kenum tsùm hinyeté érum, iné siss ipuch nî áshingai dâl manimi. Iné dâl manâssetté essé bâsha lel etimi tairùmâner thur nidili nimi. Jáh jotoomùtser hulching manâss dila, bârenin huzar dâkùloo ámùloo tomun etté wulljia senum. Ooé jotoomutsé hulching ápih senoomun. Etté tsùm chookné dâ gùchêyum.

Translation.

Yesterday a certain man told me that a hawk had perched on a walnut tree, on which I went and caused two men to sit there. They sat till nightfall, after which they came, and as soon as it was sleeping time I took lights and went, taking six men with me. We approached gently and sat a long time. After a time I sent one man, who having approached climbed up carelessly. The hawk was alarmed by his climbing up so that it flew away. I told the boys they should get a torch and see if the hawk had perched somewhere else on the trees. The boys said there was no torch, so being unable to say anything I went home to sleep.

2.

Sáboor jeh ishkârer niyum, sùndo siss jâkât doobum. Jâkât áltáts bâzishoyki toomákun bim. Etsé bâzisho hun serunké, áltáts táljo, dâ mishindo gowoo donimiyun. Itsyeté iské sissé kât hághoorké bâzisho hâhler ootsooyum, dâ hikùm ooé jeh etté gâher niyum. Phâlis kenum tsùm donun girîk yotsoomun. Kaṇsh maiyimi ipuch nimen hun ooyùm iltorengé giriyun dellum. Hín sissuné essé nîun hâh yekal nimi. Jáh elleh mùm dâ matân dishuner niyum elleh deshkultum-etté tupp manimi ooyùm bùnun yâré gùchoomun. Yettùm gùntsùloo phâlisun bêsko thânùm chishun-etté nimen dâ phâlis donun girîk yotsoomun. Elleh bârenussùloo sirgâné sissik etté gâh-ùloo joochoobum jáh yotsum, umma ooé yon-uss owlenoomun miṇ mes-goosoomun huzâr dùshmoyok maimen etté-gunné hâh yekal nimen.

Translation.

Yesterday I went out hunting, and five men came with me. I had two hawks and a gun with me. The hawks caught one hare, two pigeons and six partridges. After that I sent three men home with my horse and the hawks and went up the valley with the others. After a short time we saw a herd of wild goats. We crept close, and I shot one wild goat with large horns. One man having taken it up went towards home. I went on to a further place and on night coming on we slept under a big rock. The next day we ascended a very steep (*lit.* little-sloping) and high mountain, and saw a small herd of wild goats. While looking at them I saw some men coming along the valley, but was not able to recognize them, and fearing lest they should be enemies we went towards home.

3.

Koolto taiy khut niyabum bârenáké hin sissun tòmunetté yetté doosoobum, tairùmâner taiy dullum hín sissun gharichoomé dîmi ipuch dî dogharùsimi "oom yetté bess doosoobâ ?"

Iné senimi "bess bessun munna dila." Senussùloo dâ iné senimi "áwá, jáh munna etaba jâ koleh oomé be bi." Iné senimé "shooa, jeh yetté doosaba bareyum bessun echoomáké, joo." Etté senuss-etté yârùm iné multsimi.

Multsâssùloo yettùm inéke multsimi tairùmâner yârùm ine yettum iné yekal daiyok dellimi. Etsé daiyo-tsùm hun dunnun delluss-kât yettùm iné iyetusetté yemi.

Yeyessùloo yettùm inéké yâré dîmi, dî inéké dunnuné iné iyetusùloo dellimi. Essé delluss-kât phâlisun iyetus khárimi, mooltun dîmi, tairùmâner etté puchùm khoté puchùm siss doo phut otoomun.

Etté bùshaié Chârboo elleh bum oyon gutti nùmá Tarangfah ipuch nimen. Iné Tarangfáh ooé ustum etuss owlenimi.

Iné Tarangfah ké nîa Wuzeeré ipuch nimen, niyussùloo Wuzeer hâhle ápum. Wuzeeré supooyârer dogharùsoomun "Wuzeer um nibaiya ?"

Supooyâr ooer senoomun "Wuzeer koleh ápai Thum ipuch nibai;" Ellémoo gharichoomé Thum ipuch nimen.

Thumké Wuzeeré oltâlik gutti nùma bum, bârenumké gharichoomé bùt sissik doomun, opuch joochumké áltun sissiké mooltun dîbùllum.

Thumké Wuzeer doghârùsoomun, kooé be manoomun. Ellémoo Tarangfah áwul-tsùm âkhirer oyon chegah etimi: tairùmâner Thumke Wuzeeré ustum né oltâlik etté hùnum oyonoomun.

Translation.

To-day I had gone down the valley and saw a man who was climbing (*lit.* going out) on a tree, so that a man came calling up the valley and having come close asked him, "Why, have you climbed up ?"

He said, "why, what is forbidden ?" On his saying this he (the other one) also said, "Yes, I had forbidden it; what business have you here ?" (*lit.* what is to you in this of mine ?) He said, "Well, I have climbed up, I will see what you can do. Come." On his saying this the one below abused him.

On his abusing, the one above also gave abuse, so that the one below threw stones towards the one above. From throwing those stones one stone hit the head of the one above.

On being hit (*lit.* receiving) the one above came down; having come, he also struck him (the other) on the head with a stone. That one with beating had his head a little wounded, and blood came, so that men, having come from this side and that side, separated them.

The Charboo of the village was there, and all having got together went to the Tarangfah. The Tarangfah was not able to settle the case (*lit.* to make judgment).

The Tarangfah having taken them went to the Wuzeer. On going, the Wuzeer was not at home. They asked the Wuzeer's family, "Where has the Wuzeer gone ?"

The family told them, "The Wuzeer is not here; he has gone to the Thum." They telling it (to one another) went to the Thum.

The Thum and the Wuzeer were both together and saw many men come talking; (when) they came near (they saw that) two men were bleeding. The Thum and and Wuzeer asked them "What has happened ?" They enquired from first to last the whole (circumstances) of the Tarangfah, so that the Thum and Wuzeer having awarded judgment fined (*lit.* took goods from) both.

VOCABULARY.

All pronominal verbs, nouns, &c., are given in the 3rd person, and marked (*pron.*)

Numeral verbs are given in the singular and marked (*num.*)

Some substantives are alike in both numbers, but the plural forms of a few are omitted.

The plural forms of all the adjectives are omitted.

To be able ...	ùlenuss.
Above ...	mudull.
To abuse ...	multsâss.
Account ...	chegah *f.*
Acid ...	shùkoorùm.
Active ...	hùmalkùm.
To advise ...	kanow etuss.
After ...	ilji.
Afterwards ...	its-yeté.
Again ...	dâ.
Air ...	ghol *f.*
Alert ...	lel.
All ...	oyon.
Alongside of ...	ilut.
Although ...	ákhanâ.
Always ...	hamêsh.
And ...	dâ, nâ.
Anger ...	imoskish *f.* (*pron.*)
Angry ...	imos (*pron.*)
To be angry ...	imos manâss (*pron.*)
Another ...	thùm.
Another time ...	yetùm dum.
Answer ...	joowâb.
To answer ...	joowâb etuss.
Ant ...	kòn *m.*, koyo *pl.*
Anxiety ...	sumba *f.*
Anxious ...	goonêsh.
Apart ...	îtsé.
Apple ...	bált, bálting *pl.*
Apricot ...	joo, jông *pl.*
Arm ...	ishuck *f.* (*pron.*), ishuckichung *pl.*
Arms (weapons) ...	samân *f.*
Army ...	hol *m.*
To arrive ...	deshkultuss (*pron.*)
Arrow ...	hùnts *m.*, hùntsé *pl.*
To ask ...	dighârùsuss (*pron.*)
To ask for ...	doomaruss.
Ass ...	jakùn *m.*, jakoyo *pl.*
Aunt (father's sister) ...	intsoo *f.* (*pron.*)
,, (mother's sister) ...	imi *f.* (*pron.*)
Autumn ...	duttoo *f.*

Avalanche	...	shál
Away	...	phut
Back	...	iwuldus *m.* (*pron.*)
Bad	...	ghonaikish.
Barley	...	hurri *f.*
Bat	...	tatâpul *m.*, tatâpulsho *pl.*
To be	...	manâss.
Bean	...	rabòng *m.*
Bear	...	yâṇ *m.*, yâmùts *pl.*
Beard	...	ingyi *f.* (*pron.*)
To beat	...	idelluss (*pron.*), delluss.
Beautiful	...	tultus.
Because	...	besské, bessunké.
To become	...	manâss.
Before	...	yèr, sor.
To begin	...	soormunuss.
Behind	...	ilji.
Belly	...	yool *m.*, yooling *pl.* (*pron.*)
Beloved	...	shildâto.
Below	...	sirgân.
To betray	...	efilenuss.
Betrothal	...	hâr *f.*
Between	...	mákùch.
Bird	...	bring *m.*, bringants *pl.*
Bitter	...	ghákowm.
Black	...	mâtùm.
Blind	...	shon.
Blood	...	mùltun *f.*
To blow	...	phoo etuss.
Blue	...	aiyesh shikum.
Blunt	...	phut.
Body	...	idim *m.*, idimisho *pl.* (*pron.*)
Bone	...	iltin *m.*, iltinjo *pl.* (*pron.*)
To be born	...	dîmunuss (*pron.*)
Both	...	oltâlik.
Boundary	...	dir *f.*, diring *pl.*
Bow	...	amé *f.*, jjaming *pl.*
Boy	...	hillus *m.*, hilesho *pl.*
Brain	...	mutto *f.*
Brass	...	shikurk rîl *f.*
Brave	...	es-dághânùs (*pron.*)
Bread	...	shóró *m.*
To break	...	yelluss.
Breath	...	hish *f.*
Brick	...	dishtik *m.*, dishtikisho *pl.*
Bride	...	garôni *f.*
Bridegroom	...	garôno *m.*
Bridle	...	tabung *f.*
Bridge	...	bush *m.*, bushunts *pl.*
To bring	...	dit-thuss (*num.*), doosooyuss.

Broad	... duldullùm.
To be broken	... khấruss, gulluss.
Brooch	... rîl *f.*, rîlisho *pl.*
Brother	... echoom., echookon *pl.* (*pron.*)
Brown	... gooro.
Reddish-brown	... soormai.
Bull	... her *m.*, herants *pl.*
Bullet	... deedoo *m.*, deedoomùts *pl.*
To burn (*trans.*)	... eskolâss (*pron.*)
To burn (*intrans.*)	... golâss.
But	... umma.
Butterfly	... bitun *m.*, bitaiyo *pl.*
To buy	... gushetuss (*pron.*)
By	... tsùm (*suffixed.*)
To call	... kow etuss.
Calling	... kow *f.*
Camel	... oont *m.*
Care	... shung *f.*
Careless	... áshingai.
Cattle (*collectively*)	... booer.
Charm	... toomer *f.*, toomeri *pl.*
Cheek	.... imookùsh *f.*, imookeyùng *pl.* (*pron.*)
Chin	... isun *m.*, isunisho *pl.* (*pron.*)
Circle	... bidiro-kishi *m.*
Clarionet	... sùrnai *m.*, tooták *m.*
Clean	... praiyish.
Clever	... ilchikooin (*pron.*)
Clothes	... guttoo *m.*, guttong *pl.*
Cloth goods	... hùnum *f.*
Cloud	... khorùn *m.*
Cock	... bîro kerkâmùts *m.*
Cold	... chagoorùm.
Colour	... rung *f.*
To come	... jooyess.
Confidence	... buchik *f.*
Copper	... bârdùm rîl *f.*
Corner	... shùti *f.*, shùting *pl.*
Four-cornered	... wálto shùting.
Corpse	... gootis *m.*, gootisho *pl.*
Cough	... kùs *f.*
To count	... itsenuss (*pron. num.*)
Courage	... bâghdoori *f.*
Cousin	... echoo *m.*, iyus *f.*
Cow	... booah *f.*, booants *pl.*
To creep	... kâṇsh manâss.
Crooked	... gunder.
Crow	... gân *m.*, gaiyo *pl.*
Cultivation	... bùshai *f.*
Custom	... chôl *f.*
To dance	... giretuss.

Dancing	...	nut *f.*
Dangerous	...	náro.
Darkness	...	tootung *f.*
Daughter	...	êy *f.*, êyùshunts *pl.* (*pron.*)
Daughter-in-law	...	ikhâkin *f.* (*pron.*)
Day	...	gùnts *f.*
Mid-day	...	dogoyi *f.*
To-day	...	koolto.
Deaf	...	ghùt.
Death	...	mârun *f.*
Deceit	...	nefilen *f.*
Deceitful	...	gultung-kish.
To deceive	...	efilenuss (*pron.*)
Destitute	...	tárák.
Dew	...	pùnts *f.*
To die	...	îyruss (*pron.*)
Different	...	fhâr.
Difficult	...	mùshkil.
Dirty	...	trek.
Disposition	...	itsir *f.* (*pron.*)
To divide	...	itsé etuss.
Divorce	...	phut.
To do	...	etuss.
Dog	...	hook *m.*, hookaiy *pl.*
Door	...	hing *f.*, hingeng *pl.*
Down	...	khut.
Dreadful	...	bághèrk.
Dream	...	yooljî *f.*, yooljing *pl.* (*pron.*)
To drink	...	minâss.
Drum	...	dudung *m.*, dudungisho *pl.*
Dry	...	bùm.
Eagle	...	germoon *m.*, germoyo *pl.*
Ear	...	iltùmál *f.*, iltùmáling *pl.* (*pron.*)
Earth	...	tik *f.*
The earth	...	bîrdi *f.*
Earthquake	...	boonyul *f.*
East (sunrise)	...	jill.
Easy	...	sucho.
To eat	...	shiyuss (*num.*), sheyuss.
Eclipse	...	grân *m.*
Edge	...	ing, ingisho *pl.*
Egg	...	ting *m.*, tingaiyo *pl.*
Elbow	...	isùsùn *m.*, isùsùnisho *pl.* (*pron.*)
Elephant	...	husto *m.*, hustomùts *pl.*
Empty	...	kùsh.
Enemy	...	dùshmun *m.*
To enter	...	giess.
To envy	...	koos etuss.
Envy	...	koos *f.*
Equal	...	bubber.

Evening ...	sáboor *f.*
Ever ...	béshál.
Everybody ...	oyon.
Everything ...	oyon.
Ewe ...	bellis *m.*, bellisho *pl.*
Except ...	bágèr.
Eye ...	ilchin *m.*, ilchinùts *pl.* (*pron.*)
Eyebrow ...	iltâns *m.* (*pron.*)
Eyelash ...	irpùr *m.* (*pron.*)
Face ...	ishkil *f.* (*pron.*)
Family ...	supooyâr *m.*, hùmooyin *m.*
To fall ...	iwulluss (*pron.*)
Far ...	muttun.
Fat (*subs.*) ...	biss *m.*
Fat (*adj.*) ...	dághânùs.
Father ...	yoow *m.*, yootsáro *pl.* (*pron.*)
Father ... (*as a form of address*)	aiyah, (*as a mark of respect*) bábá.
To be fatigued ...	iwáruss (*pron.*)
Fault ...	tis *f.*
Fear ...	bîietai *f.*
To fear ...	esgoosâss (*pron.*)
Feather ...	pergoo *f.*, pergoochung *pl.*
To feed ...	yooshiyess (*pron.*)
Female ...	sōntch *m.*, sōntchomùts *pl.*
Fig ...	phâg.
Fight ...	birgah *f.*
Finger ...	emish *m.*, emishiunts *pl.* (*pron.*)
To finish ...	phushetuss (*pron. num.*)
Fire ...	phoo *f.*, phoming *pl.*
First ...	yerkomâs.
Fish ...	choomoo *m.*, choomoomùts *pl.*
Flock (of birds) ...	brin *m.*
Flour ...	dághôn *f.*
Flower ...	askoor *f.*, askooring *pl.*
Flute ...	gubbi *m.*, gubbiunts *pl.*
To fly (as a bird) ...	thur delluss.
Following ...	its-yeté.
Foot ...	yootis *m.*, yooting *pl.* (*pron.*)
For ...	gunné (*suffixed.*)
To forget ...	tillêluss (*pron.*)
Forgetfulness ...	till *f.*
Fort ...	kun *m.*, kununts *pl.*
Foster kindred ...	ooshum.
Fowl ...	kerkâmùts *m.*, kerkâmùsho *pl.*
Fox ...	loyṇ *m.*, loyṇmùts *pl.*
Friend ...	shùgoolo *m.*
Friendship ...	shùgoolâr *f.*
From ...	tsùm (*suffixed.*)
Frost ...	gámoo *m.*
Fruit ...	phámùl *m.*, phámùlisho *pl.*

Full	...	shuck.
Fur	...	bishkeh *f.*
Garden	...	bussi *f.*, bussisung *pl.*
Generous	...	es-shokùm (*pron.*), *lit.* wide-hearted.
Gentle	...	jool.
To get	...	iyêyess (*pron.*)
Girl	...	dussin *f.*, dussiwunts *pl.*
To give	...	yooyess (*pron.*)
To go	...	niyuss.
To go out	...	doosuss.
Goats (*collectively*)	...	hooyess *m.*
He-goat	...	huldun *m.*
She-goat	...	sigir *m.*, sigirisho *pl.*
Wild goat	...	giri *m.*, girîk *pl.*
God	...	dummun.
Gold	...	genish *f.*
Good	...	tultus.
Grape	...	gaing *f.*, gainging *pl.*
Grandfather	...	epi *m.* (*pron.*)
Grandmother	...	epi *f* (*pron.*)
Grass	...	shikah *f.*, shikaing *pl.*
Gratitude	...	minadâri *f.*
Great	...	ooyùm.
Green	...	jùt shikum.
Grief	...	pidik.
To grieve	...	pidik manâss.
Gun	...	toomák *m.*, toomákishs *pl.*
Gunpowder	...	milliung *f.*
Hail	...	aiyer *m.*
Hair	...	igoyiung *f.* (*pron.*)
Half	...	tráng.
Hand	...	irîng *f.*, irîngchung *pl.* (*pron.*)
Right hand	...	doyom *f.*
Left hand	...	gôm *f.*
Handle	...	yun *m.*, yununts *pl.*
Happiness	...	shùriâr *f.*
Happy	...	shùriêsh.
To be happy	...	esgoorâss (*pron.*)
Hard	...	dung.
Hare	...	ser *m.*, serunts *pl.*
Hatred	...	gut *f.*
Hawk	...	gutchunch *m.*, gutchunchisho *pl.*
Head	...	iyetis *m.*, iyetisho *pl.* (*pron.*)
To hear	...	dêyaluss (*pron.*)
Heart	...	es *m.* (*pron.*)
The Heavens	...	aiyesh *f.*
Heavy	...	tsoom.
Heel	...	ighân (*pron.*)
Hen	...	sōntch kerkâmùts *m.*
Herd	...	dòn *m.*

Here ... koleh.
High ... thânùm.
To hit (as with a gun or a stone) yeyess.
Hollow ... pùsh.
Hope ... duck *f.*
Horse ... hághoor *m.*, hághoorints *pl.*
Horse-shoe ... sârpo *f.*, sârpomùts *pl.*
Hot ... guroom.
House ... hâh *f.*, hâhichung *pl.*
How ... beltùm.
How many ... bérùmân.
How much ... bérùm.
Humble ... ashâtoo.
Hunger ... chum *f.*
Hungry ... chumini.
Hundred ... tah *f.*
To hunt ... ishkur etuss.
To be hurt ... ikoluss (*pron.*)
Husband ... mooyer *m.*, mooyerisho *pl.* (*pron.*)

Ice ... gámoo *m.*
Idle ... butt.
If ... ákân, huzâr.
To be ignorant ... ákhenuss.
To be ill ... gális manâss.
Illness ... gális *m.*
Independent ... es-goorùm (*pron.*)
Industrious ... dùrùskùn.
Infant ... jotis *m*, jotùmùts *pl.*
Instead of ... dishùloo.
Iron ... chîmer *f.*

Judgment ... ustum *f.*
To join ... desmâss (*num.*)

Kettledrum ... dâmul *m.*, dâmulisho *pl.*
To kick ... dapiski delluss.
To kill ... eskanuss (*pron.*)
King ... thum *m.*, thummo *pl.*
King's son ... gùshpoor *m.*, gùshpoorisho *pl.*
Knee ... idoomùs *m.*, idoomùsisho *pl.* (*pron.*)
Knife ... chùr *m.*, chùrunts *pl.*
To know ... henuss.

Lame ... gowoo.
Language ... bâsh *f.*, bâshisho *pl.*
To laugh ... ghasâss.
Lead ... nâng *f.*
To learn ... henuss.
To leave ... phut etuss.
Leg ... bussin *f.*, bussining *pl.*

Level	...	bubber.
Lie	...	ghultung *f.*
Life	...	jî *f.*
Light (*subs.*)	...	sung *f.*
Light (*adj.*)	...	hùmalkùm.
Lightning	...	tumlum *f.*
Like	...	joowun.
Line	...	kishi *m.* (*a line of men*), jin *f.*
Lip	...	îyl *f.*, îyling *pl.* (*pron.*)
A little	...	phâlis.
Liver	...	ekin *f.*, ekining *pl.* (*pron.*)
Loins	...	eshting (*pron.*)
Long	...	goosunùm.
Long (*in sound*)	...	birángo.
To look at	...	bârenuss.
Love	...	shool *f.*
To love	...	shool etuss.
Low	...	chutt.
Maid	...	choomùtker *f.*, choomùtkersho *pl.*
To make	...	etuss (*pron. num.*)
Male	...	biro *m.*, biromùts *pl.*
Man	...	siss *m.*, sissik *pl.*; hir *m.*, hirikunts *pl.*
Young man	...	châkùr *m.*, châkùrsho *pl.*
Old man	...	jut *m.*, jutoo *pl.*
Mare	...	bowom *m.*, bowomisho *pl.*
Marriage	...	gèr *f.*
To measure	...	ighunuss.
Meat	...	chup *f.*
Medicine	...	mili *m.*, milimùts *pl.*
Melon	...	gowun, booer *m.*
Mid-day	...	dogoyi *f.*
Midnight	...	tráng thup *f.*
Milk	...	mámoo *f.*
Mill	...	yeng *m.*, yengisho *pl.*
Miserly	...	es chedùm (*pron.*), *lit.* narrow-hearted.
Mist	...	koorts *f.*
Moon	...	hálunts *m.*
New moon	...	tsai *m.*
Month	...	ishah *f.*
Half month	...	tunts *f.*
Morning	...	sordi *b.*
Moth	...	pirun *m.*
Mother	...	imi *f.*, imitsáro *pl.* (*pron.*)
Mother (*as a form of address*)	...	zùzi, mámán̲.
Mountain	...	chish *m.*, chishming *pl.*
Mouse	...	girkis *m.*, girkisho *pl.*
Mouth	...	ikhát *f.*, ikháting *pl.* (*pron.*)
Much	...	bùt.
So much	...	tairùm.

This much	...	ákoorùm.
Mud	...	tághâ *f.*
Mulberry	...	birunsh, biráng *pl.*
Muscle	...	girkis *m.* (*literally* a mouse).
Music	...	harîp *f.*, harîping *pl.*
Must	...	awájè.
Nail (finger)	...	yoorî *m.*, yooriunts *pl.* (*pron.*)
Name	...	îk *f.*, îkin *pl.* (*pron.*)
Narrow	...	thároпum, chedùm.
Near	...	ásir (*for objects*), ipuch (*for persons*) (*pron.*)
Neck	...	esh *m.* (*pron.*)
Nephew	...	îyi *m.*, îyoo *pl.* (*pron.*)
Never	...	khus bé.
New	...	tōsh.
Niece	...	êy *f.*, êyùshunts *pl.* (*pron.*)
Night	...	thup *f.*
No	...	bé.
Nobody	...	menké bé.
None	...	besská bé.
North	...	shimâl.
Nose	...	imoopùsh *m.*, imoopùsho *pl.* (*pron.*)
Not	...	ápi, ápai, ápo.
Nothing	...	bessun ápi.
Now	...	mootoo.
Of	...	é (*suffixed.*)
Old	...	mên.
On	...	eté (*suffixed.*)
One (person)	...	kùts.
Only	...	thih, khus.
Open	...	bâto.
To open	...	dinseruss (*num.*)
Oppression	...	zùlum *f.*
Or	...	yah.
To order	...	hùkum etuss.
Other	...	thùm.
Out	...	holé (*suffixed.*)
Over	...	yet, uté, utùm (*suffixed.*)
Owl	...	hoo *m.*, hooisho *pl.*
To be pained	...	ikholuss (*pron.*)
Palace	...	táng *f.*, tángichun *pl.*
Palm (of the hand)	...	ituttus (*pron.*)
Partridge	...	gowoo *m.*
Peach	...	chùkder, chùkdering *pl.*
Pear	...	pêshoo, pêshoomùts *pl.*
To penetrate	...	êluss (*pron.*)
Perhaps	...	maiymi.
To permit	...	hùkum etuss.
Pigeon	...	tál *m.*, táljo *pl.*

Pity	...	jâk *f.*
Place	...	dish *f.*
To place	...	osuss.
Play	...	gireli *f.*
To play (a game)	...	girâtuss.
To play (on an instrument)	...	egaruss (*num.*)
Pleasant tasting	...	ooyum.
To please	...	shùriâr etuss.
To be pleased	...	esgoorâss (*pron.*)
Plough	...	hersh *f.*, herisho *pl.*
Point	...	ittun *m.*, ittunisho *pl.*
Praise	...	tikâni *f.*
Pride	...	digásherkish *f.*
To produce	...	desmenuss (*num.*)
To promise	...	kât etuss.
Proud	...	muchâr, digásher.
To pull	...	jáshetuss (*pron. num.*)
Quail	...	ghoon *m.*, ghooyo *pl.*
Quality	...	tákpah *f.*
Quarrel	...	chull *f.*
Queen	...	gánish *f.* gánunts *pl.*
Quick	...	hùmalkùm.
Rain	...	herált *f.*
Ram	...	kárêlo *m.*, kárêlomùts *pl.*
To read	...	senuss.
Ready	...	rull.
To receive	...	iyêyess (*pron.*)
To recognize	...	iyênuss (*pron.*)
To reconcile	...	desmâss (*num.*)
Red	...	bârdùm.
Relation	...	ùskoon *m.*, ùskoyo *pl.*
Relationship	...	ùskooni *f.*
To remember	...	eset gunuss (*pron.*)
Remembrance	...	gùsilo *m.*
To return	...	talinuss.
Reward	...	goorin.
Rice	...	bron *m.*
Rich	...	gummus.
Ringlets	...	gîkyoo *m.*
To rise	...	diêess, dâl manâss.
River	...	sindah *f.*, sindáming *pl.*
Road	...	gun *f.*, guning *pl.*
Rock	...	bùn *m.*. bùnisho *pl.*
Roof	...	tesh *f.*, teshing *pl.*
Rope	...	gushk *m.*, gushko *pl.*
Rotten	...	mên.
Round	...	bidiro.
Rough	...	jecherum.
To run	...	gâtsuss, haiyetuss.

Sad	... sùpùsh.
Saddle	... tilyun *f.*
Sand	... soh *f.*
Sarcasm	... chùdo *f.*
To say	... gharâss.
To scatter	... shellâss.
To search	... yegooyess.
To search for	... iyegooyess (*pron.*)
To see	... iyétsuss (*pron.*), yétsuss (*num.*)
Seed	... boh *f.*
To sell	... gushetuss (*pron.*)
To send	... éruss (*pron.*)
To separate	... itsé etuss.
Servant	... shedder *m.*, sheddershoo *pl.*
Shadow	... yel *f.*
Shame	... shiker *f.*
Sharp	... hirùm.
Sheep (*collect.*)	... belisho.
Wild sheep	... yetul *m.*
Short	... kùt.
Shoulder	... ipoing *f.*, ipoingisho *pl.* (*pron.*)
To shout	... icher etuss.
Shut	... tum.
To shut	... ifoosuss (*pron.*)
Side	... king *m.*, kingen *pl.*
On this side	... kitti.
On that side	... itti.
Alongside	... îlut.
Sigh	... hâṇsh *f.*
Silent	... chook.
Silk	... chooshi, sikkim *f.*
Silver	... boori *f.*
Sinew	... jowah *m.*, jowámùts *pl.*
To sing	... gáring etuss.
Singing	... gur *f.*
Sister	... iyus *f.* iyustáro *pl.* (*pron.*)
To sit	... hrootuss.
To cause to sit	... erootus (*pron.*)
Skin	... butt *f.*, butting *pl.*
Sky	... aiyesh *f.*
Slave	... siss.
Sleep	... dáng *f.*
To sleep	... gùchêyuss.
Sloping	... bêsko.
Slow	... butt.
Slowly	... tullân.
Small	... jot, echagon.
Smoke	... tuss *f.*
Smooth	... shigishùm.
Snake	... tòl *m.*, tòlunts *pl.*
Sneeze	... thiùṇ *f.*
Snow	... gé *f.*

Soft	...	hililùm.
Some	...	phookun.
Somebody	...	menun.
Something	...	bessun.
Son	...	îyi, *m.*, îyoo *pl.* (*pron.*)
Son-in-law	...	erer *m.* (*pron.*)
Sorrow	...	pidik *f.*
Soul	...	jî *f.*
Sound	...	icher *f.*, ichering *pl.*
South	...	janoob.
Spade	...	bel, booi *f.*
Spoon	...	dôri, kuppun *m.*
Spring	...	gároo *f.*
To stand	...	tsut diêess.
Star	...	ási *m.*, ásimùts *pl.*
Stern	...	dowom.
Stone	...	dun *m.*, daiyo *pl.*
Storm	...	tofân *f.*
Straight	...	tsun.
Straw	...	kùrk *f.*
Strength	...	shát *f.*
Strong	...	shátillo.
Stupidity	...	owdoomunuss *m.* (*lit.* inability to produce.)
Suitable	...	yeshki.
Summer	...	shini *f.*
To summon	...	deruss (*pron.*), yegooyess (*num.*)
Sun	...	sah *m.*
Sweet	...	gusherum.
Swift	...	hirùm.
To swim	...	thum delluss.
Sword	...	guttunch *f.*, guttunchtâng *pl.*
Tail	...	isùmál *m.* (*pron.*)
To take	...	tsùyess.
To take away	...	itsooyess (*pron.*)
To take hold	...	donuss.
To take out	...	diyoosuss (*pron.*)
To take up	...	iyenuss (*pron.*), yenuss, gunuss (*num.*)
To teach	...	ékinuss (*pron. num.*)
To tell	...	senuss.
Temper	...	itsir *f.*, itsiring *pl.* (*pron.*)
That one (*applied to animals or objects*)	...	ess *m.*, et *f.*
That one (*applied to human beings*)	...	in.
That (*relat.*)	...	be.
Then	...	etôloo.
There	...	elleh.
Therefore	...	khoté gun.
Thick	...	dághânùs.
Thin	...	dikootùm.

To think	...	sumba etuss.
Thirst	...	ooyooṇyâr *f.*
Thirsty	...	ooṇyooṇyooṇ.
This one (*applied to animals or objects*)	...	khos *m.*, khot *f.*
This one (*applied to human beings*)	...	kin.
Thought	...	goonêsh *f.*
Throat	...	book *m.*, bookunts *pl.*
To throw	...	phull etuss (*num.*), wushiyuss.
To throw away	...	lip etuss.
To throw down	...	khut wushiyuss.
Thumb	...	láfoot *m.*, láfootisho *pl.*
Thunder	...	tingtong *f.*
Thus	...	ákil, taiyi.
Till	...	kâshinger, tung.
Time	...	ken *f.*
Timid	...	es-goosâs (*pron.*)
Tin	...	kalai *f.*
To	...	er (*suffixed.*)
Toe	...	emish *m.*, emishiunts *pl.* (*pron.*)
Together	...	gutti.
To-morrow	...	chimden, jimel.
The day after to-morrow		hipùlto.
Tongue	...	yoomùs (*pron.*)
Tooth	...	imé *m.* (*pron.*)
Touch	...	jook etuss.
Towards	...	yekál (*suffixed.*)
Tree	...	tòm *f.*, tòming *pl.*
Truth	...	tsun *f.*
To try	...	esaluss (*pron.*)
Ugly	...	ghonaikish.
To be unable	...	owlenuss.
Uncle (father's brother)		oyùm bábá (*older*), echegon bábá (*younger*) *m.*
Uncle (mother's brother)		iṇgoo *m.* (*pron.*), nunné (*form of address.*)
Under	...	yâr (*suffixed.*)
Unless	...	bagèr.
Upright	...	tsut.
Valley	...	bârsil *f.*, taiy *f.*
Vein	...	báris *m.*, bárisho *pl.*
Very	...	bùt.
Very well	...	tultus.
Village	...	girum *f.*, girumisho *pl.*, bùshai *f.*
Vine	...	goorbi *f.*, goorbing *pl.*
Voice	...	kow *f.*, kowunts *pl.*
Vulture	...	gussir *m.*, gussirisho *pl.*
Wall	...	bull *f.*, bulling *pl.*
Walnut	...	tilli *f.*, tillung *pl.*

Walnut tree ...	bul *f.*, bulling *pl.*
Water ...	tsil *f.*, tsilming *pl.*
Weak ...	áshâto.
Weakness ...	ásháteyâr *f.*
To weep ...	heruss.
West (sunset) ...	boor.
Wet ...	hághùm.
What ...	bessun, be.
Wheat ...	gùr *f.*
When (*interrog.*) ...	béshál.
When (*relat.*) ...	kenùloo.
Where (*interrog.*) ...	ámùloo, ám.
Which one (*applied to animals or objects*)	ámis *m.*, ámit *f.*
Which one (*applied to human beings*) ...	ámin.
Whip ...	thùr *f.*, thùryung *pl.*
White ...	boorùm.
Who (*interrog.*) ...	ámin.
Why ...	bess.
Wide ...	shokùm.
Widow ...	gyoos *f.*, gyoosho *pl.*
Widower ...	gyoos *m.*, gyoosho *pl.*
Wife ...	yoos *f.*, yoosindáro *pl.* (*pron.*)
Wind ...	tish *f.*
Window ...	dárî *f.*, dárîmichung *pl.*
Wine ...	mell *f.*
Wing ...	gullgi *f.*, gullgichung *pl.*
Winter ...	baiy *f.*
Wisdom ...	ilchinkoon *m.* (*pron.*)
Wise ...	âkil.
Wish ...	ruck *f.*
To wish ...	ruck etuss.
With ...	kât (*suffixed.*)
Within ...	ùloo, lé. (*suffixed.*)
Without ...	á (*prefixed.*)
Woman ...	gùs *f.*, gùshiunts *pl.*
Old woman ...	jut *f.*, jutoo *pl.*
Wood ...	gáshil *m.*, gáshiling *pl.*
Wool ...	sheh *f.*, shehmichung *pl.*
Work ...	dùrô *f.*
To work ...	dùrô etuss.
World ...	dùnyât *f.*
To wound ...	ikháruss (*pron.*)
To write ...	girminuss.
Year ...	yôl *f.*
Yellow ...	shikerk.
Yes ...	áwá.
Yesterday ...	sáboor.
The day before yesterday ...	mâlto

Numerals.

	Masculine.	*Feminine.*	*For human beings only.*
1	hun	hik	hin
2	áltáts	álto	áltun
3	ùsko	iski	iské
4	wálto	wálti	
5	sùndo	sindi	
6	mishindo	mishindi	
7	tullo	tullé	
8	áltámbo	áltámbi	
9	hùncho	hùnti	
10	tôromo	tôrimi	
11	tùrmah-hun		
12	,, -áltáts		
13	,, -ùsko		
14	,, -wálto		
15	,, -sùndo		
16	,, -mishindo		
17	,, -tullo		
18	,, -áltámbo		
19	,, -hùncho		
20	áltèr		
21	áltèr-hun		
30	áltèr-tôrom		
40	álto -áltèr		
50	álto -áltèr-tôrom		
60	iski -áltèr		
70	iski -áltèr-tôrom		
80	wálti-áltèr		
90	wálti-áltèr-tôrom		
100	tah		
200	álto-tah		
1000	sâṇs		

APPENDIX B.

SHINA

(*Gilgit dialect*).

SKETCH OF GRAMMAR.

THE SUBSTANTIVE.

Substantives are either masculine or feminine. Those relating to human beings and animals are according to sex; for others there is no rule.

Both numbers have two forms, the nominative and the oblique; the dative and ablative are expressed by postpositions added to the oblique form. In some words elision is used. The plural is formed by adding *î*, or changing the terminal *o* into *é*.

	Singular.		*Plural.*	
Nom.	a house	gôt.	houses	gôtî.
Gen.	of a house	gôté.	of houses	gôtô.
Dat.	to a house	gôté-té.	to houses	gôtô-té.
Acc.	a house	gôt.	houses	gôtî.
Abl.	in a house	gôté-roo.	in houses	gôtî-éroo.
	on a house	gôté-ájé.	on houses	gôtî-ájé.
	with a house	gôté-sâti.	with houses	gôtî-sâti.
	for a house	gôté-kâryoo.	for houses	gôtî-kâryoo.
	from a house	gôté-joh.	from houses	gôtî-joh.

Nom.	a man	mánùjo.	men	mánùjé.
Gen.	of a man	mánùjé.	of men	mánùjo.
Dat.	to a man	mánùjé-té.	to men	mánùjé-té.
Acc.	a man	mánùjo.	men	mánùjé.
Abl.	in a man	mánùjo-roo.	in men	mánùjé-roo.
	on a man	mánùjo-ájé.	on men	mánùjé-ájé.
	with a man	mánùjo-sâti.	with men	mánùjé-sâti.
	for a man	mánùjo-kâryoo.	for men	mánùjé-kâryoo.
	from a man	mánùjo-joh.	from men	mánùjé-joh.

The noun in the genitive is placed before the governing noun, as: *áshpé* shish "The horse's head."

THE ADJECTIVE.

The adjectives with few exceptions terminate in *o* in the masculine, and *i* in the feminine, and precede the substantive, as :

a weak man	. ashâto manùjo.	a good woman	. mishti chai.

PRONOUNS.

	Nom.	Gen.	Dat.	Acc.	Abl.
I	mah (*intrans.*) másé (*trans.*)	main	mahté	mah	mah joh, &c.
Thou . . .	tooh (*intrans.*) toosé (*trans.*)	tai	tooté	tooh	tooh joh, &c.
He (*far*) . .	roh (*intrans.*) rosé (*trans.*)	resai	resáté	roh	rosé joh, &c.
He (*near*) . .	nooh (*intrans.*) noosé (*trans.*)	nesai	nesáté	nooh	noosé joh, &c.
She (*far*) . .	réh (*intrans.*) resé (*trans.*)	resai	resáté	réh	résé joh, &c.
She (*near*) . .	néh (*intrans.*) nésé (*trans.*)	nesai	nesáté	néh	nésé joh, &c.
We . . .	béh (*intrans.*) bésé (*trans.*)	asai	asoté	beh	asojoh, &c.
You . . .	tsoh (*intrans.*) tsosé (*trans.*)	tsai	tsoté	tsoh	tsoh joh, &c.
They (*far*) . .	rih (*intrans.*) risé (*trans.*)	rinai	rineté	rih	riné joh, &c.
They (*near*) . .	nih (*intrans.*) nisé (*trans.*)	nimai	nimeté	nih	niné joh, &c.

The Reflective Pronoun is formed by adding *áki,* as :

I myself . .	máh áki.	they themselves . .	nih áki.

Demonstrative Pronouns have two forms in the nominative, according as they are used with a transitive or intransitive verb, and the third person, both singular and plural, has two forms according to whether the object or subject is far or near.

The Interrogative Pronoun is declined as follows ; there is no distinction of gender in the plural :—

Singular.		*Plural.*	
Nom. who *or* which .	kô, *mas.* kê, *fem.*	who *or* which . .	kaiyi.
Gen. of whom, &c. .	kôsé, *mas.* kêsé, *fem.*	of whom, &c. . .	kênooṇ.
Dat. to whom, &c. .	kôsé-té, *mas.* kêsé-té, *fem.*	to whom, &c. . .	kaiyenoté.
Acc. whom, &c. .	kô, *mas.* kê, *fem.*	whom, &c. . .	kaiyi.
Abl. from whom, &c.	kôsé-joh, *mas.* kêsé-joh, *fem.*	from whom, &c. .	kaiyené-joh.

The Relative is expressed by *tő,* as :

I who went . . .	máh gâs *tő.*	The horse which I saw.	áshpo páchîgás *tő.*

THE VERB.

The verb is generally very regular with terminations expressing tense and person. A few verbs like BOJOYKI "to go" form the past tenses irregularly, as: *gâs* "I went," *gânùs* "I have gone."

The infinitive present always ends in *oyki.* In all tenses except the future, and in the infinitive and imperative moods the singular has a masculine and a feminine form.

The passive or a causal verb is formed by interpolating *ár* before the terminal *oyki*, as: *koyki* "to eat," *k*AR*oyki* "to be eaten" or "to cause to eat."

A noun of agency is formed by adding *k* to the infinitive, as: *koyki*K "one who eats," *toyki*K "one who does."

A verbal noun is also formed by using the infinitive present with postposition, as:

with the doing	toyki-sâti.	from the eating	koykî-joh.

for the striking . . . . . shidoyki-kâryoo.

ACTIVE VOICE.

INFINITIVE MOOD.

Present.		*Future.*	
to strike	shidoyki.	to be about to strike	shidoyki beyi.

Past.

to have struck . . . . . shidoyki asoo.

PARTICIPLES.

Present.		*Future.*	
striking	shidôjé.	being about to strike	shidoyki bé.

Past.

having struck . . . . shidé.

GERUND.

by *or* from striking . . . . . . shidôbil.

SUPINES.

possibly to strike	shidoyki ájé.	meet to strike	shidoyki hánó.

must strike . . . . shidoyki áwájé.

INDICATIVE MOOD.

Present.

Singular.		*Plural.*	
I am striking	shidémùs (*m.*) shidémis (*f.*)	we are striking	shidonus.
thou art striking	shidéno (*m.*) shidéné (*f.*)	you are striking	shideyânut.
he, she, it is striking	shideyânoo (*m.*) shideyânî (*f.*)	they are striking	shidénen.

Imperfect.

Singular.		*Plural.*	
I have been striking .	shidémasùs (*m.*) shidémasis (*f.*)	we have been striking .	shidonasus.
thou hast been striking	shideyaso (*m.*) shideyasé (*f.*)	you have been striking	shideyasut.
he, she, it has been striking.	shideyasoo (*m.*) shideyasî (*f.*)	they have been striking	shidénasé.

Pluperfect.

I had struck . .	shidégâsùs (*m.*) shidégisis (*f.*)	we had struck . .	shidégises.
thou hadst struck .	shidégâso (*m.*) shidégisé (*f.*)	you had struck . .	shidégiset.
he, she, it had struck	shidégasoo (*m.*) shidégisî (*f.*)	they had struck . .	shidégisé.

Perfect.

I struck . . .	shidêgás (*m.*) shidêgis (*f.*)	we struck . . .	shidêges.
thou struckest . .	shidêgá (*m.*) shidêgé (*f.*)	you struck . . .	shidêget.
he, she, it struck .	shidêgoo (*m.*) shidêgî (*f.*)	they struck . . .	shidêgé.

Præterite.

I have struck . .	shidégânùs (*m.*) shidéginis (*f.*)	we have struck . .	shidégenes.
thou hast struck .	shidégâno (*m.*) shidéginé (*f.*)	you have struck . .	shidégenet.
he, she, it has struck .	shidégunoo (*m.*) shidéginî (*f.*)	they have struck . .	shidégené.

Future.

I will strike . . .	shidum.	we will strike . .	shidôn.
thou wilt strike . .	shidé.	you will strike . .	shidyât.
he, she, it will strike .	shideyi.	they will strike . .	shiden.

IMPERATIVE MOOD.

strike thou . . .	shidé.	strike you . . .	shidya.
let him, her, it strike .	shidota.	let them strike . .	shidota.

CONDITIONAL MOOD.

The conditional mood is expressed by adding *ájé* "perhaps" to the indicative mood in all its forms :

Present.		*Imperfect.*	
I may be striking, &c.	shidémùs ájé, &c.	I may have been striking, &c.	shidémasùs ájé, &c.

Pluperfect.

I should have struck . . . shidégâsùs ájé, &c.

Perfect.		*Præterite.*	
I may have struck, &c.	shidêgás ájé, &c.	I may have struck, &c.	shidégânùs ájé, &c.

Future.

I may strike . . . . . shidum ájé, &c.

PASSIVE VOICE.

Infinitive Mood.

Present.		*Future.*	
to be struck . . .	shidaroyki.	to be about to be struck.	shidaroyki bé beyi.

Past.

to have been struck . . . shidaroyki asùloo.

Participles.

Present.		*Future.*	
being struck . . .	shidarojá.	being about to be struck.	shidaroyki bé.

Past.

having been struck . . . . . shidîtoo bé.

Gerund.

by *or* from being struck . . . . shidarôbil.

Supines.

possibly to be struck .	shidaroyki ájé.	meet to be struck .	shidaroyki awájé

must be struck . . . . . . shidaroyki háno.

Indicative Mood.

Present.

Singular.		*Plural.*	
I am being struck	shidîjùmùs (*m.*) shidîjimis (*f.*)	we are being struck .	shidîjinus.
thou art being struck	shidijeno (*m.*) shidijiné (*f.*)	you are being struck .	shidîyâjut.
he, she, it is being struck.	shidijinoo (*m.*) shidijinî (*f.*)	they are being struck .	shidéjenen.

Imperfect.

I was being struck	shidîjumasùs (*m.*) shidîjimisis (*f.*)	we were being struck	shidojunasus.
thou wast being struck.	shidîjaso (*m.*) shidîjasé (*f.*)	you were being struck	shidojunasut.
he, she, it was being struck.	shidîjasoo (*m.*) shidîjisî (*f.*)	they were being struck	shidéjenasé.

Pluperfect.

I had been struck .	shidarêgásùs (*m.*) shidarêgìsis (*f.*)	we had been struck .	shidarégises.
thou hadst been struck.	shidarégáso (*m.*) shidarégisé (*f.*)	you had been struck .	shidarégiset.
he, she, it had been struck.	shidarégásoo (*m.*) shidarégisî (*f.*)	they had been struck	shidarégisé.

Perfect.

Singular.		*Plural.*	
I was struck	shidarêgás (*m.*) shidarêgis (*f.*)	we were struck	shidarêges.
thou wast struck	shidarêgá (*m.*) shidarêgé (*f.*)	you were struck	shidarêget.
he, she, it was struck	shidarêgoo (*m.*) shidarêgî (*f.*)	they were struck	shidarêgé.

Præterite.

I have been struck	shidarêgânùs (*m.*) shidarêginis (*f.*)	we have been struck	shidarêgenes.
thou hast been struck.	shidarêgâno (*m.*) shidarégìné (*f.*)	you have been struck	shidarêgenet.
he, she, it has been struck.	shidarêgunoo (*m.*) shidarêginî (*f.*)	they have been struck	shidarêgené.

Future.

I will be struck	shidarum.	we will be struck	shidarôn.
thou wilt be stuck	shidaré.	you will be struck	shidaryât.
he, she, it will be struck	shidareyi.	they will be struck	shidaren.

IMPERATIVE.

be thou struck	shidaré.	be ye struck	shidarya.
let him, her, it be struck	shidarota.	let them be struck	shidarota.

CONDITIONAL MOOD.

The conditional mood is formed as in the active voice by adding *ájé* to all forms of the indicative.

Conjugation of the verb "TO BE."

The verb "TO BE" is defective, the only existing forms being as follows:

Present.

Singular.		*Plural.*	
I am	hánùs (*m.*) hánis (*f.*)	we are	hánus.
thou art	háno (*m.*) háné (*f.*)	you are	hánut.
he, she, it is	hánoo (*m.*) hanî (*f.*)	they are	háné.

Past.

I was	ásùs (*m.*) ásis (*f.*)	we were	ásus.
thou wast	aso (*m.*) asé (*f.*)	you were	ásut.
he, she, it was	asoo (*m.*) asî (*f.*)	they were	ásé.

There is an alternative form of the past tense without any change of meaning.

Singular.		*Plural.*	
I was	ásùlùs (*m.*) ásilis (*f.*)	we were	ásilus.
thou wast	ásùlo (*m.*) ásilé (*f.*)	you were	ásilut.
he, she, it was	ásùloo (*m.*) ásilî (*f.*)	they were	ásilé.

Other forms are supplied by the verb "TO BECOME."

Conjugation of the verb "TO BECOME."

INFINITIVE MOOD.

Present.		*Future.*	
to become	boyki.	to be about to become	boyki beyi.

Past.

to have become . . . . boyki ásoo.

PARTICIPLES.

Present.		*Future.*	
becoming	beyanoo.	being about to become	boyki bé.

Past.

having become . . . . bé.

GERUND.

by *or* from becoming . . . . bilo.

SUPINES.

possibly to become	boyki-ájé.	meet to become	boyki-áwájé.

must become . . . . . . boyki háno. / boykinoo.

INDICATIVE MOOD.

Present.

Singular.		*Plural.*	
I am becoming	bùmùs (*m.*) bùmis (*f.*)	we are becoming	bonus.
thou art becoming	bénoo (*m.*) béné (*f.*)	you are becoming	bânut.
he, she, it is becoming	beyanoo (*m.*) beyanî (*f.*)	they are becoming	bénum.

Imperfect.

I was becoming	bomásùs (*m.*) bomásis (*f.*)	we were becoming	bonásus.
thou wast becoming	beso (*m.*) besé (*f.*)	you were becoming	bâsut.
he, she, it was becoming.	beyáso (*m.*) beyasî (*f.*)	they were becoming	bénásé.

An alternative form of the tense is *bomásùlùs*, &c.

Pluperfect.

Singular.		*Plural.*	
I had become .	bigâsùs (*m.*) bigîsis (*f.*)	we had become .	bigêsus.
thou hadst become	bigâso (*m.*) bigêsé (*f.*)	you had become .	bigêsut.
he, she, it had become	bigoosoo (*m.*) bîsî (*f.*)	they had become	bigêsé.

An alternative form of the 3rd pers. sing. mas. is *boogoosoo*.
An alternative form of the tense is *bigásùlùs*, &c.

Perfect.

Singular.		*Plural.*	
I became . .	bigás (*m.*) bigis (*f.*)	we became . . .	biges.
thou becamest .	bigá (*m.*) bigé (*f.*)	you became . . .	biget.
he, she, it became	bigoo (*m.*) bigî (*f.*)	they became . . .	bigé.

Alternative forms of the 3rd person singular are *boo*, *boogoo*, and *booloo*.
An alternative form of the 3rd person plural is *bilé*.

Præterite.

Singular.		*Plural.*	
I have become .	bigânùs (*m.*) bigînis (*f.*)	we have become .	bigênus.
thou hast become	bigânoo (*m.*) bigêné (*f.*)	you have become .	bigênut.
he, she, it has become	bigoonoo (*m.*) bigînî (*f.*)	they have become	bigêné.

Alternative forms of the 3rd person singular are *boonoo* and *booloonoo*.
An alternative form of the 3rd person plural is *bilêné*.

Future.

Singular.		*Plural.*	
I shall become . . .	bôm.	we shall become . .	bôn.
thou shalt become . .	bé.	you shall become . .	bât.
he, she, it shall become .	béyi.	they shall become . .	bén.

IMPERATIVE MOOD.

become thou	bo.	become ye . . .	bâ.
let him, her, it become . .	bota.	let them become . .	bota.

CONDITIONAL MOOD.

The conditional mood is formed by adding *ájé* "perhaps" to all forms of the indicative mood.

THE NEGATIVE AND THE INTERROGATIVE.

"No" is expressed by *nen*, and "not" by *né*, but in an indefinite sense by *nùsh*.

The interrogative is expressed by adding *á* to the verb, or if it already terminates in *á* by lengthening it to *ắ*, as :

Is this your horse? No . . .	Anoo tai áshpo hánoá? *Nen*.
Have you a horse? No . . .	Too kuch áshpo hánoá? *Nùsh*.
I will not go	*Né* bájum.
Shall I go?	Máh bájùm*á*?
Hast thou gone?	Too g*ắ*?

Sometimes the verb is omitted and the *á* suffixed to the noun as :

Is this your horse? . . . . Anoo tai áshpoá.

THE ADVERB.

Adverbs are formed from adjectives by changing the final *o* into *ắr* or *yắr*, as :

sharp . . .	tîno.	sharply . . .	tîn*ắr*.
slow . . .	abâto.	slowly . . .	abat*yắr*.
swift . . .	laowko.	swiftly . . .	laowky*ắr*.

EXAMPLE.

Dazoto máh sùtùsùs aiyâketé manoojo kulli shongo wutto. Másé rinain hilling paroojî rinon kutchi gâs. Gé chukumto woi ájé kulli bênásé. Aiy bêyé aiyêbé kulli bênásé. Ek si woi kêt háreso, ek rosé nowâreté phuttung téásoo. Máh ifai aiyno kulli chùk táré. Bainoté woi tráng té sámáré máh wâtùs. Máh gutteji rih gá gé. Ken ik ájo chukumto nê hilling tenásé. Máh hoon bé rinon wâré gâs: gés chukumto eksé ek dê, eksé eki chîloo tser tigoosoo. Másé aiy bêyé kullijoh phutt tarêgás. Phutt táré kùjêgás, tén másé woi sámáré sùbêyé yoopáré gâsùs, nê keh kulli biget. Âdé rêgás, rinájo eksé rêgoo máh tai moreji bé gâsùs, aiyâketé woi bun boogoo. Máh nê înláji gé chukumto rosé woi booté áko wâre farêgoosoo; máh gé phuttung tigás. Rosé máh tung tigoo, másé gá tung tigás, aiyâketé rosé máté shong tigoo; másé gá hutt harigâsùs, main hut rosé giriroo go, chîloo tser booloo.

Translation.

At mid-day I was sleeping when the noise of men fighting came to me. On hearing their noise I went to them. Having gone I saw that they were fighting about water. The two were fighting with one another in this way. One was taking the water below, the other was breaking (away the earth) in this direction. I arrived and silenced both their quarrelling. Having divided the water between the two, I came (back). After a time I saw they were again making a noise. Having risen I went towards them; (and) on going I saw one beating the other (*lit.* one beating one): one had torn the clothes of the other. I separated the two from fighting. Having separated them I asked how "I having divided the water (and) reconciled you two went, why have you again quarrelled?"

I spoke thus, one (of them) said, "Having done your order I went, so that the water was closed to me." Having again gone to the watercourse,* I saw that the other (*lit.* he) had turned the whole of the water towards himself; having gone I opened it. He pushed me away, I also pushed him, so that he struck me; I also lifted (*lit.* took) my hand, my hand entered the hem of his shirt, (and) his clothes were torn.

---

* *Inl* is literally the place where water is drawn off from a watercourse. It also means the eye of a needle.

VOCABULARY.

To be able	... boyki.
Above	... ájî.
To abuse	... shádoyki.
Account	... chéghah *m.*
Accustomed	... hittoo.
Acid	... chùrko.
Active	... laowko.
To advise	... kanow toyki.
After (time)	... ájo.
,, (place)	... guttaji, phuttoo.
Again	... nê.
Air	... ôsh´*f.*
Alert	... turâr.
All	... booté.
Alongside of	... bil.
Also	... gah.
Although	... ákhanâ.
Always	... desgo.
And	... neh.
Anger	... ròsh *m.*
Angry	... ròsh.
To be angry	... ròsh boyki.
Another time	... áji noo dum.
To answer	... joowâb doyki.
Ant	... pillili *f.*
Anxiety	... sumbá *m.*
Anxious	... sumbákish.
Apart	... yoolo.
Apple	... phulla *m.*
Apricot	... jooi (fruit *m.*, tree *f.*)
Arm	... shâkho. *m.*
Arms (weapons)	... samôn *f.*
Army	... sîṇ *m.*
Arrangements	... samôn *f.*
To arrive	... ifayoyki.
Arrow	... kon *m.*
To ask	... kùjoyki.
To ask for	... bichoyki.
Ass	... jakoon *m.*
Aunt (father's sister)	... papî.
,, (mother's sister)	... mâ.
Autumn	... sharô *m.*
Avalanche	... ninâl *f.*
Away	... phutt.
Back	... dâki.
Bad	... kutcho, khajeto.

Barley	...	yo. *m*.
Bat	...	tatâpul *m*.
To be	...	boyki.
Bean	...	rabong *m*.
Bear	...	îtch *m*.
Beard	...	daiyn̥ *f*.
To beat	...	shidoyki.
Beautiful	...	millalyoo.
Because	...	djek toh.
To become	...	boyki.
Before (*time*)	...	yer (*suffixed*).
Before (*place*)	...	yer (*suffixed*).
To begin	...	sùtoy ki.
Behind	...	phuttoo.
Belly	...	dèr *f*.
Below	...	kirî.
To betray	...	hulwoyki.
Betrothal	...	hâr *f*.
Between	...	mujjah (*suffixed*).
Beyond	...	pár.
Body	...	dim *m*.
To bind	...	tuk toyki.
Bird	...	bùng *m*.
To bite	...	chupoyki.
Bitter	...	chitto.
Black	...	kino.
Blind	...	sheow.
Blood	...	lel *m*.
To blow	...	phoo toyki.
Blue	...	aghai nîlo.
Blunt	...	phutt.
Bone	...	áti *m*.
To be born	...	joyki.
Both	...	bêyé.
Boundary	...	dir *f*.
Bow	...	dânoo *m*.
Boy	...	shùdâr *m*.
Brain	...	mato *m*.
Brass	...	hulliroo rîl *f*.
Brave	...	hiyélo.
Bread	...	tiki *f*.
To break	...	pùtoy ki.
Breast	...	chùchi ; titîro.
Breath	...	shân̥ *m*.
Brick	...	dishtik *f*.
Bride	...	hillâl *f*.
Bridegroom	...	hillalô *m*.
Bridle	...	guppî *f*.
Bridge	...	so *f*.
To bring	...	atoyki.
Broad	...	châlo.

To be broken	...	pùtejoyki.
Brooch	...	chummá *m*.
Brother	...	já *m*.
Brown	...	gooro.
Bull	...	dôno *m*.
Bullet	...	diroo *m*.
To burn	...	loopoyki.
To bury	...	khutoyki.
But	...	umma.
Butterfly	...	phuttoi *f*.
To buy	..	krinoyki.
By	...	joh (*suffixed*).
To call	...	hoh toyki.
Calling	...	hoh *m*.
Camel	...	oont *m*.
Care	...	shòng *m*.
Cat	...	boosh *m*.
Cattle (*collectively*)	...	gowîlé.
Charm	...	toomer *m*.
Cheek	...	haròm *f*.
Chin	...	chòm *m*.
Circle	...	bidiriko *m*.
Clarionet	...	surnai *f*.
Clean	...	sâf.
Cleverness	...	tinyâr *m*.
To catch hold	...	lamoy ki.
Clothes	...	chîloo *m*.
Cloud	...	niyèr.
Cock	...	kòn kroch *m*.
Cold	...	shidalo.
Colour	...	rong *m*.
To come	...	woyoyki.
Copper	...	léloo rîl *f*.
Corner	...	shùtî *m*.
Four-cornered	...	chârshùtî.
Corpse	...	koonoo *m*.
Cough	...	koo *f*.
To count	...	kaloyki.
Courage	...	mùshelai *f*.
Cousin	...	já, sah.
Cow	...	go *f*.
To creep	...	kaṇsh boyki.
Crooked	...	kôlò.
Crow	...	kâṇ *m*.
Custom	...	chôl *m*.
To cut	...	cherub toyki.
To dance	...	nutádoyki.
Dancing	...	nut *f*.

Dangerous	...	bijetai.
Dark	...	tùtung.
Darkness	...	tùtung *m*.
Daughter	...	dî *f*.
Day	...	dés *m*.
Mid-day	...	trang soori, dázo.
To-day	...	ácho.
Deaf	...	kooto.
Death	...	mâren *f*.
To deceive	...	hulwoyki.
Deceitful	...	jibgullo.
Destitute	...	lîcho.
Dew	...	púts *m*.
To die	...	miroyki.
Different	...	yùlo.
Difficult	...	mùshkil.
Dirty	...	chekráto.
Disposition	...	hittoo *m*.
To divide	...	samaroyki.
Divorce	...	talâh *m*.
To do	...	toyki.
Dog	...	shoo *m*.
Door	...	dur *m*.
Down	...	kiri.
Dream	...	sântcho *m*.
To drink	...	pioyki.
Drum	...	durrung *m*.
Dry	...	shùko.
Dust	...	ùdoo.
Eagle	...	káké *m*.
Ear	...	kon *m*.
Earth	...	sùm *m*.
The earth	...	bîrdi *f*.
Earthquake	...	bùṉyiâl *f*.
East (sunrise)	...	jill béyi *m*. (*lit* "it will be evident").
Easy	...	sácho.
To eat	...	koyki.
Eclipse	...	grâṇ *m*.
Edge	...	shing *m*.
Egg	...	hánné *f*.
Elbow	...	bakùni *f*.
Elephant	...	husto *m*.
Empty	...	pooṇshko.
Enemy	...	dùshmun *m*.
Enmity	...	dùshmuni *f*.
To enter	...	ároo bojoyki.
Envy	...	gutt *m*.
Equal	...	barâbár.
To make equal	...	yoopoyki.
To escape	...	mùchoyki.

Evening ... shâm *f.*
Ever ... khuss.
Everybody ... bùté manùjé.
Everything ... hár djek.
Ewe ... eji *f.*
Except ... oré.
Expectation ... chákánî *f.*
Eye ... achi *m.*

Face ... mùkh *m.*
Family ... supooyâr.
To fall ... dijoyki.
Far ... door.
Fat (*subs.*) ... mî *f.*
Fat (*adj.*) ... tolo.
Father ... mâlo *m.*
Father (*as a form of address*). bâbo.
To be fatigued ... shùmoyki.
Fault ... aib *m.*
Fear ... bijetai *f.*
To fear ... bijoyki.
Feather ... pùrgoo *f.*
To feed ... ùnoyki.
Female ... sòntch.
Fig ... phâg *m.*
Fight ... bîrgah *m.*
To fight ... kulli toyki.
To fill ... shuck toyki.
Finger ... agooi *f.*
To finish ... phush toyki.
Fire ... ágâr *m.*
First . ... poomooko.
Fish ... chimoo *m.*
Flock (of birds) ... brin.
Flour ... ânt.
Flower ... phùner *f.*
Flute ... torooyi *f.*
To fly (as a bird) ... thur doyki.
Following ... guttéjí.
Foot ... pá *m.*
For ... kâryoo.
Forehead ... nîlow.
To forget ... amùshoyki.
Fort ... kôt *m.*
Foster-kindred ... ùnîlo mâlo, &c.
Fowl ... kerkâmùsh *f.*
Fox ... loyṇ.
Friend ... shoogálo *m.*
Friendship ... shoogályâr *f.*
From ... joh (*suffixed*).

Frost	...	shidaloo *m.*
Fruit	...	méwá *m.*
Full	...	shuck.
Fur	...	jutt *f.*
Garden	...	tsagoh *m.*
Generous	...	hyooshîlo.
Gently	...	shòng.
To get	...	dog boyki.
Girl	...	mùlai *f.*
To give	...	doyki.
To go	...	bojoyki.
To go out	...	dòroo bojoyki.
Goats (*collectively*)	...	lutch.
He-goat	...	mooger *m.*
She-goat	...	aiy *f.*
Wild goat	...	sherrah.
God	...	Dabon.
Gold	...	son.
Good	...	mishtùṇ *m.*, mishti *f.*
Grape	...	jutch *f.*
Grass	...	kutch *m.*
Great	...	buddo.
Green	...	jùt nîlo.
Grief	...	gòm *m.*
To grieve	...	phidik boyki.
Gun	...	tùmák *m.*
Gunpowder	...	bilen.
Hail	...	aiṇyer.
Hair	...	jákùr *f.*
Half	...	tráng, châk.
Hand	...	hut *f.*
Right hand	...	dushino *m.*
Left hand	...	kuboo *m.*
Handle	...	dono *m.*
Happiness	...	shùryâr *m.*
Happy	...	shùryâr.
Hard	...	kùro.
Hare	...	ooshaiṇyoo *m.*
Hatred	...	koos *m.*
Hawk	...	baiyoṇsh *f.*
Head	...	shish *m.*
Health	...	ráhát *m.*
To hear	...	parejoyki.
Heart	...	hyo *m.*
The heavens	...	aghai *f.*
Heavy	...	agooroo.
Hen	...	sòntch kerkâmùsh *f.*
Herd	...	dòn.
Here	...	âni.

High	...	ùtullo.
To hit (as with a gun or a stone).		dijoyki.
Hope	...	oomêd *f.*
To hope	...	oomêd toyki.
Horse	...	áshpo *m.*
Horse shoe	...	sârpo *m.*
Hot	...	tâto.
House } Home }	...	gôt *m.*
How	...	kyoh.
How many	...	kutchâkuk.
How much	...	kutchâk.
Humble	...	môro.
Hunger	...	ooyanâr *f.*
Hungry	...	ooyano.
Hundred	...	shul.
To hunt	...	duroo doyki.
Husband	...	báro.
Ice	...	gumùk *m.*
Idle	...	abâto.
If	...	ákhân.
To be ignorant	...	ná sùnoyki.
Ill	...	rogoto.
To be ill	...	rogoto boyki.
Illness	..	rogotyâr *f.*
In	...	éroo, bul (*suffixed*).
Industrious	...	gresto.
Infant	...	shùdâr.
To injure	...	nooksân toyki.
Instead of	...	dishéro.
Iron	...	chîmer *m.*
Judgment	...	ustòm *m.*
To jump	...	prig doyki.
Justice	...	insâf.
To join	...	mishoyki.
Kettledrum	...	dâmul *m.*
To kick	...	pachootyâr doyki.
To kill	...	mároyki.
King	...	râ.
King's wife	...	sônê.
King's son	...	gùshpoor.
King's daughter	...	rá-i-dî.
Knee	...	kùtoo *m.*
To kneel	...	kootiáshki baiyoyki.
Knife	...	khatâroo *m.*, khatâr *f.*
To know	...	sùṇyoyki.
Knowledge	...	sùṇyoyki *m.*

Lame	...	kùdo.
Language	...	bâsh *f.*
Large	...	buddo.
Late	...	choot.
To laugh	...	haiyoyki.
To lie down	...	paroyki.
Lead	...	nâng *m.*
Leaf of a tree	...	páto.
To learn	...	sichoyki.
To leave	...	phutt toyki.
Leg	...	patâloo *m.*
To let go	...	phutt toyki.
Level	...	parùlo.
Lie	...	khulté *m.*
To lay down	...	poyki.
Life	...	jîl *f.*
To lift	...	hon toyki.
Light (*subs.*)	...	sung *m.*
Light (*adj.*)	...	laowko.
Lightning	...	bîchùsh *f.*
Like	...	paroloo.
Line	...	tsir *f.*
Lip	...	ōnti *f.*
Little	...	chon.
A little	...	âpoo.
Liver	...	yùm *m.*
Long	...	jigo.
To look at	...	chakoyki.
To lose	...	naiyoyki.
Love	...	shool *m.*
To love	...	shooltoyki.
Low	...	lâto.
To make	...	toyki.
Male	...	bîro *m.*
Man	...	manùjo *m.*
Young man	...	châkŭr *m.*
Old man	...	jero *m.*
Mankind	...	jùk.
Mare	...	bâm *f.*
To marry	...	ger toyki.
Marriage	...	ger *f.*
To measure	...	toloyki.
Meat	...	mos *m.*
Medicine	...	bilen.
Melon (water)	...	booer *m.*
Melon (musk)	...	gon *f.*
Mid-day	...	tráng soori, dázo.
Mid-night	...	tráng râti.
Milk	...	dùt *m.*
Mist	...	ùdoo *m.*

To mix	...	mishoyki.
Moon	...	yoon *f.*
Month	...	mâz *m.*
Half month	...	putch *m.*
More	...	moots.
Morning	...	loshtiko, chel bùji *m.*
Moth	...	prononˌ *m.*, prenoonˌ *pl.*
Mother	...	mâ *f.*
Mother (*as a form of address*).		âjé.
Mountain	...	tshîsh *m.*
Mouse	...	mooj *f.*
Mouth	...	aiyṇ *f.*
To move (*trans.*)	...	lung toyki.
To move (*intrans.*)	...	lung boyki.
Much	...	bodô.
So much	...	achâk.
Mud	...	tọh *m.*
Mulberry	...	maronch *m.*
Muscle	...	mooj *m.*
Music	...	hárîp̣ *f.*
Naked	...	nunno.
Nail (finger)	...	noro *m.*
Name	...	nóm *m.*
Narrow	...	irooto.
Near	...	kutch.
Neck	...	shuck *m.*
Nephew	...	pùtch *m.*
Never	...	khussné.
New	...	nowoo.
Niece	...	dî *f.*
Night	...	râti.
No	...	neṇ.
Nobody	...	koh nùsh.
Noise	...	hilling *f.*
None	...	nùsh.
North	...	shimâl *m.*
Nose	...	náto *m.*
Nothing	...	khuss, djeká nùsh.
Now	...	ten.
Of	...	é (*suffixed*).
Old	...	prononˌ.
On	...	ájî.
Owl	...	hoo *m.*
Only	...	gùtcho.
Open	...	bâto.
To open	...	toroyki, phuttung toyki.
Or	...	yá.
To order	...	bundish toyki.

Out	...	doroo.
Over	...	ájî (*suffixed*).
Pain	...	shilán.
To be pained	...	shiloyki.
Palace	...	râko *m*.
Partridge	...	kaṇkalo *m*.
Peach	...	chookanâr *m*.
Pear	...	peshé *m*.
Perhaps	...	áji.
Pigeon	...	kùnooli *f*.
Pity	...	nirai *f*.
Place	...	dish *f*.
To place	...	choroyki.
Plain	...	dâs.
Play	...	halibon *m*.
To play (a game)	...	halibon toyki.
To play (on an instrument).		bushoyki.
Pleasant tasting	...	ispow.
To please	...	shùriâroyki.
Pleased	...	shùriâr.
To be pleased	...	shùroyoyki.
Pleasure	...	shùraiyoon.
Plough	..	hull *m*.
Point	...	chùroo *m*.
To praise	...	siffut toyki.
To prepare	...	têyâr toyki.
Pride	...	badyâr *f*.
To produce	...	diloojoyki.
To promise	...	kát toyki.
Proper	...	chòl.
Proud	...	muchâr.
To pull	...	jákáloyki.
Punishment	...	saza.
To push	...	tung toyki.
Quarrel	...	hilling *f*.
To quarrel	...	kulloyki.
Queen	...	sônê *f*.
Quickly	...	laowko.
Rain	...	ajo *m*.
Ram	...	karêlo *m*.
To read	...	rayoyki.
Ready	...	têyâr.
To receive	...	layoyki.
To recognize	...	dushtoyki.
To reconcile	...	yoopoyki.
Red	...	léli.
Relation	...	ùskoon *m*.

Relationship ... ùskùni *f.*
To remember ... hiyêjé toyki.
Remembrance ... hiyijá *m.*
To return ... faroyki.
Reward ... goorin *m.*
Rice ... briùṇ *m.*
Rich ... poyôno.
Ring ... kickin.
Ringlets ... toroiy *f.*
Ripe ... puckoto.
To be ripe ... puchoyki.
To rise ... ùthoyki, hoon boyki.
River ... sin *f.*
Road ... pòn *m.*
Rock ... giri *f.*
Roof ... tesh *f.*
Rope ... bâli *f.*
Rotten ... krido.
Round ... bidiro.
Rough ... chichâro.
To run ... hai toyki, ùchoyki.

Sad ... sùpùsh.
Saddle ... tilén *m.*
Sand ... sigel *f.*
Sarcasm ... chùdo *m.*
To say ... bushoyki.
To scatter ... shijoyki.
To search for ... ùdaroyki.
To see ... pushoyki.
Seed ... bî.
Self ... ákî, áko.
To sell ... gâtch doyki.
To send ... chanoyki.
Separate ... chido.
To separate ... yùlo toyki.
Servant ... shudder *m.*
Shadow ... chijôt *f.*
Shame ... lush *f.*
Sharp ... tîno.
Sheep (*collectively*) ... ejîlé.
Wild sheep ... oorin.
Short ... kùto.
Shoulder ... piow *m.*
To shout ... shogṇo toyki.
Shut ... tum.
To shut ... gunoyki.
Side ... khing *f.*
On this side ... anoowári.
On that side ... aiyoowári.
Alongside ... bil.

Sigh	... hish *f.*
Silent	... manooker, chook.
Silk	... sikkim *f.*
Silver	... roop *m.*
Sinew	... jowa *m.*
To sing	... gai doyki.
Singing	... gai *f.*
Sister	... sah *f.*
To sit	... baiyoyki.
Skin	... chōn *m.*
Slave	... maristun *m.*
Sleep	... nir *f.*
To sleep	... soyki.
Sloping	... besko.
Slow	... abâto.
Slowly	... choot, agooroo.
Small	... chùno.
Smoke	... doom *m.*
Smooth	... pîchiliko.
Snake	... jon *m.*
Sneeze	... jaiṇ *f.*
Snow	... hin *m.*
Soft	... mâwo.
Solid	... sâṇro.
Solstice	... hallôl *f.*
Some	... ápùk.
Somebody	... koh manùjo.
Something	... djekek.
Son	... pùtch *m.*
To soothe	... shiloyki.
Soul	... jîl *f.*
Sound	... shongo *m.*
South	... janoob *m.*
Spade	... bel *f.*
Speech	... mor *m.*
Spoon	... kuppaiy *f.*
Spring	... bazôno *m.*
To stand	... tsukootoyki.
Star	... tároo *pl.*, táré *m.*
Stern	... doomôngi.
Stone	... but *m.*
Storm	... tofân *m.*
Straight	... sòncho.
Strength	... shut *m.*
To strike	... { shidoyki. / doyki. / shong toyki. }
Strong	... shâtillo.
Stupidity	... kum ákilî *f.*
Suitable	... yeshki.
Summer	... wâlo *m.*

Summer solstice	...	wâlo hallôl.
To summon	...	ho toyki.
Sun	...	soori.
Sweet	...	môro.
Swift	...	lâowko.
To swim	...	thum doyki.
Sword	...	kunger *f.*
Tail	...	pacho *m.*
To take	...	haroyki.
To take away	...	nikáloyki.
To take hold	...	lamoyki.
To take up	...	hùn toyki.
To teach	...	sicharoyki.
To tear	...	tser toyki.
To tell	...	rayoyki.
That (*relat.*)	...	oh *pl.* rih.
Then	...	esoroo.
There	...	âli.
Therefore	...	anussé kâryoo.
Thick	...	toloo.
Thin	...	abrîlo.
To think	...	sumbá toy ki.
Thirst	...	waiyâl *f.*
This one	...	noo anoo.
Those two	...	aiy bêye.
Thought	...	khaiyâl *m.*
Throat	...	shoto *m.*
To throw	...	phull toyki, wiyoyki.
To throw away	...	lipp toyki.
To throw down	...	naravioyki.
Thumb	...	ágooi *f.*
Thunder	...	ting tong *m.*
Thus (*this way*)	...	áde.
,, (*that way*)	...	aiyîbé, aiyé.
Till	...	to, té.
Time	...	ken *f.*
Timid	...	bîjâto.
Tin	...	kalai *f.*
To	...	té (*suffixed*).
Toe	...	ágooi *f.*
Together	...	gutti.
To-day	...	acho.
To-morrow	...	loshtâki.
The day after to-morrow		loshtá chiring.
Tongue	...	jip *m.*
Tooth	...	dòn *m.*
Touch	...	jook *f.*
To touch	...	jook toyki.
Towards	...	khing, wâre (*suffixed*).
Treacherous	...	hulwoykik.

Tree	...	tòm *m.*
Truth	...	soontch *m.*
To try	...	siloyki.
To turn	...	faroyki.
Turning	...	fhâr.
Ugly	...	kutcho.
To be unable	...	dùboyki.
Uncle (father's brother)		mâlo.
Uncle (mother's brother)		mowl.
Under	...	kiri (*suffixed*).
Unless	...	oré.
Upright	...	tsuck.
Valley	...	gah *m.*, butzel *f.*
Vein	...	nâr *f.*
Very	...	bòdô.
Very well	...	shoh, mishtùṇ.
Village	...	het, girom *f.*
Vine	...	goorbi *f.*
Voice	...	masho *m.*
Vulture	...	koowâṇroo *m.*
Wall	...	kùt *m.*
Walnut	...	acho *m.*
Water	...	woi *m.*
Water-mill	...	yùr *f.*
Weak	...	ashâto.
Weakness	...	ashâto *m.*
To weep	...	royki.
West (sunset)	...	boor beyi *m.* (*lit.* "it will be down").
Wet	...	ajo.
What	...	djek.
Wheat	...	goom.
When (*interrog.*)	...	káré.
When (*relat.*)	...	káré.
Where (*interrog.*)	...	kôni.
Which	...	koh.
Whip	...	tùr *f.*
White	...	shaiyo.
Who (*interrog.*)	...	koh.
Why (*interrog.*)	...	keh.
Wide	...	shîlo.
Widow / Widower	...	gyoos.
Wife	...	gren *f.*
Wind	...	ôsh *f.*
Window	...	darî *f.*
Wine	...	mo *m.*
Wing	...	putchâli *f.*
Winter	...	yôno.

Winter solstice	...	shini hallôl.
Wise	...	dânά.
Wish	...	ruck *m.*
To wish	...	ruck toyki.
With	...	sâti (*suffixed*).
Within	...	mujjah.
Wolf	...	shâṇ.
Woman	...	chai *f.*
Old woman	...	jerî *f.*
Young moman	...	chùmùtkir.
Wood	...	jùk *m.*
Wool	...	jutt *f.*
Wool (*pushm*)	...	báphoor *f.*
Work	...	kòm *m.*
To work	...	kòm toyki.
The world	...	dùniyát *f.*
To wound	...	zukum doyki.
To write	...	likoyki.
Year	...	ewêlo.
Yellow	...	halijo.
Yes	...	áwá.
Yesterday	...	bullá.
The day before yesterday.		ichî.

Numerals.

1	ek.
2	doo.
3	ché.
4	chár.
5	poin.
6	shâ.
7	sut.
8	átsh.
9	now.
10	daiy.
11	ekaiy.
12	baiy.
13	tchoiṇ.
14	tchowndaiy.
15	punzaiy.
16	shoiṇ.
17	sutaiṇ.
18	áshtaiṇ.
19	kúnî
20	bî.
21	bî gah ek.
30	bî gah daiy.
40	doo bî.
50	doo bî gah daiy.
60	ché bî.
70	ché bî gah daiy.
80	châr bî.
90	châr bî gah daiy.
100	shul.
1000	sâṇs.

APPENDIX C.

CHILISS.

Spoken in the Indus Valley.

DECLENSIONS.

THE NOUN.

	Singular.		*Plural.*	
Nom.	a house	gôt	houses	gôté.
Gen.	of a house	gôtân	of houses	gôtōṇ.
Dat.	to a house	gêt too	to houses	gôtōṇ.
Acc.	a house	gôt	houses	gôté.
Abl.	from a house	gôt hundé	from houses	gôtōṇ hundé.

PRONOUNS.

PERSONAL.

	Nom.	Gen.	Dat.	Acc.	Ablative.
I	má	miṇ	miṇ	miṇ	miṇ hundé.
thou	too	teṇ	tî	tî	tî hundé.
he, she *or* it	ùṇ	ashâṇ	ashî	ashî	ashî hundé.
We	beh	azâṇ	azoṇ	azoṇ	azoṇ hundé.
You	tùs	tsâṇ	tsoṅ	tsoṇ	tsoṇ hundé.
They	iṇ	iṇwâṇ	iyoṇ	iyoṇ	iyoṇ hundé.

THE VERB.

Conjugation of the verb "To Strike."

ACTIVE VOICE.

Infinitive Mood.

Present.		*Future.*	
to strike	kotōṇ	about to strike	kotōṇ hōndo

Past.

to have struck . . . . kotōṇ aso.

Participles.

Present.		*Future.*	
striking	kotâṇ	being about to strike	kotōṇ hoshato.

Past.

having struck . . . . koté.

Supines.

meet to strike	kotōṇ owzânto	must strike	kotōṇ tho.

Indicative Mood.

Present.

Singular.		*Plural.*	
I am striking	kotân tho (*m.*) kotân thi (*f.*)	we are striking	kotânthé.
thou art striking	kotân tho (*m.*) kotân thi (*f.*)	you are striking	kotânthé.
he, she, it is striking	kotân tho (*m.*) kotân thi (*f.*)	they are striking	kotânthé.

Imperfect.

I was striking	kotân aso (*m.*) kotân asi (*f.*)	we were striking	kotânasé.
thou wast striking	kotàn aso (*m.*) kotân asi (*f.*)	you were striking	kotânasé.
he, she, it was striking	kotân aso (*m.*) kotân asi (*f.*)	they were striking	kotânasé.

Pluperfect.

I had struck	kotôaso (*m.*) kotîasi (*f.*)	we had struck	kotôasé.
thou hadst struck	kotôaso (*m.*) kotîasi (*f.*)	you had struck	kotôasé.
he, she, it had struck	kotôaso (*m.*) kotiasi (*f.*)	they had struck	kotôasé.

Perfect.

Singular.		*Plural.*	
I struck	kotô (*m.*) kotî (*f.*)	we struck	kotô (*m.*) kotî (*f.*)
thou struckest	kotô (*m.*) kotî (*f.*)	you struck	kotô (*m.*) kotî (*f.*)
he, she, it struck	kotô (*m.*) kotî (*f.*)	they struck	kotô (*m.*) kotî (*f.*)

Præterite.

I have struck	kotetsô (*m.*) kotetsé (*f.*)	we have struck	kotetsô (*m.*) kotetsé (*f.*)
thou hast struck	kotetsô (*m.*) kotetsé (*f.*)	you have struck	kotetsô (*m.*) kotetsé (*f.*)
he, she, it has struck	kotetsô (*m.*) kotetsé (*f.*)	they have struck	kotetsô (*m.*) kotetsé (*f.*)

Future.

I will strike	kotéshatho (*m.*) kotéshethi (*f.*)	we will strike	kotéshethé.
thou wilt strike	kotéshatho (*m.*) kotéshethi (*f.*)	you will strike	kotéshethé.
he, she, it will strike	kotéshatho (*m.*) kotéshethi (*f.*)	they will strike	kotéshethé.

IMPERATIVE MOOD.

strike thou	koté	strike you	kotyah.
let him, her, it strike	kotōnté	let them strike	kotyâṇ.

CONDITIONAL MOOD.

The conditional mood is formed by adding *giné* "why" to the indicative mood in all its forms, as:

I may be striking	kotântho giné.
I may have been striking	kotânaso giné.

PASSIVE VOICE.

INFINITIVE MOOD.

Present.		*Future.*	
to be struck	kotezōṇ	to be about to be struck.	kotezōṇ hōndo.

Past.

to have been struck	kotezōṇ asoo.

PARTICIPLES.

Present.		*Future.*	
being struck	kotezâṇ	being about to be struck.	kotezōṇ hoshato.

Past.

having been struck	kotyâṇ.

SUPINES.

meet to be struck	kotezōṇ owzântho.
must be struck	kotezōṇ tho.

INDICATIVE MOOD.

Present.

Singular.		*Plural.*	
I am being struck	kotezōntho (*m.*) kotezainthi (*f.*)	we are being struck	kotezânthé (*m.*) kotezainthiá (*f.*)
thou art being struck	kotezōntho (*m.*) kotezainthi (*f.*)	you are being struck	kotezânthé (*m.*) kotezainthiá (*f.*)
He, she, it is being struck.	kotezōntho (*m.*) kotezainthi (*f.*)	they are being struck	kotezânthé (*m.*) kotezainthiá (*f.*)

Imperfect.

Singular.		*Plural.*	
I was being struck	kotezōṇ aso (*m.*) kotezaiṇsi (*f.*)	we were being struck	kotezâṇsé (*m.*) kotezéṇasiá (*f.*)
thou wast being struck	kotezōṇ aso (*m.*) kotezaiṇsi (*f.*)	you were being struck	kotezâṇsé (*m.*) kotezéṇasiá (*f.*)
he, she, it was being struck.	kotezōṇ aso (*m.*) kotezaiṇsi (*f.*)	they were being struck	kotezâṇsé (*m.*) kotezéṇasiá (*f.*)

Pluperfect.

I had been struck	kotezaso (*m.*) kotezasi (*f.*)	we had been struck	kotezâsé (*m.*) kotezasiá (*f*).
thou hadst been struck	kotezaso (*m.*) kotezasi (*f.*)	you had been struck	kotezâsé (*m.*) kotezasiá (*f.*)
he, she, it had been struck.	kotezaso (*m*) kotezasi (*f.*)	they had been struck	kotezâsé (*m.*) kotezasiá (*f.*)

Perfect.

Singular.		*Plural.*	
I was struck . . .	kotezo (*m.*) kotizî (*f.*)	we were struck .	kotezé (*m.*) koteziá (*f.*)
thou wast struck .	kotezo (*m.*) kotizî (*f.*)	you were struck .	kotezé (*m.*) koteziá (*f.*)
he, she, it was struck .	kotezo (*m.*) kotizî (*f.*)	they were struck .	kotezé (*m.*) koteziá (*f.*)

Præterite.

I have been struck .	koté-âṇso (*m.*) koté-énasi (*f.*)	we have been struck .	koté-âṇso (*m.*) koté-énasi (*f.*)
thou hast been struck .	koté-âṇso (*m.*) koté-énasi (*f.*)	you have been struck	koté-âṇso (*m.*) koté-énasi (*f.*)
he, she, it has been struck	koté-âṇso (*m.*) koté-énasi (*f.*)	they have been struck	koté-âṇso (*m.*) koté-énasi (*f.*)

Future.

I shall be struck .	kotezáshatho (*m.*) kotezéshethi (*f.*)	we shall be struck	kotezéshethé.
thou shalt be struck	kotezáshatho (*m*). kotezéshethi (*f.*)	you shall be struck	kotezéshethé.
he, she, it shall be struck . . .	kotezáshatho (*m.*) kotezéshethi (*f.*)	they shall be struck	kotezéshethé.

Imperative Mood.

be thou struck . . .	kotiá.	be ye struck . . .	kotiâṇ.
let him *or* her be struck . .	kotiōnthé.	let them be struck . .	kotiōnthé.

The Conditional Mood.

The conditional mood is formed as in the active by adding *giné* to the indicative in all its forms.

Portions of the defective verb "To Be."

Indicative Mood.

Present.

Singular.		*Plural.*	
I am	tho (*m.*) thi (*f.*)	we are	thé (*m.*) thiá (*f.*)
thou art	tho (*m.*) thi (*f.*)	you are	thé (*m.*) thiá (*f.*)
he, she, it is	tho (*m.*) thi (*f.*)	they are	thé (*m.* thiá (*f.*)

Past.

I was	aso (*m.*) asi (*f.*)	we were . . .	asé (*m.*) asiá (*f.*)
thou wast	aso (*m.*) asi (*f.*)	you were	asé (*m.*) asiá (*f.*)
he, she, it was . . .	aso (*m.*) asi (*f.*)	they were	asé (*m.*) asiá (*f.*)

Conjugation of the verb "To Become."

Infinitive Mood.

Present.		*Future.*	
to become	hōṇ.	to be about to become .	hōṇ hōndo.

Past.

to have become . . . . hôṇ aso.

Participles.

Present.		*Future.*	
becoming	hoâṇ.	being about to become .	hōṇshatho.

Past.

having become . . . . . hōṇ

Supine.

meet to become . . . . . owzântho.

Indicative Mood.

Present.

I am becoming . .	hoântho (*m.*) hoânthi (*f.*)	we are becoming .	hoânthé (*m.*) hoânthiá (*f.*)
thou art becoming .	hoântho (*m.*) hoânthi (*f.*)	you are becoming .	hoânthé (*m.*) hoânthiá (*f.*)
he, she, it is becoming	hoântho (*m.*) hoânthi (*f.*)	they are becoming .	hoânthé (*m.*) hoânthiá (*f.*)

Imperfect.

I was becoming . .	hoânaso (*m.*) hoânasi (*f.*)	we were becoming .	hoânasé (*m.*) hoânasiá (*f.*)
thou wast becoming .	hoânaso (*m.*) hoânasi (*f.*)	you were becoming .	hoânasé (*m.*) hoânasiá (*f.*)
he, she, it was becoming	hoânaso (*m.*) hoânasi (*f.*)	they were becoming .	hoânasé (*m.*) hoânasiá (*f.*)

Pluperfect.

I had become . .	hōndoaso (*m.*) hōndîasi (*f.*)	we had become . .	hōndéasé.
thou hadst become .	hōndoaso (*m.*) hōndîasi (*f.*)	you had become .	hōndéasé.
he, she, it had become	hōndoaso (*m.*) hōndîasi (*f.*)	they had become .	hōndéasé.

Perfect.

I became . . .	hōndo (*m.*) hōndi (*f.*)	we became . .	hōndé (*m.*) hündé (*f.*)
thou becamest . .	hōndo (*m.*) hōndi (*f.*)	you became . .	hōndé (*m.*) hündé (*f.*)
he, she, it became .	hōndo (*m.*) hōndi (*f.*)	they became . .	hōndé (*m.*) hündé (*f.*)

Præterite.

I have become . .	hōntho (*m.*) hōnthi (*f.*)	we have become .	hônthé (*m.*) hōnthiá (*f.*)
thou hast become .	hōntho (*m.*) hōnthi (*f.*)	you have become .	hônthé (*m.*) hōnthiá (*f.*)
he, she, it has become	hōntho (*m.*) hōnthi (*f.*)	they have become .	hônthé (*m.*) hōnthiá (*f.*)

Future.

I shall become	hoshatho (*m.*) hoshathi (*f.*)	we shall become	hoshathé.
thou shalt become	hoshatho (*m.*) hoshathi (*f.*)	you shall become	hoshathé.
he, she, it shall become	hoshatho (*m.*) hoshathi (*f.*)	they shall become	hoshathé.

IMPERATIVE MOOD.

become thou	hōṇ.	become ye	hooṇ.
let him, her, it become	hōnthé.	let them become	hōnthé.

CONDITIONAL MOOD.

The conditional mood is formed by adding *giné* to all forms of the indicative mood.

VOCABULARY.

After ... putyoṇ
All ... bùté.
Always ... mùdâm.
Angry. ... rosh.*
To be angry ... rosh hōṇ.
Arm ... bákwi *pl.*, bákwiyé *f.*
To arrive ... chêlōṇ.
To ask ... pùtsōṇ.
Back ... dow *pl.*, dowé *m.*
Bad ... lácho *m.*, láchi *f.*
To be ... hōṇ.
To become ... hōṇ.
Before ... mùtùko.
To begin ... shùroo keṇ.

Belly ... dhèr *pl.*, dhèré *f.*
Between ... mázé (*suffixed*).
Bird ... ming *m.*
Black ... kishùṇ *m.*, kishiṇ *f.*
Blue ... nîlo *m.*, nîli *f.*
Body ... soorut *pl.*, sooruté *f.*
Bone ... hâd *pl.*, hádé *m.*
Boy ... leko *m.*
Brave ... hikooro *m.*, hikoori *f.*
Bread ... gôli *f.*
To break ... sharōṇ.
Bridge ... seyo.
To bring ... yōṇ.
Brother ... já.
To buy ... ginōṇ.
By ... hundé (*suffixed*).

To call ... lùkōṇ.
Cheek ... koki *pl.*, kookiyé *f.*
Clean ... sâf.
Cold ... too *m.*, tooi *f.*
To come ... yōṇ.
To count ... kâlōṇ.
To cut ... kōṇ.

Darkness ... tumaiy *f.*
Daughter ... dhi *f.*
Day ... dîs *m.*
To-day ... âz.
Death ... merg *m.*
To deceive ... bhálōṇ.

* Many adjectives are the same in both genders.

To die ... márōṇ.
Difficult ... sukt.
Dirty ... pálît.
To do ... karaiṇ ; kyōṇ *m.*, keṇ *f.*
Dog ... kùtsùro *m.*
Donkey ... khur *m.*
Door ... der *m.*
To drink ... po-ōṇ.
Dry ... shishêlo *m.*, shishêli *f.*

Ear ... kân *pl.*, kunné *m.*
Empty ... tish.
Evening ... neshoṇ *m.*
Eye ... áché *pl.*, eché *f.*

Face ... mùṇ *pl.*, mùṇé *m.*
To fall ... dizōṇ.
Far ... door.
Father ... mhâlo *m.*
Fear ... bihil *f.*
To fear ... bihōṇ.
To fight ... kulli keṇ.
Finger ... hángooi *pl.*, hángooyé *f.*
To finish ... tamâm kyōṇ.
Fire ... nâr *m.*
First ... mootoh.
Flower ... phùndo *m.*
To follow ... putyōn kyōṇ.
Foot ... kùr *pl.*, kùré *m.*
For ... kiryah (*suffixed*).
Forehead ... tâlo *pl.*, tâlé *m.*
Fort ... kila *m.*
Fourth ... chōrōṇ.
From ... hundé (*suffixed*).
Full ... pōṇsêlo *m.*, pōṇsêli *f.*

Girl ... leki *f.*
To give ... dyōṇ.
To go ... bazōṇ.
Goats (*collectively*) ... bukker.
He-goat ... tsatilo *m.*
Gold ... swán *m.*
Good ... shooto ; mitoo *m.*, shooti *f.*
Great ... goṇ *m.*, geṇ *f.*
Green ... zârgoon.

Hair ... bâl *pl.*, bâlé *m.*
Half ... âdo *m.*, âdi *f.*
Hand ... hât *pl.*, háté *m.*
Happy ... khùsh.
Hard ... kooro *m.*, koori *f.*

To have	...	tsaiṇ.
Head	...	shish *pl.,* shishé *m.*
To hear	...	shōṇ.
Heart	...	nyoo *pl.,* néwé *m.*
Here	...	ángeké.
Horse	...	gho *m.*
Hot	...	gurm.
House	...	gôt *m.*
Husband	...	báryo *m.*
In	...	kùn (*suffixed*).
Iron	...	tsimer *m.*
To join	...	lyoo kyōṇ.
To kill	...	mârōṇ.
King	...	râz *m.*
To know	...	purzōṇ.
To laugh	...	hâse keṇ.
To learn	...	sechōṇ.
To leave	...	phutyōṇ.
Leg	...	zâng *pl.,* zungé *f.*
Life	...	sâ *f.*
Light (*subs.*)	...	chùlo *m.*
Lightning	...	bitchesh *m.*
Long	...	jingo *m.,* jingi *f.*
To make	...	sundōṇ.
Man	...	mâsh *m.*
Young man	...	tswor *m.*
Old man	...	záro *m.*
Mare	...	ghoi *f.*
Milk	...	chîr *m.*
Moon	...	tsán *f.*
Month	...	mown *pl.,* máh *m.*
Morning	...	okhté *m.*
Mother	...	mhâli *f.*
Mountain	...	kân *m.*
Mouth	...	aiṇ *pl.,* aiṇyé *f.*
Mud	...	tsitsel *m.*
Near	...	kuts.
Neck	...	shâk *pl.,* shâké *m.*
New	...	nō *m.,* nai *f.*
Night	...	râl *f.*
No	...	neh.
Nose	...	natōr *pl.,* natōré *m.*
Now	...	hüwiṇ.
To obey	...	chêtalyōṇ.
Old	...	poorōṇ *m.,* pooreṇ *f.*
Once	...	ek hesh.
To order	...	hookum dyōṇ.

Perhaps	...	owzânto.
To promise	...	wâdá keṇ.
To pull	...	jîtyōṇ.
Rain	...	ajo *m.*
To receive	...	chálōṇ.
Red	...	lîlo *m.*, lîli *f.*
To return	...	pateyōṇ.
To rise	...	ùtyōṇ.
River	...	sîn *f.*
Road	...	pán *f.*
To run	...	mádé keṇ.
Sand	...	sigil.
To say	...	manōṇ.
Second	...	doyōṇ.
To see	...	pashōṇ retōṇ.
To sell	...	mùlrōṇ.
To send	...	chehōṇ.
To separate	...	tselerōṇ.
Shadow	...	tseyùl *f.*
Sheep	...	mindhul *m.*
Short	...	kátōṇ *m.*, káteṇ *f.*
Silver	...	roop *m.*
Sister	...	bihōṇ *f.*
Sleep	...	nîsh *f.*
To sleep	...	nîsh keṇ.
Slow	...	ùngooro *m.*, ungoorì *f.*
Small	...	leko *m.*, leki *f.*
Snow	...	hyooṇ *m.*
Soft	...	kùholo *m.*, kùholi *f.*
Son	...	pooch *m.*
Star	...	târ *m.*
Stone	...	bât *m.*
To strike	...	kotōṇ.
Sun	...	soori *f.*
Sweet	...	zìno *m.*, zìni *f.*
To take	...	dohoṇ.
To teach	...	páshyoṇ.
Then	...	aloṇ kyōṇ.
There	...	álgeké.
To think	...	fiker kyōṇ.
Third	...	choyōṇ.
Thrice	...	châhesh.
To throw	...	gyōṇ.
Thunder	...	tundr *m.*
To	...	too *m.*, ti *f.*, te *pl.* (*suffixed*)
Toe	...	hángooi *pl.*, hángooyé *f.*
To-morrow	...	râli.
Tongue	...	zîb *pl.*, zibé *f.*

Tooth	...	dân *pl.*, duné *m.*
Tree	...	gyoo *f.*
Twice	...	doo hesh.
Water	...	woy *m.*
To weep	...	rōṇ.
Wet	...	bilzêlo *m.*, bilzêli *f.*
What	...	gi.
When (*interrog.*)	...	kullé.
Where (*interrog.*)	...	golé.
White	...	punaro *m.*, punarì *f.*
Who (*interrog.*)	...	koṇ.
Why (*interrog.*)	...	giné.
Wife	...	geryooṇ *f.*
Wind	...	osh *f.*
Wine	...	moṇ *m.*
To wish	...	hyoo hōṇ.
With	...	mulgiri (*suffixed*).
Woman	...	geryooṇ *f.*
Old woman	...	zári *f.*
Young woman	...	pêghul *f.*
Wood	...	soo *m.*
To wound	...	jôbul kyōṇ.
Year	...	kâl *m.*
Yellow	...	pîlo *m.*, pîli *f.*
Yes	...	âṇ.
Yesterday	...	biyâli.

Numerals.

1	ek.	16	showsh.
2	doo.	17	sátâsh.
3	châ.	18	átâsh.
4	chōr.	19	unbish.
5	pâṇs.	20	bish.
6	shoh.	21	bish-oo-ek.
7	sât.	30	bish-oo-dush.
8	ât.	40	doobish.
9	now.	50	doobish-oo-dush.
10	dush.	60	chobish.
11	aiyâsh.	70	chobish-oo-dush.
12	aoowâsh.	80	chōrbish.
13	chōsh.	90	chōrbish-oo-dush.
14	tsòndush.	100	shul.
15	punjish.	1000	zir.

APPENDIX D.

TORWÂLÂK.

The language spoken in Torwâl in the Swat Valley.

DECLENSIONS.

THE NOUN.

	Singular.		*Plural.*	
Nom.	a woman . .	chî.	women . . .	chî.
Gen.	of a woman . .	chî-si.	of women . .	chî-á-si.
Dat	to a woman . .	chî-ké.	to women . .	chî-á-gé.
Acc.	a woman . .	chî.	women . . .	chî.
Abl.	from a woman .	chî-má.	from women . .	chî-á-má.
Nom.	a house . .	shir.	houses . . .	shir.
Gen.	of a house . .	shir-si.	of houses. . .	shir-á-si.
Dat.	to a house . .	shir-wá.	to houses. . .	shir-á-wá.
Acc.	a house . . .	shir.	houses . . .	shir.
Abl.	from a house .	shir-á.	from houses . .	shir-á.

PERSONAL PRONOUNS.

	Nom.	Gen.	Dat.	Acc.	Abl.
I	á	mî	mágé	mai	mámá.
Thou	tooh	chi	tégé	tai	tai-má.
He, she *or* it . . . {	heh	issah	esské	ess	ez-má.
	tiyah	tissah	tesské	tess	tez-má.
We	mah	mùn	mogé	mah	mo-má.
You	toh	tùn	togé	toh	to-má.
They . . . . {	iyah	iyásah	iyáké	iyân	iyah-má.
	tiyah	tiyásah	tiyáké	tiyân	tiyah-má.

N. B.—There are no distinctions of gender. The two forms of the 3rd person singular and plural are employed according to whether the person or object is "near" or "remote."

VERBS.

Conjugation of the verb "To Strike."

ACTIVE VOICE.

Infinitive Mood.

Present.		*Future.*	
to strike . . .	kùdoosá.	about to strike . .	kùd bâdooi.

Past.

to have struck . . . . kùdoosá áshoo.

PARTICIPLES.

Present.		*Future.*	
striking . . .	kùdùdoot.	being about to strike	kùdoosá hoo.

Past.

having struck . . . . kùdùgé.

GERUNDS.

on striking . . . . kùdoojet
from *or* by striking . . . . kùdoomá.

INDICATIVE MOOD.

Each tense has only two forms, *viz.*, masculine and feminine, which are the same in all persons.

Present.	*Pluperfect.*	*Præterite.*
kùdádoo (*m.*)	kùdooshoo (*m.*)	kùdel (*m.*)
küdüdji (*f.*)	küdîshi (*f.*)	küdil (*f.*)
Imperfect.	*Perfect.*	*Future.*
kùdoosáshoo (*m.*)	kùdoo (*m.*)	kùdnin (*m.*)
küdùsáshi (*f.*)	kidi (*f.*)	küdnin (*f.*)

IMPERATIVE MOOD.

Singular.	*Plural.*
2. kùd.	2. kùdá.
3. kùdé.	3. kùdâ.

CONDITIONAL MOOD.

The conditional mood is formed by adding *kyah* "perhaps" to the indicative mood in all its forms, as:

I may be striking . . . . kùdádoo kyah.

PASSIVE VOICE.

The passive is formed by the use of the auxiliary verb *bajoosa* "to go," as:

to be struck . .	kùdùgé bajoosá	I am being struck .	kùdá bajùdoo.

VOCABULARY.

To be able	...	hâda hôsá.
Abuse	...	gál.
To abuse	...	gál dyoosá.
Accustomed	...	âded.
Acid	...	chùk *m.*, chik *f.*
Active	...	tulkh.
After	...	pásh.
Again	...	bî.
Air	...	hilâ *m.*
Alert	...	hùjâ *m.*, hüjè *f.*
All	...	bùd.
Alongside	...	kyuṇ.
Although	...	ágárki.
Always	...	herdî.
And	...	o-ow.
Anger	...	joshil *f.*
Angry *	...	josh.
To be angry	...	josh kowôsá.
To answer	...	jùwâb dyoosá.
Ant	...	pél *f.*
Anxiety	...	piger *m.*
Anxious	...	fikerdâr.
Apart	...	wek.
Apple	...	bebai *f.*
Apricot	...	áshai *f.*
Arm	...	békin *f.*
To arrive	...	ábôsá.
Arrow	...	kân *m.*
To ask	...	kùjoosá.
Ass	...	godô *m.*, gedê *f.*
Aunt (father's sister)	...	pábî *f.*
Aunt (mother's sister)	...	mâsho *f.*
Autumn	...	shet *m.*
Avalanche	...	himâl *m.*
Away	...	choh.
Axe	...	tùnger *m.*
Back	...	dák *m.*
Bad	...	lásh *m.*, láj *f.*
Barley	...	yo *m.*
Basket	..	chùdo *m.*
To be	...	hôsá.
Been	...	jamùng *m.*
Bear	...	oosh *m.*, îsh *f.*
Beard	...	dè *f.*

* Many adjectives are the same in both genders.

To beat	...	kùdoosá.
Beautiful	...	shijo *m.*, shijé *f.*
Because	...	isikyáh.
To become	...	hôsá.
Before	...	moonsh (*suffixed*).
To begin	...	shùroo kôsá.
Behind	...	pásh (*suffixed*).
Belly	...	dê *f.*
Between (*near*)	...	mîmi.
Between (*remote*)	...	maimo.
Bird	...	puchîn *f.*
Bitter	...	tid *m.*, tîd *f.*
Black	...	kishun *m.*, kishen *f.*
Blind	...	un *m.*, án *f.*
Blood	...	jed *f.*
To blow	...	pùgoosá.
Blue	...	nîl.
Blunt	...	book.
Body	...	soorut *m.*
Bone	...	hár *m.*
To be born	...	jyoosá.
Bow	...	bârdun *m.*
Boy	...	po *m.*
Brain	...	mîm *f.*
Brass	...	jit *f.*
Brave	...	hùkoo *m.*, hüki *f.*
Bread	...	gil *f.*
To break	...	porôsá.
Breath	...	shîsh *f.*
Bride	...	bamundir *f.*
Bridegroom	...	bamundoor *m.*
Bridle	...	mulundê *m.*
Bridge	...	seh *f.*
To bring	...	anoosá.
Broad	...	bizin *m.*, bizîn *f.*
To be broken	...	pooroosá.
Brother	...	bâ *m.*
Bull	...	gô *m.*
Bullet	...	gôli *m.*
But	...	médé.
Butterfly	...	puttung *m.*
By	...	má (*suffixed*).
To call	...	chát kôsá.
Camel	...	ùd *m.*, üd *f.*
Charm	...	teyis *f.*
Cheek	...	bogùl *m.*
Chin	...	hágel *f.*
Circle	...	chesh *f.*
Clean	...	shijoo *m.*, shiji *f.*
Clothes	...	bishut *m.*

Cloud ... ágâ *m.*
Cock ... kùgoo *m.*
Cold (*subs.*) ... shidul *m.*
Cold (*adj.*) ... shidahoo *m.*, shidaihi *f.*
Colour ... râng *m.*
To come ... yôsá.
Copper ... támbâ *m.*
Corner ... gùd *m.*
Corpse ... zinâs *m.*
Cough ... kán *m.*
To count ... lékoosá
Country ... wuttun *m.*
Courage ... hikoo *m.*
Cow ... gâ *f.*
To creep ... tátáshoosá.
Crooked ... kol *m.*, kel *f.*
Crow ... kágh *m.*
Custom ... dustoor *m.*

Dagger ... choo *m.*
To dance ... nâr kôsá.
Dancing ... nâr *m.*
Dangerous ... káternâk.
Darkness ... ánchik *f.*
Daughter ... doo *f.*
Dawn ... lobyât *m.*
Day ... dî *f.*
Mid-day ... badùshkâr *m.*
To-day ... ayùdi.
Deaf ... boo *m.*, bü *f.*
Death ... merg *m.*
Deceit ... chul *m.*
To deceive ... baderôsá.
Destitute ... hwah.
Dew ... pullus *m.*
To die ... maiyoosá.
Difficult ... mùshkil.
Dirty ... ánatôl *m.*, ánitel *f.*
To dismount .. wôsá.
To do ... kôsá.
Dog ... kùjoo *m.*, kijî *f.*
Door ... derwâz *m.*
Down ... ládoot.
Dream ... sen *f.*
To drink ... poosá.
Drum ... dunduk *m.*
Dry ... shùgil.

Ear ... kán *m.*
Earth ... sùng *m.*
Earthquake ... boomel *m.*

East	...	mushshrikh
Easy	...	soogâh *m.*, sùgè *f.*
To eat	...	kowoosá.
Eclipse	...	tundergyát *m.*
Edge	...	tîn *f.*
Egg	...	ân *m.*
Elbow	...	tih *f.*
Empty	...	toosh.
Enemy	...	dùshmun *m.*
To enter	...	ùshoosá.
Envy	...	ghumâz *m.*
Equal	...	báràber.
Equinox	...	hámál *m.*
Evening	...	nyáshâm *m.*
Ever	...	kyeh.
Everybody	...	bùd mâsh.
Everything	...	bùd siz.
Ewe	...	ê *f.*
Eye	...	áshi *f.*
To fall	...	lár bajoosá.
Family	...	gun *m.*
Far	...	doo.
Fat (*subs.*)	...	mih *f.*
Fat (*adj.*)	...	bâr *m.*, bèr *f.*
Father	...	bâp *m.*
Fault	...	ep *f.*
Fear	...	bid *f.*
Feather	...	pet *m.*
Female	...	chî *f.*
Fight	...	dák *m.*
To find	...	sai kôsá.
Finger	...	ângî *f.*
To finish	...	tomâm kôsá.
Fire	...	ungâh *m.*
First	...	mooṇsh
Fish	...	máj *m.*
Flower	...	pushoo *m.*
Flute	...	bîsh *f.*
To fly (as a bird)	...	shijoosá.
Following	...	pásh.
Foot	...	koo *m.*
For	...	kyah (*suffixed*).
To forget	...	ámáshoosá.
Forgetfulness	...	ámosh *m.*
Fort	...	kálâ *m.*
Fox	...	poosh *m.*, pîsh *f.*
Friend	...	dôs *m.*
Friendship	...	dosti *f.*
From	...	ámá (*suffixed*).
Frost	..	kùlékùlé *f.*

Fruit ... mewâ *m.*
Full ... poonil.

Garden ... bâgh *m.*
Generous ... hùkoo *m.*, hüki *f.*
Girl ... serán *f.*
To give ... dyoosá.
To go ... bajoosá.
To go out ... bâgé nikoosá.
He-goat ... birát *m.*
She-goat ... chel *f.*
Gold ... lùrzer *m.*
Good ... ghōrâh.
Grape ... dásh *m.*
Grass ... gâ *m.*
Gratitude ... shùkùr *m.*
Great ... gun *m.*, gen *f.*
Green ... pihîl.
To grieve ... zùchoosá.
Gun ... toobook *m.*
Gunpowder ... dâroo *m.*

Hail ... mek *f.*
Hair ... bâl *m.*
Half ... ur.
Hand ... hât *m.*
Right hand ... sùbun hât *m.*
Left hand ... ábun hât *m.*
Handle ... dun *m.*
Happiness ... khâdî *f.*
Happy ... khùsh *m.*, khesh *f.*
Hard ... koo *m.*, kü *f.*
Hare ... hoosî *m.*
Hatred ... boghùz *m.*
Head ... shōh *m.*
Health ... kairut *m.*
To hear ... bùjooṣá.
Heart ... hü *f.*
Heat ... germî *f.*
The heavens ... azmân *m.*
Heavy ... oogoo *m.*, ügü *f.*
Hen ... kügî *f.*
Herd ... gun : gullah *m.*
Here ... met.
High ... ootál *m.*, ootil *f.*
Hope ... oomet *f.*
Horse ... gho *m.*
Hot ... gurm.
House ... shir *f*
How ... kyul, kál.
How many ... kidé.

How much	...	kidát gen.
Humble	...	hü gháríb.
Hunger	...	bùsh *m.*
Hungry	...	bùshowhoo *m.*, bùshaihi *f.*
Husband	...	bé *m.*
Ice	...	ôsh *m.*
Idle	...	narâz.
If	...	ákhir.
Illness	...	nájùrtyáh *m.*
In	...	konîm (*prefixed*).
Industrious	...	kumâder *m.*, kumâdèr *f.*
Infant	...	lit.
Iron	...	chimoh *m.*
To kick	...	paiṇ dyoosá.
To kill	...	mowoosá.
King	...	pâdshâh *m.*
Knee	...	kùré *m.*
Knife	...	châgoo *m.*, kerah *f.*
To know	...	jánoosá.
Knowledge	...	hoojâ *m.*
Lame	...	kùd *m.*, küd *f.*
Land	...	darin *f.*
Language	...	bât *m.*
To laugh	...	hásoosá.
Lead	...	sigah *m.*
To learn	...	chùjoosá.
To leave	...	chowoosá.
Leg	...	jung *m.*
To let go	...	chôsá.
Lie	...	lobo *m.*
Life	...	sâ *m.*
Light (*subs.*)	...	loj *m.*
Light (*adj.*)	...	oopùr *m.*, ipîr *f.*
Lightning	...	bijmot *m.*
Lip	...	dùd *m.*
A little	...	ashùr.
Liver	...	jagô *m.*
Long	...	jik *m.*, jîk *f.*
To look at	...	pushoosá.
Love	...	yâr *m.*
To love	...	dôsti kôsá.
Low	...	chit *m.*, chît *f.*
Maid	...	butkoomâ *f.*
Male	...	nariná *m.*
Man	...	mesh *m.*
Young man	...	zùwâṇ *m.*
Old man	...	derg *m.*

Mankind	...	mâsh.
Mare	...	ghé *f.*
Meat	...	mâs *m.*
Medicine	...	dáwah *m.*
Mid-day	...	badùshkâr *m.*
Mid-night	...	urjât *m.*
Milk	...	chüî *f.*
Mist	...	dùr *m.*
Moon	...	yùn *m.*
New moon	...	nem *f.*
Full moon	...	pin *f.*
Month	...	mah *m.*
Morning	...	jut *m.*
Mother	...	yê *f.*
Mountain	...	chai *m.*
Mouse	...	moosh *m.*
Mouth	...	èṇ *m.*
To move (*trans.*)	...	pergoosa.
Much	...	cher.
So much	...	essum.
This much	...	mussum.
Mud	...	öj *m.*
Mulberry	...	toot *m.*
Music	...	dunduk-o-bîshi *m.* (*literally* "drum and flute").
Nail (finger)	...	nōk *m.*
Name	...	nâm *m.*
Narrow	...	chùn *m.*, chin *f.*
Near	...	nyuṇ.
Neck	...	chaiyoṇ *m.*
Nephew	...	bowoosh *m.*
Never	...	hecherinah.
New	...	num.
Niece	...	beyîsh *f.*
Night	...	jât *m.*
No	...	nâ.
Nobody	...	nákâmnah.
North	...	kùtùb *m.*
Nose	...	nât *m.*
Nothing	...	nokoynah.
Now	...	méré.
Of	...	i-si (*suffixed*).
Old	...	lájing.
On	...	jet (*suffixed*).
Open	...	baiyel.
To open	...	olôsá.
Or	...	yah.
To order	...	bundoosá.
Out	...	baiyim (*prefixed*).
To overthrow	...	jùjoosá.

Peach	...	â *m.*
Pear	...	tòngoo *m.*
Perhaps	...	kyah.
Pigeon	...	nîlgolê *f.*
Pity	...	hidej *f.*
Place	...	pöt *m.*
Play	...	nerer *m.*
To play (a game)	...	noroosá.
To please	...	khùshoosá.
Pleased	...	khùjâ.
To be pleased	...	khùjah hôsá.
Plough	...	höl *m.*
Point	...	pid *f.*
To pour	...	taloosá.
Praise	...	sipad *m.*
Pride	...	loyichâr *m.*
To produce	...	hâda hôsá.
To promise	...	wai kôsá.
Proud	...	loyi.
To pull	...	jigáloosá.
Quarrel	...	lât *m.*
Quarter	...	chùdeh.
Queen	...	khoonzah *f.*
Rain	...	ágâ *m.*
Rainbow	...	inhân *m.*
Ram	...	midhál *m.*
Ready	...	tiah.
To receive	...	powoosá.
Red	...	lohoor *m.*, lihîr *f.*
Relation	...	doomsah *m.*
Relationship	...	kámwâl *m.*
To remember	...	yâdoosá.
Remembrance	...	yát *m.*
To return	...	pádgé boosá.
Rice	...	tunôl *m.*
Rich	...	ishtamun.
To rise	...	ùshoosá.
River	...	nád *m.*
Road	...	pân *m.*
Roof	...	tel *f.*
Rope	...	keh *f.*
Rough	...	zigh.
Round	...	koror *m.*, kerer *f.*
To run	...	daiṇ dyoosá.
Sad	...	ghumjun *m.*, ghumjen *f.*
Saddle	...	kâti *f.*
Sand	...	sigul *m.*

To say	...	bánoosá.
To search for	...	birâroosá.
To see	...	boo-oosá.
Seed	...	bij *f.*
Self	...	tuṅoo.
To sell	...	biginoosá.
To send	...	pyoosá.
To separate	...	jùda kôsá.
Servant	...	noker *m.*
Shadow	...	chojol *m.*
Shame	...	sherm *m.*
Sharp	...	tîn.
Sheep	...	bogho *m.*
Short	...	kurrun *m.*, keren *f.*
Shoulder	...	kân *m.*
To shout	...	chigân gâloosá.
Shut	...	dél.
To shut	...	gunoosá.
Side	...	bárish *f.*
On this side	...	medish.
On that side	...	edish.
Alongside	...	kyuṇ.
Sigh	...	humsôs *m.*
Silent	...	ghulé.
Silver	...	oozelzer *m.*
To sing	...	git dyoosá.
Singing	...	git *f.*
Sister	...	shoo *f.*
To sit	...	baiyoosá.
Skill	...	poá *m.*
Skin	...	chum *m.*
Slave	...	gholum *m.*
Sleep	...	nîn *f.*
To sleep	...	nîn bajoosá.
Sloping	...	barîsh.
Slow	...	sot *m.*, söt *f.*
Small	...	lùd *m.*, lid *f.*
Smoke	...	dîmi *f.*
Smooth	...	pishul *m.*, pishel *f.*
Snake	...	ján *m.*
Sneeze	...	tîṇyoo *m.*
Snow	...	him *m.*
Soft	...	kumul *m.*, kemel *f.*
Solstice	...	kir *f.*
Somebody	...	kâm.
Something	...	kuchis.
Son	...	pùj *m.*
Sorrow	...	ghum *m.*
Sound	...	áwâs *m.*
South	...	nilow *m.*
Spoon	...	deh *f.*

Spring	...	basân *m.*
To stand	...	ùshoosá.
Star	...	táh *m.*
Stone	...	bád *m.*
Storm	...	tofân *m.*
Straight	...	shoosh *m.*, shîsh *f.*
Strength	...	tâgut *m.*
Strong	...	zaror.
Stupidity	...	bekoo *m.*
Summer	...	bushâ *m.*
Sun	...	sî *f.*
Sweet	...	mîd.
Swift	...	tulákh.
To swim	...	lâmôsá.
Sword	...	terbel *f.*
Tail	...	lámâd *m.*
To take	...	gushoosá.
To take away	...	neyoosá.
To take up	...	ùchoosá.
To teach	...	choojoosá.
To tell	...	lât kôsá.
That one	...	páhgah.
Then	...	tetchek.
There	...	tel.
Therefore	...	tisikyah.
Thick	...	bâr *m.*, bèr *f.*
Thin	...	joobál *m.*, joobel *f.*
Thirst	...	tish *f.*
Thirsty	...	tishowhoo *m.*, tishaihi *f.*
This	...	ágah.
Thought	...	khyâl *m.*
Throat	...	shâng *m.*
To throw	...	taloosá.
To throw down	...	lâ taloosá.
Thumb	...	angùt *m.*
Thunder	...	gedus *m.*
Thus	...	mechelé.
Till	...	tá.
Time	...	chek *f.*
Timid	...	biád.
To	...	wá, tá, ké, gé (*suffixed*).
Toe	..	ángî *f.*
Together	...	epot.
To-morrow	...	bolùdi.
The day after to-morrow		chotùgdi.
Tongue	...	jib *m.*
Tooth	...	dân *m.*
Touch	...	áwoo *m.*
To touch	...	miloosá.
Towards	...	dishah (*suffixed*).

Tree	...	tâm *m.*
Truth	...	sáj *m.*
Ugly	...	osho *m.*, eshé *f.*
Uncle (father's brother)		pejî *m.*
Uncle (mother's brother)		mâm *m.*
Under	...	ten (*suffixed*).
Unless	...	bágèr.
Up	...	ootel.
Upright	...	shoosh *m.*, shîsh *f.*
Valley	...	koo *m.*
Very	...	cher.
Very well	...	ghōrâ.
Village	...	gâm *m.*
Wall	...	kùr *m.*
Water	...	oo *m.*
Weak	...	kumzor *m.*, kemzer *f.*
Weakness	...	kumzortyah *m.*
Wedding	...	bêbâ.
Week	...	satumdì *f.*
To weep	...	jingoosá.
West	...	mugrib *f.*
Wet	...	öj *m.*, áj *f.*
What	...	kah.
Wheat	...	gomoo *m.*
When (*interrog.*)	...	kê.
When (*relat.*)	...	tetchek.
Whence	...	kedah.
Where (*interrog.*)	...	ket.
Which	...	kâmé.
White	...	oojul *m.*, oojel *f.*
Whip	...	korodah *m.*
Who (*interrog.*)	...	kâm.
Why	...	keské.
Widow	...	jem *f.*
Widower	...	jon *m.*
Wife	...	chî *f.*
Wind	...	balai *f.*
Window	...	tumboo *m.*
Winter	...	himân *m.*
Wise	...	dânah.
Wish	...	rezah *m.*
To wish	...	rezah kôsá.
With	...	sát (*suffixed*).
Without	...	bé.
Woman	...	chî *f.*
Old woman	...	dág *f.*
Wood	...	shellah *m.*

Wool	...	pám *m.*
Work	...	kám *m.*
To work	...	kám kôsá.
To write	...	ligoosá.
Year	...	kâl *m.*
Yellow	...	chùnoo *m.*, chené *f.*
Yes	...	a-âṇ.
Yesterday	...	chîdùgdi.
The day before yesterday.		ejùgdi.

Numerals.		*Ordinals.*	
1	ek.	First ...	moonsh.
2	doo.	Second ...	pâsh.
3	châ.	Third ...	tlooi.
4	choh.	Fourth ...	chotum.
5	pân.	Fifth ...	pânjum.
6	shoh.	Sixth ...	showum.
7	sát.		
8	át.		
9	nom.	Once ...	ekgonah.
10	dush.	Twice ...	doogonah.
11	ágâsh.	Thrice ...	chîgonah.
12	doowâsh.		
13	chesh.		
14	chettish.		
15	pungsh.		
16	shésh.		
17	sátâsh.		
18	átâsh.		
19	unbîsh.		
20	bîsh.		
21	ek-o-bîsh.		
30	dush-o-bîsh.		
40	doo bîsh.		
50	dush-o-doo bîsh.		
60	châbîsh.		
70	dush-o-châbîsh.		
80	choh bîsh.		
90	dush-o-choh bîsh.		
100	soh.		
1000	zer.		

APPENDIX E.

BUSHKARIK.

The language spoken in the upper part of the Swat and Punjkorah Valleys.

DECLENSIONS.

THE NOUN.

	Singular.		*Plural.*	
Nom.	a woman	îs.	women	îsâl.
Gen.	of a woman	îs-eṇ.	of women	îsâlâṇ.
Dat.	to a woman	îs-kah.	to women	îsâl-kah.
Acc.	a woman	îs.	women	îsâl.
Abl.	with a woman	îs-sah.	with women	îsâl-sámân.
	from a woman	îs-mah.	from women	îsâl-mah.
	by a woman	îs-rah.	by women	îsâl-rah.
	for a woman	îseṇ-ker.	for women	îsâleṇ-ker.

PERSONAL PRONOUNS.

	Nom.	Gen.	Dat.	Acc.	Ablative.
I *intrans.* / *trans.*	yah / yeh	mâ (*m.*) / meṇ (*f.*)	máké	mai	mai-sah, &c., meṇ-ker.
thou	tooh	châṇ (*m.*) / cheṇ (*f.*)	táké	tai	tai-sah, &c., cheṇ-ker.
he, *or* it	ai (*n.*) / átâṇ (*r.*)	ásâṇ	áské (*n.*) / táské (*r.*)	áseṇ (*n.*) / táteṇ (*r.*)	âs-sah, &c., áseṇ-ker.
she, *or* it	utteṇ (*n.*) / tutteṇ (*r.*)	usseṇ (*n.*) / tusseṇ (*r.*)	*as in the masculine*		
we	mah	moṇ	mâké	mah	mâ-sah, &c., meṇ-ker.
you	tah	toṇ	tâké	tah	tâ-sah, &c. toṇ-ker.
they	um (*n.*) / tum (*r.*)	ásoṇ (*n.*) / tásoṇ (*r.*)	âmké (*n.*) / tâmké (*r.*)	âm (*n.*) / tâm (*r.*)	âm-sah, &c., ásoṇ-ker.

n. and *r.* signify *near* and *remote.*

THE VERB.

Conjugation of the verb "To Come."

INFINITIVE MOOD.

Present.		*Past.*	
to come	yâgân.	to have come . . .	yâgâshoo.

PARTICIPLES.

coming.	yâgrá.	having come . . .	yâté.

GERUNDS.

from coming	yânder.	in coming . . .	yâgân maiyá.

SUPINE.

must come . . . . yâgtoo.

INDICATIVE MOOD.

Each tense has only two forms, *viz.:* masculine and feminine, which are the same in all persons.

Present.		*Perfect.*	
I am coming, &c. . .	yântoo m.) yenti (*f.*)	I came, &c. . . .	gâ (*m.*) gê (*f.*)
Imperfect.		*Præterite.*	
I was coming, &c. . .	yânshoo (*m.*) yenshi (*f.*)	I have come . .	yâtoo (*m.*) yeti (*f.*)
Pluperfect.		*Future.*	
I had come, &c. . .	yâshoo (*m.*) yeshi (*f.*)	I will come, &c. . .	yum (*m.*) yen (*f.*)

IMPERATIVE MOOD.

Singular.		*Plural.*	
come thou	yáh.	come ye	yâ.
let him *or* her come. . .	yádáh.	let them come . . .	yâdáh.

The defective verb "To Be."

INFINITIVE MOOD.

Present.

to be . . . . ashoogân.

INDICATIVE MOOD.

Present.		*Pluperfect.*	
I am, &c. . . .	too (*m.*) tooi (*f.*)	I had been, &c. . .	âshoo (*m.*) áshooi (*f.*)

Past.

I was *or* have been, &c. . . . hoo (*m.*) / hü (*f.*)

Where defective the verb "To Become" is used.

Conjugation of the verb "To Become."

Infinitive Mood.

Present.

to become . . . . . . hogâṇ.

Participles.

Present.		*Past.*	
becoming	homé.	having become . .	hooti.

Indicative Mood.

The future has more than two forms.

Present.		*Pluperfect.*	
I am becoming, &c.	hoowântoo (*m.*) hùwenti (*f.*)	I had become, &c. .	hooshoo (*m.*) hūshi (*f.*)
Imperfect.		*Perfect.*	
I was becoming .	hoowânshoo (*m.*) hùwenshi (*f.*)	I became, &c. .	hoo (*m.*) hü (*f.*)

Præterite.

I have become, &c. . . . hootoo (*m.*) / hütü (*f.*)

Future.

Singular.		*Plural.*	
I will become . . .	hom (*m.*) hoowé (*f.*)	we will become . .	hoo (*m.*) hooi (*f.*)
thou wilt become . .	hoh.	you will become . .	hoo (*m.*) hooi (*f.*)
he, she, it, will become .	hoh.	they will become . .	hoo (*m.*) hooi (*f.*)

Imperative Mood.

become thou	hoh.	become ye . . .	hô.
let him, her, it, become . .	hodah.	let them become . .	hohdah.

Conjugation of the verb "To Do" *or* "To Make."

Infinitive Mood.

Present.		*Past.*	
to do.	karoogâṇ.	to have done . . .	karoogâshoo.

Participles.

doing	karâ.	having done	kâ.

Gerunds.

from doing . . .	karoogerer.	in doing . . .	karoog maiyá.

Indicative Mood.

The future has more than two forms.

Present.		*Pluperfect.*	
I am doing, &c.	karântoo (*m.*) karenti (*f.*)	I had done, &c.	kirshi (*m.* & *f.*)
Imperfect.		*Perfect.*	
I was doing, &c.	karânshoo (*m.*) karenshi (*f.*)	I did, &c.	kir (*m.* & *f.*)
		Præterite.	
		I have done, &c.	kirti (*m.* & *f.*)

Future.

Singular.		*Plural.*	
I will do	káruṇ (*m.*) káreṇ (*f.*)	we will do	kári (*m.*) káreṇ (*f.*)
thou wilt do	káreṇ (*m.*) káreṇ (*f.*)	you will do	kárâṇ (*m.*) káreṇ (*f.*)
he, she, it, will do	kárâṇ (*m.*) káreṇ (*f.*)	they will do	kárâṇ (*m.*) káreṇ (*f.*)

IMPERATIVE MOOD.

do thou	ker.	do ye	kerah.
let him, her, it, do	kerdah.	let them do	kerdah.

EXAMPLES.

Come here	Âté yah.
Go away	Nikki choh.
A sharp sword	Tîn terbêl.
A brave man	Düt mîsh.
A good knife	Ren kâter.
A good horse	Ghor rân.
A great river	Gen nádh.
Three small swords	Tlâ lüküt terbâl.
I saw ten big trees	Mai dush gân tum lüch.
I have a good gun	Másé ren tobâk tooi.
I have a wound on my hand.	Meṇ ther-ráh perâr too.
What is your name?	Châṇ kah nám?
Whence have you come?	Kunti yâgá?*
Where are you going to?	Kun káh buchân too?
Is this your horse?	Aiṇ ghor chânā?*
No; it is my father's horse.	Nah, aiṇ ghor mâ bábá.
What is your father's name?	Châṇ bábá kah nám?
Give me something	Máké kichá dah.
I come from Bushkar.	Bushkâti yântoo.
I am going to Chitral.	Yah Châtlâl-ké buchântoo.
Is the road good?	Pund ren tooi?
No, there is much snow.	Nah, him bár too.
The land in Kalam is good.	Gâl Kalâmah rentooi.
It is two days' journey from Rashkot to Kalam?	Râshkoti Kalâmai doo dos pund too?
I am hungry	Yah bùchágâltoo.
Give me some bread	Máké kichá gyül dah.
What do you want?	Káh bah tântoo?
I will beat you	Yeh tai renum.
Call that man here	Tettuṇ mîsh tâker.
Tell him to come	Táské munooyahdah.
He has struck me; he is my enemy.	Ai mai renâgh; ai mâ ghálîm.
He took the gun from me.	Ai mai-mah tobâk gin.
His gun is better than mine.	Usseṇ tobâk meṇ tobâk ren tooi.
We will go with him	Mah âs-sah chom.
Bring two horses from them.	Âm-mah doo ghor gyah.

* The terminal *a* marks the interrogative.

VOCABULARY.

To be able	... hâsá hogâṇ.
Accustomed	... ádât.
Although	... lôlá poorá.
And	... o.
Angry	... rosh.
To be angry	... rosh karoogâṇ.
To ask	... kojâgâṇ.
Ass	... guddá *pl.*, guddâ *m.*; *fem. form* guddai.
Aunt (father's sister)	... pep. *pl.*, pepoo *f.*
,, (mother's sister	... meṇsh *pl.*, meṇshoo *f.*
Away	... nikki.
Back	... tung *m.*
Bad	... lulh *m.*, lelh *f.*
Battle-axe	... tong *pl.*, tongât *m.*
To be	... ashoogâṇ.
Beard	... dér *f.*
To beat	... renágâṇ.
Beautiful	... rân soorut *m.*, ren soorut *f.*
Because	... khâsá.
To become	... hogâṇ.
Belly	... dâr *m.*
Bird	... shîṇsh *pl.*, shînshâr *f.*
Black	... küshün *m.*, kishin *f.*
Blind	... shâhr *m.*, shihr *f.*
Blood	... rut.
Blue	... nül *m.*, nil *f.*
Body	... soorut *m.*
Bone	... hád *m.*
Bow	... kân *pl.*, kânâr *m.*
Boy	... jâták *pl.*, jâtáko *m.*
Brave	... düt *m.*, dit *f.*
Bread	... gyül.
To break	... chinjoogâṇ.
To bring	... ánoogâṇ.
Broad	... bissün *m.*, bissin *f.*
Brother	... jâ *pl.*, johoo *m.*
Bull	... goh *pl.*, gô *m.*
By	... rah (*suffixed*).
To call	... takeroogâṇ.
Clean	... pâkhîzá.
Cloud	... âgah *m.*
Cock	... kùkùr *pl.*, kùkùrbâl *m.*
Cold	... shùdul *m.*, shidil *f.*
To come	... yâgâṇ.
To count	... gunoogâṇ.

Cow	gâ, *pl.* gai *f.*
Custom	dustoor *m.*
To cut	chinoogâṇ.
Dagger	choor, *pl.* choorbâr *m.*
Dark	chün.
Darkness	enchook *m.*
Daughter	birê, *pl.* birêshâl *f.*
Day	dos.
To-day	âj.
Deaf	por *m.*, bür *f.*
Deceit	bâderoogh.
Destitute	ghárîb.
To die	maroogâṇ.
Difficult	bùshüt.
Dirty	nowl.
Disposition	kákoom *m.*
To do	karoogâṇ.
Dog	kùchùr, *pl.* kùchùrbâl *m.*, *fem. form* kichir.
To drink	poogâṇ.
Dry	shok *m.*, shök *f.*
Ear	kán *m.*
Earth	sùm *m.*
Easy	soogâr *m.*, soogér *f.*
To eat	kâgâṇ.
Egg	án *m.*
Elbow	bákün *m.*
Elephant	het *f.*
Empty	chun *m.*, chin *f.*
Enemy	ghálîm.
To enter	ichoogâṇ.
Ewe	îr *f.*
Eye	âch, *pl.* ech *f.*
To fall	chor karoogâṇ.
Far	door *m.*, dür *f.*
Father	bâp, *pl.* bâpoo *m.*
Fault	âb *m.*
Fear	büt *m.*
To fear	byoogâṇ.
Female	thlöhl *f.*
Fifth	pânchum.
Fight	jâr ; yoor *m.*
To fight	járâṇ.
Finger	ángoor, *pl.* ángoorâl *m.*
Fire	ángâr *m.*
First	owál.
Fish	muts, *pl.* mutsin *m.*
Flower	phond *m.*

To follow	...	notoogâṇ.
Foot	...	kŭr *m.*
For	...	ker (*suffixed*).
Fort	...	kôt.
Fourth	...	chōt.
Fowl	...	kŭkŭr, *pl.* kŭkŭrbâl.
Fox	...	lomaiy *m.*
From	...	ti (*place*), mah (*person*) *suffixed.*
Full	...	poojâl *m.*, poojil *f.*
Garden	...	bâgh.
Girl	...	baih, *pl.* birêshâl *f.*
To give	...	dâgâṇ.
To go	...	buchoogâṇ ; choogâṇ.
Goats (*collectively*)	...	châl.
He-goat	...	bür.
She-goat	...	cher.
God	...	khŭdai.
Gold	...	lohoozer *m.*
Good	...	rân *m.*, ren *f.*
Great	...	gân *m.*, gen *f.*
Green	...	pâlá *m.*, pále *f.*
Gun	...	tobâk, *pl.* tobek *f.*
Hand	...	ther *f.*
Happiness	...	khŭshéli *f.*
Hard	...	tukker *m.*, tukkir *f.*
Hare	...	hŭsooi *m.*
Head	...	tōs, *pl.* tōsilân *m.* ; *fem. form* tês.
To hear	...	bŭjoogâṇ ; lüchgâṇ.
Heart	...	hikooker, *pl.* hikookerâl.
Heavy	...	
Hen	...	kikir, *pl.* kikirbâl *f.*
Herd	...	bukker.
Here	...	âté.
High	...	ootull *m.*, ootill *f.*
Hope	...	oomât *m.*
Horse	...	ghor, *pl.* ghorâl *m.*
Hot	...	tutt *m.*, tett *f.*
House	...	shŭt *f.*
How	...	kol.
Hungry	...	bŭch.
To be hungry	...	bŭchágogâṇ.
Ice	...	osh.
If	...	ákhür.
To be ill	...	bilâgogâṇ.
Illness	...	bilegâr *m.*
In	...	ah (*suffixed*).
Infant	...	lookoot, *pl.* lookootor *m.*
Iron	...	chimer *m.*

To kill	...	mâroogâṇ.
King	...	râj, *pl.* râjem *m.*
Knee	...	koot *m.*
Knife	...	kâter, *pl.* kâtêr *f.*
Land	...	gâl.
To laugh	...	hásoogâṇ.
Lead	...	tsüz *f.*
To leave	...	choroogâṇ.
To let go	...	tâgâṇ.
To lift	...	ùchoogâṇ.
Light (*subs.*)	...	chull ; loh *m.*
Lightning	...	tunder *m.*
Long	...	lük *m.*, lik *f.*
To look at	...	pushoogâṇ.
Low	...	kuttung *m.*, kutting *f.*
Maid	...	bâdeṇ, *pl.* bâden isâl *f.*
To make	...	karoogâṇ.
Male	...	thohl *m.*
Man	...	mîsh, *pl.* mánùsh *m.*
Young man	...	bádân, *pl.* bâdân *m.*
Old man	...	gánâr, *pl.* gánârât *m.*
Mare	...	ghür, *pl.* ghorâl *f.*
Marriage	...	jin *f.*
Meat	...	mâs.
Milk	...	chür *f.*
Moon	...	chán *m.*
Month	...	mâ.
Mother	...	yê *f.*
Mountain	...	zum, *pl.* kán *m.*
Much	...	bár.
Mouth	...	aiñy *f.*
Name	...	nám.
Narrow	...	tung *m.*, teng *f.*
Near	...	nîher.
New	...	num *m.*, nim *f.*
Night	...	rât.
No	...	nah.
Nose	...	názor *f.*
Nothing	...	kai nah.
Old	...	poorán *m.*, pooren *f.*
On	...	ùjùm.
To open	...	mùchâgâṇ.
Or	...	yah.
To be pained	...	bilegárâṇ.
Pigeon	...	nîlbot *m.*
Pleased	...	khosh.
To promise	...	woi karoogâṇ.

Quarrel	...	tupoo *m.*
To quarrel	...	tupoogâṇ.
Queen	...	hōnzá, *pl.* hōnzâ *f.*
Rain	..	mùchook *m.*
Ram	...	mùnâr.
Ready	...	têyâr.
To receive	...	lâgâṇ.
Red	...	lohoo *m.*, lehi *f.*
To remember	...	shimeroogâṇ.
Rich	...	ishtamun *m.*, ishtamen *f.*
River	...	nádh, *pl.* nidh *f.*
Road	...	pund *m.*
Rock	...	tok, *pl.* tchen *m.*
Rope	...	kâröt *f.*
To run	...	dâghâṇ.
Sad	...	kuppá.
Sand	...	sügüt *f.*
To say	...	munoogâṇ.
Second	...	pátai.
To see	...	pushoogâṇ ; lüchgâṇ.
To send	...	tulloogâṇ.
Servant	...	nôker, *pl.* nôkeroo.
Shame	...	shurm.
Sharp	...	tén *m.*, tîn *f.*
Sheep (*collect.*)	...	âr.
Short	...	chùnùt *m.*, chünüt *f.*
Shoulder	...	kân *m.*
Silent	...	lân.
To be silent	...	lân buchoogâṇ.
Silver	...	punnerzer *m.*
Sister	...	ishpo, *pl.* ishpowoo *f.*
To sit	...	baiyoogâṇ.
Skin	...	chum.
Sky	...	ásmân *f.*
Slave	...	golâm, *pl.* golâmân.
To sleep	...	nîn buchoogâṇ.
Small	...	lookoot *m.*, lüküt *f.*
Smoke	...	démî.
Snow	...	him.
Soft	...	kômul *m.*, komil *f.*
Something	...	kichá.
Son	...	po, *pl.* pül *m.*
Sound	...	háwâz *m.*
To stand	...	itoogâṇ.
Star	...	târ *m.*
Stone	...	but, *pl.* bâtin *m.*
Storm	...	topân *m.*
To strike	...	renágâṇ.
Strong	...	mokum *m.*, mokem *f.*

Stupid ...	gáront *m.*, gárent *f.*
Sun ...	sür *f.*
Sword ...	terbêl, *pl.* terbâl *f.*
To take ...	gushoogâṇ.
To take away ...	nâgâṇ ; gunoogâṇ.
That ...	uttâṇ ; tettuṇ.
Then ...	uttâṇ klâk ; tettiṇ klâk.
There ...	ashùmbâ.
Therefore ...	tesseṇker.
To think ...	toloogâṇ.
Thirsty ...	tlùch.
This ...	aiṇ.
Thought ...	khaiyâl *m.*
To throw ...	taloogâṇ.
Third ...	tlooi.
Thunder ...	good goodai *m.*
Thus ...	aiṇchellah ; uttâṇchellah.
Time ...	klâk.
Timid ...	biât *m.*, biet *f.*
To ...	kah ; ké ; sé.
To-morrow ...	rét.
The day after to-morrow	tlüd.
Tongue ...	jib.
Tooth ...	dun, *pl.* dân *f.*
Tree ...	tâm, *pl.* tum *m.*
Ugly ...	lâl soorut *m.*, lel soorut *f.*
Uncle (father's brother)	*if older*, gân bâp ; *if younger*, lookoo bâp.
,, (mother's brother)	môt, *pl.* moloo *m.*
Under ...	toowah.
Valley ...	gull ; kâd.
Very ...	bár.
Water ...	oo *m.*
Weak ...	ajùz.
To weep ...	rongoogâṇ.
To weigh ...	toloogâṇ.
Wet ...	ull *m.*, ell *f.*
What ...	kah.
When (*interrog.*) ...	kwun.
Whence ...	kunti.
Where (*interrog.*) ...	kunkah.
White ...	punner *m.*, punnir *f.*
Who (*interrog.*) ...	kum.
Why ...	kîk.
Wife ...	kumudîn, *pl.* yür *f.*
Wind ...	bâlá *m.*
Wine ...	mud *m.*

To wish	...	rezai karoogâṇ.
With	...	sah (*suffixed*).
Woman	...	îs, *pl.* îsâl *f.*
Old woman	...	gánîr, *pl.* gánîrküt *f.*
Wood	...	shellah *f.*
Wound	...	zákoom; perâr.
To write	...	chùndoogâṇ.
Year	...	kâl.
Yellow	...	choner *m.*, chonir *f.*
Yes	...	ōṇ.
Yesterday	...	jâl.
The day before yesterday.		âlhî.

Numerals.

1 ák.
2 doo.
3 tlâ.
4 chor.
5 pânch.
6 shoh.
7 sut.
8 uch.
9 nom.
10 dush.
11 ikâhá.
12 bâhá.
13 tloho.
14 chōn.
15 pánjá.
16 shôr.
17 satâhá.
18 uchâhá.
19 unbîsh.
20 bîsh.
21 ák-o-bîsh.
30 dush bîsh.
40 doo bîsh.
50 dush-o-doo bîsh.
60 tlâ bîsh.
70 dush-o-tlâ bîsh.
80 chor bîsh.
90 dush-o-chor bîsh.
100 pânch bîsh.

APPENDIX F.

GOWRO.

Spoken by the Gawáré in the Indus Valley.

DECLENSIONS.

THE PRONOUN.

	Nom.	Gen.	Dat.	Acc.	Ablative.
I . .	mah (*intrans.*) méh (*trans.*)	miâṇ	mâṇ	mah	mási, from me, &c.
thou . .	too (*intrans.*) teh (*trans.*)	tâṇ	tê	too	toosi.
he, she, it .	oh (*intrans.*) eh (*trans.*)	tashâṇ	ùshé	oh	ùshi.
we . .	beh (*intrans.*) asoṇ (*trans.*)	asâṇ	asé	beh	asoṇsi.
you . .	tùs (*intrans.*) tùsoṇ (*trans.*)	tùsâṇ	tùsé	tùs	tùsoṇsi.
hey . .	seh (*intrans.*) seoṇ (*trans.*)	sewâṇ	seweṇ	seh	sioṇsí.

Conjugation of the verb "To Go."

Infinitive Mood.

Present.		*Past Participle.*	
to go	bayoṇ.	having gone . . .	baigá.

Indicative Mood.

Present.

Singular.		*Plural.*	
I am going . .	bayoṇ (*m.*) baiṇ (*f.*)	we are going . .	beṇ.
thou art going . .	bayon (*m.*) baiṇ (*f.*)	you are going . .	beṇ.
he, she, it is going .	bayon (*m.*) baiṇ (*f.*)	they are golng . .	beṇ.

Imperfect.

Singular.		Plural.	
I was going	bayoṇs (*m.*) bayiṇsi (*f.*)	we were going	beṇs.
thou wast going	bayoṇs (*m.*) bayiṇsi (*f.*)	you were going	beṇs.
he, she, it was going	bayoṇs (*m.*) bayiṇsi (*f.*)	they were going	beṇs.

Pluperfect.

I had gone	bayéaso (*m.*) bayéaswî (*f.*)	we had gone	bayéasé.
thou hadst gone	bayéaso (*m.*) bayéaswî (*f.*)	you had gone	bayéasé.
he, she, it had gone	bayéaso (*m.*) bayéaswî (*f.*)	they had gone	bayéasé.

Perfect.

I went	bayégá (*m.*) bayégi (*f.*)	we went	bayégé.
thou wentst	bayégá (*m.*) bayégi (*f.*)	you went	bayégé.
he, she, it went	bayégá (*m.*) bayégi (*f.*)	they went	bayégé.

Præterite.

I have gone	bayétho (*m.*) bayéthi (*f.*)	we have gone	bayéthé.
thou hast gone	bayétho (*m.*) bayéthi (*f.*)	you have gone	bayéthé.
he, she, it has gone	bayétho (*m.*) bayéthi (*f.*)	they have gone	bayéthé.

Future.

I will go	baybōṇsh.	we will go	baybîzesh.
thou wilt go	baybish.	you will go	baybiyâṇsh.
he, she, it will go	baybish.	they will go	baybiyâṇsh.

IMPERATIVE MOOD.

go thou	bá.	go ye	byá.

Conjugation of the defective verb "TO BE."

INDICATIVE MOOD.

Present.

Singular.		Plural.	
I am	thoo (*m.*) twî (*f.*)	we are	thé.
thou art	thoo (*m.*) twî (*f.*)	you are	thé.
he, she, it is	thoo (*m.*) twî (*f.*)	they are	thé.

Past.

I was	asoo (*m.*) aswî (*f.*)	we were	asé.
thou wast	asoo (*m.*) aswî (*f.*)	you were	asé.
he, she, it was	asoo (*m.*) aswî (*f.*)	they were	asé.

Future.

Singular.		*Plural.*	
I will be . . .	gōṇsh.	we will be . . .	geṇs.
thou wilt be . .	gōṇsh.	you will be . .	geṇs.
he, she, it will be .	gōṇsh.	they will be . .	geṇs.

Conjugation of the verb "To Become."

Infinitive Mood.

Present.

to become . . . . . . gahoṇ.

Indicative Mood.

Present.

Singular.		*Plural.*	
I am becoming . .	hoṇ (*m.*) hwiṇ (*f.*)	we are becoming .	heṇ.
thou art becoming .	hoṇ (*m.*) hwiṇ (*f.*)	you are becoming .	heṇ.
he, she, it is becoming	hoṇ (*m.*) hwiṇ (*f.*)	they are becoming .	heṇ.

Imperfect.

I was becoming . .	hoṇs (*m.*) hwiṇs (*f.*)	we were becoming .	heṇs.
thou wast becoming .	hoṇs (*m.*) hwiṇs (*f.*)	you were becoming .	heṇs.
he, she, it was becoming	hoṇs (*m.*) hwiṇs (*f.*)	they were becoming .	heṇs.

Pluperfect.

I had become . .	hiṇasoo (*m.*) hiṇaswî (*f.*)	we had become . .	hiṇasé.
thou hadst become .	hiṇasoo (*m.*) hiṇaswî (*f.*)	you had become .	hiṇasé.
he, she, it had become	hiṇasoo (*m.*) hiṇaswî (*f.*)	they had become .	hiṇasé.

Perfect.

I became . . .	hingá (*m.*) hingî (*f.*)	we became . .	hingé.
thou becamest . .	hingá (*m.*) hingî (*f.*)	you became . .	hingé.
he, she, it became .	hingá (*m.*) hingî (*f.*)	they became . .	hingé.

Præterite.

I have become . .	hiṇthoo (*m.*) hiṇthî (*f.*)	we have become .	hiṇthé.
thou hast become .	hiṇthoo (*m.*) hiṇthî (*f.*)	you have become .	hiṇthé.
he, she, it has become .	hiṇthoo (*m.*) hiṇthî (*f.*)	they have becowe .	hitṇhé.

Future.

Singular.		*Plural.*	
I will become . .	hiṇbōṇsh.	we will become . .	hiṇbijish.
thou wilt become .	hiṇbesh.	you will become .	hiṇbeṇsh.
he, she, it will become .	hiṇbesh.	they will become .	hiṇbeṇsh.

IMPERATIVE MOOD.

become thou . .	hooṇ.	become ye . . .	hyâṇ.

VOCABULARY.

Above	...	ootalo.
Abuse	...	kunzul.
To advise	...	nusîhat gōṇ.
After	...	putter.
Again	...	nootî.
All	...	tol.
Although	...	agâr.
Always	...	hullul.
And	...	ow.
Angry	...	rosh.
To be angry	...	roshōṇ.
Another	...	dooi.
Apple	...	bábow.
Arm	...	bakoowiṇ.
Arms (weapons)	...	aiyok.
To arrive	...	áprōṇ.
To ask	...	taposgōṇ,
Ass	...	khur.
At	...	más (*suffixed*).
Aunt (father's sister)	...	phai.
,, (mother's sister)	...	mâsai.
Autumn	...	sháro.
Back	...	dow.
Bad	...	letch.
Barley	...	yow.
To be	...	hōṇ.
Beard	...	daiy.
To beat	...	kotōṇ.
Beautiful	...	shondo.
Because	...	getah.
To become	...	gahōṇ.
Before	...	áger.
To begin	...	shùroo gōṇ.
Belly	...	der.
Below	...	lâto.
Betrothal	...	munsrow.
Bird	...	papai.
Black	...	keno.
Blood	...	rât.
Blue	...	nîloo.
Body	...	soorut.
Bone	...	hâr.
Both	...	supdoo.
Boundary	...	kân.
Boy	...	molôt.
Brain	...	mutt.

Brave	...	zerwâl.
Bread	...	joowé.
To break	...	sharōṇ.
Bridge	...	syoo.
To bring	...	yâṇ.
Brother	...	jyooṇ.
Bull	...	goo.
But	...	wálé.
To buy	...	genōṇ.
To call	...	sâtōṇ.
Cheek	...	mùṇ.
Clean	...	dêyah.
Clothes	...	chîloo, zoro.
Cold	...	shilî.
To come	...	yōṇ.
To count	...	lekōṇ.
Cow	...	gow.
Crow	...	kow.
Custom	...	mîrâs.
Darkness	...	tumaiṇ.
Daughter	...	dî.
Day	...	dîs.
To-day	...	âz.
Death	...	merêgah.
To deceive	...	bérōṇ.
To die	...	marōṇ.
Difficult	...	grân.
Dirty	...	mult.
To do	...	gōṇ.
Dog	...	kùsùr.
Door	...	der.
To drink	...	pōṇ.
Dry	...	shikélo.
Ear	...	kân.
To eat	...	kaiyōṇ.
Egg	...	átah.
Elbow	...	toongri.
Empty	...	chōṇ.
Evening	...	nêshōṇ.
Everybody	...	tol-loo.
Except	...	bê
Eye	...	utch.
Face	...	mùṇ.
To fall	...	pârtōṇ.
Far	...	door.
Father	...	bâ.
Fault	...	aib.

Fear	...	byoo.
To fear	...	bîyōṇ.
Fight	...	kálî.
To fight	...	káligōṇ.
Finger	...	angooi.
To finish	...	poorgōṇ.
Fire	...	nâr.
Fish	...	mutsah.
Flour	...	ow.
Flower	...	phono.
To follow	...	putter tillōṇ
Foot	...	koor.
Forehead	...	tâlo.
Fort	...	kelow.
From	...	si (*suffixed*).
Fruit	...	mêwa.
Full	...	poṇ.
Garden	...	bâgh.
Girl	...	molôti.
To give	...	deyōṇ.
To go	...	bayōṇ ; tillōṇ.
Goat	...	sâli.
Gold	...	zer.
Good	...	nik.
Great	...	gōnt.
Gun	...	nâli.
Hair	...	bâl.
Half	...	áré.
Hand	...	hât.
Right hand	...	dáchoṇ hât.
Left hand	...	kùsh hât.
Happy	...	khùshâl.
Hard	...	koor.
Hawk	...	bâz.
Head	...	shish.
To hear	...	shōṇ.
Heart	...	hêyo.
Heavy	...	ogùr.
Here	...	izé.
High	...	joogo.
Horse	...	gho.
Hot	...	gurm.
House	...	goo.
How	...	girung.
How many How much	... ...	} kutti.
Hunger	...	joṇ.
Husband	...	bâryooṇ.

If	...	ké.
In	...	kun *(suffixed)*.
Iron	...	tsimber.
To join	...	exêgōṇ.
To kill	...	mârōṇ.
King	...	rájâ.
Knee	...	kùt.
Knife	...	chùrkulli ; khatâr.
To know	...	perzōṇ.
To laugh	...	hassōṇ.
Lead	...	sikah.
To learn	...	cheshōṇ.
To leave	...	gérōṇ.
Leg	...	sait ; záng.
Lie	...	bèr.
Life	...	rùh.
Light (*subs.*)	...	chow.
Light (*adj.*)	...	ooshâlo.
Lightning	...	milyoṇ.
Lip	...	bōt.
A little	...	tsōti.
Long	...	joogo.
Maid	...	pêgál.
To make	...	sanōṇ.
Man	...	mésh.
Young man	...	loong.
Old man	...	záro.
Mare	...	ghooî.
Meat	...	mâs.
Medicine	...	dâroo.
Milk	...	chir.
Moon	...	yooṇ.
Mother	...	yâ.
Mountain	...	kân.
Mouth	...	aiṇ.
Much	...	jow.
So much	...	hoti.
This much	...	iti.
Mud	...	tsitsil.
Nail (finger)	...	nâk.
Name	...	nowṇ.
Near	...	leh.
Neck	...	mutti.
New	...	loong.
Night	...	roh.
No	...	nah.

Nobody ... kooz.
None ... kis.
Nose ... nut.
Nothing ... kis sîz.
Now ... itîr.

To obey ... manōṇ.
Of ... sâṇ *(suffixed)*.
Old ... poroṇ
Or ... ki.
To order ... hookum gōṇ.
Over ... ootalo.
Owl ... goongé.

Pear ... tângoo.
Pigeon ... kowtari.
To place ... rachōṇ.
Plough ... hull.
Praise ... sifát.
To promise ... wâdah gōṇ.
To pull ... jekōṇ.

Rain ... ájo.
Ready ... têyâr.
To receive ... chaiyōṇ.
Red ... lyoo.
To return ... tillōṇ.
Rice ... tullùng.
To rise ... otyōṇ.
River ... sind.
Road ... pân.
Roof ... chull.
Rope ... kyoo.
To run ... jōṇ.

Sand ... sigil.
To say ... alōṇ.
To see ... retōṇ.
Seed ... bî.
To sell ... moldeyōṇ.
To send ... chiyōṇ.
To separate ... undérōṇ.
Servant ... nôker.
Shadow ... shêlah.
Sheep ... î.
Short ... katoṇ.
Shoulder ... tsánoo.
On this side ... in.
On that side ... páré.
Silver ... ozulzer.
Sister ... bhaiṇ.

Skin	...	sâm.
Slave	...	dim.
Sleep	...	sùt.
To sleep	...	heldōṇ.
Slow	...	motoṇ.
Small	...	pelōnto.
Smoke	...	dùṇ.
Snake	...	sâp.
Snow	...	heyoṇ.
Soft	...	kâṇwál.
Some	...	gi.
Somebody	...	gi mōsh.
Something	...	gi sîz.
Son	...	pooch.
To sow	...	bōṇ.
Spring	...	basând.
Star	...	târ.
Stone	..	bât.
Storm	...	baiyo.
Strength	...	koowát.
To strike	...	kotōṇ.
Summer	...	reyoo.
Sun	...	soorî.
Swift	...	gurándé.
Sword	...	terwâli.
To take	...	sheyōṇ.
To teach	...	pushōn.
That	...	oh.
Then	...	ti.
There	...	pârozé.
Therefore	...	aiṇ subub.
These	...	êyooṇ.
To think	...	fikrgōṇ.
Thirst	...	cheshoṇ.
This	...	aiṇ.
Those	...	syooṇ.
Throat	...	shungnarai.
To throw	...	ladōṇ.
Thunder	...	tunder.
Thus	...	aiṇ shân.
Till	...	tuk.
Time	...	wákt.
To	...	té (*suffixed*).
Toe	...	ángooi.
To-morrow	...	bâlil.
Tongue	...	zîb.
Tooth	...	dând.
Towards	...	kooch.
Tree	...	bich.
Truth	...	sâtsé.

Uncle (father's brother)	kâkah.
Uncle (mother's brother)	mâmah.
Under ...	lâto (*suffixed*).
Very ...	jow.
Village ...	gaoṇ.
Wall ...	koor.
Water ...	wî.
Weak ...	kumzor.
To weep ...	rooidyōṇ.
Wet ...	bilzélo.
What ...	gi.
Wheat ...	gooṇ.
When (*interrog.*) ...	kanoṇ.
Whence ...	goyâṇ.
Where ...	koṇzé.
Whip ...	tùr ; kororo.
White ...	ozullo.
Who ...	koh.
Why ...	get.
Wife ...	mùlai.
Wind ...	hawaiy.
Wine ...	moh.
Winter ...	hewând.
To wish ...	mungōṇ.
With ...	exé (*suffixed*).
Woman ...	mùlai.
Old woman ...	zerî.
Wood ...	sōṇ ; káshâk.
To wound ...	kapōṇ.
Yellow ...	pîloo.
Yes ...	âṇ.
Yesterday ...	dōsh.

Numerals.

1	ek.
2	doo.
3	chooah.
4	tsor.
5	pâṇs.
6	shoh.
7	sât.
8	ât.
9	noh.
10	dush.
11	aiyâsh.
12	dwâsh.
13	chish.
14	tsundùsh.
15	pánjish.
16	shoowesh.
17	satâsh.
18	âtâsh.
19	ùmbish.
20	bish.
21	ekánbish.
30	deshánbish.
31	aiyâshánbish.
32	dwâshánbish.
40	doobish.
41	ektal doobish.
42	dootal doobish.
50	deshándoobish.
60	chobish.
70	deshán chobish.
80	tsor bish.
90	tsor bish ándesh.
100	shao.
1000	zer.

APPENDIX G.

NARISATI.

Spoken by the Gubbers in the Chitral Valley.

VOCABULARY.

Alive ... jântah.
All ... sômî.
Alone ... yekùlah.
Always ... hamêshah.
To ask ... koodâwá.
Ass ... guddah.

Back ... dâkah.
Bad ... kuts.
To be ... tîná.
Beard ... dâri.
To beat ... shiâwá.
Bird ... pechîn.
Black ... kántsah.
Blind ... shîrah.
Blood ... gutto.
Blue ... nîlah.
Boy ... zâták.
Bread ... gnùshti.
To bring ... anâwá.
Brother ... blaiyo.
Bull ... gah.

Cheek ... killunto.
Clean ... rogh.
Cold ... shalah.
To come ... já, *imp.* jai.
Copper ... rîd.
Cow ... golung.

Dagger ... khatâro.
Darkness ... handâdoop.
Day ... dés.
Mid-day ... tsekeli dés.
To-day ... noondés.
Dead ... mîsunt.
Death ... merg.
To die ... mitâná.
Difficult ... mùshkil.
Dirty ... malùtah.
To do ... kerâwá.
Dog ... shùnah.

Ear ... kumtah.
Earth ... soom.
Easy ... asân.
To eat ... joowâwá, *imp.* jô.
Egg ... byoo.
Evening ... shâm.
Eye ... itsin.

Face ... mook.
Far ... dùrâré.
Father ... bâp.
Fire ... angâr.
Foot ... koor.
Forehead ... târunputtah.
Fort ... kolah.
Friend ... yâr.
Fruit ... mêwah.

Girl ... téokoori.
To give ... siâwá.
To go ... dîká, *imp.* dî.
Goats (*collectively*) ... plung.
He-goat ... enni.
Gold ... sôn.
Good ... baiy.
Great ... dol.
Gun ... tôbuk.

Half ... tsekeli.
Hand ... hust.
Hard ... kuttenah.
Head ... showootah.
To hear ... shùnâwá, *imp.* shùn.
Heart ... hidah.
The heavens ... asmân.
Here ... ántî.
High ... dáro.
Horse ... ghorah.

Hot	...	tápoo.
House	...	ámah.
How	...	shilah.
How much	...	kuttah.
Ill	...	nájoor.
Iron	...	chîmer.
To kill	...	marâwá.
Lame	...	kootah.
Lead	...	sik.
Life	...	phook.
Light (*subs.*)	...	plull.
Lip	...	nokah.
Long	...	ligâlo.
Low	...	mâlo.
To make	...	sázâwá.
Man	...	mânoos.
Young man	...	lowri.
Mare	...	ghorî.
Mid-day	...	tsekeli dés.
Midnight	...	tsekeli yil.
Milk	...	chir.
Moon	...	mâsoi.
More	...	loh.
Morning	...	sahâr.
Mother	...	jai.
Mountain	...	dahâr.
Mouth	...	hâṇsi
So much	...	ántah.
Near	...	nerah.
New	...	zoowân.
Night	...	yil.
No	...	nai.
Nose	...	nâsi.
Old	...	dugah.
Rain	...	wâsh.
Red	...	looterah.
River	...	nendi.
Road	...	pōnt.
To say	...	jâwá.
To see	...	tâwá ; bâlá.
To send	...	shâwá.
Sheep	...	érah.
Silver	...	rùp.
Sister	...	sussi.

Skin	...	gulh, gôtsi.
Small	...	polah.
Soft	...	chiringah.
Star	...	târo.
Stone	...	wutt.
Sun	...	soorî.
Sword	...	towrâli.
There	...	ántiné.
Thing	...	tìz.
This	...	woi.
To-morrow	...	sabârah dés.
Tongue	...	zib.
Tooth	...	dōnt.
Tree	...	mootoh.
Village	...	lum.
Water	...	owoo.
What	...	kî.
Wheat	...	gom.
When (*interrog.*)	...	kôl.
Where (*interrog.*)	...	kêné.
White	...	oozellah.
Who (*interrog.*)	...	kareli.
Why	...	kênah.
Wind	...	wádimon.
Woman	...	shigâli.
Wood	...	dâr.
Yes	...	eh.
Yesterday	...	dosùki dés.
Young	...	zoowân.

Numerals.

1	yek.	11	jáss.
2	doo.	12	báss.
3	shê.	13	showáss.
4	tsoor.	14	tsooduss.
5	pânts.	15	pinchuss.
6	shoh.	16	shoruss.
7	sut.	17	suttuss.
8	usht.	18	ushtuss.
9	noo.	19	inîsh.
10	duss.	20	ishi.

Pronouns.

I	...	moi.	We	...	âmma.
Thou	...	tooi.	You	...	mé.
He, she, *or* it	...	en.	They	...	émé.

APPENDIX H.

KHOWAR.

The language spoken by the Kho in the Chitral Valley.

[This is the language called Arnyiah by Dr. Leitner.]

SKETCH OF GRAMMAR.

THE SUBSTANTIVE.

In both numbers there are two forms the nominative and the oblique. The genitive and accusative in the singular, and the genitive in the plural, are signified by the simple oblique form, the dative and ablative by the oblique form with postpositions added.

There are no distinctions of gender.

	Singular.		*Plural.*	
Nom.	a horse . .	istor.	horses . . .	istor-ân.
Gen.	of a horse .	istor-oh.	of horses . .	istor-ân oh.
Dat.	to a horse .	istor-oté.	to horses . .	istor-ân té.
Acc.	a horse . .	istor-oh.	horses . . .	istor-ân.
Voc.	oh horse . .	eh istor.	oh horses . .	eh istor-ân.
Abl.	on a horse .	istor-oh-sōrá.	on horses . .	istor-ân-sōrá.
	in a horse .	istor-oh-undrêni.	in horses . .	istor-ân-undrêni.
	with a horse .	istor-oh-sùm.	with horses . .	istor-ân-sùm.
	for a horse .	istor-oh-buchun.	for horses . .	istor-ân-buchun.
	from a horse .	istor-oh-sur.	from horses . .	istor-ân-sur.

The noun in the genitive is placed before the governing noun, as: *moshoh* sor "the man's head."

THE ADJECTIVE.

The adjective precedes the noun and has no terminations distinctive of number, as:

a strong man . .	koowatîn mōsh.	swift horses . . .	tároo istor.

PRONOUNS.

Pronouns have mostly two forms, a nominative and an oblique form. The genitive and accusative are signified by the oblique form without postpositions; the dative and ablative by the oblique form with postpositions applied.

The PERSONAL and DEMONSTRATIVE PRONOUNS are declined as follows:—

	NOM.	GEN.	DAT.	ACC.	VOC.	ABL.
I . . .	áwá	má	máté	má	——	má sōrá.
Thou . .	too	tá	táté	tá	eh tù	tá sōrá.
He (*near*) .	haiyá	hamoh	hamoté	hamoh	——	hamoh sōrá.
she (*further*)	hess	horoh	horoté	horoh	——	horoh sōrá.
or it (*far*) .	hásé	hattoghoh	hattoghoté	hattoghoh	——	hattoghoh sōrá.
We . .	ispah	ispah	ispáté	ispah	——	ispah sōrá.
You . .	bissah	bissah	bissáté	bissah	eh bissah	bissah sōrá.
They (*near*) .	hamit	hamitun	hamitunté	hamitun	——	hamitun sōrá.
„ (*further*)	het	hetun	hetunté	hetun	——	hetun sōrá.
„ (*far*) .	huttet	huttetun	huttetunté	huttetun	——	huttetun sōrá.

The REFLECTIVE PRONOUN is formed by adding the syllable *tun*, as:

I myself	*áwátun.*	we ourselves . . .	*ispahtun.*
Thou thyself . . .	*tootun.*	you yourselves . .	*bissahtun.*
He, she *or* it, himself, &c.	*haiyátun.* *hesstun.* *hásétun.*	they themselves . .	*hamittun.* *hettun.* *huttettun.*

THE INTERROGATIVE PRONOUN.

Which horse went ?	*Kī* istor baghai.	Whose horse is this ?	Haiyá istor *kùs.*

The RELATIVE is expressed by *ki*, as:

I who went	Áwá *ki* baghestum.
This is the man you saw	Haiyá mōsh too *ki* poshirosho.

THE VERB.

The verb is generally very regular, with terminations expressing tense and person, except in the perfect tense, which is often irregular in its derivation. The infinitive active always terminates in *iko*, *îko*, or *éko*.

The passive is formed by using *biko* "to become" as an auxiliary verb.

A causal verb is formed by changing *i* in the infinitive into *é* or if the infinitive already terminates in *éko* by interposing *é*, as:

to stand	rùp*iko.*	to cause to grieve . .	kro*éko.*
to cause to stand . . .	rùp*éko.*	to run	d*éko.*
to grieve	kro*íko.*	to cause to run . . .	dê-*éko.*

A noun of agency is formed by adding *ák* to the root of the verb, as: *korák* "one who does" from *koriko* "to do," *piyák* "one who drinks" from *piko* "to drink."

A verbal adjective is formed by adding *wár* to the root, as: *dikwár* "suitable to the striking."

A verbal noun is formed by using the infinitive present with postpositions, as:

in the beating . . .	diko mùji.	with the beating .	diko sùm.
by „	diko sōra.	for „ . .	diko buchun.

Conjugation of the verb "To Strike."

Infinitive Mood.

Present.		*Future.*	
to strike	diko.	to be about to strike	diko boi.

Past.

to have struck . . . . diko oshoi.

Participles.

Present.		*Future.*	
striking	dyow.	being about to strike	diko biti.

Past.

having struck . . . . diti.

Gerunds.

in striking	dyowah.	from *or* by striking	dikah.

Supines.

possibly to strike	diko-á-kyah.	meet to strike	diko-bush.

must strike . . . . diko-sher.

Indicative Mood.

Present.

Singular.		*Plural.*	
I am striking	domun.	we are striking	dosiun.
thou art striking	dosun.	you are striking	domiun.
he, she, it is striking	doyun.	they are striking	doñun.

Imperfect.

I was striking	diôshtum.	we were striking	diôshtum.
thou wast striking	diôsho.	you were striking	diôshtami.
he, she, it was striking	diôshai.	they were striking	diôshani.

Pluperfect.

I had struck	dirooshtum.	we had struck	dirooshtum.
thou hadst struck	diroosho.	you had struck	dirooshtami.
he, she, it had struck	dirooshai.	they had struck	dirooshani.

Perfect.

I struck	prestum.	we struck	prestum.
thou struckest	prá.	you struck	prestami.
he, she, it struck	prai.	they struck	práni.

The perfect is also used as a future præterite, as :

I shall have struck . . . . prestum.

Præterite.

Singular.		*Plural.*	
I have struck	dityasùm.	we have struck	dityasùsi.
thou hast struck	dityasùs.	you have struck	dityasùmi.
he, she, it has struck	dityasùr.	they have struck	dityasùni.

Future.

Singular.		*Plural.*	
I will strike	dom.	we will strike	dosi.
thou wilt strike	dos.	you will strike	domi.
he, she, it will strike	doi.	they will strike	doni.

IMPERATIVE.

strike thou	det.	strike you	dioor.
let him, her, it strike	diâr.	let them strike	deni.

CONDITIONAL MOOD.

Present.		*Perfect.*	
I may be striking, &c.	domun-á-kyah.	I may have struck, &c.	prestum-á-kyah.
Imperfect.		*Præterite.*	
I may have been striking, &c.	diôshtum-á-kyah.	I may have struck, &c.	dityasûm-á-kyah.
Pluperfect.		*Future.*	
I may have struck	dirooshtum-á-kyah.	I may have struck, &c.	dom-á-kyah.

THE PASSIVE VOICE.

INFINITIVE MOOD.

Present.		*Future.*	
to be struck	diko-biko.	to be about to be struck	dik-biko-boi. din-boi.

Past.

to have been struck . . . . dik-biko-oshoi.

PARTICIPLES.

Present.		*Future.*	
being struck	diroo. dyono.	being about to be struck	diek biti.

Past.

having been struck . . . . dinbiti. dyonobiti.

GERUNDS.

in being struck	diroowah.	from *or* by being struck	dik bikah.

SUPINES.

possibly to be struck	dik-biko-á-kyah.	meet to be struck	dik-biko-bush.

must be struck . . . . dik-biko-sher.

INDICATIVE MOOD.

Present.

Singular.		*Plural.*	
I am being struck	dinbômum.	we are being struck	dinbosiun.
thou art being struck	dinbosun.	you are being struck	dinbomiun.
he, she, it is being struck	dinboyun.	they are being struck	dinboñun.

Imperfect.

Singular.		*Plural.*	
I was being struck . .	dinbôshtum.	we were being struck	dinbôshtum.
thou wast being struck .	dinbôsho.	you were being struck .	dinbôshtami.
he, she, it was being struck	dinbôshai.	they were being struck .	dinbôshani.

Pluperfect.

I had been struck .	dinbirooshtum.	we had been struck .	dinbirooshtum.
thou hadst been struck	dinbiroosho.	you had been struck	dinbirooshtami.
he, she, it had been struck.	dinbirooshai.	they had been struck	dinbirooshani.

Perfect.

I was struck . .	diestum.	we were struck . .	diestum.
thou wast struck . .	diesta.	you were struck . .	diestami.
he, she, it was struck .	diestai.	they were struck .	diestani.

Alternative Form.

I was struck . . .	dinôstum.	we were struck . .	dinôstum.
thou wast struck . .	dinôsta.	you were struck . .	dinôstami.
he, she, it was struck .	dinôstai.	they were struck . .	dinôstani.

Præterite.

I have been struck . .	dinbityasùm.	we have been struck .	dinbityasùsi.
thou hast been struck .	dinbityasùs.	you have been struck .	dinbityasùmi.
he, she, it has been struck	dinbityasùr.	they have been struck .	dinbityasùni.

Future.

I shall be struck . .	dinbom.	we shall be struck	dinbosi.
thou shalt be struck .	dinbos.	you shall be struck .	dinbomi.
he, she, it shall be struck	dinboi.	they shall be struck .	dinboni.

IMPERATIVE MOOD.

be thou struck . . .	dinbos.	be you struck .	dinbor.
let him, her, it be struck .	dinbâr.	let them be struck . .	dinbâni.

CONDITIONAL MOOD.

Present.		*Perfect.*	
I may be being struck, &c.	dinbomun-á-kyah.	I may have been struck, &c.	dimôstum-á-kyah.
Imperfect.		*Præterite.*	
I may have been being struck, &c.	dinbôshtum-á-kyah.	I may have been struck, &c.	dinbityasùm-á-kyah.
Pluperfect.		*Future.*	
I may have been struck, &c.	dinbiroosh-tum-á-kyah.	I may be struck, &c. .	dibom-á-kyah.

Conjugation of the verb "TO BE."

There are two verbs "TO BE," both of which are defective. The first *assiko* is used for animate beings, and the second *shiko* for inanimate beings only. The latter is used as an auxiliary verb also. The only existing forms are as follows:

For animate beings only.

Infinitive Mood.

Present.		*Future.*	
to be	assiko.	to be about to be	assiko-boi.

Past.

to have been . . . . assiko-oshoi.

Gerunds.

In being	assowah.	from being	assikah.

Supines.

possibly to be	assiko-á-kyah.	meet to be	assiko-bush.

must be . . . . assiko-sher.

Participles.

Present.		*Future.*	
being	assow.	being about to be	assiko biti.

Past.

having been . . . . ?

Indicative Mood.

Present.

Singular.		*Plural.*	
I am	assûm.	we are	assûsı.
thou art	assûs.	you are	assûmi.
he, she, it is	assûr.	they are	assûni.

Pluperfect.

I had been	assirooshtum.	we had been	assirooshtum.
thou hadst been	assiroosho.	you had been	assirooshtami.
he, she, it had been	assirooshai.	they had been	assirooshani.

Past.

I have been	assistum.	we have been	assistum.
thou hast been	assista.	you have been	assistami.
he, she, it has been	assistai.	they have been	assistani.

Conditional Mood.

Present.		*Pluperfect.*	
I may be, &c.	assûm-á-kyah.	I should have been, &c.	assirooshtum-á-kyah.

Past.

I might have been, &c. . . . . . . assistum-á-kyah.

For inanimate objects only.

Infinitive Mood.

Present.		*Future.*	
to be	shiko.	about to be	shiko-biti. shak-biti.

Past.

to have been . . . . shiko-oshoi.

GERUNDS.

in being . . . showah. | from *or* by being . . shikah.

SUPINES.

possibly to be . . shiko-á-kyah. | meet to be . . . shiko-bush.
must be . . . . shiko-sher.

PARTICIPLES.

Present. *Future.*

being . . . . show. | about to be . . . shikobiti.

Past.

having been . . . . shiti.

INDICATIVE MOOD.

Present. *Past.*

it is . . . . sher. | it has been . . . oshoi.

Pluperfect.

it had been . . . . sirooshoi.

CONDITIONAL MOOD.

Present. *Past.*

it may be . . . sher- á-kyah. | it might have been . oshoi-á-kyah.

Other forms are supplied by the verb "TO BECOME."

Conjugation of the verb "TO BECOME."

INFINITIVE MOOD.

Present. *Future.*

to become . . . biko. | to be about to become . biko sher.

Past.

to have become . . . . . . bow oshoi.

PARTICIPLES.

Present. *Future.*

becoming. . . . bowah. | being about to become . biko biti.

Past.

having become . . . . biti.

SUPINES.

possibly to become . biko-á-kyah. | meet to become . . biko-bowah.
must become . . . . biko-bush.

INDICATIVE MOOD.

Present.

Singular.		*Plural.*	
I am becoming	bomun.	we are becoming	bosiun.
thou art becoming	bosun.	you are becoming	bomiun.
he, she, it is becoming	boyun.	they are becoming	boñun.

Imperfect.

I was becoming	bôshtum.	we were becoming	bôshtum.
thou wast becoming	bôsho.	you were becoming	bôshtami.
he, she, it was becoming	bôshai.	they were becoming	bôshani.

Pluperfect.

I had become	birooshtum.	we had become	birooshtum.
thou hadst become	birooshò.	you had become	birooshtami.
he, she, it had become	birooshai.	they had become	birooshani.

Perfect.

I became	hôstum.	we became	hôstum.
thou becamest	howa.	you became	hôstami.
he, she, it became	hoya.	they became	hôni.

Another form of the 3rd pers. sing. is *hőr.*

Præterite.

Singular.		*Plural.*	
I have become	bityasùm.	we have become	bityasùsi.
thou hast become	bityasùs.	you have become	bityasùmi.
he, she, it has become	bityasùr.	they have become	bityasùni.

Future.

I will become	bôm.	we will become	bôsi.
thou wilt become	bôs.	you will become	bômi.
he, she, it will become	boi.	they will become	bôni.

IMPERATIVE MOOD.

become thou	bôs.	become ye	bôr.
let him, her, it become	bai.	let them become	bâni.

CONDITIONAL MOOD.

The conditional mood is formed by adding *á-kyáh* to all forms of the indicative.

Assiko is also employed to signify possession, as: *Máté ioo istor assùni* "I have two horses," *literally* "To me two horses are."

THE NEGATIVE.

This simple negative is expressed by *nō.* "Not" is expressed by *noh* in a definite sense, and by *nikki* in an indefinite sense, as:

Is this your horse? No	Haiya tá istor assùrá? *Nō.*
Have you a horse? No	Tá istor assùra? *Nikki.*
I will not go	Áwá *noh* bîm.

THE INTERROGATIVE.

The interrogative is expressed in the same way as in Shina and Boorishki by adding *á* to the verb, or if it already terminates in *á* by lengthening it to *ấ*, as :

Shall I go?	Ấwá bîm*á*?
Hast thou given?	Too pr*ấ*.

Sometimes the verb is omitted and the *á* suffixed to the noun, as :

Is this your horse?	Haiya tá istor*á*?

ADVERBS.

There are no adverbs ; their place is supplied by the past participle of the verb *Biko* "to become," as : *Het blush*-BITI *hani* "They came slowly," *literally* "They having become slow, came."

EXAMPLES.

I.

1. What is your name? . .	Tá kyâkh nâm.
2. My name is Jabín .	Má nâm Jabîn.
3. Whence have you come? . .	Koorâr hâ?
4. My home was at Chitral, but now I live in Gilgit. .	Má door Chitrârah oshoi, hánisen Gilitah gityasùm.
5. What do you want? . .	Kyâkh mushkisun.
6. I do not know . . .	Hùsh nákom.
7. Is that your horse? . .	Hess tá istorá?
8. Yes, my father gave it to me .	Jum, má tutt máté dityasùr.
9. Your horse is better than your brother's.	Tá brâroh istoroh sur tá istor jum.
10. This house is mine . .	Haiyá khuttun má.
11. When did you build it? .	Kyáwát kordoosho.
12. It was built five years ago	Pònch sâl hor kori.

II.

Yesterday I went to hunt, with me two horses were, one dog was, one hawk was, (and) with me four servants were.	Oozen áwá boghdooshtum ishkâr, másùm joo istorân assistani, î rêni assistai, î yoorj assistai, másùm chor duck assistani.
(As) we were going a quail made a noise, I "the dog let go" called out ; the quail came out, the hawk I let go and he took it.	Ispah boghôshtum î bertî háwâz árer, áwá rêni chucké mushkeshtum ; bertî nisai, yoorj lâkistum dosistai.
On his taking it the *kalamấs* I did : the *kalamấs* having done another quail came out. On (its) coming out the hawk I let go ; very far having taken it he was not able (to seize it).	Dosiko† kalamâs* arestum : kalamâs koriko† îdî bertî nisai. Nisiko† yoorj lâkistum boh doodéri álti noh obistai.

* The *kalamas* is the ceremony of giving the head of the captured bird to a hawk

† The use of the infinitive is to be noted.

From his not being able I sorry became. Upon which wild ducks having come on a pool settled. I the hawk having taken went (and) near having become let him go.

Nobiko áwá kuffá hôstum. Harooni ulli giti chetah nishâni. Áwá yoorjoh gunni baghestum nussá bî, lâkistum.

On being let go my hawk having separated the mallard took it. With me servants were. One servant a stick having thrown (*lit.* struck) one duck killed. For the hawk having performed the *kalamás* much pleased having become we ourselves back home went.

Lâkiko má boorj nooweri tutt-ulli dosistai. Másùm duck assistani. Î duck bânen diti î ulli máristai. Boorjoté kalamâs kori boh khùshân biti, tun dooroté baghâstum.

III.

Oozen áwá Nomaloté boghdooshtum, terah biko Nomalik másùm shurti ghâl koriko rai areni. Másùm ghâl koráká noo astani. Hamooniki ispah sòt jùn hôstum, sòt Nomalik honi, te ghâl arestum, ghâl koriko ispah beshistai. Ki ispah beshêko ispáté shurti prâni, ispah shurtiyo jùti wa ghâl arestum. Ghâl koriko ispah osht biroshai, Nomaliko troi biroshai; má istor boh bé tâkát biti tor hor. Má istor tor biko áwá yoh khamistum. Wa ispah beshorooshtum harooni mùji má istor kiji biko noh obestai. Áwá istoroh húnoh bicheri istoroh sōrá oogh darestum. Oogh driko má istor tsuck jum hor.

Translation.

Yesterday I had gone to Nomal; on arriving there a man of Nomal desired to make a wager at polo with me. I had no (good) polo players with me. However, we were seven young men, and the Nomal men were seven; so we played polo. In playing we won (*lit.* exceeded). On account of our winning they gave us the wager, and we after eating the wager played again. In playing we won eight games (*lit.* became eight), and the Nomal men won three; my horse being much exhausted fell down. On my horse falling I dismounted. And we won to such an extent that my horse was unable to move. I undid the horse's saddle and poured water on the horse. By pouring water my horse became a little better (*lit.* a little well).

VOCABULARY.

To be able	...	hostâr giko ; biko.
Above	...	tòrik.
Abuse	...	dishloo.
To abuse	...	dishloo koriko.
Accustomed	...	âdut ; fehl.
Acid	...	shùt.
Active	...	tároo.
To advise	...	nasihat koriko.
After	...	áchâr ; áchi.
Again	...	wâ.
Air	...	howl.
Alert	...	hùsh.
All	...	chik.
Alongside of	...	prashowulti.
Always	...	háránùs.
Although	...	wâghumki.
And	...	wá.
Anger	...	khármi.
Angry	...	kahár.
To be angry	...	kahren biko.
Another	...	îdî.
To answer	...	jùwâb diko.
Ant	...	pillili.
Anxiety	...	khiyâl.
Anxious	...	fikir doonuk.
Apart	...	tunhâ.
Apple	...	pálogh.
Apricot	...	jooli.
Arm	...	bâzoo.
Army	...	bol.
To arrive	...	toriko.
Arrow	...	weshoo.
To ask	...	bushur koriko.
Ass	...	gordokh.
At	...	ah (*suffixed*).
Aunt (father's sister)	...	betch.
Aunt (mother's sister)	...	betch.
Autumn	...	shároh.
Avalanche	...	resht.
Away	...	lâké.
Axe (war)	...	tápârzing.
,, (wood)	...	bárdokh.
Back	...	krem.
Bad	...	shoom.
Barley	...	siri.
Basket	...	beloo.

To be	...	assiko ; shiko.
Bean	...	rámbogh.
Bear	...	ōrts.
Beard	...	rigish.
To beat	...	diko.
Beautiful	...	chùst.
Because	...	ketchah ki.
To become	...	biko.
Before	...	nuss.
To begin	...	shùroo koriko.
Behind	...	áchâr.
Belly	...	khoyânoo.
Below	...	mùri.
Between	...	mùji.
Bird	...	jándâr.
Bitter	...	trōk.
Black	...	shah.
Blind	...	kánoo.
Blood	...	leh.
To blow	...	phooîko.
Blue	...	òtch.
Blunt	...	mùtoo.
Body	...	huddum.
Bone	...	kol.
To be born	...	ajiko.
Bow	...	dron.
Boy	...	duck.
Brain	...	mâz.
Brass	...	loh.
Brave	...	pùr dil.
Bread	...	shápìk.
To break	...	chiko (*intrans.*) ; chiniko (*trans.*)
Breath	...	hah.
Brick	...	ùshtoo.
Bride Bridegroom	... ...	} shábok.
Bridle	...	iwis.
Bridge	...	sér ; telsiri.
To bring	...	ángiko.
Broad	...	biroghun.
Brother	...	brâr.
Brown	...	jigári.
Reddish brown	...	krooyâlo.
Bull	...	reshoo.
Bullet	...	weshoo.
But	...	hamùni.
Butterfly	...	pùlmùdùk.
By	...	sur.
To call	...	hooi diko.
Camel	...	oot.

Cattle (*collectively*)	...	leshoo.
Charm	...	tawîz.
Cheek	...	mùkh.
Chin	...	zenákh.
Circle	...	rogh.
Clean	...	puzgá.
Cleverness	...	kùshkorák.
Clothes	...	zupp.
Cloud	...	kot.
Cock	...	nári kookoo.
Cold (*subs.*)	...	ooshàki.
Cold (*adj.*)	...	ooshuck.
Colour	...	rung.
To come	...	gîko.
To come out	...	nisiko.
Copper	...	doorúm.
Corner	...	boorj.
Four-cornered	...	chârákht.
Corpse	...	jussut.
Cough	...	kopik.
To count	...	ishùmárêko.
Country	...	wullát.
Courage	...	pùr dili.
Cousin	...	brâr *m.*, ispoosâr *f.*; (as forms of address) lull *m.*; kai *f.*
Cow	...	leshoo.
To creep	...	rookooshiko.
Crooked	...	koli.
Crow	...	kâgh.
Curls (of hair)	...	preshoo.
Custom	...	miruss.
Dagger	...	mehmoodi.
To dance	...	poniko.
Dancing	...	ponik.
Dangerous	...	kuturnâk.
Darkness	...	chooi.
Daughter	...	joor.
Dawn	...	wálah bêlo.
Day	...	ánùs.
Midday	...	granish.
To-day	...	hanùn.
Deaf	...	karootoo.
Death	...	brik.
Deceit	...	fun.
Deceitful	...	chùngâk.
To deceive	...	fun diko.
Destitute	...	chùn.
Dew	...	prájgâr.
To die	...	briko.

Difficult	... mùshkil.
Dirty	... názgùsti.
Disposition	... féhl.
To dismount	... khwumiko.
To do	... koriko.
Dog	... rêni.
Donkey	... gordok.
Door	... bitt.
Down	... pust.
Dream	... kùshp.
To drink	... pîko.
Drum	... dôl.
Dry	... chùchoo.
Eagle	... saiyoorj.
Ear	... kâr.
Earth	... chùti.
The earth	... bùm.
Earthquake	... bôlmùji.
East	... nisiko.
Easy	... áskân.
To eat	... jùbiko.
Eclipse	... grah.
Edge	... dum.
Egg	... aikùn.
Elbow	... koorkoon.
Empty	... khâli.
Enemy	... dùshmun.
To enter	... ootiko.
Envy	... ghumâz ; mùzir.
Equal to	... burki.
Equinox	... hummál.
Evening	... shumma.
Ever	... kyawát.
Everybody	... chikmosh.
Everything	... chikjinâri.
Ewe	... keli.
Eye	... ghutch.
Family	... roiwáloo.
To fall	... tor biko.
Far	... doodéri.
Fat (*subs.*)	... zâkh.
Fat (*adj.*)	... tùl.
Father	... tutt.
Fault	... gùnah.
Fear	... bùrtooik.
Feather	... pùtch.
Female	... istrî ; kiméri.
Fig	... kowitt.

Fight	...	gutt.
To find	...	lêko.
Finger	...	chámoot.
To finish	...	kùlêko ; kùl koriko.
Fire	...	ungâr.
Fish	...	mátsih.
Flock (of birds)	...	röm.
Flour	...	peshiroo.
Flower	...	gumboori.
Flute	...	surnai ; boloo.
To fly (as a bird)	...	ùlîko.
To follow	...	áchi giko ; áchi bîko.
To cause to follow	...	chuckêko.
Following	...	áchá.
Foot	...	pong.
For	...	buchun (*suffixed*).
To forget	...	roksiko.
Forgetfulness	...	roksi.
Fort	...	noghôr.
Fowl	...	kahuck.
Fox	...	pooshi.
Friend	...	dost.
Friendship	...	dostî.
From	...	râr âr (*to inanimate*) ; sur (*to animate objects ; suffixed*).
Frost	...	merôj.
Fruit	...	mêwah.
Fur	...	zùsh.
Full	...	tip.
Garden	...	goorzen.
Generous	...	lùt herdî.
To get	...	lêko.
To get up	...	rùpiko.
Girl	...	koomoroo.
To give	...	diko.
To go	...	bîko.
To go out	...	bêdibîko.
Goats (*collectively*)	...	leshpai.
He-goat	...	titch.
She-goat	...	pai.
Wild goat	...	mroi.
God	...	Khùdai.
Gold	...	sorùm.
Good	...	jum.
Grape	...	droch.
Grass	...	jösh.
Gratitude	...	shùkùr.
Great	...	lùt.
Green	...	sôz.
To grieve	...	kroîko.

Gun	...	tooik.
Gunpowder	...	wés.
Hail	...	kochùni.
Hair	...	poor.
Half	...	phutt.
Hand	...	host.
Righthand	...	horski host.
Lefthand	...	koli host.
Handle	...	gon.
Happiness	...	khùshâni.
Happy	...	khùsh.
Hard	...	dung.
Hare	...	gholdi.
Hatred	...	mùzir.
Hawk	...	yoorj.
Head	...	sor.
Good health	...	tundroosti.
To hear	...	kárá diko.
Heart	...	herdî.
Heat	...	péchi.
The heavens	...	âsmân.
Heavy	...	khaiyi.
Hen	...	istrî kookoo.
Herd	...	röm.
Here	...	yah ; yerah ; haiyerah ; yoh.
High	...	jung.
Hollow	...	khâli.
Home	...	door.
Hope	...	ooméd.
To hope	...	ooméd koriko.
Horse	...	istor.
Horse-shoe	...	nâl.
Hot	...	petch.
House	...	khuttun.
How	...	ketchah.
How many	...	kundoori.
How much	...	kundoori lot.
Humble	...	ájiz.
Hunger	...	choowi.
Hungry	...	choowî.
Hundred	...	shōr.
To hunt	...	ishkâr koriko.
Husband	...	mōsh.
Ice	...	yôs.
Idle	...	kahál.
If	...	wâghum.
Illness	...	chaiyek.
In	...	undrêni (*suffixed*).

Industrious	...	korùmgâr.
Infant	...	tsuck.
Iron	...	chimoor.
Kettle-drum	...	dummunâ.
To kick	...	pedingung diko.
To kill	...	máriko.
King	...	mihter.
King's son	...	mihter jow.
Knee	...	zânoo.
Knife	...	kooten.
To know	...	hùsh koriko.
Knowledge	...	ukùlmin.
Lame	...	khùtoo.
Land	...	boom.
Waste land	...	kùch.
Language	...	looh.
To laugh	...	hosiko.
Lead	...	háziz.
To learn	...	chichiko.
To leave	...	lákiko.
Leg	...	dék.
To let go	...	lâkiko.
Level	...	barobár.
Lie	...	chángâk.
Life	...	jun.
Light (*subs.*)	...	roshti.
Light (*adj.*)	...	lots.
Lightning	...	bilphukk.
Like	...	ghonah.
Lip	...	shoon.
Little	...	tsuck.
A little	...	kum.
Liver	...	shoghoon.
Long	...	drùng.
To look at	...	poshiko.
Love	...	yâr.
To love	...	dosti koriko.
Low	...	pust.
Male	...	nári.
Man	...	mōsh.
Young man	...	jùwân.
Old man	...	zâroo.
Mankind	...	roi.
Mare	...	mádiân.
Marriage	...	jêri.
To measure	...	nimêko.
Meat	...	pùshoor.
Medicine	...	illâj.

Mid-day	...	granish.
Midnight	...	chooi barobâr.
Milk	...	shîr.
Mist	...	gert.
Moon	...	muss.
Newmoon	...	nogh.
Halfmoon	...	phátooki.
Fullmoon	...	pánjerush.
Month	...	muss.
Morning	...	chooichi.
Moth	...	yoorum ; postwâzùr.
Mother	...	nun.
Mountain	...	zom.
Mouse	...	kálow.
Mouth	...	uppuck.
To move (*intrans.*)	...	kiji biko.
Much	...	boh.
So much	...	horoo burki.
This much	...	hámoo burki.
Mud	...	zah.
Mulberry	...	márátch.
Muscle	...	kálow pùsho.
Music	...	dôl bôloo.
Must	...	bush.
Nail (finger)	...	doghoor.
Name	...	nâm.
Narrow	...	turung.
Near	...	shoi ; nussá.
Neck	...	gerdun.
Nephew	...	nowis.
Never	...	kyawát di noh.
New	...	nokh.
Niece	...	nowis.
Night	...	chooi.
No	...	nō.
Nobody	...	kahnoh.
North	...	heppreshá.
Nose	...	nusskâr.
Not	...	neki.
Nothing	...	kedrákh noh.
Now	...	hánisen.
Of	...	o-(*suffixed*).
Old	...	práno.
On	...	ai ; sōrá (*suffixed*).
Open	...	hùrî.
To open	...	bicheriko.
Or	...	yá.
To order	...	bundêko.
Out	...	béri (*suffixed*).

To overthrow	...	châghaiko.
Owl	...	boo.
To be pained	...	chumiko.
Palace	...	baipush.
Partridge	...	kooloo.
Peach	...	girgálogh.
Pear	...	tong.
People	...	jùn.
Perhaps	...	kyah.
Pigeon	...	kor.
Pity	...	ján polik.
Place	...	jugâ.
To place	...	lekiko.
Play	...	ishtùk.
To play (a game)	...	ishtùk koriko.
Pleasant tasting	...	zowáloo.
To please	...	khùsh koriko.
Pleased	...	pissun.
To be pleased	...	khùsh biko.
Plough	...	kishîni.
Point	...	poor.
To pour	...	driko.
Praise	...	siffut.
Pride	...	tákáboori.
Prince	...	mihterjow.
Princess	...	khoonzá joori.
To produce	...	hostâr giko.
To promise	...	wâda koriko.
Proud	...	tukáboor.
To pull	...	jingaiko.
Quail	...	bertî.
Quarrel	...	kùt.
Quarter	...	nuss.
Queen	...	khoonzá.
To be quick	...	tuzzêko.
Rainbow	...	drinháno.
Rain	...	boshik.
Ram	...	wurkálo.
To read	...	rêko.
Ready	...	taiyâr.
To receive	...	lêko.
Red	...	krooi.
Relation	...	kumdâr.
Relationship	...	kumdâri.
To remember	...	herdî koriko.
Remembrance	...	yád.
To return	...	ácheguriko.
Rice	...	grinj.

Rich	...	khoowátin.
Ring	...	pùlùngùsht.
To rise	...	rùpiko.
River	...	sin.
Road	...	pon.
Roof	...	isprâz.
Rope	...	shimêni.
Round	...	pindoroo.
Rough	...	shen.
To run	...	dêko.
Sad	...	ghumgîn.
Saddle	...	hùn.
Sand	...	shùghoor.
To say	...	rêko.
To search for	...	mushkiko.
To see	...	loliko ; poshiko.
Seed	...	bih.
Self	...	tun.
To sell	...	bizemiko.
To send	...	woshêko.
To separate	...	noweriko.
Servant	...	shudder ; duck.
Shadow	...	chákh.
Shame	...	shurm.
Sharp	...	tookùnoo.
Sheep (*collectively*)	...	leshpai.
Wild sheep	...	rōn.
Short	...	iskooldi.
Shoulder	...	kootoo.
To shout	...	kooj koriko.
Shut	...	korî.
To shut	...	botiko.
Side	...	troski.
On this side	...	haiyawulti.
On that side	...	hêwulti.
Alongside	...	práshowulti.
Sigh	...	shároo.
Silent	...	phik.
Silver	...	drochum.
Sinew	...	poi.
To sing	...	bushêko.
Singing	...	bashôno.
Sister	...	ispoosâr.
To sit	...	nishiko.
Skin	...	post.
Slave	...	maristun
Sleep	...	porik.
To sleep	...	poriko.
Sloping	...	koli.
Slow	...	káhál.

Small	... tsuck.
Smoke	... kùshùn.
Smooth	... ushipoko.
Snake	... aiy.
Sneeze	... ùshtoorkik.
Snow	... him.
Soft	... plush.
Solstice	... yerwân.
Somebody	... kah.
Something	... kedrákh.
Son	... jow.
Sorrow	... kuffai.
Sound	... áwâzá.
South	... yeppreshá.
Spade	... bel.
Spoon	... kippini.
Spring	... bosùn.
To stand	... rùpiko.
Star	... istári.
Stern	... dung.
Stone	... bōt.
Storm	... tofân.
Straight	... hōsk.
Strength	... koowát.
Strong	... koowátin.
Stupidity	... békoo.
Summer	... grishpoh.
Sun	... yor.
Sweet	... shirîn.
Swift	... tároo.
To swim	... ùsnêko.
Sword	... kongôr.
Tail	... roon.
To take	... dosiko.
To take away	... áliko.
To take up	... ai } koriko. / áhi } koriko.
To teach	... chichêko.
To tell	... reko ; gush koriko.
That	... hess ; heh.
Then	... husséwákt.
There	... herah ; terah.
Therefore	... hámoobuchun.
These	... hámit.
Thick	... bösk.
Thin	... jokh.
Thirst	... trùshni.
Thirsty	... trùshná.
This	... haiyá.
Thoes	... het.

Thought	...	khiyâl.
Throat	...	book.
To throw	...	petsiko ; drêko.
To throw down	...	driko.
Thumb	...	lotro chámoot.
Thunder	...	bùmbérùsh.
Thus	...	hámùsh.
Till	...	tá ; bîkáput.
Time	...	wákt.
Timid	...	boortwâ.
Tin	...	kalai.
To	...	ròté (*suffixed*). òté.
Toe	...	chámoot.
Together	...	îbiti.
To-morrow	...	pingáchooi.
The day after to-morrow		pingá.
Two days after to-morrow.		shoo pingá.
Three days after to-morrow.		ortiri.
Tongue	...	ligîni.
Tooth	...	don.
Touch	...	torik.
To touch	...	toriko.
Towards	...	wulti.
Treacherous	...	fund.
Tree	...	kun.
Truth	...	hōsk.
Ugly	...	durt.
Uncle (father's brother) Uncle (mother's brother)		mik.
Under	...	moolla; moolto (*suffixed*).
Unless	...	bagèr.
Up	...	jung.
Upright	...	hōsk.
Valley	...	göl ; ret.
Vein	...	yùroo.
Very	...	boh.
Very well	...	jum.
Village	...	deh.
Vine	...	droch.
Voice	...	háwâz.
Vulture	...	bizbur.
Wall	...	kánj.
Walnut	...	jòl.
Walnut tree	...	birmogh.
Water	...	oogh.

Water-mill	...	khorâ.
Weak	...	bêkoowut.
Weakness	...	bêkoowut.
Wedding	...	jêrî.
Week	...	sùd buss.
To weep	...	kuliko.
West	...	dokodiko.
Wet	...	zah.
What	...	kyâkh.
In what way	...	ketcháká.
Wheat	...	gôm.
When (*interrog.*)	...	kyáwát.
When (*relat.*)	...	husséwákt.
Whence	...	koorâr.
Where (*interrog.*)	...	koorah.
Which	...	kih.
White	...	ishpiroo.
Whip	...	chághez.
Who (*interrog.*)	...	kah.
Why	...	koh ; kyotá ; kyobuchun.
Wide	...	frákh.
Widow	...	} wesòroo.
Widower	...	}
Wife	...	bok.
Wind	...	gán.
Window	...	tsáláкh doori.
Wine	...	ren.
Winter	...	yomùn.
Wise	...	dânâ.
Wish	...	rai.
To wish	...	rai koriko.
With	...	sùm (*suffixed*).
Without	...	wé.
Woman	...	kiméri.
Old woman	...	yâroo.
Young woman	...	choomootkir.
Wood	...	dâr.
Wool	...	pùshp.
,, (pushum)	...	mùrgùlùm.
Work	...	korùm.
To work	...	korùm koriko.
The world	...	dùnyá.
To write	...	nooweshiko.
Year	...	yoorân.
Yellow	...	zerch.
Yes	...	dî ; jum.
Yesterday	...	oozen.
The day before yesterday.		dosh.

Numerals.

1	î.	16	josh c̍hoi.
2	joo.	17	josh sòt.
3	troi.	18	josh osht.
4	chor.	19	josh nyoṇ.
5	pònch.	20	bîsher.
6	choi.	21	bîsher î.
7	sòt.	30	bîsher josh.
8	osht.	40	joo bîsher.
9	nyoṇ.	50	joo bîsher josh.
10	josh.	60	troi bîsher.
11	josh î.	70	troi bîsher josh.
12	josh joo.	80	chor bîsher.
13	josh troi.	90	chor bîsher josh.
14	josh chor.	100	shôr.
15	josh pònch.		(No higher number.)

Once . . .	î bắr, &c.	Second . .	joowum.
First . . .	ắwắlum.	Third . . .	troiyum, &c.

APPENDIX I.

BUSHGALI.

[*Spoken by the Bushgali Tribe of the Siah Posh.*]

Singular.		*Plural.*	
I	*uns.*	we	*imma.*
of me	*ī.*	of us	*imma.*
thou	*tù.*	you	*sha.*
of thee	*too.*	of you	*sha.*
he *or* she	*inner.*	they	*umna.*
of him *or* her	*in.*	of them.	*umna.*

SENTENCES.

Come here	Anî uts.
Go	Î.
What is your name?	Too nom káz?
Whence have you come?	Kwâr sáshé?
Where are you going?	Kwâr inji?
Is this your horse?	In-né ooshpé too sázá?
No, it is my father's horse	Nen în tutt ooshpázé.
I am hungry	I owotá bissá.
I am not able	Ná balam.
I do not know	Ná zrenum.
What do you want?	Kai wâgùnji?
I am much pleased with him	Inné tá bidi leh assá.
He is stronger than him	Inné inné tá katoower assé.

VOCABULARY.

To be able	...	eṇstá.
Advice	...	wirip shoh.
Again	...	warekti.
Alive	...	shooweh.
All	...	pareh.
Always	...	parier
Angry	...	mujeh
To be angry.	...	mujegrá
Apple	...	purreh.
Apricot	...	tsiri.
Arrow	...	kon.
To ask	...	koodêik, *imp.* koodow.
Asleep	...	wároṇ.
Ass	...	kôre.
Astonished	...	dèr.
Aunt (father's sister)	...	jenshnùṇ (*if older than father*); kroinshnùṇ (*if younger*).
,, (mother's sister)		jenshnùṇ; kroinshnùṇ.
Awake	...	pshoois.
Back	...	pitî.
Bad	...	dugger.
Barley	...	rîts.
Battle-axe	...	kashé.
To be	...	azá.
Beard	...	dárî.
To beat	...	wîṇsá.
Beautiful	...	shingrá.
Before	...	pamûk.
To begin	...	papillestá, *imp.* papillî.
Behind	...	ptîper.
Belly	...	kitull.
To bind	...	gityá.
Bird	...	mrungzeh.
To bite	...	ajingoodá.
Black	...	jî.
Blind	...	kâṇr.
Blood	...	looî.
To blow	...	pîbuss (?)
Blue	...	kooger.
Body	...	jît.
Bone	...	uttî.
Bow	...	droṇ.
Bread	...	bootî.
To break	...	*imp.* petto.
To bring	...	owrá.

Brother ... brâ.
Bull ... asheh.
Butter ... noonî.
To buy ... gnusstá.

To call ... *imp.* wullow.
Cat ... pishush.
Chair ... bâṇ.
Cheek ... nusker.
Children ... permer.
To choose ... chîrá.
Clean ... adoobá.
To clean ... pâk kará.
Cloud ... nîro.
Cock ... ṇî kukkuk.
Cold ... shelleh.
To come ... atsendá.
Copper ... deryoo.
To count ... gareyá, *imp.* garô.
Country ... gùl.
Cow ... goh.
Crooked ... skùr.
Crow ... kôr.

Dagger ... kátrá.
Daily ... pareṇgájer.
Dancing ... nut.
Darkness ... undereh.
Daughter ... jù.
Day ... gájer.
Mid-day ... samogájer.
To-day ... shprùkájer.
Dead ... murreh.
Deaf ... asingá.
Death ... murreṇ.
Deceit ... mijuṇ.
Delicate ... shingrá.
Destitute ... garîb.
To die ... márá.
Difficult ... zôr.
Dirty ... dugger.
To do ... kará, *imp.* kishî.
Dog ... koorî.
To drink ... pîyá.
Dry ... dariss.

Ear ... kur.
Earth ... pullul.
Easy ... asán.
To eat ... yeṇrá.
Egg ... ajow.

Elbow	... areptî.
Enemy	... dùshmun.
Enough	... bess.
To escape	... *imp.* moghoo.
Evening	... shâm.
Exceedingly	... bilook.
Eye	... acheṇ.
Face	... nusker.
To fall	... *imp.* ùṇgé.
Far	... badùr.
Father	... tutt.
Fatigued	... gátrer.
Fear	... vidirik.
Feather	... puttyoo.
To fight	... sooch kará.
Finger	... angiùr.
To finish	... sangaiyá, *imp.* wazingow.
Fire	... angâ.
Flower	... pùsh.
Foolish	... cháteh.
Foot	... kyùr.
Forehead	... mùn.
Fort	... kullah.
Fowl	... kukkuk.
Fox	... vrigi.
Friend	... solî.
From	... tá.
Fruit	... kuchoowich.
Girl	... jùk.
To give	... prestá, *imp.* pitush.
To go	... éṇrá.
To go away	... gooá.
Goat	... wuzzeh.
God	... Imbrá.
Gold	... son.
Good	... leh.
Grand-father	... wow.
Grand-mother	... waiy.
Grape	... druss.
To grasp	... gootá.
Great	... ôl.
Green	... nîleṇ.
Gun	... tuppko.
Hair	... jù.
Half	... echleh.
Hand	... doosht.
Hard	... kugger.
Head	... sheh.

To hear ... sùngaiyá.
Heart ... zurreh.
The Heavens ... dih.
Heavy ... alùngah.
Hen. ... ishtri kukkuk.
Here ... ánî.
High ... ooreh.
To hope ... tummá.
Horse ... ooshp.
Hot ... tuppî.
House ... ámah.
How ... kaisteh.
How much ... kai kùnj.
Hungry ... ōtah.
Husband ... much.

Ibex ... mrang.
Ice ... sheh.
Immediately ... tupp tùch.
Infant ... âti.
Iron ... chîmoh.

To kick ... pâṇwîá.
To kill ... jeṇsá.
Knee ... zâṇ
Knife ... kuttah.
To know ... poorjá.

Lame ... kùter
Lead ... tùtch
To learn ... *imp.* remookshé.
To leave ... nummustá, *imp.* nummoo.
Life ... shooṇ.
Light (*subs.*) ... rôch.
Light (*adj.*) ... lôger.
Lightning ... pilsir.
Lip ... yùsht.
Long ... dergrùṇ.
Loose ... chîleṇ.
Low ... wùreh.

Maid ... drooik.
To make ... kará, *imp.* kishî.
Man ... muncher.
Young man ... loot.
Old man ... poordok.
Mare ... ishtri ooshp.
Meat ... anah.
Melon ... cárboozah.
Mid-day ... samogájer.
Mid-night ... samorut.

Milk	...	zooh.
Moon	...	más.
More	...	bilook.
Morning	...	dullkeh.
Mother	...	nùṇ.
Mountain	...	dâ.
Mouth	...	ashî.
This much	...	inné gek.
Naked	...	limungsteṇ.
Nail (finger)	...	nácheṇ.
Name	...	nom.
Near	...	toreh.
New	...	nooî.
Night	...	rudder.
No	...	nêṇ.
Noise	...	chow.
Nose	...	nasùr.
To obey	...	shtálá.
Of	...	
Oil	...	anooh.
Old	...	pùkùlah.
Only	...	gitok ti.
To order	...	húkum prestá.
Pain	...	brazeṇ.
To pant	...	shoshotîná.
Pear	...	tōng.
Pleased	...	shōtik.
To be pleased	...	shōtîná.
To pull	...	*imp.* nooksow.
Quickly	...	tupp tùch.
Rain	...	ughul.
Ram	...	nî.
Red	...	zeruṇ.
To remain	...	*imp.* ootiow.
Remaining	...	pootiber.
Rich	...	urreh.
River	...	nunni.
Road	...	pùt.
Rock	...	ôlwutt.
To run	...	achooná.
Sand	...	syoo.
To say	...	kurrá.
To see	...	âshkrá.
Seed	...	bî.
To sell	...	vretch kōṇsá.

To send	...	namiá, *imp.* namoo.
Servant	...	shudder.
Sheep	...	weh.
Short	...	moteh.
Shoulder	...	tâs.
To show	...	*imp.* warow.
Sick	...	brazower.
Silver	...	âryoo.
To sing	...	*imp.* dummoo.
Sister	...	sùs.
To sit	...	nijeṇstá.
Skin	...	goochum.
Slave	...	bári ; lowndoh.
Sleep	...	pshooik.
To sleep	...	pshooik kará.
Slow	...	dùnger.
Small	...	permùstùk.
Smoke	...	dyùm.
Snow	...	zîm.
Soft	...	wiogh.
Son	...	pùthr.*
Sorry	...	boodabuss.
Star	...	rishtah.
Stone	...	wutt.
Straight	...	shtull.
Strong	...	leh.
Sun	...	soo.
Swift	...	shatrùmoh.
Sword	...	tùrwâch.
That	...	soor.
There	...	ákî.
Thirsty	...	opik.
This	...	inné.
To throw	...	*imp.* ashoo.
Thunder	...	oodrun.
Tight	...	áreṇ.
Toe	...	angiùr.
To-morrow	...	dullkinkájer.
Tongue	...	dits.
Tooth	...	doot.
Tree	...	kunnah.
Trouble	...	guttreṇ.
Ugly	...	duggerker.
Uncle (father's brother)		jenshtutt (*if older than father*) ; kroinshtutt (*if younger*).
Uncle (mother's brother)		mum.

* In this instance the *th* is pronounced as in English.

Very	...	bilook.
Village	...	grâṃ.
Voice	...	kot.
Walnut	...	yamùṇ.
Water	...	owgh.
In this way	...	kittok ti.
In that way	...	soorokti.
Weak	...	tatrer.
Wet	...	zilleh.
What	...	kai.
Wheat	...	gōm.
When (*interrog.*)	...	kooî.
Where (*interrog.*)	...	kwer.
White	...	kashîr.
Who (*interrog.*)	...	káchî.
Why	...	ki.
Wife	...	shtri.
Wind	...	dummoo.
Wise	...	kshùleh.
To wish	...	mujjen kōṇsá.
Woman	...	jùker.
Old woman	...	poordîk.
Wood	...	dow.
Yellow	...	âdr.
Yes	...	lugieṇ.
Yesterday	...	dùskájer.
Young	...	lùt.

Numerals.

1	ek.	18	ashtits.
2	dù.	19	nits.
3	tré.	20	witsi.
4	shtah.	21	witseo.
5	pōch.	22	wits-a-dù.
6	shoh.	30	wits-a-dùts.
7	soot.	31	wits-a-yenits.
8	ōṇsht.	40	dùwits
9	nooṇ.	50	dùwits-a-dùts.
10	dùts.	60	tréwits.
11	yenits.	70	tréwits-a-dùts.
12	dits.	80	shtah wits.
13	trits.	90	shtah wits-a-dùts.
14	shtrits.	100	pōchùtsi.
15	pachits.	200	dùts witsi.
16	shits.	400	hazâr.
17	satits.		

once	êwer.
twice	dùwer.
thrice	tréwer.

APPENDIX J.

YIDGHAH.

Spoken in the upper part of the Ludkho valley, and in Munjan.

DECLENSIONS.

	Singular.		*Plural.*	
Nom.	a house . . .	kyê.	houses . . .	kyê-i.
Gen.	of a house . .	kyê	of houses . . .	kyê-i.
Dat.	to a house . .	ná kyê-en.	to houses . . .	ná kyê-ef.
Acc.	a house . . .	kyê	houses . . .	kyê-i.
Abl.	from a house . .	ze kyê-en.	from houses . .	ze kyê-ef.

Nom.	a horse . . .	yasp.	horses . . .	yasp-i.
Gen.	of a horse . .	yasp.	of horses . . .	yasp-i.
Dat.	to a horse . .	ná yasp-en.	to horses . . .	ná yasp-ef.
Acc.	a horse . . .	yasp.	horses . . .	yasp-i.
Abl.	from a horse . .	ze yasp-en.	from horses . .	ze yasp-ef.

PERSONAL PRONOUNS.

	Nom.	Gen.	Dat.	Acc.	Abl.
I	zoh	mun	námun	vámun	jámun.
thou	too	toh	nátoh	vitoh	jitoh.
he, she *or* it . . .	yoh *n.*	ámun *n.*	nùmun *n.*	vùm *n.*	jùmun *n.*
	woh *d.*	eyen *d.*	neyen *d.*	veh *d.*	jeyen *d.*
	hooroh *r.*	áwun *r.*	nowun *r.*	voh *r.*	jowun *r.*
we	mâkh	ámâkh	nomâkh	vomâkh	jámâkh.
you	mâf	ámâf	nomâf	vomâf	jámâf.
they	yeh *n.*	ámuf *n.*	nùmuf *n.*	vùmùv *n.*	jùmùv *n.*
	weh *d.*	aiyef *d.*	neyef *d.*	vev *d.*	jev *d.*
	hooreh *r.*	o-of *r.*	no-of *r.*	vov *r.*	jo-ov *r.*

N, *d*, *r* stand for *near*, *distant*, *remote*. There are no distinctions of gender.

Conjugation of the verb "To Strike."

Infinitive Mood.

Present.		*Past.*	
to strike	jiah.	to have struck	jiah bush.

Participles.

Present.		*Past.*	
striking	dîé.	having struck	jioh.

Indicative Mood.

Present Future.

Singular.		*Plural.*	
I am striking *or* will strike	dahum.	we are striking, *or* will strike	dahum.
thou art striking *or* wilt strike	déhé.	you are striking, *or* will strike	dahuf.
he, she *or* it is striking *or* will strike	déhé.	they are striking, *or* will strike	dáhát.

Imperfect.

Singular.		*Plural.*	
I was striking	jî-ermstum.	we were striking	jî-erstum.
thou wert striking	jî-tstet.	you were striking	jî-efstef.
he, she *or* it was striking	jî-erstoh.	they were striking	jî-etstet.

Pluperfect.

I had struck	jigum vioh.	we had struck	jigum vioh.
thou hadst struck	jigá vioh.	you had struck	jiguf vioh.
he, she *or* it had struck	jî-vioh.	they had struck	jî-vioh.

Perfect.

I struck	jî-em.	we struck	jî-em.
thou struckest	jît.	you struck	jî-ef.
he, she *or* it struck	jîoh.	they struck	jî-et.

Præterite.

I have struck	jigum.	we have struck	jigum.
thou hast struck	jiget.	you have struck	jiguf.
he, she *or* it has struck	jî.	they have struck	jî-é.

Imperative Mood.

Singular.		*Plural.*	
strike thou	dihé.	strike you	dihè.
let him, her *or* it strike	dihé.	let them strike	dihé.

The passive voice is formed by the use of the auxiliary verb *kshiyah* "to go," as; *jiah kshiyah* "to be struck."

The interrogative is formed by adding *á* to the verb in all its forms.

[Note.—The above does not exhaust all the forms of the verb, but they are the only ones of the correctness of which I could be sure.]

Present Future of the verb SHOOAH "To Become."

Singular.		*Plural.*	
I become	shom.	we become	shom.
thou becomest	shoo-ît.	you become	shof.
he, she *or* it becomes	shoo-ît.	they become	shot.

Present tense of the verb ASTAH "To Be."

Singular.		*Plural.*	
I am	astet.	we are	astet.
thou art	astet.	you are	astet.
he, she *or* it is	astet.	they are	astet.

Past tense used with both verbs.

I was *or* became	bîm.	we were *or* became	bîum.
thou wast *or* becamest	bît.	you were *or* became	bî-if.
he, she *or* it was, *or* became	bîoh.	they were *or* became	bî-it.

SENTENCES.

1. What is your name?	Toh nâm ches mîn.
2. This is my brother.	Moh mun vrai mîn.
3. My brother has two good horses.	Mun vraiyen loh ghushé yaspi astet.
4. His sword is better than mine.	Eyen kùgoren mun kùgor ghushé astet.
5. I want to go to my home.	Ná kyê-en kshiyah muns khiyâl astet.
6. How far is it from here?	Ze moloh chemin looroh astet.
7. It is twenty days' journey.	Mùntroh pádoh wîstoh mîkh.
8. I told him that I could not çome to-day.	Mun nowun ishtum zoh door ágoyah chi wizidum.
9. What do you want?	Nátoh koyi raist.*
10. Why do you ask me this	Too moh vámun chî pîstet.
11. I can run faster than he can.	Zoh eyen tîz gházum.

* A corruption of *rai astet.*

VOCABULARY.

To be able ...	wizidah.
Above ...	boorghoh.
Abuse ...	ástiah.
To abuse ...	ástiah kerah.
Accustomed ...	âdet.
Acid ...	trishpoh.
After (place) ...	shpuchin.
After (time) ...	bád.
Again ...	dir.
To agree ...	kábùl kerah.
Air ...	howl
Alive ...	zindoh.
All ...	ámbá.
Alone ...	ifkîgoh.
Alongside of ...	péchirum.
Although ...	wáhgumki.
Amongst ...	dokomulun.
And ...	oo.
Anger ...	khuffoh.
Angry ...	kyahèr.
To be angry ...	kyahèr kerah.
Another ...	dir.
Answer ...	joowâb.
To answer ...	joowâb kerah.
Ant ...	moorghoh.
Anxiety ...	fikir.
Anxious ...	fikiri.
Apple ...	ámoonoh.
Apricot ...	chîré
Arm ...	lust.
Arms (weapons) ...	yarâkh.
To arrive ...	rásîah.
Arrow ...	láspikh.
To ask ...	pîstah.
To ask for ...	dellah.
Asleep ...	lowádum.
Ass ...	khoroh.
Astonished ...	hairân.
Aunt (father's sister)	kokoh.
,, (mother's sister) ...	kok lùghdoh.
Autumn ...	paiz.
Awake ...	jibîm.
Away ...	lok.
Back ...	pishchoh.
Bad ...	dölk ; nashker.
Barley ...	yershiyoh.

Battle-axe	...	toower.
To be	...	ástah.
Bear	...	yersh.
Beard	...	yárzoh.
To beat	...	jîah.
Beautiful	...	sooráti.
Because	...	chemin.
To beeome	...	shooah.
Before (time)	...	piroh.
Before (place)	...	psároh.
To begin	...	dùftah.
Behind*	...	boorgoh.
Belly	...	oojùt.
Below*	...	psároh.
Between	...	domulun.
To bind	...	troghdah.
Bird	...	zōrzoh.
To bite	...	nághuvdah.
Bitter	...	tulkh.
Black	...	noroh.
Blind	...	yâdhé.
Blood	...	înoh.
To blow	...	phooah.
Blue	...	âkshin.
Blunt	...	mighioh.
Body	...	tonoh.
Bone	...	yestoh.
To be born	...	ájistah.
Both	...	ábeli
Bow	...	droon.
Boy	...	poor.
Brain	...	mâghs.
Brass	...	miss.
Brave	...	báhâdùr; poordùl.
Bread	...	nughun.
To break	...	vristchah.
Breast	...	fùz ; ischînah.
Breath	...	dom.
Brick	...	ùshtoo.
Bride Bridegroom	... ...	shábok.
Bridle	...	ávlân.
Bridge	...	yêyah.
To bring	...	ávrah.
Broad	...	ookwah.
To be broken	...	vristchah kshiyah.
Brooch	...	chámoh.
Brother	...	vrai.

* The words for *above* and *behind* are identical, so also are those for *below* and *before.*

Brown ... boodeki.
Bull ... kyâkh.
Bullet ... pish.
To burn (*trans.*) ... pùfah.
To burn (*intrans.*) ... gùvdah.
To bury ... dizdah.
But ... ámah.
Butter ... muskoh.
Butterfly ... kotiah.
Business ... hōrt.
To buy ... sodah kerah.
By ... zá; zé (*prefixed*).

To call ... oosháwah.
Camel ... shtùroh.
Careless ... bî fikir.
Cat ... pishkoh.
Charm ... toomâr.
Cheek ... kelikoh.
Chin ... zánâkh.
To choose ... chùvdah.
Clean ... pághzghoh.
Clothes ... chupun; weroh.
Cloud ... mîgh.
Cock ... ner kireh.
Cold ... yōkh.
Colour ... rung.
To come ... ágoyah.
To converse ... gupdah.
Copper ... loh.
Corner ... shùngah.
Four-cornered ... chârboorsh.
Corpse ... jussut.
To cough ... khiftah.
Cough ... kofah.
To count ... yoomrah.
Courage ... himut.
Cow ... ghowoh.
Crooked ... chop.
Crow ... khùn.
Cultivation ... zirahát.
Custom ... dustoor.
To cut ... tùrdah.

Dagger ... mamoodighoh.
Daily ... mîsh mîsh.
To dance ... drùvdah.
Dark ... tîroh.
Daughter ... lùghdoh.
Day ... mîsh; mîkh.
Mid-day ... mîshen.

To-day	...	door.
Dead	...	mooroh.
Deaf	...	ghoo.
Death	...	mōrgh.
Deceit	...	fun.
To deceive	...	fun jiah.
Dew	...	prejgâ.
To die	...	moorah.
Difficult	...	mùshkil.
Dirty	...	budrooyi.
To divide	...	bâghdah.
To do	...	kerah.
Dog	...	gulv.
Door	...	lùvor.
Dove	...	migyah ; kùmrî.
Dream	...	koovun.
To drink	...	shumdah.
Drum	...	doomòmoh.
Dry	...	ùshk.
Dust	...	kutter.
Ear	...	ghoo.
Earth	...	ghoroi.
The earth	...	zámîn.
Earthquake	...	moojevt.
Easy	...	askân.
To eat	...	khoorah.
Egg	...	orgooh.
Elbow	...	rezé.
Empty	...	kháli.
Enemy	...	dùshmun.
Equal	...	vesputch.
To escape	...	rùstah.
Evening	...	shám.
Everything	...	hárchîz.
Ewe	...	moowogh.
Eye	...	chum.
Face	...	rooi
Family	...	ájgál.
To fall	...	chestah.
Far	...	looroh.
Fat (*subs.*)	...	subrim.
Fat (*adj.*)	...	lunduk.
Father	...	tutt.
To be fatigued	...	pokhùftah.
Fear	...	tors.
To fear	...	dùriyah.
Feather	...	poona.
To feed	...	korovdah.
Female	...	shîoh.

Fight	...	difah.
To fight	...	diftah.
Finger	...	ogùshtchoh.
To finish	...	kùlás kerah.
Fire	...	yoor.
First	...	áwul.
Fish	...	kòp.
Flour	...	yârah.
Flower	...	gùl.
Foolish	...	bîákil.
Foot	...	pelloh.
For	...	ná (*prefixed*).
Forehead	...	pishâneh.
To forget	...	permistchah.
To forgive	...	bukshindá kerah.
Fort	...	lizokh.
Fowl	...	keryoh.
Fox	...	roosoh.
Friend	...	dost.
To frighten	...	dùroh wùvdah.
From	...	ze ; zá (*prefixed*).
Fruit	...	mêwá.
Full	...	pùr.
Garden	...	bâghá.
Girl	...	lúghdoh.
To give	...	liah.
To go	...	kshiyah.
To go out	...	koochah.
He-goat	...	firghámoh.
She-goat	...	vizoh.
Wild goat	...	nukchîr ; shùmonná ; trowoo.
Gold	...	tillá.
Good	...	ghushé.
Grape	...	agidroh.
Grandfather	...	páp.
Grass	...	oosh.
Great	...	ùstùr.
Green	...	sōvz.
Grief	...	ghom.
To grieve	...	ghumzah.
Gun	...	tùfuk.
Gunpowder	...	dârooi.
Hail	...	moorghik.
Hair	...	poghoh.
Half	...	nîm.
Hand	...	lust.
Right hand	...	horzooh lust.
Left hand	...	chop lust.
Handle	...	dustoh.

Happiness	...	feryoh.
Happy	...	ghushi.
Hard	...	sukt.
Hare	...	sîgh.
Hawk	...	pùz.
Head	...	poosir.
Healthy	...	tázghoh.
To hear	...	doghùjah.
Heart	...	zil.
Heavy	...	ghárkh.
Hen	...	kiryoh.
Here	...	málé ; moloh.
High	...	bilund.
Honey	...	agibîn.
Hope	...	hoomit.
Horse	...	yasp.
Horse-shoe	...	chowlî.
Hot	...	pich.
House	...	kyê.
How	...	chemin.
How many	...	chund.
How much	...	chund.
Hunger	...	wákhrâkh.
Hungry	...	ooshiá.
Hundred	...	shōr.
Husband	...	shfoh.
Ice	...	láksir.
If	...	wáhgum.
To be ignorant	...	bîákél shooah.
Ill	...	lorooh.
To be ill	...	lorooh shooah.
Illness	...	lorovoh.
In	...	dé ; dir.
Infant	...	rizá.
Iron	...	rispin.
To join	...	jùftah.
To jump	...	ùstùschah.
Justice	...	insuf.
Kettledrum	...	tabîlaghah.
To kick	...	polingi jiah.
To kill	...	máschah.
King	...	mishtir.
Knee	...	zik.
To kneel	...	dozânoh kerah.
Knife	...	keroh.
To know	...	wizedah.
Lame	...	shell.

Language	...	zabân.
To laugh	...	khudiyah.
Lead	...	kâlub.
Leaf of a tree	...	punùk.
To learn	...	wùksah.
To leave	...	lákrah.
Leg	...	pîshchen.
Lie	...	chopî.
Life	...	ján.
Light (*subs.*)	...	arùngoh.
Light (*adj.*)	...	sùbùk.
Lightning	...	aroonwoh.
Like	...	mooâfik.
Lip	...	pârshik.
A little	...	kestah.
Liver	...	jiger.
Long	...	ván.
Loose	...	wussá.
To lose	...	gibuvdah.
Low	...	pöst.
Maid	...	chimitkeryoh.
To make	...	kerah.
Male	...	ner.
Man	...	merer.
Young man	...	joowân.
Old man	...	zor.
Mare	...	maiyághoh.
To marry	...	wálkh kerah.
Marriage	...	wálkh.
To measure	...	muvdah.
Meat	...	ghùsh.
Medicine	...	dârooi.
Melon	...	kárboozé.
Mid-day	...	mîshen.
Midnight	...	kshowoh barâber.
Milk	...	kshîrá.
Mill	...	khirwoh.
To mix	...	vidághdah.
Moon	...	moghoh.
Month	...	moogh.
More	...	ziáté.
Morning	...	sáher.
Mother	...	nînoh.
Mountain	...	pêfer.
Mouse	...	perkh.
Mouth	...	pookhor.
To move (*trans.*)	...	moojivdah.
To move (*intrans.*)	...	mooghdah.
Much	...	jáhân.
So much	...	harooni.

This much	...	yendah.
Mulberry	...	meretch.
Muscle	...	bùzgah ; ilîrah.
Music	...	doomámághah.
Naked	...	shilokh.
Nail (finger)	...	anákná.
Name	...	nâm.
Near	...	násdîk.
Neck	...	shilleh.
Never	...	hêch kùloh nah.
New	...	nooé.
Night	...	kshowoh.
No	...	nah.
Nobody	...	kidichi, *acc.* vokohchi.
Noise	...	háwâz.
Nose	...	fiskoh.
Not	...	chi.
Nothing	...	hêch kùch.
Now	...	wuss.
Of	...	i.
Old	...	zor ; telt.
On	...	mál ; skoh.
Only	...	fukut.
Open	...	kùshâdah.
To open	...	wiyetah.
Oppression	...	zilm.
To order	...	hùkùm kerah.
Out	...	dokùchoh.
Path	...	pâdoh.
Pain	...	lorová.
Partridge	...	jōrjoh.
Pear	...	kyoghoh.
Perhaps	...	îyah.
Pigeon	...	ko-woo.
To place	...	ùstaiyah.
Plain	...	pistoh.
Play	...	khudî.
To play (a game)	...	khudiyah.
Pleased	...	khùsh.
To be pleased	...	ferioh shooah.
Plough	...	sporoh.
To plough	...	sporoh kerah.
Point	...	sōr.
Poor	...	ghárîb.
To praise	...	shah básh kerah.
To prepare	...	têyâr kerah.
Pride	...	tákáboori.
Promise	...	wâdoh.

To promise ... wâdoh kerdah.
Proud ... tákáboor.
To pull ... kistchah.

Queen ... hunzâghoh.
Quick ... jelt.

Rain ... novoh.
Ram ... pleshyeh.
To read ... ishtah.
Ready ... têyâr.
To receive ... priviah.
To recognize ... wizidah.
Red ... sùrkoh.
To remain ... oozaiyah.
Remaining ... bùsh.
To remember ... yâd kerah.
To return ... ghostchah.
Rice ... shálì.
Rich ... dowlutmund.
Ring ... pergùshchoh.
Ringlets ... kùjkah.
Ripe ... pishai.
River ... dáriyow.
Road ... pádoh.
Rock ... ùstùrgher.
Roof ... ischik.
Rope ... tunow.
Rotten ... fshî.
Round ... perwákin.
To run ... gházdah.

Saddle ... pulun.
Sand ... sigioh.
To search ... tálásh kerah.
To see ... ùjùrah ; listchah.
Seed ... tooghùm.
Self ... koyah.
To sell ... perîstah.
To send ... khùzdah.
To separate ... wettah.
Servant ... shuddá.
Shadow ... sághoh.
Shame ... sherm.
Sharp ... tùrghoh.
Sheep (*collect.*) ... pleshyî.
Short ... kookyoh.
Shoulder ... sùvdoh.
To show ... nishân kerah.
Shut ... bot.
Sick ... lorová.

On this side	...	moloh ; skêkirah.
On that side	...	oloh ; skimkirah.
Sigh	...	házá.
Silent	...	khâmosh.
Silver	...	rùpêoh.
Sinew	...	righoh.
To sing	...	fágîkah.
Sister	...	yikhoh.
To sit	...	niástah.
Skin	...	kuruss.
Sky	...	asmînoh.
Slave	...	huddá.
Sleep	...	loghát.
To sleep	...	loghádah.
Slow	...	káhl ; shùm.
Small	...	rîzah.
Smoke	...	looî.
Snake	...	îj.
Sneeze	...	khirfoi.
To sneeze	...	khirfah.
Snow	...	werfoh.
Soft	...	molaim.
Some	...	kustah.
Somebody	...	kidi- ; *acc.* vokoh.
Son	...	pooser.
Sorry	...	kuffoh.
To sparkle	...	lápessah.
Spoon	...	kufchî.
To speak	...	gup jiah.
Spring	...	psîdroh.
To stand	...	jùbah.
Star	...	sittâreh.
Stone	...	gher.
Storm	...	toofân.
Straight	...	hoorzook.
Strength	...	koowut.
Strong	...	zool.
Suitable	...	mùnasîb.
Summer	...	wároh.
Sun	...	mîrá.
Sweet	...	kshùnt.
Swift	...	ielt ; tùnd ; tîz.
Sword	...	kùgor.
Tail	...	lùm.
To take	...	ghordah.
To take hold	...	futtah.
To take up	...	borghah.
To teach	...	wùksah.
To tell	...	ishtah.
That	...	woh.

That (*relat.*)	...	zoh.
There	...	hooré.
Thick	...	lövs.
Thin	...	tùnkâ ; dölk.
Thirst	...	trishp.
Thirsty	...	trùshná.
This	...	moh.
Throat	...	ghōrdoghoh.
To throw	...	lughádah.
Thumb	...	nárungúsht.
Thunder	...	tânder.
Thus	...	mulmin.
Tight	...	troghoh.
Time	...	wákt.
To	...	ná (*prefixed*).
Toe	...	ogùshtchoh.
Together	...	yoojê.
To-morrow	...	yâmoh.
The day after to-morrow		woyoo yâmoh.
Tongue	...	zevir.
Tooth	...	lud.
Towards	...	kirah.
Tree	...	drákht.
To try	...	asmùn kerah.
Trouble	...	musháká t.
Ugly	...	budrooyi.
Uncle (father's brother)		bai.
Uncle (mother's brother)		bai.
Under	...	shtáhan.
Valley	...	durrah.
Vein	...	rerik.
Very	...	jáhân.
Very well	...	ghushé.
Village	...	lámoh.
Vine	...	agidroh.
Voice	...	ùshtùm.
Wall	...	khaiyoh.
Walnut	...	oghoozoh.
Water	...	yowgh.
Weak	...	sùst.
To weep	...	khshiyah.
West (sunset)	...	mághrib.
Wet	...	khùst.
What	...	koyi ; tsi ; ches.
Wheat	...	ghádum.
When (*interrog.*)	...	kùloh.
Where (*interrog.*)	...	koo ; kshoo.
White	...	spî.

Whip	...	chintoh.
Who (*interrog.*)	...	kyum.
Why	...	chî.
Widow	...	wosoroh.
Widower	...	wosoroh.
Wife	...	ooloh.
Wind	...	wooikh.
Window	...	derbuchoh.
Wine	...	bōghmuz.
Wing	...	verzghoh.
Winter	...	zemistân.
Wise	...	lânawoh.
Wish	...	rai.
With	...	lá ; lé ; (*prefixed*).
Within	...	dekheh.
Without	...	dokùchoh.
Wolf	...	wùrgh.
Woman	...	jinkoh.
Old woman	...	żorikoh.
Wood	...	skùt.
Wool	...	pum.
Work	...	hōrkun.
Wound	...	zōkhm.
To write	...	nooishah.
Year	...	sâloh.
Yellow	...	zît.
Yes	...	ō.
Yesterday	...	ùzîr.
The day before yesterday		shirîzen.
Young	...	joowân.

Numerals.

1	yoo.
2	loh.
3	shùroi.
4	chîr.
5	pânsh.
6	ookshoh.
7	ávdoh.
8	áshchor.
9	no.
10	luss.
11	luss-yoo.
12	luss-loh.
13	luss-shùroi.
14	luss-chîr.
15	luss-pânsh.
16	luss-ookshoh.
17	luss-yávdoh.
18	luss-yáshchor.
19	luss-no.
20	wîstoh.
21	wîstyoo.
30	wîst-oo-luss.
40	loh wîst.
50	loh wîst-oo-luss.
60	shùroi wîst.
80	chîr wîst.
100	shōr.